M000029344

ABINGDON PREACHER'S ANNUAL 1992

ABINGDON PREACHER'S ANNUAL 1992

COMPILED AND EDITED BY

John K. Bergland

ABINGDON PRESS
Nashville

ABINGDON PREACHER'S ANNUAL 1992

This book is printed on acid-free paper.

ISBN 0-687-00568-X
ISSN 1047-5486

MANUFACTURED IN THE UNITED STATES OF AMERICA

To ***Ed Tindell***
Kay Bundy
Marlin Stewart
Karen Barkman
Jackie Barnett
David Padgett
Dot Wyatt
and the countless unnamed laypersons who, like them, honor the Word of God and faithfully support preaching.

Contents

□

SECTION II:

SERMON RESOURCES

Section III:

Indexes

Preface

□

On a Sunday several years ago, I chatted with the distinguished New Testament scholar W. D. Davies outside Duke University Chapel. We were discussing the Sunday sermon. Without praise or blame, my colleague observed, "Preaching appears to be an easy task, but it's not!"

Minister's who preach every Sunday morning and face the demand to prepare a new sermon to be delivered before the same hearers know that they have a difficult task. When one considers the awesome responsibility of being a servant of the Word of God, the trust becomes menacing.

Is it burden or joy? Is sermon preparation a delight, or is it raw duty? When Alexander Gerschenkron ended his notable career as a professor at Harvard, he reflected on his life's work, saying: "I seriously considered staying in the shipyard. I like the contact with the anonymous mass of Americans. And the work doesn't follow you at night into your dreams. Is scholarship pleasure or pain? If someone cuts your leg off, you know it's pain, but with scholarship you never know" (Henry Rosovsky, *The University: An Owner's Manual* [New York: W. W. Norton, 1990], p. 213).

This book will not make preaching painless or easy. It's not intended to do so. For preachers who feel the word of God within them like "fire in their bones," painless preaching is never a possibility. Like Jeremiah, they can only say, "I am weary of holding it in; indeed, I cannot" (Jer. 20:9).

Every preacher needs a starting place—some revealed truth, some felt need, some occasion, some assigned mission—that will inspire and prompt the sermon. If the only reason one stands to preach in the church is that it's 11:00 o'clock on Sunday morning, there is little hope that preaching will be significant in the cause of Christ or in the lives of people.

This book assumes that there is a gentle and steady reason for preaching that is always compelling. It is the response to the important question, "Is there any word from God today?" The Bible holds a central place in such preaching.

For many ministers, it is the beginning place, and they find the

New Common Lectionary to be a helpful point of contact with Holy Scripture. Week-in and week-out, they refer to it for the Sunday Lessons. *Abingdon Preacher's Annual* is primarily based on this lectionary. This volume follows Cycle C and the Advent lessons of Cycle A for the year 1992.

For every Sunday of the church year, this book provides:

1. The Old Testament, New Testament and Gospel Lessons assigned to each Sunday.
2. A brief summary of each lesson.
3. A discussion related to the texts, referred to as "Interpretation and Imagination."
4. A complete sermon related to one of the lectionary lessons.
5. The Psalm assigned for each Sunday and a responsive call to worship from that Psalm.
6. Prayers for the day and suggested hymns.

I have written for each Sunday of the year the theme sentence, lesson summaries, and sermon starters ("Interpretation and Imagination"). I have also suggested the hymns and written some of the prayers.

The ministers who have provided the sermons for *Abingdon Preacher's Annual* are broadly based both geographically and denominationally. The sermons are not necessarily their best. These sermons are the products of genuine reverence for the Word of God and reflect the varieties of gifts and graces that exist among servants of the Word.

Some of the sermon contributors are well known and have addressed congregations numbering in the thousands. Others are relatively unsung, but not unimportant. The sermons of bishops, homiletics professors, chaplains, media preachers, and church leaders will be found in this book alongside the sermons of local priests and pastors.

Although most of the sermons are either explicitly expository or textually thematic, not every sermon is clearly related to the Sunday Lessons. Some simply address a topic related to the lessons. Some sermons relate to the Sunday (such as Independence Sunday) rather than to the Sunday Lesson. The narrative style of Larry Grimes (which reminds me of the stories of Garrison

Keillor) at first seems detached from the lesson, but there's a that's-the-way-it-is quality about his parables from West Virginia that has a compelling relevance.

Complete schedules of the Scripture texts and hymns for the year are included in Section II. Suggestions for funeral sermon texts and topics, additional aids for worship, and the essay "The Move from Text to Sermon" are also found in that section.

This is not "my" book, but our book. Abingdon editors Paul Franklyn and Sally Sharpe have refined, challenged, and corrected the material. Copy editor Linda Allen has managed every page of the publication. Many authors have provided sermons and prayers. Bob Bergland, who is an able minister and my steady son, has assisted in this project. Marcia Moritz, Emma Faircloth, Lisa Bryant, and Debra Sepp have provided competence as word processors, typists, and correspondents.

I have discovered personally and solemnly the perils that plague preaching. I know well the pitfalls that beguile preachers, and I have fallen victim to many of them. Who dares to speak for God? Who can worthily proclaim the good news of Christ week in and week out? But this is our occupation, our obligation, and our opportunity. May God grant you insight and boldness equal to the task.

John K. Bergland
Pentecost 1990

Section I:

□

FIFTY-TWO SUNDAY SERMONS

JANUARY 5, 1992

□

Second Sunday After Christmas

The past belongs to us. It's our history. We've lived it, and we can't change it. The future belongs to God—to the God of new dawning light and life, the one who gives power to become.

The Sunday Lessons

Jeremiah 31:7-14: With a bold, "Thus says the Lord," Jeremiah proclaims that God will save God's people. A remnant of the scattered exiles will be gathered from the farthest parts of the earth. Even the weak and wounded will return. "Hear, O nations," the Lord has scattered and will gather the flock. God will give joy instead of sorrow. God's saving ways are described: God will ransom, will redeem.

Ephesians 1:3-6, 15-18: Paul's hymn proclaims that God has blessed us. God has destined us to be children, has bestowed grace and forgiveness, and has made known a plan for the universe, which is "to unite all things in Christ." The Apostle gives thanks for those who know this through faith in Christ, who have "the eyes of your heart enlightened" (v. 18).

John 1:1-18: John's prologue proclaims that the Word was before there was anything, that the Word was agent for everything made, and that the Word gives both life and light. The Word has not been overcome by darkness. This true light (rejected by people who were God's own) gives power to all who believe—power to become children of God. "The Word became flesh and lived among us" (v. 14).

Interpretation and Imagination

January takes its name from a god of the Romans named Janus, who had two faces. With one he looked to the past; the other faced the future. In January we remember what has been given to us and decide how we will fill the empty pages of the new chapter that is just beginning.

Today we consider three passages. Each suggests a different beginning of the same salvation story. Jeremiah looks back and sees a remnant of scattered exiles whose sadness will turn to joy. Paul writes to Gentile outcasts who have been chosen to be God's own children. John begins in cosmic history and then proclaims that light and life have come into the world and that God has become human.

Looking back with a negative attitude of resentment and regret, one may see only scattered exiles, Gentile outcasts, and one rejected by his own people. When that cynicism must face the future, it is made weak by its fear.

Some of Paul's images are impossible to comprehend rationally, such as having the eyes of your heart enlightened. But there is deep meaning in that phrase. It implies an intuitive encounter and speaks with the confidence of faith (seeing is believing). You, too, may see God in the story of a remnant people, God present in new communities of faith, God in the cosmic order, and God in the immediacy of light.

WHAT A DESTINY!

Ephesians 1:3-6, 15-18; John 1:1-18

A SERMON BY REGINALD W. PONDER

The Epistle lesson for this Sunday prior to Epiphany in 1992 is a message of great hope and challenge for the Church, for each Christian believer. The so-called Epistle to the Ephesians is addressed to the entire Church of the first century and not solely to one congregation or assembly of believers at Ephesus. Although the Pauline authorship of the letter is discredited by some, I tend to affirm its authenticity. If Paul did not write this letter to the Church at large, he should have.

The Gospel lesson for the day is the beautiful prologue to the Fourth Gospel. It is John's story of the incarnation of God's grace and love in the person of Jesus of Nazareth. The message anticipates the epiphany of Jesus, the showing forth of his nature, with these incomparable words: "And the Word became flesh and lived among us, and we have seen his glory, the glory as of a father's only son, full of grace and truth."

The most exciting message of the lessons of this day is that we, you and I, have the potential placed within us by the prevenient grace of God to live as sons and daughters of God. This is the gospel, the good news, that bursts forth from the pages of Scripture and the tradition of our faith to greet us as we worship together at the beginning of this new year.

The Epistle lesson begins with words of grace, affirming the blessedness of God as well as the fact that we have been given spiritual blessings in Christ Jesus. These blessings are showered upon us (*eulogia*), as opposed to those that evolve or grow up in us like fruit. As the people of God, we are freely given countless blessings that enrich and empower our lives and our living. What an exciting focus for our worship as we begin the new year! Let us affirm our blessings from God.

These blessings are the free gift of God's grace. They are not a reward for our faithfulness or our righteousness, in spite of what some may say. We need to learn how to enjoy these blessings.

In addition to our being blessed in Christ, we are also chosen (*edeledzato*), which means that we are selected from the crowd, picked out from a group. When I was a child in school, my favorite time was recess. Each day we went through the same ritual: Two persons, usually the largest boys in the class or the best ball players, took turns choosing members for their teams until all the players were chosen. Although this pattern was repeated day after day, we each felt a certain thrill in hearing our names called, especially if we were among the first called. We would run to line up behind our captain for the day.

What Paul is saying in this lesson is that Jesus is calling our names and asking us to line up on his side as we live our lives. To line up behind Jesus is to live in a special way, "holy and blameless." The claim on our lives to live like Jesus seems to offend some, but I believe that it is imperative if we are to be effective witnesses for Jesus today.

The concept of being chosen is not unique to Paul. Peter, the other primary patriarch of the Church, wrote: "But you are a chosen race, a royal priesthood, a holy nation, God's own people"

(I Pet. 2:9). Again, the words *chosen* and *holy* are prominent. There is no question that both Paul and Peter determined that the chosen believers in Jesus Christ, the members of the Church, were called to be special people, to live lives that were different from those of other persons in the crowd. Indeed, God chose them and chooses us from all the rest to be disciples of the risen Christ.

What this means is that we are a chosen people. God has called us out from the crowd to live in a special way. We are to live like Jesus—to be holy and blameless in our behavior. Each of us has been hand-picked by God to live in the presence of God.

Francis Asbury wrote as he set sail for America: "What am I going to do?" He answered his own question, "To live to God and help others so to do." Why has God chosen you?

In my years as a pastor, I have known a few persons who have possessed a sense of calling, of being chosen. Early in my ministry one such person had a profound influence on me. When I was appointed to his church, I was the fifth pastor the charge had had in six years. Not everyone wanted me. Some wanted a pastor with more experience. But Jimmy put his hand on my shoulder and said, "I believe that God has sent you to be our pastor, and I know that he has told me to help you be the best pastor you can be." You can imagine what that did for me as a young pastor. It is even more remarkable that Jimmy lived up to his promise, and together we had a great ministry with that congregation.

We have been blessed and chosen, but there is more. We have been given a precious destiny by God—that is, we are to be God's sons and daughters through faith in Jesus Christ. Through the adoption of faith, we become God's own offspring, God's children. Perhaps this is the best news that we have to share with each other and with the world.

God, through the gift of his son, Jesus, has given us a special place in the Master-plan. Everyone who believes that Jesus is the Savior-Son shares in that destiny. This destiny is available to each person in the world, if that person will make a faith commitment to believe in Jesus and follow him as Lord of life.

Listen to what Paul wrote: "He destined us for adoption as his children through Jesus Christ, according to the good pleasure of his will, to the praise of his glorious grace that he freely bestowed on us" (Eph. 1:5-6).

The destiny that God has afforded us in the Church is not a reward for our exemplary behavior. Not at all! Rather, it is an act of love, of *agape*. It is a gift of grace. I believe that God wants every person in the world to receive that perfect gift of grace and love. What we must do is enjoy and celebrate that gift so that others will want to share it—to be sons and daughters of God, too. Wasn't it of this divine destiny that Fanny Crosby was thinking when she wrote "Blessed Assurance"?

> Blessed Assurance, Jesus is mine!
> O what a foretaste of glory divine!
> Heir of salvation, purchase of God,
> Born of his Spirit, washed in his blood.
> This is my story, this is my song.
> Praising my Savior, all the day long.

To these familiar words, the Apostle added his prayer for the Church, God's sons and daughters:

> I have heard of your faith in the Lord Jesus and your love toward all the saints, and for this reason I do not cease to give thanks for you as I remember you in my prayers. I pray that the God of our Lord Jesus Christ, the Father of glory, may give you a spirit of wisdom and revelation as you come to know him, so that, with the eyes of your heart enlightened, you may know what is the hope to which he has called you, what are the riches of his glorious inheritance among the saints. (Eph. 1:15-18)

That "glorious inheritance" is none other than our being the sons and daughters of God. Therefore, my sisters and brothers, let us go out into the world and act as God's own children.

By the miracle of God's gracious love bestowed on us by Jesus and through the adoption of faith, you and I are God's children. The way we act will determine how some people feel about God and relate to God. What a joyous privilege it is to be God's children! Will you join me as we seek to live as God's sons and daughters to the praise and glory of God?

Suggestions for Worship

Call to Worship (Ps. 147:12-15):

MINISTER: Praise the LORD, O Jerusalem! Praise your God, O Zion!

PEOPLE: For he strengthens the bars of your gates; he blesses your children within you.

MINISTER: He grants peace within your borders; he fills you with the finest of wheat.

PEOPLE: He sends out his command to the earth; his word runs swiftly.

Act of Praise: Psalm 147:12-20.

Suggested Hymns: opening hymn: "Go, Tell It on the Mountain"; second hymn: "We Three Kings"; closing hymn: "Who Is He in Yonder Stall."

Opening Prayer: Almighty God, you were before the beginning and are beyond all time, and you have come into the days of our lives in the bright shining light of your Son. Those who are wise behold your light and adore your majesty. Grant that the star of your truth and righteousness will lead us to Christ, and move us to offer our gifts and ourselves in worship and praise through Jesus Christ our Lord. Amen.

Pastoral Prayer: O God of infinite grace and goodness, you have blessed us in many ways. We are children of blessing and hope. In blessing you have called us apart to be your children and to live holy lives. It seems such a difficult thing to do, but when we look at the life of Jesus we realize that he is our example and our guide. He tells us to be perfect, and we shudder at that prospect. It is as if you are asking us to give up something precious, our sin.

Holy God, help us to know that when we seek to live like Jesus and to be the holy persons that you created us to be, it is then that we experience the exciting joy of being your sons and daughters. May others learn to praise you because of the goodness and the God-likeness they see in us. Today we claim that we are your children. Help us to live so even as we follow the perfect example of Jesus our risen Savior. Amen.

JANUARY 12, 1992

□

First Sunday After Epiphany (Baptism of the Lord)

Discouragement and depression are all too common among us. New confidence, new vision, new hope, and new power are what we need and want. Spiritual power attended Christ's baptism and empowered his mission.

The Sunday Lessons

Isaiah 61:1-4: This is the passage Jesus read in the synagogue in Nazareth (see Luke 4:14-21). Associated with God's year of Jubilee, it is a royal decree of amnesty and release. Those who hear will receive a mantle of praise instead of a faint spirit.

Acts 8:14-17: Philip's hearers in Samaria believed the gospel and were baptized. Peter and John were sent from Jerusalem to minister to the new converts. They prayed for them, "that they might receive the Holy Spirit" (v. 15) and laid hands on them. The believers, first baptized in the name of Jesus only, then received the Spirit.

Luke 3:15-17, 21-22: Verses repeated from the Gospel lesson of third Sunday in Advent tell of John the Baptist's contrast of his baptism to the one the Christ will give. "I baptize you with water. . . . He will baptize you with the Holy Spirit and fire" (v. 16). When John the Baptist baptized Jesus, the heavens opened and the Holy Spirit descended on Jesus.

Interpretation and Imagination

The doctrine of the Holy Spirit and the related teachings of sanctification and Christian perfection have from time to time been troubling doctrines for the church. Many Christians ignore these terms, seldom speaking them and paying little attention when hearing them.

This is understandable. So many insane things have been done in the name of the Spirit; so many unchristian attitudes have been manifested by those claiming holiness; so many wrongs and sordid imperfections have been fostered by the elitism of those confident of their perfection. It is not surprising that we turn aside from these teachings with some fear.

But it will be a tragic loss if we abandon this great New Testament truth, a reality that we desperately need. Perhaps if we claim Isaiah's "mantle of praise instead of a faint spirit," we can shake our fear and apathy. Or if we could begin with the innocence of Philip's Samaritan converts we, too, might gain a desire for this power and purity.

Since we cannot begin there, let us begin with our baptism. We honor our baptism. We want it to be a covenant of heart and mind and will. But our love is without passion, our thought without enlightenment, and our will without strength until we are baptized with the Holy Spirit. When we experience the power of God's presence in our covenant, we take on the goodness of one who knows the power of the Spirit.

ON THE TIPTOE OF EXPECTATION

Luke 3:15-17, 21-22

A SERMON BY REGINALD W. PONDER

Epiphany is a season of excitement, of unveiling, of showing forth the glory and majesty of the Son of God. No experience in Epiphany is more filled with this sense of excitement than the remembrance of the baptism of Jesus, and the remembrance of our own baptism.

Luke's record of the baptism of Jesus embodies this excitement. In fact, there is an air of enthusiasm in the Jordan valley before Jesus appears. The translators of the *New English Bible* captured this mood when they translated the first part of the Luke 3:15: "The people were on the tiptoe of expectation." What was the reason for their excitement, their expectation?

Since the time of David, the Jews had been expecting a Messiah, a Savior king who would restore their nation to its place of prominence in the Middle East. Each time a baby boy was born into a Jewish family, especially to a descendant of David, the parents would look into the baby's eyes and ask prayerfully, "Could it possibly be that our son might be the Messiah?" For nine centuries this ritual had been repeated.

Then came John, the son of Zechariah and Elizabeth. He was different. He certainly was a man of God. His preaching was so powerful that some of the leaders came from Jerusalem to the Jordan to be baptized. John told his hearers to *repent*, to turn from their wicked ways and return to following God's ways—the laws and commandments. As he preached and baptized, the people became excited. A buzz ran through the throng. "Can it be that John is the Messiah?" they questioned one another. Luke records, "The people were on the tiptoe of expectation, all wondering about John, whether perhaps he was the Messiah" (Luke 3:15 NEB).

When I was a lad, my Uncle Johnny took me to watch the Greensboro Patriots play baseball. It was the highlight of my summer to go to the games with him, and since he had no children, he liked to take me. When I went to the games, I noticed that a group of boys always gathered behind the outfield fence. They would chase the balls that were hit over the fence and take them to a man who watched the gate at the end of the fence in return for being allowed to sit in the stands and watch the game.

Some of the boys would stand on crates or on each other's shoulders in order to watch the game. Others would watch through holes in the fence. They were the most enthusiastic fans at the stadium. Every time the Patriots did something, they cheered. They cheered when the team was hopelessly behind and many of the paying customers had left the park. They even cheered for the errors. They watched every play "on the tiptoe of expectation."

What a lesson that experience has taught me about life. How wonderful it would be if you and I had the hope in our hearts to face life every day "on the tiptoe of expectation"!

Today, I preach to you "on the tiptoe of expectation." Why? Let me share my reasons with you.

First of all, I stand on the tiptoe of expectation because I believe that God is in charge of the world. The Epiphany and baptism of Jesus remind us that God has not forgotten us or forsaken the world. God loves us and sent his Son Jesus into the world to show us that love. John reminds us in the Fourth Gospel: "For God so loved the world that he gave his only Son, so that everyone who believes in him may not perish but have eternal life" (John 3:16).

Hurricanes, tornadoes, and earthquakes devastate towns and cities. Major airplane crashes and other accidents claim hundreds of lives. The epidemic of drug and alcohol abuse continues to destroy thousands of lives. When we read and hear of all of these tragedies and experience others in our own lives, we wonder whether God really cares. But the message of Epiphany is that he does. God does care! The hymn writer Maltbie D. Babcock had it right when he wrote:

> This is my Father's world.
> O let me ne'er forget,
> That though the wrong seems oft so strong,
> God is the ruler yet.

Because God is in charge of the world, I stand on the tiptoe of expectation!

Second, I stand on the tiptoe of expectation because God sent Jesus, and I know that Jesus is the Messiah, the Christ, the Savior. We have an advantage over those persons who went to the Jordan to hear John preach. We know who the Messiah is. We know that Jesus of Nazareth is the Messiah—the Son of God. We don't have to wonder about who the Savior is. We have met him and have claimed him as the Lord and Savior of our lives. There is no question as to the importance and meaning of such assurance: "blessed assurance, Jesus is mine!"

It is my prayer that each person here this morning will claim or renew the claim of Jesus as her or his personal Savior. Open your heart and let Jesus come into your life right now! It will bring you the greatest joy you can know. It will raise you to your tiptoes!

Third, I stand on the tiptoe of expectation because Jesus sends the Holy Spirit to guide and strengthen my life and the lives of all those who believe in him. Yes, the Christian believer has a special gift. It is the gift of God's Holy Spirit, who comes into our lives when we believe in Jesus and are baptized in his name. The Holy Spirit is God's promise of strength and power to enable us to live in these difficult days.

God does not promise us an exemption from the trials and troubles of the world. Such has not been my experience, nor was it the experience of Paul, the early martyrs, or most of the Christians I have known. In fact, the promise is that we will have these troubles. But God also promises that he will send his Holy Spirit to guide and strengthen us in our times of testing. All that we have to do is to open our hearts to receive this precious gift. Once you receive the gift of the Holy Spirit, you will be on your tiptoes, too.

Finally, I stand on the tiptoe of expectation because God has called us, the Church, to be his messengers and his servants in our broken and hurting world. What a great privilege it is for us to be God's agents of reconciliation and healing in our world. I have many privileges as a Christian, but none is more important or more exciting than the privilege of touching someone's life with the joy and hope of the Gospel of Jesus Christ. This happens when one shares the grace of God's love with another person by telling or showing her or him the love of Jesus. It happens when one loves another person who is in need or who is depressed or hurting. It happens when one feeds the hungry or gives warmth or hope to the poor and needy. Jesus cares, and so does his Church. We are an extension of his love in the world, and there is nothing that gives us greater excitement.

The people were on the tiptoe of expectation! What about you? You know what I have been talking about, don't you? Of course, it's baptism. Your baptism! I am talking about your claiming the providential power of God, which enables you to declare that God is in charge of the world. I am talking about your claiming Jesus as your own Messiah and Savior. I am talking about your opening your life to receive the guidance and empowerment of the Holy Spirit. I am talking about your commitment of your life to be a servant of the risen Christ in our broken and hurting world. Yes, I am asking you to claim anew this day your own baptism. If you have never been baptized, I call on you in the name of Jesus the Savior to talk with me or some other Christian you trust about how you can be baptized and live the rest of your life on the tiptoe of expectation.

I love a ball game. It's exhilarating. The fans get excited and yell and cheer. They stand up and shout. They lose themselves in their enthusiasm. People used to do that in Church. Why have we stopped? Are we afraid of what God might do with our lives? Are we frightened by the possibility of life on a higher plane, on tiptoe?

I wonder whether you and I, whether the Church, will ever get that excited about the tremendous opportunity we have to transform the world through the power, love, and grace of Jesus Christ and his Holy Spirit. All the people were on the tiptoe of expectation! I am. Will you join me today?

Suggestions for Worship

Call to Worship (Ps. 29:1-2):

MINISTER: Ascribe to the LORD, O heavenly beings,

PEOPLE: ascribe to the LORD glory and strength.

MINISTER: Ascribe to the LORD the glory of his name;

PEOPLE: worship the LORD in holy splendor.

Act of Praise: Psalm 29.

Suggested Hymns: opening hymn: "Jesus! the Name High over All"; second hymn: "Majestic Sweetness Sits Enthroned"; closing hymn: "We've a Story to Tell to the Nations."

Opening Prayer: O God, you have manifested your glory through your only Son and have made us to be your own people by the waters of baptism. Bless your church today. Inspire, strengthen, and send your servants into the whole world. Let your mercy be known to those who do not know you. By the power of the Holy Spirit, help us to be the light of the world, that children of all nations will turn to you and the salvation offered by our Lord Jesus Christ. Amen.

Pastoral Prayer: God of all creation, we worship you this morning on the tiptoe of expectation. What a good and loving parent you are to us, your children. By your grace we have been called to worship. In your grace we experience the joys of our baptism. Through your grace we are sent into the world to be in ministry in the name and love of Jesus, our Christ.

Fill us today with the power of your Holy Spirit as we remember the baptism of Jesus and our own baptisms. We claim the ministry of every baptized Christian. May that ministry be in tune with the mind and spirit of our risen Savior. May that ministry reach out to every person in the world without regard of age or gender, race or color, need or station in life.

You have called your Church to be your servant in the world. Equip us today by your grace for that servanthood, that ministry. In the name of Jesus Christ our Savior we pray. Amen.

JANUARY 19, 1992

□

Second Sunday After Epiphany

John's prologue declares, "We beheld his glory." The first manifestation of Christ's glory was at a wedding in Cana when the wine failed. His disciples saw and believed.

The Sunday Lessons

Isaiah 62:1-5: The city of Zion will be restored, and nations and kings will see its glory. No more will the city be termed a forsaken and desolate woman, but rather, "My Delight" and "Married" (v. 4). God will rejoice over Zion as the bridegroom rejoices over the bride.

I Corinthians 12:1-11: The Corinthian church was marked by some highly visible gifts of the Spirit. Paul noted their variety, but pointed to a single source and a single purpose. God inspires all as a manifestation of the Spirit for the common good. The utterance of wisdom, healing, prophecy, and tongues are some of the gifts Paul mentioned.

John 2:1-11: A wedding in Cana was the setting of Jesus' first miracle. The wine had run short, and he turned water into better wine. The miracle is a sign of an underlying reality, a manifestation of Christ's glory. When ordinary things fail, like wine at a wedding or water at the well or bread in the wilderness, the life-giving power of Christ can be manifest.

Interpretation and Imagination

In contemporary times, when the relationship of a man and a woman is valued more for personal pleasure and individual satisfaction than for family and belonging, it is difficult to live into a text that refers to an unmarried woman as being forsaken. Among Hebrews, the Levirate specified that a widow left childless should become the wife of the dead man's brother, to bear his progeny and preserve the inheritance.

We don't think of an unmarried, childless woman as being desolate. Quite the contrary. We are a people who teach birth control methods and sterilize the fertile. For us, eternal life has little significance as life that prevails in the midst of barrenness and death. It has come to mean the preservation and well-being of "my life" if it is in conflict with other life.

The ancient church, honoring Mary as the mother of Christ and referring to the church as the bride of Christ, found divine approval of marriage in this text. Our marriage ritual makes reference to the wedding at Cana. It may be noted that the pious Essenes, who in Jesus' day considered themselves the only true representatives of the high priestly tradition, did not marry. Neither did Jesus or Paul, but the first sign of Christ's glory, described as life-giving and radiant in the prologue, was manifest among family at a wedding.

The issue was not earth-shattering. The wine had run out, and the party would soon be over. Such was the setting for the first miracle of the cosmic Christ.

WHEN THE WINE FAILS

John 2:1-11

A SERMON BY JOHN K. BERGLAND

"This is the happiest day of my life," she said. Some days are like that; they're special. There are great days in all of our lives. What have been the wondrous moments and principal occasions for you? Can you recall the most wonderful day of your life? For me such days are filled with extraordinary hope and joy.

Life involves many happy affairs—the birth of a child, the gatherings of Christmas, a summer vacation, high school graduation. It is often said that to love and be loved is the greatest happiness in the world. For most of us, then, the most significant movement of hope and joy is our wedding day. It's the day we celebrate before God and all our friends the love in our life. Marriage vows are the most profound vows one can make. No other vows are more tender, none more sacred. No other pledge will so radically shape and claim an individual. The two become one. A home is born. A haven for family is founded. Your place to be is situated. But, alas, in too many marriages and in so many lives the wine fails.

Wine, with its sparkle and zip, has long been the symbol of hope and joy. It's the beverage of choice for promises and toasts. In ancient Israel it was the primary ingredient of a wedding feast. So important was wine to a feast that the chief steward was the one entrusted with its selection. He ordered it. He tasted it first. He served it. He poured it.

At a wedding in Cana in Galilee, Jesus and his disciples were present as guests. It was there that a social calamity began to unfold. In the midst of the celebration, Jesus' mother came to him, saying, "They have no more wine." The supply of wine had given out. We don't know why, and the scriptures don't tell us why. Did the chief steward order too little? Did those hearty fishermen disciples drink too much? Whatever the reason, the wine supply had failed, and the wedding celebration would soon end. The party was almost over.

The Gospel of John is filled with symbolism. Every story has meanings that go three and four levels deep. Symbolically the wine running out suggests that the celebration of hope and joy had ended. Now life would return to the ordinary. The symbol is compelling. Birth, baptism, marriage, and burial are the recorded dates in vital records. In these days of your life, marriage is the day for a party. But the wine fails.

Something like this happens to all of us. The sparkle, the bubble, the promise, the hope, and the joy all end. Sooner or later life closes in on all of us. The shine wears off. Dreams go away unrealized. Promising ventures end in bankruptcy. Romances end with broken hearts. Marriages fail. Leaders are voted out. Careers crest without a crown.

Surely this is the fabric of our finite lives and of all creation. Springtime turns brown with summer. Autumn splendor lies buried beneath the snows of winter. Morning gives way to evening.

In our own lives we experience it. The resiliency of a young body will be slowed by brittle bones and aging muscles. The strength of a mature hand will give way to weakness. A life-beating heart will be stopped by death. What is the most important thing in all your life? Is it not the good gift of those you love and who love you? But every relationship ends. It ends with your death or with the death of the one you love. The wine fails, but this is only the beginning of the story.

John's Gospel carries a wonderful message of life—new life in Christ. The first miracle, the changing of water into wine, was the first manifestation of Christ's life-giving power and glory. The disciples believed in him. Christ's power transforms. Darkness is pushed back by the light. Fear becomes faith. Sadness is turned to joy. Death yields to new life. Christ changes the ordinary into the glorious. The water became wine.

Six stone jars sat near to the entrance of the house in which the wedding took place. Each probably held twenty to thirty gallons. Jesus said to the servants, "Fill the jars with water." They filled them to the brim. "Now take some of it to the chief steward," Jesus said. The master of the banquet called the bridegroom aside to ask, "Why have you saved the best till now?" Usually hosts brought out the choice wine first and then served the cheaper wine after the guests had drunk too much to tell the difference.

We would not profit from the reading of this lesson if the only truth we gathered was that life and joy run out on us. But that's not why we remember this story. This is the good news. Jesus has the authority to provide for every need, and in God's providence the best is yet to be. There are three evidences in the miracle story that provide spiritual guides for our faith and practice.

The first is that Jesus Christ is the author and finisher of life. Christ acts. He does not simply react. He does not let human problems and shortages define his agenda or claim his power. When his mother told him of the need for more wine, he almost rudely replied, "That's no concern of mine. My time has not yet come."

The church and all who minister in Christ's name will be helped if they, too, can learn not to let the failures and needs of this world define their agenda. Christ was never indifferent to need, but it was from fulfilled truth, not from emptiness, that he took his marching orders. It was God's infinite power, not humankind's finite predicament, that centered Christ's mission and manifested his glory.

The second truth evident in the lesson is that we should begin with what we already have and use it all. The stone jars were commonplace. The water was on hand. The servants used all of it, filling the jars to the brim. It was Montaigne who wrote in *Essays*:

"Whenever your life ends, it is all there. The advantage of living is not measured by length, but by use: some men have lived long and lived little: attend to it while you are in it. It lies in your will, not in the number of years, for you to have lived enough."

How sad it is when we are melancholy in the midst of joy, and dead when we are still alive. There is truth in the counsel, "Grab all the gusto." Use every circumstance, every opportunity, every day to it's fullest.

Consider, finally, this truth: The best is yet to be. This is a primary tenet of faith. Pilgrims and saints throughout the ages have lived by this assurance. Confident that the future belongs to God and that the new creation is better than the old, the new Jerusalem more glorious, the new heaven and the new earth more sustaining, they applaud the moment and let it go. They recognize the temporary for what it is. This is wise Christian counsel, "Celebrate the temporary." The Apostle Paul says it like this: "Forgetting what lies behind and straining forward to what lies ahead, I press on toward the goal for the prize of the heavenly call of God in Christ Jesus" (Phil. 3:13-14). The best is yet to be.

Three principles are appropriate for marriages that have lost their sparkle: (1) Don't over react. Don't focus on your problems and needs. You'll likely add to them and take them into tomorrow. Take control of your lives and decide what you want to be. (2) Take advantage of the "givenness" of today. Use every common and ordinary thing in your life to the fullest. (3) Look to the future with confidence. In courtship, couples plan for their future, dreaming about a life together. If there is emptiness now, just let it go. Dare to believe that the best is yet to be.

I watched with wonder the remarkable joy that was evident in a couple who had been married for almost fifty years. There wasn't one thing negative about them. Moreover, they had learned to kiss with their eyes. They had shared many yesterdays, but for them life was not defined by painful memories. They were always planning something together, confident that their joy could be new every morning.

In the ancient city of Gerasa, later called Jerash, a great Christian church was built in the fourth century. Near the entrance of the church there was a pool. Citizens of the city came there every day to get water. But on one special day of the year, the first miracle of our Lord was remembered. The water was replaced with wine.

Before a recent wedding, friends, family, and the wedding party gathered for a dinner following the rehearsal. Many toasts were lifted to the bride and the groom. These toasts called for long life, happiness, health, and prosperity and welcomed a new son or a new daughter. Then a grandfather stood to speak. The room became quiet, and he toasted them saying, "May the very best day of your courtship be like the very worst day of your marriage. The very best to you my dears."

The best is yet to be. With God there is always more.

Suggestions for Worship

Call to Worship (Ps. 36:5-7, 9):

MINISTER: Your steadfast love, O LORD, extends to the heavens, your faithfulness to the clouds.

PEOPLE: Your righteousness is like the mighty mountains, your judgments are like the great deep; you save humans and animals alike, O LORD.

MINISTER: How precious is your steadfast love, O God! All people may take refuge in the shadow of your wings. . . .

PEOPLE: For with you is the fountain of life; in your light we see light.

Act of Praise: Psalm 36:5-10.

Suggested Hymns: opening hymn: "See the Morning Sun Ascending"; Second hymn: "I Love to Tell the Story"; Closing hymn: "Spirit of Faith, Come Down."

Opening Prayer: From the ordinary places of our daily lives and from the depths of our human need we cry out to you, O Lord. Hear the prayers of your people. There is no good thing we can do to merit your favor. There is no righteousness we can claim to entreat your blessing. Therefore, we come like the beggar who prays. Our hands are empty, reaching out to receive. Our faces are turned to you, seeking your gifts through Jesus Christ our Lord. Amen.

Pastoral Prayer: Almighty God, we praise you today because your love never ends, because your truth endures forever. You know who we are and from where we have come today. Some of us are numbered among the faithful. Some of us are half faithful, some unfaithful. Some of us are still strong and confident because we have plenty. Some of us are worried because we fear that our resources will fail. Some of us are embarrassed because failure has already found us.

But now we are before you, and we pray the same prayer. You have created each of us and all of us. Our lives are alike in the transient and temporary ways of humanity. Our need for your grace is the same, for we have all sinned. We all must die and die alone. Therefore, hasten to hear us; be quick to heal and forgive; and send forth your truth. Fill us with your Spirit and save us through Jesus Christ our Lord. Amen.

JANUARY 26, 1992

□

Third Sunday After Epiphany

The word of God, read and preached, is the subject of these lessons. It is a word of both judgment and grace.

The Sunday Lessons

Nehemiah 8:1-4*a*, 5-6, 8-10: Tradition teaches that Ezra originated the synagogue service. This passage describes how the scribe Ezra read the book of the law to all who could understand. The people stood when it was opened. Ezra blessed God for its insights, and the people answered, "Amen," with uplifted hands. Then they bowed in worship. Others read from the book and interpreted its meaning.

I Corinthians 12:12-30: Paul referred to the church as the body of Christ. The body has many members, each different, but each important. Discord is not found among members of the same body. Apostles, prophets, teachers, healers, those with the ability to speak in different languages, and interpreters are all members of the same body.

Luke 4:14-21: Jesus began his ministry in Galilee, teaching in the synagogues. At the synagogue in Nazareth, he read from Isaiah concerning the beginning of Jubilee—release for the captives. Having the people's complete attention, he announced, "Today this scripture has been fulfilled in your hearing" (v. 21). Christ himself announced the coming of the new age.

Interpretation and Imagination

An ancient proverb declares, "More men adore the sun rising than the sun setting." When one watches the coronation of a king or the inauguration of a president, the proverb seems to be true. Witness the coming of a new coach, the joy of a new love, or the excitement of a new anything. All seem to declare that we always welcome a new day.

But when the new begins to challenge our old values and habits, our adoration is likely to be short-lived. At first, Jesus was welcomed into the synagogue in Nazareth just as he was thronged throughout Galilee and later greeted with hosannas in Jerusalem. But then the people learned that his good news also had a word of judgment. Liberty for the oppressed meant loss for the oppressor.

These lessons tell of the word of God being declared with fresh insight and meaning. The community of faith should question and will question: "How do we know this is the word of God for us?" Perhaps the first test is this: "Does it offend or challenge?"

WHERE DOES JESUS FIT IN?

Luke 4:14-21

A SERMON BY RALPH K. BATES

After a Sunday evening worship service, I walked to the fellowship hall for a covered-dish dinner. After dinner I was approached by my Sunday school teacher, who asked me a very startling question: "Ralph, do you know God?" I had no earthly idea how to answer that question. Finally, in a defensive way, I said, "You can't know God." She quietly reassured me that it was possible and convinced me that I should give it a try. At that time, I did the only thing I knew how to do. My simple, yet sincere, prayer was "O God, if you are knowable, then I'm going to know you." That started a journey that is still in process.

One of the difficulties of knowing Jesus is finding new ways for him to fit into a modern life-style. Like a giant jigsaw puzzle, I had problems putting the pieces together. Just about the time things started to fit together, they started to pull apart. There were times when I didn't know what to do with him or without him. C. S. Lewis was right when he called Jesus "a transcendental interferer" in his book *Surprised by Joy*.

The people in Jesus' hometown of Nazareth had the same problem. They welcomed him and sang his praises until his words rankled their feelings. It was acceptable for him to read the synagogue lesson from Isaiah, but when he identified himself as the fulfillment of that prophecy, that was too much. It is no wonder that, when he rolled up the scroll, gave it back to the attendant, and sat down, all eyes in the synagogue were fixed on him.

For many reasons, Jesus did not fit in. The Gospels tell us so.

> He was in the world, and the world came into being through him; yet the world did not know him. He came to what was his own, and his own people did not accept him. (John 1:10-11)

> [Mary] gave birth to her firstborn son and wrapped him in bands of cloth, and laid him in a manger, because there was no place for them in the inn. (Luke 2:7)

> Foxes have holes, and birds of the air have nests; but the Son of Man has nowhere to lay his head. (Matt. 8:20)

It's not easy to fit Jesus into human experience. It's very confusing theologically to understand how God was in Christ reconciling us to himself. Is Jesus God? The New Testament declares that the "Word became flesh and lived among us, and we have seen his glory, the glory as of a father's only son, full of grace and truth" (John 1:14).

His words about loving our enemies, announcing good news to the poor, releasing prisoners, restoring sight to the blind, and freeing broken victims are not on our wavelength. We do not have the time, concern, or energy to stoop to the needs of the poor, maimed, lame, blind, and outcast.

We admire him from a distance; we give him lip service; and occasionally we offer a helping hand. But we can't always find a place where he fits in. So the question becomes more real when we ask ourselves honestly, "Where does Jesus fit it?"

Although I have not put all of the pieces of the puzzle together, there are a few pieces that fit beautifully. There are some areas of life where Jesus is a perfect fit.

Jesus fits in where he is invited. Jesus loved to invite others to be a part of his life. He said that God loved to invite us to be in relationship and friendship. Jesus talked about the king who gave a party for his son. The invitations went out, but the people refused to come. Why? Matthew gave the following reasons: "But they made light of it and went away, one to his farm, another to his business, while the rest seized his slaves, mistreated them, and killed them" (Matt. 22:5). Some were too busy with their work to care; others were murderous. John, writing in Revelation 3:20, gave us a classic picture of Jesus standing at the heart's door, knocking and waiting for an invitation to enter. Do you care?

I was reluctant to invite Jesus into my life because of what I had heard about him. I often heard him described as being critical, demanding, legalistic, and judgmental. To tell the truth, I avoided him like the plague. However, when I met him, I was surprised. There is a difference between hearing about a person and meeting that person.

I found him to be loving, compassionate, and caring. For the first time I felt accepted and included. There were no sermons, no impossible demands, no unrealistic commands. There were no shoulds, oughts, or musts; there was only a supportive, nurturing Presence. I found a friend. I found someone who believed in me. When others said no, he said yes. When others gave up, he held on. He saw in me more than I saw in myself. When I met Jesus, he invited me to follow him. It was the greatest day of my life.

I once found a poem by an unknown author which expresses my surprise:

I was young when I met the Master,
But I know the skies were more clear and vivid blue than any I had seen.
A holy hush trembled upon the hills and the world was new.
A silent music swept my feet with an ecstasy that was too deep for human words.
I walked for a while in a Churchyard where I met Jesus.
The joy I felt was a flame that swept my heart with a holy fire.

I don't know about you, but I would follow a person like Jesus to hell and back. So before you make up your mind that Jesus doesn't fit, make sure you meet him first.

Jesus fits in where he is accepted. We are so big on acceptance. Much of our acceptance, however, is exclusive. We accept persons who look like us, act like us, think like us, and pray like us. We talk about pluralism, melting pots, openness, *glasnost*, and the beauty of differences. This is a step in the right direction.

Oh, we try hard to accept the presence of Jesus. We include him in the blessings of our celebrations. As a minister, I am called upon to bless all kinds of occasions. Sometimes I wonder why we try so hard to fit Jesus in with an invocation. I read that a minister once offered the invocation at a college football game. In the prayer, he invited God to take time from his busy schedule to watch the football game. When he finished the prayer, the phone rang in the booth. When the minister said, "Hello," the voice on the other end responded, "This is God, what channel?"

Although we have difficulty accepting Jesus, he accepts us unconditionally. I know that I am accepted by him. There are times when I don't deserve to be accepted, when I have difficulty believing that someone could love me in spite of my unloving ways. I have felt that I have been unacceptable in the eyes of others, but I have never felt that I was unacceptable to Jesus. Because of that, I could follow such a person through the gates of eternity. You may not accept Jesus for many reasons, but never forget that he accepts you.

Jesus fits in where he is free to use his gifts. One of the alarming statements in the New Testament is about the time Jesus spent in Nazareth, "He did not do many deeds of power there, because of their unbelief" (Matt. 13:58). It is amazing what Jesus can do with us and for us when he is allowed the freedom of using his gifts. Have you ever found yourself in a place where your gifts were not appreciated? Do you remember how you felt? How paralyzed you were? Do you remember being in a situation where your gifts were appreciated and eagerly anticipated? Do you remember the way life poured from you and brought healing to yourself and to those around you?

Jesus brings new life to everything he touches. I have always wondered what would have happened in Nazareth—or what would happen in Birmingham, or New York, or California—if Jesus were allowed the freedom to release his gifts among us.

Jesus fits into our lives where he is needed. If you ever need Jesus, then you will understand where he fits in. Most of the time, we can get through life on our own wits; we can depend on ourselves to come through when things get tough. Number one will be adequate; however, there will come times when we need resources greater than our own. If we ask for his help, he'll be there for us in ways we will not believe. Since becoming a

Christian, I have never had to ask, "Well, Jesus, where were you when I needed you?"

Our needs vary from time to time, and I have found that Jesus meets our needs in the most surprising ways. Last year I suffered a heart attack and had bypass surgery. The recuperation period was somewhat intimidating. Although I felt the gracious Presence of Christ with me, I had difficulty fitting my life into the plan that was before me. During the following summer, I spent time reading, praying, and seeking to renew my spiritual life. One July day, I got up early and sat by a rushing mountain stream in North Carolina. I carried with me a book by Bruce Larson, entitled *A Call to Holy Living.* On that morning I read a story that spoke to me in a powerful way. I would like to share it with you.

> An old friend who had a great impact on my life died about 10 years ago. She was born in the lap of luxury. She actually grew up in New York's Waldorf-Astoria Hotel, the child of millionaire parents. Her life began to go awry just after her first marriage. She traveled with the wrong crowd, got hooked on drugs and alcohol and promiscuous sex, and finally divorced her husband. Her money, her health, and her luck all ran out and, in despair, she attempted suicide. At that point she phoned her former husband and told him her situation. "Why, I have nothing left." His response? "It's OK, Gert, I'll take care of it."
>
> On that very day, enough money was deposited in her bank account to last her through the rest of her life. Her ex-husband was at that time president of Merrill-Lynch. The woman was Gert Behanna, lay evangelist and author of *The Late Liz,* who, some three miserable marriages later, found faith in Jesus Christ and became part of the new humanity that Paul describes for us in Ephesians. (Bruce Larson, *A Call to Holy Living*. Augsburg Publishing House, 1988, p. 25).

That's the way Jesus meets our needs. When we run out of resources he says, "Don't worry, I'll take care of it." There are enough resources to last us a lifetime, and they have been deposited in our account. They simply need to be claimed. That was what I needed to hear.

Do you have trouble trying to fit Jesus into your life? First, meet him, and you will be surprised by how well all things will fit together.

Suggestions for Worship

Call to Worship (Ps. 19:7, 9):

MINISTER: The law of the LORD is perfect, reviving the soul;

PEOPLE: **the decrees of the LORD are sure, making wise the simple . . .**

MINISTER: the fear of the LORD is pure, enduring forever;

PEOPLE: **the ordinances of the LORD are true and righteous altogether.**

Act of Praise: Psalm 19:7-14.

Suggested Hymns: opening hymn: "When Morning Gilds the Skies"; second hymn: "Standing on the Promises"; closing hymn: "O Zion, Haste."

Opening Prayer: Gracious God, you have created us with the potential for many moods. Sometimes we are cast down and at other times lifted up. In fearful and wonderful ways you have given us the capacity to be victims or victors. There are times when we feel good about ourselves, and there are times when we devalue our worth. We confess that we are unworthy of your love. We break down as individuals, break up as families, break off as nations, and refuse to let you break into our lives. We have abandoned you, but you have not abandoned us. We have made room for you on the cross, but little room in our hearts. Forgive us when we ignore you and become indifferent to your love. In the name of Christ our Lord, amen.

Pastoral Prayer: Eternal God, we are privileged to come into your Presence with thanksgiving and praise. You have graciously given the gift of life to us, and you have allowed us to have freedom of choice and chance. You have invited us to express our concerns and have generously involved yourself in those areas where you are invited, needed, and accepted. Thank you for being sensitive to our freedom and for refusing to break-in, manipulate, and control.

When we take time to know you, we are surprised at your graciousness and love. Although you are all-powerful, you limit yourself to protect our freedom. Although you are all-seeing, you do not "rush in where angels fear to tread." Although you are all-knowing, you do not take away the consequences of our actions. Thank you for trusting us to work out our own salvation with fear and trembling.

Yet, there is a great need for your involvement in our world. We need to know that your ultimate plan cannot be aborted; that faith, hope, and love are eternal; and that history has meaning and purpose. We need you to be involved in the political arena to aid those who lead us to be men and women of integrity, to give guidance to assemblies and institutions that they may be worthy of their names, and to instruct our world leaders in the way of peace and good will.

We invite you to be a part of our world and to use your gifts to bring us to a greater understanding of Jesus Christ, that we may enthusiastically answer his call to follow him. Through your leadership, may new doors of opportunity open to us, new roads of purpose lead us further down the road, and new insights lead us to greater fulfillment. In your holy name we pray. Amen.

FEBRUARY 2, 1992

□

Fourth Sunday After Epiphany

A prophetic word is always needed but seldom wanted.

The Sunday Lessons

Jeremiah 1:4-10: The call of the Lord came to Jeremiah: "Before I formed you in the womb I knew you. . . . I appointed you a prophet" (v. 5). The young Jeremiah, who would for more than twenty years remain unshakable in his commitment, at first answered, "I do not know how to speak" (v. 6). The Lord God put words in the mouth of the prophet.

I Corinthians 13:1-13: Though one may speak like an angel and have prophetic powers and understand all mysteries, without love, one is only a noisy gong. Paul wrote it personally, saying, "[Without love] I am a noisy gong or a clanging cymbal" (v. 1). His beautiful and compelling description of love concludes with the promise that faith, hope, and love abide.

Luke 4:21-30: Jesus was rejected in his own town. Preaching in the synagogue at Nazareth, he proclaimed that God would heal, feed, and set free the outsiders they despised. He told how Elijah fed the widow at Zarapath in Sidon and healed the leprosy of the Syrian captain. The congregation was filled with wrath.

Interpretation and Imagination

Tomorrow never comes. It is what's about to happen and what is happening now that makes a difference. A promise that only applies to a distant future benefits no one and costs little. A restaurant manager dared to advertise with a big sign that said, "Free lunch tomorrow!" But tomorrow never comes.

The Word of God is never like that, although some weak substitutes are. God's Word is immediate and compelling. It is eventful—happening now. All of us have experienced a language happening. "Come in"; "Sit down"; and "You're fired" are word events. They change things. They make a difference. They are immediate. They are happening now.

When Jesus announced in Nazareth that Isaiah's promise of good news and deliverance was "today fulfilled in your hearing," his preaching became a happening, a word event. When the Word of God claimed the life and being of the prophet Jeremiah, his prophecy became a troubling encounter for the prophet as well as for his hearers.

A prophet's message may be intriguing when it speaks of things to come. When the prophet's message becomes immediate (the popular label for such witness is "telling it like it is") there is quick response, and often immediate rejection.

There are many qualities unique to prophetic preaching or witness. It challenges the status quo. It seems to side with the outside or even the enemy (the preaching of both Jesus and Jeremiah are examples). It holds little or no regard for either praise or blame. It claims the awful authority of God. It implies or may even declare judgment. And it is always eventful, immediate, happening now.

The Old Testament and Gospel lessons tell of the way in which prophets are rejected and of Jesus' rejection at Nazareth. The Epistle lesson, with its emphasis on the enduring power of love, teaches us how to speak the prophetic and saving Word of God. Christ is the supreme example of prophetic preaching—never rejoicing in the wrong, always rejoicing in the right; never impatient, though always immediate, bearing all things, believing all things, hoping all things.

When the Word of God is spoken or lived out in this way, it may be rejected, but it will not be denied.

ABANDONMENT

Luke 4:28-30

A SERMON BY RALPH K. BATES

Have you ever been abandoned? *Abandon* is an ugly word with an ugly meaning. To abandon is to forsake utterly, to give up all concern, to cast away or to leave without any intention of reclaiming, to banish. The word is surfacing more and more in our world—political prisoners are banished to forgotten prisons, children are abandoned by parents, lovers are forsaken, friends are cast aside, victims are assaulted and left to die.

Jesus experienced a form of abandonment when he went back to his hometown synagogue in Nazareth. His words infuriated the people. They were so angry that they dragged him through the city to a cliff, where they intended to throw him off headfirst. His words of inclusiveness hooked their prejudice. They could not stand the fact that God had healed Naaman, a leper from Syria, and did not heal the lepers in Israel. Jesus, feeling this rejection so keenly, remarked, "No prophet is accepted in his own country."

A newspaper carried three articles stating that three newborn babies were found in garbage dumps where they had been abandoned. In the same paper there was a report that a father carried his six-year-old son to the lobby of a hospital and left him with no intention of returning. Another article told of a husband and wife who went partying for the weekend and left their newborn baby to starve to death. A television program dramatized abandonment when a mother, influenced by her new boyfriend, let her thirteen-year-old son out at a gas station in San Francisco and abandoned him while he went to the restroom.

Abandonment has many faces. We pull away from people who hook our prejudices; who refuse to live up to our expectations, who shun or ignore us; who intimidate, manipulate, and seek to control us; who persecute and abuse us. Life is rampant with abandonment.

Why do we abandon each other? I can understand that we have our differences, that we grow angry and get upset with each other, but why do we go to the extreme of abandonment, to leave without intention of reclaiming?

There may be as many reasons for abandonment as there are persons. Harsh things happen to us, and slowly we lose our sensitivity to relatedness. Then we give ourselves permission to act without conscience. We become hard, defensive, and unforgiving. We strike back in ways that seem to hurt the most.

In my early years of ministry, I married a young couple who appeared to be deeply in love. Two weeks later I answered a 7:00 A.M. knock at the parsonage door. When I opened the door, I saw the young husband standing with tears in his eyes. Without explanation he cried out, "If she only knew how much she hurt me, she would never have left me." When I talked to the bride, her callous reason was, "He was just not what I wanted."

During the 1960s I served a church on a college campus and worked on a master's degree in psychology. I took an exciting course in abnormal psychology. The professor met with all interested students one night a week to answer questions. One Tuesday evening the conversation turned to religion. One young student leaned his chair against the wall, looked at me, and let it all hang out: "I came to the university wanting to be a Christian. I went to a student group at a certain church. They started telling me what I had to do to be a part of their group." With anger in his face, he remarked, "I decided I didn't want Jesus as my Savior."

Why do we abandon each other? Who knows?

Although we don't always know why we abandon others, we certainly can feel the hurt and pain that accompany rejection and banishment. Sometimes I wonder whether we recognize the ugly things we do to each other when we abandon each other. Listen to the following stories, and you be the judge.

Jim is a minister who has served the church for twenty years. He was called to a large metropolitan church to follow the minister who had started that church some thirty years earlier. At first he was met graciously and enthusiastically. The crowds came to hear his effective sermons. But Jim did not administrate the way his predecessor had. The talk started, the crowds decreased, the money slowed, support dwindled. Do you think Jim felt abandoned?

Phil and Sally have been married for fifteen years. At first they were very happy. Their communication was exceptional, and they seemed to be off to a happy journey together. Through the years Phil became disappointed in his profession. He began to drink at night, and after supper he would sit silently and watch television. Conversation dried up. Do you think Sally felt abandoned?

Lucy and Tom started their relationship with conflict. Tom could do nothing right. She stayed on his case for years. Then she started withholding affection and keeping Tom at arms length. Do you think Tom feels abandoned?

Bill is a crackerjack salesman. He has made the company thousands of dollars. Now, he is getting older, and his sales are dropping off. Recently, the boss gave Bill's territory to a younger person, demoting Bill in job status and salary. Do you think Bill feels abandoned?

John and Myra have been married forty years. John retired at sixty-five. They made their plans for travel and leisure time together. Six months after retirement John became the victim of a fast-growing cancer. Three months later, he was dead. Do you think Myra feels abandoned?

The story has a thousand faces. Each of us has his or her own story to tell. We are not always sure why we have been abandoned, but we have to live with the hurt and pain. We all have experiences in all of our lives that are too broken to mend. It has been my experience that we have to learn to trust God with those experiences.

Since abandonment seems to be a universal experience, how can we learn to manage ourselves and the hurt and pain that come from forsakenness?

Jesus was abandoned by his own people. He went to his own people, but they did not receive him. He was forsaken by the members of the synagogue. It helps to know that abandonment happens to everyone, including our Lord. It helps to know that it need not be the end of the world. There is always someone who will accept us, take us in, and help us to feel that we are wanted and that we belong. There is love out there, believe it or not.

We can identify with Jesus because he suffered abandonment on our behalf. The writer of Leviticus tells us about the scape goat that carried the sins of Israel into the desert of Azazel on the Day of Atonement:

> Then Aaron shall lay both his hands on the head of the live goat, and confess over it all the iniquities of the people of Israel, and all their transgressions, all their sins, putting them on the head of the goat, and sending it away into the wilderness. . . . The goat shall bear on itself all their iniquities to a barren region; and the goat shall be set free in the wilderness. (Lev. 16:21-22)

What a desolate picture—abandoned on my behalf. In the New Testament the image is different, but the experience is the same. This time it is Jesus hanging on the cross, abandoned for us: "From noon on, darkness came over the whole land until three in the afternoon. And about three o'clock Jesus cried out with a loud voice, 'Eli, Eli, lema sabachthani?' that is, 'My God, my God, why have you [abandoned] me?' " (Matt. 27:45-47).

Why? The answers are not always forthcoming. However, there is one thing we can count on: God never abandons us. Obviously, he did not abandon Jesus. Our experiences of abandonment can make us more sensitive to the issue and more aware of the ways we relate to each other.

This insight was brought home to me through a conversation with my son-in-law, who is a psychiatrist. We were walking down the beach at the close of a wonderful day. I asked him, "Now that you have finished your studies and are a practicing psychiatrist, what have you learned that stands out in your memory?" He replied, "I have learned that there is no growth without suffering." As we talked he shared that he was in search of the genuinely holy. Then he told me about a young woman with whom he was working, who had been abandoned by her father. I asked, "What did you say to her?" He said that he had reassured her that he would never leave or abandon her. As I thought about his search for "the holy" and his reassurance that he would never abandon this woman, a thought came to my mind, which I shared: "David, you have been searching for that which is genuinely holy—well that is it. Genuine holiness is God's reassurance that he will never abandon us."

What Jesus felt in the synagogue in Nazareth we may feel today in our modern world. When we experience abandonment, we can be assured of one thing: Jesus knows, he understands, and he will never leave nor forsake us.

Suggestions for Worship

Call to Worship (Psalm 71:1, 3-4):

MINISTER: In you, O LORD, I take refuge;

PEOPLE: let me never be put to shame. . . .

MINISTER: Be to me a rock of refuge, a strong fortress, to save me. . . .

PEOPLE: Rescue me, O my God, from the hand of the wicked, from the grasp of the unjust and cruel.

Acts of Praise: Psalm 71:1-6.

Suggested Hymns: opening hymn: "O For a Thousand Tongues to Sing"; second hymn: "Sweet Hour of Prayer"; closing hymn: "Take My Life, and Let It Be."

Opening Prayer: O God, you are our refuge. Our home is always with you. O Christ, who, though rejected, homeless, and alone, was never lonely, draw us closer unto yourself. Teach us to love as you have loved, to welcome those who reject us, and to pray for those who resent us. Forbid, O Savior Christ, that we should in any way turn you away from our homes and our sanctuary today. Have mercy upon us. Amen.

Pastoral Prayer: Eternal and gracious God, You have invited us to come and worship in your sanctuary. The joy of worship brings delight to our minds and growth to our souls. To be with you is to be disturbed with the joy of elevated thoughts. In your presence, all the world looks different. Our problems are more solvable, our confusion is clarified, our emptiness is filled, and our lives are enriched by the adequate expression of your grace. You are truly a very present help in time of trouble; you hide us in your pavilion; you give us peace in the midst of the swirling storms. You give us stability when the foundations are shaky, and you give us confidence to go on when we are tempted to run away.

Oh God, fill your people with the courage to help the weak, to lift up the fallen, to clothe the naked, and to feed the hungry. Give us the courage of our convictions and the endurance for the journey of life. May the words of our mouths, the intentions of our minds, and the actions of our lives be acceptable and pleasing to you. In the maddening maze of daily routine, help us to find the path that leads to insight, management, and sanity. Help us to use all our strength by allowing you to be our inner companion and supportive friend. Thank you for that part of you that will never leave us or forsake us, for that part of you that stands firm when we are shaking, for that part of you that is always there when we need you. Thank you that we have never had to say, "Where were you, God, when we needed you?"

In the name of Christ our Lord, amen.

FEBRUARY 9, 1992

□

Fifth Sunday After Epiphany

Those who witness the manifestation of God's power and glory are left with a sense of unworthiness, and they cannot escape the divine claim upon their lives.

The Sunday Lessons

Isaiah 6:1-8 (or 13): In the year the king died, the young Isaiah was in the Temple and "saw the Lord sitting on a throne, high and lofty" (v. 1). Surrounded by the holiness of God, he sensed his own unworthiness, "Woe is me!" (v. 5). Isaiah was cleansed, called, and commissioned.

I Corinthians 15:1-11: The church at Corinth questioned Christ's Resurrection. Paul considered it basic to the gospel and noted the appearances of the risen Christ. Paul, too, felt unworthy, "I am the least . . . unfit to be called an apostle" (v. 9).

Luke 5:1-11: The call of the first disciples was by the Sea of Galilee. Jesus had been teaching from Simon's boat and then said, "Put out into the deep water and let down your nets" (v. 4). After the amazing catch of fish, Simon was overwhelmed by a sense of the divine. Like the young Isaiah, he was aware of his unworthiness: "Go away from me, Lord, for I am a sinful man!" (v. 8).

Interpretation and Imagination

William E. Sangster, a scholar-evangelist of England, once observed, "It is not always bliss to have your prayers answered." He referred to Isaiah, who prayed for light and then trembled in the presence of God's glory when it appeared. He called the sermon "The Pain of Answered Prayer."

We may ask God for an awareness of his presence, but we must realize that any real manifestation of divine power and glory is likely to upset our world and our personal agendas. It will reveal our unworthiness, make claims on our personal programs, deny us comfort, and possibly even undo our career status and ecclesiastical privilege.

If all of this sounds heavy and uninviting (and it is), recall the burning coal from the holy altar. It touches lips and makes them new. Remember the response of our Lord to Peter's confession, "Depart from me, I am a sinful man." He took that fisherman, and his self-depreciation, and made him a fisher of men and the rock upon which God built the church.

EXHAUSTED BUT EMPOWERED

Luke 5:1-11

A SERMON BY THOMAS H. TROEGER

His body ached from lack of sleep,
and his joints were stiff
from being out on the water
through the chill of the night,
from standing
and sitting
then standing again for long hours in a boat.
And I doubt there was any way that he,
Simon Peter,
could mask the exhaustion in his voice
when Jesus told him to put out to deep water
and he answered:
"Master, we were hard at work all night and caught nothing;
but if you say so, I will let down the nets."
All that effort and not one thing to show for it.
You know how life goes:
You work and you work and you work,
and sometimes it all adds up to nothing.
You work and you work and you work
to help your child become accepting of every kind of person.
Then one night at supper you hear:
"I don't like so-and-so at school."
You ask who so-and-so is,

only to discover it is a child of another race
or from a foreign country.
Then you understand what Simon felt when he said:
"Master, we were hard at work all night and caught nothing."
All that effort and not one thing to show for it.
Or maybe you try to get a project started in your neighborhood—
a counseling agency, a drug rehab program,
a youth center, a tutoring service,
a home for the homeless.
You take around petitions.
You enlist volunteers.
You talk to civic organizations.
You write letters to the paper.
Then the funding fails to come through.
Or some group shows up at the city council
with posters reading:
"Not in my back yard."
And out of your heart arises a prayer that sounds like Simon Peter's
first response to Jesus:
"Master, we were hard at work all night and caught nothing."
All that effort and not one thing to show for it.
I think of the church for whom Luke wrote his Gospel
some two generations after the resurrection of Christ.
How hard they had worked!
They had worked and worked and worked.
They had preached.
They had taught.
They had healed.
They had shared bread and wine and even their possessions.
But things had not come out the way they had hoped.
They had expected Christ's imminent return.
They had told people, as he had,
that the kingdom was on the way,
that God's intention for the world would soon be realized.
And what did the church have to show for it all?
The kingdom was still nowhere in sight.
If anything,
what with the persecutions
and the scorn they faced,
it seemed farther away than ever.

There was probably a great sigh of recognition
when Luke's congregation heard Simon Peter say:
"Master, we were hard at work all night and caught nothing."
All that effort and not one thing to show for it.
Simon Peter, however, did not stop with the acknowledgment of his exhaustion.
He continued:
"But if you say so, I will let down the nets."
Peter's response involves more than just a second effort,
more than the old cliche:
"If at first you don't succeed,
try, try again."
The translation of Peter's words,
"But if you say so, I will let down the nets,"
is too lightweight in English.
It fails to communicate the heft of Luke's meaning.
The phrase "if you say so" is better rendered:
"But at your creative word I will let down the nets."
A creative word,
a power for good,
for truth,
for love,
has been set loose in the universe.
Although Simon's initial efforts failed,
he tried again
because Christ's gracious power will bring to completion
the work that Simon was called to do:
"But at your creative word I will let down the nets."
Although their initial efforts appear to have fallen short,
Luke's church will try again
because Christ's gracious power will bring to completion
the work they are called to do:
"But at your creative word I will let down the nets."
And although you and I have not realized our best goals,
we will try again;
we will persist to teach tolerance;
we will persist in ministering to those in need,
because Christ's gracious power will bring to completion
the work we are called to do:
"But at your creative word I will let down the nets."

This trust in the creative word of Christ is far more than wishful thinking.
Such faith is nurtured by what we can observe in our own experience.
Recall those times when you thought you were defeated
and you had no more strength to carry on.
But you did.
Bitter times
when you were convinced you could not forgive.
But you did.
Sacrificial times
when you said you had given all you could
and could give no more.
But you did.
Dangerous times
when you said you lacked the courage to do justice
and you would not stick out your neck once again.
But you did.
If you think back to these times,
if you consider all that has been best in your life,
you will discover that at such times there was within you
a presence,
a power,
a holy strength
that was more than your ability.
It was what Paul calls grace:
"By God's grace I am what I am."
And when we identify this grace in our lives,
then we do not claim it as our own selfish possession.
But, like Paul, we come to see that
this presence,
this power,
this holy strength that infuses our energies,
this irresistible desire to do what is right
is nothing less than a gift of the risen Christ.
It is the creative word that calls us, saying:
"Put out into deep water and let down your nets for a catch."
In the presence of this word we are utterly honest
about our exhaustion:

"Master, we were hard at work all night and caught nothing."
And in the presence of this word
we are empowered to persist in our efforts
to make a more just and compassionate world.
We join with Simon Peter and declare:
"But at your creative word I will let down the nets."

Suggestions for Worship

Call to Worship:

MINISTER: I will praise you, O LORD, with all my heart;

PEOPLE: We will praise your name for your love and your faithfulness,

MINISTER: For you have exalted above all things, your name and your word.

PEOPLE: Let us sing of the ways of the LORD, for the glory of the LORD is great.

Act of Praise: Psalm 138.

Suggested Hymns: opening hymn: "Jesus Calls Us"; second hymn: "Lord, I Want to Be a Christian"; closing hymn: "Take Up Thy Cross."

Opening Prayer:
Holy, holy, holy are you, O God.
  Stars and planets, land and ocean,
  atoms and galaxies—all that exists—
  is filled with your glory.
We come to praise you, as the source of everything:
  the breath that fills us with breath,
  the pulse that gives our hearts their pulse,
  the love that makes our love more than passing affection.
Before your presence, O Holy and Mysterious One,
  we see how imperfect we are:
  that we are people whose speech and deeds
  fall far short of your commands and our highest hopes.

Touch our hearts, our minds, our lips
with the purifying fire of your truth,
that we with confidence may respond to your grace,
saying, "Here we are. Send us."
Send us with light to a world that is in darkness.
Send us with peace to a world that is at war.
Send us with grace to a world that lives by vengeance.
Send us with faith to a world that is in doubt,
until every creature and every nation shall
join the song of the seraphim, chanting:
Holy, holy, holy are you, O God.
Stars and planets, land and ocean,
atoms and galaxies—all that exists—
is filled with your glory. Amen.

Pastoral Prayer:

O God, whose presence means more to us than life itself,
we pray with the psalmist: "Do not abandon what you have made."
We fear being alone,
alone with our violent thoughts,
alone with our griefs,
alone with the doubts that sap our energies.
Yet, even as we recognize our fear of being alone,
we remember others who feel abandoned:
prisoners of conscience,
members of divorced families,
those who are dying without a circle of support,
those who are mourning by themselves.
Through us and through the silent and unseen ministries of your Spirit,
invade our lonely, yearning, bleeding world.
Become incarnate again in the touch of a hand,
in acts of compassion
in words of sympathy
that all may know what the psalmist knows:
that "your love endures for ever, Lord." Amen.

February 16, 1992

□

Sixth Sunday After Epiphany

Abiding peace and contentment, "blessedness," have more to do with being faithful than being fulfilled.

The Sunday Lessons

Jeremiah 17:5-10: Jeremiah, trying to persuade hearers to be faithful to God, refers to God as a life-giving stream in the desert. Blessed are those who trust God. They will be like a tree planted by the water.

I Corinthians 15:12-20: Some Corinthians said there was no resurrection of the dead. Paul replied that if we have hope for this life only, we are to be pitied. "If Christ has not been raised, your faith is futile" (v. 17). But Christ has indeed been raised from the dead, the "first fruits" of those who have fallen asleep.

Luke 6:17-26: These are Luke's beatitudes and part of Jesus' teaching in the sermon on the plain. There are four: blessed are the poor; blessed are those who hunger; blessed are those who weep; and blessed are those who are excluded. Luke also lists four woes: woe to those who are rich; woe to those who are well fed; woe to those who laugh; woe to those of whom all speak well.

Interpretation and Imagination

The marks of good fortune are luxury and leisure, power and popularity. Every story with a happy ending includes these qualities of life. These are the standards by which we measure success.

Therefore, we conclude: How fortunate are those who have enough money to hire servants. How fortunate are those who dine at the finest tables. How fortunate are those who are so much in control that they can laugh in the face of every limitation. How fortunate are those who have the approval and favor of many friends.

Jesus taught that these things are not benefits, but burdens. How hard it is for a rich person to enter the kingdom. How hard it is for a proud person to receive God's gift of mercy.

Luke's beatitudes include four. Matthew's Gospel (Matt. 5:1-11) lists nine. Luke's are more direct than Matthew's. They refer more to standards of living than to spiritual attitudes.

Who are the poor and the hungry? Are they persons who cannot afford to buy everything they want? No, they are persons who do not have what they need.

Who are those who weep? Persons whose hearts are broken by bereavement and loss; spoiled children who cry in order to get their way. There is a kind of weeping referred to as "holy mourning." These are tears of a contrite heart.

The "beggar who prays" is a sculpture made in clay by a sixteen-year-old German boy, Erdmann-Michael Hinz. The figure is lean, ragged, and bent. Everything about him speaks of poverty. His hands, overly large and very empty, and his face, uplifted and imploring, are the shape of his prayer and, therefore, his blessing. He knows he has nothing to give and can only receive.

THE BLESSED, THE CURSED, AND THE CHURCH

Luke 6:17-26

A SERMON BY PAUL T. STALLSWORTH

According to the Bible, there are two basic types of people in this world. There are the blessed, and there are the cursed. The blessed, as far as the Bible is concerned, are blessed by God. They have God's favor for one reason or another. Having received divine approval, the blessed are promised future happiness by the Lord. On the other hand, there are the not so fortunate, the cursed. The cursed have fallen out of favor with God. They are divinely disapproved. Their future ends in God's judgment—most likely in God's angry judgment.

The Old Testament is loaded with statements on the blessed

and the cursed. For example, Jeremiah declared that "those who trust in the LORD" (17:7) are blessed. The prophet also stated that "those who trust in mere mortals" (17:5) are cursed. The psalmist also knew of the blessed and the cursed:

> Happy are those
> who do not follow the advice
> of the wicked
> (Ps. 1:1)

The psalmist then stated that "the wicked will not stand in the judgment" (1:5). The wicked, in other words, are cursed.

Early in his public ministry, Jesus of Nazareth joined Jeremiah and the psalmist in setting forth who are the blessed and who are the cursed. In Luke 6 Jesus pronounces blessings on some and curses, or woes, on others. But the strange thing about Jesus' pronouncement in Luke is who gets what. Looking into the faces of his most loyal followers, Jesus announces that the poor, the hungry, the weeping, and the hated are blessed. He also announces that the rich, the full, the laughing, and the popular are cursed. Woe to them, Jesus says.

"What?" we protest in a hurry. That does not make sense! Poor people, hungry people, weeping people, and hated people cannot possibly be blessed. And the rich, the full, the laughing, and the popular cannot possibly be cursed.

The Bible does not directly answer our protest. It is silent. But the silence of the Bible beckons us to look more closely at its word.

According to Luke, when Jesus issued these blessings and curses, he was preaching a sermon. He was not in the middle of a private conversation. Nor was he lecturing before a group of eager theology students in a Jerusalem classroom. Instead, he preached a sermon to a multitude of his ragtag followers somewhere out on a Galilean prairie. His sermon, which sounds something like Matthew's rendition of the Sermon on the Mount, is commonly called the Sermon on the Plain.

Luke tells us that the day before preaching his Sermon on the Plain, Jesus had hiked up a mountain to do some serious praying. After praying all night long, he invited some of his followers to join him up on the mountain. From his followers assembled on the mount, Luke informs us, Jesus chose twelve men to be his "apostles." In his account, Luke was careful to use the word *apostles.* Luke could have called the twelve "disciples," but instead he called them "apostles." Luke called the chosen "apostles" because he knew that Jesus would later send them out to preach the gospel of the kingdom of God. It is these apostles who became "witnesses [for Jesus Christ] in Jerusalem, in all Judea and Samaria, and to the end of the earth" (Acts 1:8). After selecting the twelve—Simon Peter, Judas Iscariot, and the other ten—Jesus led them and all of the not-chosen others back down the mountain. There they joined a massive crowd of followers. Then, after miraculously healing the sick among them, Jesus stood to preach a sermon, the Sermon on the Plain.

The Sermon on the Plain, Luke reports, was the very first sermon Jesus preached. Therefore, in this sermon the stakes for Jesus and for his cause are high. In this sermon Jesus laid out, as exactly and as clearly as he could, what the kingdom of God is all about. Jesus had to get his message right. After all, this sermon would establish the direction of the rest of his earthly ministry and the direction of the ministry of the apostles. It would establish the direction of the Church through the ages.

Since the Sermon on the Plain is a sermon, it is meant for us, brothers and sisters, just as much as it was meant for the apostles and disciples of old.

> Blessed are you poor. . . . Blessed are you who are hungry now . . . on account of the Son of Man. . . . But woe to you who are rich. . . . Woe to you who are full now. . . . Woe to you who are laughing now. . . . Woe to you, when all speak well of you. (Luke 6:20-26)

There is a blessing of the down-and-out taking place—then and now. And there is a cursing of the upward-and-onward taking place—then and now.

Now let's be honest. Jesus' blessings and curses rub us the wrong way, don't they? They come across as a little too judgmental for our modern and refined tastes. We are more comfortable with a nonjudgmental style of Christianity. You know the message of the gospel of nonjudgment: "God made me in all of my uniqueness. God loves me just the way I am; therefore, I should try to be a little nicer to others." But then comes that very unpleasant refrain from the preacher on the plain: "Blessed are you who are poor. . . . But woe to you who are rich." That is simply too judgmental for us.

Jesus' blessings and curses rub us the wrong way for a second reason. Not only do they come across as judgmental, but also they judge *us*. You see, *we are rich.* I know it is hard to believe that we are rich when we look at our checkbooks. But look again. Look at our cars. Look at our houses—our vacation houses, our vacations, our color televisions, our VCRs, our CD players, and on and on. In the global village, we certainly live north of the tracks.

We are full now. Our daily question is not whether we are going to have something to eat. Our daily question is what we are going to have to eat, or where we are going to dine out.

We are happy now. We run around town with smiles on our faces and jokes in ready reserve—at least most of the time.

We are well-liked. We have never been put down, we have never been persecuted, because of our faith in Christ. We can feel the heat of these curses. They burn a bit too close to home.

So, what exactly was Jesus trying to tell us with these blessings and curses? What was Jesus trying to tell the Church through his blessings and his curses?

With the blessings and curses of the Sermon on the Plain, Jesus was charging the Church to look squarely at God. Jesus' blessings and curses are not primarily about us. Jesus' blessings and curses do not tell us what we must do to enter the kingdom of God. Jesus' blessings and curses are about God and who God is and what God is doing in this world. Preaching on the plain, Jesus showed us how strange God is. God blesses you who are poor. God blesses you who are hungry. God blesses you who are weeping. God blesses you who are hated for the sake of Christ.

Our God blesses these people—these real, live, smelly, stomach-growling, tear-streaked, sometimes-jailed people. He blesses these people by visiting them. God the Son visited the down-and-out in Luke's day. God the Spirit visits the down-and-out today. And finally, at the end of time, God the Father will visit this motley crew at his heavenly banquet table. This is God, announced Jesus.

God also pronounces misery on those of us who seem to have made it. God pities us if all we have is a lot of money and a lot of things. God pities us if all we have is a plentiful table and a cup that is running over. God pities us if all we do is try to escape suffering

punishment are the favored responses to wrong doing and crime. This is the primary purpose of our prisons. The New Testament teaching "Do not repay evil for evil" (Rom. 12:17; Heb. 10:38; I Pet. 3:9) is a familiar concept to Christians, but it is not common practice.

In his book *Love or Perish,* Dr. Smiley Blanton refers to humanity's constant flux between war and peace, achievement and destruction, prosperity and poverty. He illustrates his point with the philosopher Schopenhauer's view of humanity—that we are like a herd of porcupines huddling together to keep warm. If they get too close, their quills prick and give pain to one another; if they get too far apart, they freeze to death. Only constant shifting can enable them to determine what position will avoid both extremes.

It is possible to move from hostility to hospitality; to set aside treachery, betrayal, and ill will in favor of sympathy and trust. Christ is our finest example and our best teacher. Remember how he said

> You have heard that it was said "An eye for an eye and a tooth for a tooth." But I say to you, Do not resist an evildoer. But if anyone strikes you on the right cheek, turn the other also. . . . Give to everyone who begs from you, and do not refuse anyone who wants to borrow from you. (Matt. 5:38-42)

THE CHRISTIAN LOVE LIFE

Luke 6:27-38

A SERMON BY PAUL T. STALLSWORTH

As Christians living in the United States, we are confident that we have arrived at a fairly good way of being Christian and modern at the same time. For some time we have held Christianity and modern life together by talking quite a bit about love. But, modern Christians that we are, we have not been content to talk about love in the ways the Bible talks about love. So we have forever updated what we think love is all about. That, of course, has prevented us from coming across as too fundamentalist in this society of ours, which prides itself on being progressive.

Our new and allegedly improved understandings of love have

borrowed freely, and unconsciously, from the world around us. Since "ethics" is the rage these days on the university campus and on the pages of our newspapers, we Christians find ourselves talking quite a bit about ethics. For more than a few of us, the word *ethics* has become as important as the word *love*. As far as we are concerned, ethics is displacing, or replacing, love. We act as if "You shall be ethical" has been added to the Ten Commandments.

We Christians have a no-nonsense way of talking about and doing ethics today. We talk about ethics by discussing moral choices and decisions that many have to make at one time or another. When we are especially thoughtful, we reflect on "decision humankind"—that is, how we make, or how we ought to make, the moral choices that we have to make. When we get into moral decision making, we lay out the reasons—the advantages and the disadvantages, the costs and the benefits—for making the moral choices that we make.

Mixed in with our discussion of ethics and choices and decision making is the theme of individual rights. We simply assume, as do most citizens of the United States, that all of the constitutional rights (as well as many nonconstitutional rights) belong to us. Indeed, like most Americans, we Christians believe that all kinds of individual rights should be asserted—at the office, in the classroom, at the grocery store, in the living room, at the train depot, on the interstate, and so on. Some of us have probably taken classes in assertiveness training. Individual rights and our assertion of individual rights help to shape our way of being ethical.

The idea of relationships also shapes our way of being ethical. A Christian hospital executive recently mentioned to me, "At our hospital we are not much interested in rules. Here at the hospital we are interested in relationships. In fact, we have found that rules often get in the way of genuine relationship. Rules often harm meaningful relationships." And, as an aside, did you ever notice how often today people talk about having "a relationship"?

With this kind of an ethical background, how do we, as Christians, usually love our neighbor today? Usually, and I trust that this is not too far from the mark, we love our neighbor by being nice to the people we think we should be nice to. In most cases, this means that we are nice to the people who will probably be nice to us. Our love is usually a soft form of enlightened self-interest. Our love is usually the stuff of common sense.

Now if, by chance someone would do something against us, our love, which starts out as enlightened self-interest, suddenly becomes much more self-interested than enlightened. In the midst of what we see as a personal offense against us, we react by instinct almost immediately against our offender. These offenses happen all of the time. For example, if you do not exceed the speed limit by at least ten miles per hour, usually the driver in the car behind you will try to urge you to drive faster. What is usually your reaction to that? To honk back or to offer a condescending wave of the hand to the honker or to mutter some not-so-nice comments about the irate driver who does not appreciate your law-abiding habits. As far as we are concerned, this is simply a commonsense response to an aggressive driver on a crowded street. It is in line with the way we understand, talk about, and do love; we are nice to someone until we are shown reason to be otherwise. Then we slip into a look-out-for-number-one mode. That is the way we are.

But then along comes Jesus, preaching the Sermon on the Plain. In the first part of the sermon, Jesus reveals a picture of the God who, strangely enough, blesses the unlucky of this world while pronouncing woes on the lucky. After revealing a glimpse of who God is, Jesus moves on to show how his apostles, his disciples, his people, his church should live in obedience to this God. This is the practical, how-does-this-apply-to-our-lives section of the sermon that we North American Christians find most interesting. Jesus begins, "But I say to you that listen, Love your enemies" (Luke 6:27*a*). Surely knowing that not everyone will hear him, Jesus preaches, "Love your enemies." What a strange thing to say. Nevertheless, Jesus says it, and Jesus does not halfheartedly say it. He commands it. Jesus commands his Church: "Love your enemies."

Do you see what is going on here? Our Lord Jesus Christ is commanding his people, us—you and me—to love our enemies. This is nothing short of an assault on us, for Jesus is assaulting our usual way of living and loving. By commanding us to love our enemies, Jesus is telling us that, whether we recognize them or not, we have enemies. But most of the time we cover up the fact of our enemies by avoiding them and by being nice to everybody who is nice to us. Could each of us come up with a personal enemies list? According to the command of Christ, we could. Indeed, as Christians we should know exactly who our enemies are.

Jesus' command to love our enemies assaults our modern ways of living and loving in a deeper sense. After all, Jesus is not interested in ethics. He is interested in love. But Jesus is not interested in our kind of love. He is interested in the love that he describes and practices. Jesus is not interested in our moral choices and our ethical decision-making processes. He is interested in our being a people who love as he loved. Jesus is not interested in our individual rights. He is interested in the claims that he and our neighbor, even our enemies, have on us. Jesus is not interested in our relationships without rules. He is interested in our being related to God by becoming "children of the Most High" (Luke 6:35). Jesus is not interested in our calculating, subtle forms of enlightened self-interest. He is interested in our being interested in the interests of our enemies. "Love your enemies," you see, is an assault on us.

On the lips of Jesus, "love your enemies" is not a challenge for us to create yet another humanitarian program that tries to uplift a specific group of people. "Love your enemies" is not a call for some do-gooding. Nor is it a call for us to exercise, through the strength of our own will power, extraordinary moral virtue. "Love your enemies" is, as Karl Barth wrote, a "marching order never to allow rejection or opposition which they [the disciples of Christ] encounter to divert them from their accepted role as witnesses of the kingdom" (*Church Dogmatics*). Likewise, with "love your enemies," Jesus commands us to be single-minded about being his witnesses for the kingdom of God in the world—no matter what the world is doing, no matter what the world is doing to us.

If someone wrongs us, we are commanded not to retaliate in kind against that person. If someone hates us, we are commanded to do good to that person. If someone curses us with a foul word, we are commanded to return a good word. If someone abuses us, we are commanded to pray for, not against, the abuser. If someone strikes us on one cheek, we are commanded to turn the other cheek, not to enlist a lawyer and drag the assailant to court. If someone steals from us, we are commanded to offer the thief more of our possessions. And if someone begs from us, we are commanded to give to that person. "Love your enemies," the

Lord commands us. "Love your enemies" not because it will benefit you in the end. "Love your enemies" not so that you can be proven to be more righteous than the next guy. "Love your enemies" because in doing so you can be merciful. "Love your enemies" because that is what Jesus desires of us.

Friday night is always the big night out for high-school students. One Friday night back in the mid 1960s in Garden City, Kansas, a group of the local high school seniors, many of whom were athletes, happened upon a group of freshmen and sophomores. One of the seniors was looking for one of the sophomores. The senior, who was the center on the varsity basketball team, had some strong words with the sophomore over a girlfriend. After issuing a series of warnings and threats, the senior took a swipe at his perceived adversary and made contact. The sophomore, who was a devout Christian, stood his ground and cooly offered up the other side of his face to the senior's fist. The Friday night spectators who had gathered around this duel were stunned by the gesture. He had heard his Lord's command to "love your enemies," and he had obeyed.

Jesus commands us to love our enemies. That is something we are not now doing. If we were honest before God, we would wonder whether we are capable of loving our enemies. Hearing one thousand sermons on this passage from Luke will not make us able to love our enemies. Merely trying just as hard as we can to love our enemies will likely result in absolute failure. So what can we do?

We can seek to be converted, or turned around, by Christ. On our own, as we are, given our habits and our inclinations, we cannot possibly love those who oppose us. But through the crucifying and resurrecting power of God in Christ, our fevered desires to defeat our enemies can be eliminated and the burning desire to care for our enemies can be received.

Our Lord, and our Lord alone, gives us everything we need to love our enemies. He gave us a new start through our baptism into his death and resurrection. He gives us nourishment with his own body and blood through the bread and the cup of Holy Communion. He speaks to us through the Scriptures—read, preached, and taught. He gives us the Church, through which we are trained, sometimes painfully, into a new way of living and loving. Everything that we need to love our enemies has been and is being given. All we lack is a new heart. That, also, he will give to us if we will but ask him.

Loving our enemies, brothers and sisters, begins in this household of faith. As you certainly know, it is often more difficult to love our enemies in our own church than it is to love enemies outside our church. Still, that is Christ's command. Too often we succumb. That, my friends, is sin of which we are guilty and for which we must seek forgiveness. We must be converted.

God's word for us today is simple. It is unqualified. It is straight. It is difficult: *Love your enemies.* But by the merciful and converting power of God—working through his Word, his sacraments, and this church—it is possible for us to obey. *Love your enemies.* Amen.

Suggestions for Worship

Call to Worship:

MINISTER: Delight yourself in the LORD, and he will give you the desires of your heart.

PEOPLE: Commit your way to the LORD; trust in him and he will do this:

MINISTER: He will make your righteousness shine like the dawn; the justice of your cause like the noonday sun.

PEOPLE: Be still before the LORD and wait patiently for him.

MINISTER: A little while, and the power of evil will fail.

PEOPLE: But the meek will inherit the earth and enjoy great peace.

Act of Praise: Psalm 37:1-11.

Suggested Hymns: opening hymn: "Christ for the World We Sing"; second hymn: "In Christ There Is No East or West"; closing hymn: "Where Charity and Love Prevail."

Opening Prayer: O Lord, we praise you for creating this world and then for entering into it in a relentless search for the lost and for the deceived. We praise you for finding us. We praise you for becoming, in Jesus Christ, our righteousness. We praise you for saving us from the bondage of sin and death, from our self-chosen ways and our self-devised projects for security.

Through your Holy Spirit, grant us, we pray, the humility and the desire to hear you and to trust you and to obey you. In Jesus' name. Amen.

Pastoral Prayer: O Father, for this day of resurrection and for this service of resurrection, we give you thanks. For giving us earth and sun and moon and stars to enjoy, we give you thanks. For giving us breath after breath, minute after minute, year after year, we offer up our thanks to you. For work to do, for meals to cook, for families and friends and enemies, for sermons to write, for hills and mountains to climb, for sales to attempt, for books to read, for miles to drive, for games to win and lose, for time to rest, for music to play, for conversations to join, we give you thanks. Enlarge and deepen our gratitude for your infinite gifts, we pray.

Father, because of your mercy, your Son is our Lord and Savior. May we, because of your Spirit, see him truly and hear him rightly. We ask that your Son would create fresh unity in his Church and among his churches on earth. May the unity provided by Christ assist the Church in holding high the cross as a judgment of all of the false prophets and counterfeit salvations of our day. Assist the Church also in proclaiming the Resurrection of Christ as the clearest sign of genuine hope in this world.

Sustain us, O Lord, in doing what you command and in avoiding what is destructive to us and to our communities. Through your severe mercy challenge us, change us, and push us on to perfection. Lead us daily out of our self-absorption. Place upon us the yoke of obedience so that we might serve you more faithfully in the vocations and duties that you bestow upon us.

Prepare us to suffer and to be with the suffering. May your Holy Spirit protect our brothers and sisters who are near death or who experience afflictions of the mind. May you grant them blessings of the kingdom even as they experience the terrors of this life.

We pray this in the name of Jesus Christ, who was and is and will always be our salvation in this world and in the world to come. Amen.

MARCH 1, 1992

□

Last Sunday After Epiphany (Transfiguration)

When the radiance of heaven touches earth, we recognize familiar things, but never comprehend the mystery.

The Sunday Lessons

Exodus 34:29-35: After forty days and nights on Mount Sinai, Moses' "face shone because he had been talking with God" (v. 29). At first the people were afraid to come near him, just as they feared the nearness of God. Moses called them to him, gave them the Commandments, and then covered his face with a veil. Why did he veil his face *after* he had spoken to the people?

II Corinthians 3:12–4:2: Paul interpreted Moses' veiled face. He contrasted the Sinai revelation and the old covenant, "a fading splendor," with the abiding glory of Christ. He concluded that we, with unveiled faces, are being changed into his likeness.

Luke 9:28-36: First-century Christians loved to retell the transfiguration story. Their confessed Messiah was rejected, humiliated, denied, and finally crucified. The account of Moses' prayers on the mountain, the cloud, the shining glory, and the voice from heaven helped them to know, in the face of suffering, that God is Lord.

Interpretation and Imagination

A generation ago (1956) Paul Tillich quoted an intellectual leader of the day, who said, "I hope for the day when everyone can speak again of God without embarrassment." Tillich challenged that statement, asking, "Is an unembarrassed use of the divine name desirable? Is an unembarrassed religion desirable? Certainly not!" (*The Eternal Now*).

The theologian then wrote of our silence before God and about

God. Sometimes, we tactfully remain silent. At other times we really have nothing to say. But it is silence caused by fear and awe that prohibits thoughtful and reverent persons from speaking of God altogether. God "lives in unapproachable light, which no man has ever seen nor can see."

Without minimizing that truth or denying that glory, the Gospel lesson enables us to see God in a new light. A humble carpenter from Nazareth, on his way to humiliation and death, was at prayer on a mountain. While praying, he was transfigured, and there appeared with him two Old Testament greats: Moses and Elijah. But the glory rested in Jesus Christ, Son of God.

All things, like all persons, may be seen in a new light, which is not new at all, but rather the abiding glory of Christ.

THE TRANSFIGURATION OF OUR COMMON LIFE

II Corinthians 3:12–4:2

A SERMON BY THOMAS H. TROEGER

Remember when you were a child
and you dreamed of changing into an animal?
A bird on the wind,
a deer in the field,
flying or leaping beyond family and school.
A metamorphosis more wonderful
than a caterpillar into a butterfly.
Those childhood dreams never leave us.
They simply take new forms.
Turn on the tube and tune in the fantasies:
a perfect figure,
winning the lottery,
flying to exotic lands.
Then look in the mirror.
I don't know about you, but to speak for myself,
I will not soon be featured on life-styles of the rich and famous.
I doubt I could even make it on a religious broadcast.
When I look in the mirror, there is no evidence—
to use words from Paul the Apostle—

that I am being transfigured "from splendor to splendor."
Paul's words seem not to apply to me at all,
until I examine what he wrote and find that,
under the influence of childhood dreams
and media fantasies,
I have completely misunderstood the apostle.
According to Paul,
we are the mirror,
not the image.
As J. B. Phillips translates it:
We "reflect like mirrors the glory of the Lord."
There is a difference between
being the image
and being the mirror,
between observing ourselves
and reflecting another.
Think of the difference this way:
two people are falling in love
and are getting ready for a date with each other.
Before the date each fusses with his or her appearance.
They keep returning to the mirror
with this piece of clothing and that.
Nothing is right.
As long as they are preoccupied with their own images,
doubt and concern shadow their eyes.
Then at last they join each other's company.
The faces that had peered into the mirror,
charting every blemish and oversized pore,
are transfigured in the presence of each other.
The eyes shine.
The lines of concern relax into natural smiles.
Even the clothes that seemed like foreign costumes
drape more gracefully
as the body adjusts to a posture of confident joy.
The two people are no longer obsessed
with their own self-image in the mirror.
They have become themselves a mirror of their beloved:
They have not lost their individuality and identity,
but they each reflect back

delight, joy, concern, and affection
for the other person.
Now this is only an analogy,
and like all analogies it has its limits.
But in Spirit it illumines what Paul meant when he said
"We all reflect as in a mirror the splendour of the Lord;
thus we are transfigured into his likeness,
from splendour to splendour;
such is the influence of the Lord who is Spirit."
If the two people who are in love
have more than a passing infatuation,
then their initial radiance will deepen and mellow
through the years.
It will develop "from splendour to splendour."
I have seen this happen in marriages
and in deep and enduring friendships.
I am not thinking of love's first romantic bloom,
as wonderful as that can be.
I have in mind, rather, the simplicities
of mature wisdom:
patience with each other's foibles,
understanding how hard life can be,
faithfulness,
standing side by side in grief and joy,
being consistently gracious and fair.
These do not show up in the morning mirror
when we count another wrinkle
and regret our thickening bodies.
Yet, they are the qualities that sustain
not only a couple
or a family
but also a community.
They are at the heart of the church's common life.
Paul knew that,
but he feared the Corinthians did not.
He feared they might try to hold themselves together
by basing their common life on the law
rather than God's Spirit and grace.
He acknowledged that there was splendor to the law:
"That splendor, though it was soon to fade,

made the face of Moses so bright
that the Israelites could not gaze steadily at him.
But if so, must not even greater splendour
rest upon the divine dispensation of the Spirit?"
To understand Paul's distinction between law and Spirit,
think again of our imperfect analogy of lovers.
There are times of stress and conflict
in all human relationships.
And when we encounter them,
if we do not want to break up,
we use more formal ways of relating.
We guard what we say.
We make a point of not presuming upon the other's
usual patience
or humor
or grace.
We do not risk a hot topic.
And there is wisdom in such behavior.
There are times when the heart is too tender
and wounds are too raw to risk our usual familiarity.
We live by the law of our relationship,
not by its spirit
or its grace.
We depend on the strictures of diplomacy
instead of the customs of intimacy.
But no friendship,
no marriage,
no community
can sustain itself indefinitely on law,
even on divine law.
Life is too sad, too happy,
too complex, too unpredictable,
and so instead we must live by the Spirit
for "where the Spirit of the Lord is, there is liberty."
This liberty is not license to do whatever we feel,
to disregard all the civilities of the law.
But it is the liberty that comes from reflecting
the grace and love of God,
the liberty of lovers and friends
to be mirrors of each other,

to reflect all that is best in each other.
We may never realize our childhood dreams,
to be birds that soar upon the wind
or deer that leap through the high mountain pasture,
and we may never embody the televised fantasies of mass culture,
to be the svelte dieties of the
diet soda commercials
or to win the state lottery.
But if as a community
we rely on the grace and Spirit of our Lord,
then we will find that we are being "transfigured"—
or, to use Paul's literal word, "metamorphosed"—
into the likeness of the Lord.
This is a metamorphosis
more wonderful than our most extravagant childhood dream,
more satisfying than television's most luxurious version of the good life.
We will not see this metamorphosis in the morning mirror.
We will not be able to record it on video,
any more than Peter, James, and John
could capture the transfiguration of Christ upon the mountain.
But we will sense and feel
the transfiguration of our common life
in our words of forgiveness and our acts of love.
Then Paul's extravagant claim will be our own:
"We all reflect as in a mirror the splendour of the Lord;
thus we are transfigured into his likeness,
from splendour to splendour;
such is the influence of the Lord who is Spirit."

Suggestions for Worship

Call to Worship (Ps. 99:1-2, 9):

MINISTER: The LORD is king, let the peoples tremble. . . .

PEOPLE: The LORD is great in Zion; he is exalted over all the peoples. . . .

MINISTER: Extol the LORD our God, and worship at his holy mountain;

PEOPLE: **for the LORD our God is holy.**

Act of Praise: Psalm 99.

Suggested Hymns: opening hymn: "Christ, Whose Glory Fills the Skies"; second hymn: "Ask Ye What Great Thing I Know"; closing hymn: "Jesus Shall Reign."

Opening Prayer:
God of justice and judgment,
We know that you call us to account
as you called Moses and Samuel and Aaron,
Sarah and Deborah and Miriam.
We know that you have the highest expectations
for fairness,
for equity,
for respect for all your creatures.
We acknowledge that we have not lived up to your high standard.
We have ignored those who lack status.
We have paid more attention to the wealthy than the poor.
We have assumed
our own class,
our own race,
our own kind of people were more precious in your sight.
Cleanse us from arrogance and superiority.
Teach us to show such kindness and fairness
that all people may exalt you as Lord
and bow toward your holy mountain,
recognizing you as the source of all true justice. Amen.

Pastoral Prayer:
O Christ, who was transfigured on the mountain,
but who left the moment of glory to descend to the valley,
we recall this day how we must walk the way of the cross.
Like Peter, we would prefer to stay on the summit
to build a shrine,
to retreat to our happiest memories
of grace and glory and light.

Give us now what you had: a faithful heart;
  a heart ready to wrestle with pain and grief;
  a heart brave enough to stand up to evil;
  a heart gracious enough to give up ourselves for others;
  a heart that trusts in the resurrection power of God.
Then our lives shall be transfigured,
  and we shall seek no other glory
  than what lies beyond the cross,
  beyond our dying and our rising
  to your everlasting love. Amen.

MARCH 8, 1992

□

First Sunday in Lent

The worship of God begins with the acknowledgment of God's gifts and of our dependence on God's sovereign grace. The temptations invite us to serve and honor self.

The Sunday Lessons

Deuteronomy 26:1-11: Each year, faithful Jews were to bring some of the first fruits of the land to the "altar of the Lord." This was an acknowledgment that God had given them the land in which they lived, a land flowing with milk and honey. Their confession of dependence on God begins, "A wandering Aramean was my ancestor" (v. 5). It concludes by saying, "Now I bring the first of the fruit of the ground that you, O LORD, have given me" (v. 10).

Romans 10:8*b*-13: True faith is not only believed, but it is also professed. With your lips confess that Jesus is Lord. In your heart believe that God raised Jesus from the dead. Paul contrasted a right relationship with God, sought through keeping the laws of Moses, with a relationship dependent upon faith—faith believed and confessed.

Luke 4:1-13: The three temptations of Christ were (1) bread to satisfy physical hunger, (2) power to rule the world, and (3) a spectacular attraction. Three times Jesus rebuked the tempter: (1) People shall not live by bread alone; (2) you shall worship the Lord; (3) you shall not tempt the Lord your God.

Interpretation and Imagination

Wilderness haunts and a talking devil may tempt us to view this story as something less than real. Like the garden story of the woman and the talking snake, we want at first to say that it isn't really true; it's just a fairy tale. Then we listen to the speeches of the devil, and we know it's true—it's always true. The speeches of the snake are so much akin to the voices of temptation we hear, that we do not ask what happened. We know it happens.

Surely, the wilderness is real to us. Sometimes we dream of a place twenty miles removed from sin, and at least ten miles away from temptation. We would like to send our children to college there. But such a place does not exist. All of us know all too well the haunts of wickedness, and we've often wandered in them for a time.

The temptations are real, too. We are forever trying to turn stones into bread. Again and again we strive for power to control our own destinies and the lives of others. The quick fix and easy ways of God's wonderful miracles intrigue us and turn us away from true devotion.

The three temptations held great promise for the earthly success of Jesus' mission. Bread for the world, political control of all nations, and spectacular feats to gain the attention and affection of the masses still have great appeal for all who want to rule. Jesus chose the road to Jerusalem, the way of humiliation and suffering and the cross.

LED BY THE SPIRIT, TEMPTED BY THE DEVIL

Luke 4:1-13

A SERMON BY WILLIAM K. QUICK

The baptism of Jesus by his cousin John in the River Jordan is the beginning point of Jesus' ministry. All the Gospels agree that the Holy Spirit descended in the visual image of a dove and a voice was heard proclaiming, "This is my beloved son in whom I am well pleased." This was the turning point in Jesus' life when the truth, which he may have perceived implicitly as a boy of twelve in the Temple, became explicit. Baptism was, for him, an awakening to God's unique call and God's unique powers within him.

Following the story of Jesus' baptism, the Gospel of Luke tells the story of Jesus' withdrawal into the desert to fast and meditate for a period of forty days and nights. It was a time to think of next steps toward the divine objective.

Solitude was a necessity now. Jesus knew he must take leave from these voices to hear the One voice.

Any experience that dramatically redirects one's life naturally leads one to seek space—a time of isolation and meditation. Jesus was about to enter a cosmic battle between the forces of darkness and light. Terrible forces were let loose in the world. Now God let loose God's Son to champion the cause of righteousness and to challenge Satan. Jesus' retreat to the barren Judean hills is the prelude to this story of the temptation. Satan, with his infinitely resourceful plausibility, would try to win Jesus over to his side.

Westward from the Jordan River lay the wilderness mountains. For thirty miles north to south and fifteen miles across there was no village, no wandering herdsman, no spring of water. In the stretch of desert terrain between Jerusalem and the Dead Sea he withdrew. Then, as now, the sun sinks below the horizon and the only sound heard is the jackals' howling cries. With a stone for a pillow, God's beloved Son was foodless, homeless, alone.

The wilderness battle began. This was no staged drama, but one in which a man encountered all the craftiness of the devil.

Some Christians at this point stop and say, "Go no further. I don't believe in a devil." Many acknowledge the existence of God, but they draw the line at the devil. They find it difficult in our enlightened twentieth century to believe in a destructive, malevolent creature. I heard a great Christian layman testify once that personally he found the devil easier to believe in than God because of one thing: He had had more dealings with the devil.

There is at work in our world a diabolic force that is counter to a creative, redeeming God. I do not speak of a devil out of John Milton, horned and hoofed. But I speak of a counterforce destructive in its purpose, evident in every culture, in all ages of human history, present in every being.

The long, dark shadow of that satanic presence would now tempt Jesus. So real was the battle that Jesus would recall the experience to his disciples.

My preaching professor at Duke University once pointed out to his class the fact that Jesus' temptation was not as ours. Jesus was the Son of God, but he was tempted as a human being would have been tempted. Jesus' temptations were genuine—even as yours and mine are real. True, the time, place, and circumstances of his temptations could never be ours. But it's equally true that each of us, like him, is tempted in our calling, our daily work, along the battle lines of our own talents and gifts. The tempter is always testing our temperament—waiting for the opportune time to put us at his mercy.

Jesus was tempted in three ways. The first assault on Jesus was at the point of his personal and physical needs. Basic to life are food, water, and shelter. In the initial assault on Jesus, the devil began with bread. Jesus awoke to the gnawing pain of hunger, and the fasting only accentuated his hunger pangs.

People who have visited those desert slopes and plains know there is a whole expanse of stones, most of them identical, baked and browned by the Palestinian sun and looking uncommonly like loaves of bread. Let's put the claim to the test. "If you are God's Son, order this stone to turn into bread" (Luke 4:3 GNB). Was the devil forewarning, "Out there in Judea, Samaria, and Galilee are the world's poor and starving. You will soon hear their cry for bread. Why not demonstrate your power now? One day you will be asked to turn water into wine, so by that same power make these stones become bread!"

And why not? The authorities of the Roman Empire distributed free bread to promote Caesar's kingdom. Could not Jesus do the same to promote the kingdom of God?

How alluring! Devilishly subtle, as Satan's temptations always are. Jesus saw through the offer and turned it down. Free bread might buy additional time for Caesar, but Jesus refused, saying:

> One does not live by bread
> alone,
> but by every word that comes
> from the mouth of God.
> (Matt. 4:4)

Why did Jesus refuse? Jesus knew that our physical needs are secondary to our spiritual needs. You cannot bribe people into the kingdom by promising to meet their physical needs. While bread is a basic necessity of life, if bread is its own end the one who is well fed could end up spiritually starved.

Time and time again throughout his ministry Jesus echoed this them. Never indifferent to physical needs and to the social conditions that brought on those needs, Jesus knew that a life built around physical needs alone would collapse. History has proved it so. Ancient cultures that ruled the world all collapsed, one by one.

Jesus knew the Law and the Prophets. He remembered the word spoken generations earlier: "He humbled you by letting you hunger . . . in order to make you understand that one does not live by bread alone, but by every word that comes from the mouth of the LORD" (Deut. 8:3). We need bread, and we need it desperately. Ask the hungry and half-starved in our cities or in the Third World. But bread is not our deepest need. Fellowship with God—even if it means hunger—is our deepest need. Jesus refused to use his power to meet his own need.

Jesus returned often to this theme and promised those who would follow him the "Bread of Life" which would satisfy their hunger forever. In the upper room, during the meal we call the Last Supper, he spoke to his disciples and likened bread to his own body, which would be sacrificed for them and for every person who would henceforth live. Was he saying that bread is to the body what his truth is to the soul? "The body they may kill;/God's truth abideth still," the reformer Martin Luther would testify centuries later. Jesus, led by the Spirit, won the first battle.

The second temptation the devil offered Jesus was political power. All the kingdoms of the world with all their wealth and power would be his if he would bow down and worship Satan. From the crest of that mountain that towers over the Jordan, Jesus had a view of his world. To the east beyond Moab stretched the historic nations that had ruled the ancient world: Assyria, Babylon, Persia. When he looked to the west he could see the blue waters of the great Mediterranean around which the Roman Empire spread as well as the ancient civilizations of Egypt and Greece.

Why not build an empire greater than Rome? Why not become emperor of the world? The devil said, "It has all been handed over to me, and I can give it to anyone I choose. All this will be yours, then, if you worship me" (Luke 4:6-7 GNB).

By a simple genuflection and assent, it would all belong to Jesus. And he, God's beloved Son, could bring to pass every utopian dream of all men and women born and unborn. His statue would be in every major city in the world, his picture plastered in every town square, his name would be above all names. Here was a once-in-a-lifetime offer. This was a golden opportunity, his chance at the biggest lottery in history. What did Jesus say?

He turned the offer down. And he did it for one reason: Only God should be worshiped. His response to Satan's offer was to quote Deuteronomy 4:10:

> It is written,
> "Worship the Lord your God,
> and serve only him."
> (Luke 4:8)

Jesus knew that God's powers were to be used on God's terms. The one thing that God will not do is compromise with evil. Perhaps in that moment Jesus realized what he would later preach in a sermon to a multitude gathered on a mountain: "What does it profit them if they gain the whole world, but lose or forfeit themselves?" (Luke 9:25). Had Jesus acknowledged Satan's lordship anywhere in the world, he would have denied the total Lordship of God everywhere in the world.

Jesus was not looking for a rule by authority. History proves that external authority never wins the allegiance of men and women, nor can it last. History itself is the graveyard of nations and ideologies that sought to enslave by authority.

God seeks our will, our heart, and our obedience freely lived out in love. When these are given freely, then and only then is the work of the kingdom evident in and through us.

The devil's third temptation was that Jesus should use his power to do miracles to establish the kingdom by attracting attention to himself. Satan told him, "Use your powers to dazzle others, and they will follow you! Take the spotlight. Become a celebrity, and then you can persuade people to accept your teaching." Human nature seems addicted to signs and wonders.

The tempter took Jesus in his imagination to the Temple, to the pinnacle of the corner turret above the royal cloisters, the highest point of the Temple in the Holy City. The devil taunted Jesus, "If you are the Son of God, throw yourself down from here," reminding him that the scripture says:

> "[God] will command his angels
> concerning you,
> to protect you,"
> and

MARCH 8

"On their hands they will bear
you up,
so that you will not dash your
foot against a stone."
(Luke 4:9-11)

"There you have it, Jesus," Satan said. "God will send his angels to protect you from harm. What a sensation you will be. You'll startle the people, and they will rush into the arms of God! The headlines will be yours around the world. Every television network will have as their lead story: Dateline-Jerusalem, 'A miracle man named Jesus jumped from the highest point in the Holy City, landed unharmed amid admiring crowds and walked away without a broken limb.' You'll be sought after for every talk show in the world. International audiences will welcome you in capital cities."

Once again, Jesus responded from Deuteronomy, "It is said, 'Do not put the Lord your God to the test' " (Luke 4:12). God is not on trial. He is not to be tested. God's promises are not given to be used for selfish ends. Neither are they designed to surround us with divine protection when we choose to walk down some foolishly dangerous path. Jesus knew the Scriptures, and he knew the God of the Scriptures. He knew God's concern for him and for all creation, and he would not exploit that loving concern. The universal love of God for the righteous and the sinner was the love Jesus had come to proclaim. Our Lord refused to fall for some publicity stunt. Truth is accepted for its own sake. God will not go out of his way to work a miracle to seek to convince us. Signs and wonders will not do. Jesus asked for faith, and with that faith mountains could be moved, the blind would have sight restored, the lame would walk again, and the dead would be raised. A sign from heaven? Heavens, no! The only worthwhile sign was the truth of his message.

The devil failed to persuade Jesus to exploit his own miraculous powers in order that he might be proclaimed a miracle worker by the world. The final battle was won by Jesus.

"So," you ask, "in what ways do these temptations of Jesus speak significantly to our life today?" The struggle with evil is as real today as it was when Jesus encountered the tempter in the wilderness. The Christian is battling in everyday life this enemy of God, whom Jesus called "the ruler of the world" (John 16:11). There is a war raging in every life, in every culture, in every race.

Many question the existence of a real devil and see him only as being symbolic of the total sin of the human race. Neither I nor anyone else can offer proof for or against belief in the reality of a devil, but it is plain that Jesus believed in a devil. Our struggle against the powers of darkness is a day-to-day battle. Although the nature of the temptation experiences cannot be fully understood, they were—and are—nevertheless real.

Jesus in his battle drew from the wellsprings of his own faith. He entered the fray wearing the armor of faith. It is significant to remember the place Scripture played in this temptation encounter. The devil tried to mislead Jesus twice by a wrong use of Scripture. It was Jesus' precise knowledge of the Word of God and his deep commitment to the Truth within the Word that won the day. He recognized Satan as the liar he was—and is.

Jesus' priorities were in order. His obedience was to God. The mission would be costly. He would live as a man, but he would live in perfect obedience to God's will.

Jesus emerged victorious, and his victory encourages us in our battle with temptation that evil need not triumph. This was not the end of Jesus' struggle with evil men and systems. He was constantly assaulted throughout his ministry. He spoke of his apostles as "those who have continued with me in my trials" (Luke 22:28).

The good news for us is that Jesus continues with us in our trials. He has walked this road before us. "Because he himself was tested by what he suffered, he is able to help those who are being tested" (Heb. 2:18).

Suggestions for Worship

Call to Worship (Ps. 91:14-16):

MINISTER: They Lord says: "Those who love me I will deliver.

PEOPLE: **I will protect those who know my name.**

MINISTER: When they call to me, I will answer them. . . .

PEOPLE: **With long life will I satisfy them, and show them my salvation."**

Act of Praise: Psalm 91:9-16.

Suggested Hymns: opening hymn: "Guide Me, O Thou Great Jehovah"; second hymn: "I Am Thine, O Lord"; closing hymn: "By Thy Birth and By Thy Tears."

Opening Prayer: O God, by your Spirit you empowered Jesus to triumph over the tempter. Deliver us from easy compromise and expediency in our daily temptations. Help us to follow the One who is the way, the truth, and the life, that your will may be truly done in our lives. In Jesus' name, amen.

Pastoral Prayer: O Lord, whom to know is to love and whom to love is to serve, we gather in worship today to praise and thank you for your Presence and your Power.

Help us to pull together the fragments of our lives. There are so many broken promises, loose ends, alluring temptations.

We recognize, O God, that it is not our vices as much as our virtues that sometimes are our undoing.

We are kind to those we can patronize, unkind to those who need us most.

We are loving to those who love us and harsh to those whose ways often hide deep insecurity.

We are religious on Sunday but find it difficult to share our faith in the marketplace on Monday. We sometimes practice the golden rule and at other times worship the golden calf.

Pull our good intentions, our fragmented virtues, our feeble faith together and help us to see ourselves through the eyes of him who was tempted as we are, yet was without sin. As he found his oneness with the heavenly Father, help us to find a unity of life in the only One who makes sense in our world today.

We pray for those we have ignored and neglected.

WILLIAM K. QUICK

We recall with regret, O God, promises we have not kept, tasks we have postponed, resolutions waiting to be implemented.

Restore us. Renew us. Empower us to emerge from the wilderness of our existence, armed by your Spirit to witness for Jesus in the world lost without him. In his name, amen.

March 15, 1992

□

Second Sunday in Lent

God keeps his covenants. The steadfast love of Christ is not set aside by rejection.

The Sunday Lessons

Genesis 15:1-12, 17-18: God's promise and covenant with Abraham was a son, descendants, and a land to possess. The carcasses of animals, by ancient custom, were arranged to be a symbol of good faith on the part of covenanting persons. Use of the halved heifer, goat, and ram implied that one who broke the promise would become like them.

Philippians 3:17–4:1: The Apostle Paul asked his Philippian converts to imitate him in patterning their lives after that of Christ and the cross. Some among them, "enemies of the cross," indulged the appetites of their bodies and set their minds on earthly things. Obedient to death on the cross, Christ was glorified and will glorify us.

Luke 13:31-35: When Jesus was warned that Herod wanted to kill him, he sent word that he would continue to set people free from evil and to heal. He would not turn back from Jerusalem, even though the city was notorious for rejecting and killing prophets.

Interpretation and Imagination

Ivan was the intellectual agnostic in that trio created by Dostoevski in *The Brothers Karamazov.* He argued against the Christian faith with his brother Alyosha, a believer, with a poem he had written and titled "The Myth of the Grand Inquisitor."

The setting was Madrid in A.D. 1000. Christ had come again, and his ministry in Galilee and Jerusalem was being relived. The lame walked; the blind could see; a funeral procession was interrupted and Christ whispered, "Talitha cume." The little girl lived again. The cardinal of Madrid, dressed like a monk, suddenly pointed toward Jesus and commanded, "Arrest that man!" But now the story was different. In first-century Jerusalem he was arrested as a pretending messiah. The cardinal inquisitor ordered the arrest because he knew Jesus to be the Son of God.

In the dungeon he accused Jesus of returning to undo the little bit of authority it had taken the church one thousand years to reclaim. He condemns Jesus for his choices during the temptation; he upbraids, threatens and finally ends by sentencing him to death. Christ's only response is to reach out to the old cardinal and kiss his accusing lips.

With that the Grand Inquisitor turns for the door, throws it open, and screams, "Go and come no more. Come not at all, never, never!" Jesus goes out into the lonely streets of the city.

There is unyielding authority and power in the eternal presence of a compassionate Christ. Rejected, mocked, and crucified, Christ still loves.

I WOULD HAVE—THEY WOULD NOT

Luke 13:31-35

A SERMON BY JOHN K. BERGLAND

You don't live very long before you suffer it—rejection, that is. You're not chosen to play. You're left sitting alone at a dance. An application for admission is denied. You receive a "Dear John" letter or a notice of job termination. You're passed over for promotion. In a thousand and one subtle or brutal ways, you have experienced rejection.

Few of us, however, experience the kind of rejection that Jesus encountered in that Judean village. The local Pharisees, who wanted him to leave quickly and quietly, came to him with a warning: "Get away from here while you still can. Herod wants to kill you." Is there any rejection more absolute than that?

In Margaret Jensen's book *First We Have Coffee,* there is the touching account of her Baptist preacher father's being voted out. She describes how the news reached her. Called to the dormitory phone, she heard her sister saying, "Margaret, this is Grace."

Then after a momentous pause: "Papa has been voted out." She goes on to write: "Unable to share the family disgrace with anyone, I went to class and failed the biology exam for which I was well prepared. . . . I tried to figure out what could have gone wrong with Papa's call. In my mind, the ministry had somehow been disgraced."

For ten years he had shepherded and loved that congregation, but now they didn't want him anymore. When Margaret arrived home, she found her sister Leona furious. She explained life as she saw it for the Norwegian immigrant pastor: "They wanted an American pastor, one more geared to the changing times."

"What will you do now?" Margaret asked. Her mother's answer reflected a faith that seemed never to change: "God never fails, but it will be interesting to see how he works this one out. But now we have coffee."

Not only are pastors voted out, but it happens in every other profession as well. Henry Rosovsky, in his book *The University: An Owner's Manual*, reports that in arts and sciences at Harvard approximately eight out of ten assistant and associate professors are denied tenure. He refers to the vote, which frequently occurs at the end of a six- to eight-year term, as "explicit rejection." Being denied tenure is not a casual act. It isn't generic rejection—because you're feminine or black or old. It's not prompted by some faceless force—a corporate takeover. It isn't provoked by a reduction of staff or caused by sales that have slowed. This rejection is "carefully calculated," determined by associates and friends. It is even made public. From that point on, the scholar is "marked with a scarlet letter."

Yet, being voted out or denied tenure by colleagues pales before the menacing threat voiced by the Pharisees: "Herod the king wants you dead."

There is another style of rejection—apathy. It is more subtle, but no less painful and equally desolating. Rejection, like being voted out or denied tenure, at least takes you seriously. It recognizes and may even honor the good you have done and may yet do—the importance of your existence.

Apathy is that style of rejection that acts as though you never lived; or at best, as though you were already dead. To be unwanted, ignored, set aside, and overlooked is devastating.

The cross of Christ was cruel. The crown of thorns was heartless.

The taunting crowd was callous. But the cross was not what prompted Christ's lament. He did not bemoan his crucifixion. It was the apathy and indifference of those he came to seek and to save that broke his heart. Our scriptures, sermons, hymns, poetry, and art together describe Jesus as despised, forsaken, rejected, and alone and longing for calvary.

The Gospel of Luke portrays Christ like that. When told that Herod wanted him dead, he left the Judean village and made his way to Jerusalem. No cunning threat by the Pharisees or King Herod would turn him from his mission. Resolutely he journeyed toward that city famous for killing the prophets and stoning those sent from God.

When he looked out upon that great city of priests, Temple, and prophets, the City of God, he mourned: "Jerusalem, Jerusalem, the city that kills the prophets and stones those who are sent to it! How often have I desired to gather your children together as a hen gathers her brood under her wings, and you were not willing!" (Luke 13:34).

"Living beings reveal their grade in the scale of existence by their wants" wrote Fosdick in *The Meaning of Prayer*. Stones and clods and bricks and mortar are never disturbed by a sense of want. Inanimate things want nothing and nobody. But the tiniest glimmer of life engenders desire. Even a simple amoeba rolls around in search of food.

The presence of life brings hunger and thirst. Moreover, the higher one's quality of life, the higher is one's desire. "Ignorance is bliss," we say. Children who grow up in deprived and barren circumstances seldom reach for the stars. Can we break the cycle of poverty and despair? Our best hope for making the children receptive to life's better opportunities and challenges is in helping them to see beyond the life they know, to impart a yearning for the highest and best.

Most of us have tried to do that in our own homes. We want the best for our children, or at least we want to protect them from the least promising choices in life. So we've tried to turn them away from wrong places and wrong friends, from ways that we know will lead to unwanted pregnancies, alcohol or drug addiction, broken hearts, and wasted lives. How often we would have gathered them, and they would not.

What was it in Jerusalem that caused the people of the Holy City to acquiesce to what they wanted and renounce what they needed; to reject God's only Son and heaven's very best? What is it in our city that we desire so much that we will refuse the highest and the best?

If our only ache today is to satisfy our nearsighted shoddy longings, we too prompt the lament of Christ: "How often I would have gathered you to myself. You would not."

We're on both sides of this issue, aren't we? Sometimes we're rejected and ignored. Sometimes we're the ones who do the rejecting. Let me suggest a helpful response: Risk rejection! Risk the leap of faith! Accept the call of God!

I don't like to be rejected. Do you? In fact, I hate rejection. I never want to be left out or passed over. I dread being forgotten. If we experience rejection often, and suffer the pain of it, we soon come to fear it. We won't risk it often. And after a dozen or so rejections we won't risk anything again—ever.

Doctors tell us that our tendency to protect ourselves from pain is a natural phenomenon. The first moment we sense any discomfort we draw away from it. If something is hot or sharp we know it in an instant and draw back from it. If we're cold, we want to be warm. If we're wet, we want to be dry. If someone doesn't like us we avoid that person. If we're faced with an unpleasant confrontation, we put it off. We have learned well, and we know how to avoid pain.

A leper was left without feeling in his limbs. One day he stepped on a loose stone and turned his ankle over completely, causing a major sprain that tore away the ligaments so that the sole of his foot was pointed inward. But he walked on, never feeling the injury. In so doing, he severely damaged the ligaments. Doctors corrected it the first time, but without the protection of pain, the leper turned and sprained and tore his ankle again and again, until finally he lost his foot.

Should we then respond to the pain of rejection by playing it safe? That was not Christ's way nor has it been the way of his disciples who worthily bear the name Christian. Is not facing the rejection and apathy of the world a part of what it means to bear the cross?

James Russell Lowell described the worth of risking rejection in his poem "Slaves":

> They are slaves who fear to speak,
> For the fallen and the weak;
> They are slaves who will not choose,
> Hatred, scoffing and abuse;
> Rather than in silence shrink,
> From the truth they needs must think;
> They are slaves who dare not be
> In the right with two or three.

"I would have gathered your children," Jesus said, "like a hen gathers her chicks, but you would not." I watched the chicken hawk circle and noticed that the old mother hen had seen it, too. With a furious fuss she called seven baby chicks to herself, fluffed out her wings, and protected them with her own body. The chicken hawk dived once, and the hen cocked a wary eye, but never moved. The predator dived again, and the old hen cocked the other eye and spread her wings wider. A third time, the menacing hawk dived, and then, knowing his attack had been thwarted by the determined self-sacrifice of a mother hen, he flew away.

"In the shelter of his wings." The comfort of those words have steadied many frightened souls. The shadow side is this, "How often I would have gathered you to myself, but you would not."

Let the words of Psalm 91 be God's beckoning call today:

> You who live in the shelter of
> the Most High,
> who abide in the shadow of
> the Almighty,
> will say to the Lord, "My refuge
> and my fortress;
> my God, in whom I trust."
> For he will deliver you from the
> snare of the fowler
> and from the deadly
> pestilence;

he will cover you with his
pinions,
and under his wings you will
find refuge;
his faithfulness is a shield and
buckler.
(Ps. 91:1-4)

Suggestions for Worship

Call to Worship (Ps. 127:1):

MINISTER: Unless the LORD builds the house,

PEOPLE: those who build it labor in vain.

MINISTER: Unless the LORD guards the city,

PEOPLE: the guard keeps watch in vain.

Act of Praise: Psalm 127.

Suggested Hymns: opening hymn: "Come, Christians, Join to Sing"; second hymn: "All the Way My Savior Leads Me"; closing hymn: "Only Trust Him."

Opening Prayer: O God, we could not seek you if you had not first sought us. Sometimes we sense your presence and dimly discern your truth. Your love has called us into being; your love has revealed to us your way. Now, by the power of Christ in our midst, stir up those longings and affections that make life good, and cause us to reach forth to you, through Jesus Christ our Lord. Amen.

Pastoral Prayer: Almighty God, we turn to you for safety and refuge. Only you are God, and apart from you there is no good thing. Our sorrows increase when we fail to heed your gentle call. Our burdens grow heavy when we run after the gods of money and power. All hope fails us when we forsake your strength and love. You are the Lord, and divorced from you we have nothing that lasts.

Our lives stand in the appointment of your will, O God. You have assigned each of us our portion and our cup. You have blessed us in this good land and in the friendship of this congregation. If our lot in life is secure, it is because of your blessing. If the circumstances of our lives are in any way pleasant, it is because of your providence and care. Surely we have a delightful inheritance as your children, and we praise you for it.

We praise you, O Christ, for your counsel. In the midst of the community of your faithful, we have been called and named by your word. In the lonely places of our days, we have sensed your nearness. Even at night, your truth provides a resting place. Be always before us, O Lord, and with your gifts of faith we will not be shaken.

Our hearts are glad today, for we have sensed your presence and have rested in your peace. You have not abandoned us to our foolish ways, not to the evil that seeks to destroy us. Therefore, we will lift our voices to praise you, and in our daily walk we will seek to follow you.

Grant to us, we beseech you, O Christ, the joy of your presence now and at last the eternal pleasures found at your right hand. Keep us safe in your mercy and truth, O Lord, that we may abide forever in the shelter of your wings. Amen.

MARCH 22, 1992

□

Third Sunday in Lent

Self-righteousness and misplaced confidence are products of idolatry. So if you think you are standing, watch out that you do not fall" (I Cor. 10:12).

The Sunday Lessons

Exodus 3:1-15: At Horeb, the mountain of God, Moses turned aside to the burning bush, and God called him to "bring [God's] people, the Israelites, out of Egypt" (v. 10). Wanting the authority of God's name, Moses asked: "'What shall I say to them?' God said to Moses, 'I AM WHO I AM [I cause to be what is]'" (vv. 13-14).

I Corinthians 10:1-13: "So if you think you are standing, watch out that you do not fall" (v. 12). The Corinthians, with their baptism and Holy Communion, were not free from temptations and evil. Likening baptism to passing through the sea and communion to the supernatural food and drink of the wilderness, Paul remembered that many of their Israelite ancestors who had experienced these trials had perished.

Luke 13:1-9: In the context of settling accounts (12:58), Luke introduces two puzzling incidents. Galileans offering righteous sacrifice at Passover were not spared, but were slain by Pilate. Workers building a watchtower at a sacred place in the holy city were killed when it fell. Were they "worse sinners than all other Galileans? No, I tell you" (vv. 2-3). The parable of the barren fig tree asks, "Why should it be wasting the soil?" (v. 7).

Interpretation and Imagination

Sometimes it is a good thing to be confident and filled with hope. A small boy expects to become a strong man because of what he is and what he will be. People in bondage have visions that they will one day be free.

Yet, sometimes it is a foolish and dangerous thing to expect great things. Should anyone hope that a new car will never get old, that bodies will never wrinkle and evenings will never come? Soon and very soon, fruit trees grow old, cease to bear, and are cut down. One doesn't trust that there will be new growth on old trees.

The Zealots of Israel were motivated by a false hope. Overconfidence, the beginning place of idolatry, leads to a false sense of security and seldom to deliverance.

Penance, a theme of Lent and of these lessons, means more than giving up meat for four days. Repentance means more than a disciplined devotional life in the days before Easter. It is more than increased tithes and offerings, important as they are. Repentance means turning back to God in Christ, who is the only true Savior. Without him we all perish.

How does one turn to God? By offering faithful worship, like sacrifices at Passover? By building a church or temple or shrine? By bearing fruit in the kingdom—that is, many converts gained? No, no, a thousand times no! Twice the lesson speaks the words, "Turn from your sins" (vv. 3, 5). Turn from the sins of idolatry that ignore the sovereignty of God and our dependence on sovereign grace. "I Am Who I Am." "I cause to be all that is."

IT CAN HAPPEN TO THE BEST OF US

Luke 13:1-9; I Corinthians 10:1-13

A SERMON BY JAMES A. HARNISH

They waved the morning edition of the *Jerusalem Times* in his face. "Jesus," they asked, "did you see the headlines? Did you hear about the Galileans Pilate killed while they were offering their sacrifices?" Pilate's soldiers had sneaked into the Temple with their weapons tucked beneath their robes. When the Galileans were least expecting it, the soldiers slaughtered them. It was a tyrannical act of injustice against innocent people. And it still makes headlines today.

Jesus, did you read about the South African pastor whose home was raided because he spoke out against Apartheid? Jesus, did you see the students die in Tiananmen Square? Jesus, did you hear about the Catholic workers who were murdered in El Salvador? Jesus, did you hear about the young firemen who died in a blaze while trying to save lives? Jesus, do you remember the people who were killed in an airplane crash? Jesus, did you see the children who were gunned down on a school playground?

Jesus must have watched the morning news show over breakfast that day because he tossed another headline back to them. "What about the eighteen construction workers who died when the tower collapsed on them?" There's a story we can understand.

The people of Jerusalem were reading the headlines that day. Jesus responded with the question all of us ask: Do you think the Galileans who were killed in the Temple were worse sinners than all the others? Is there a connection between suffering and sin? Do good people prosper and evil people suffer?

There was probably no doubt in the minds of the folks who surrounded Jesus that day. They were sure of it. They accepted a strict interpretation of the Wisdom literature, which taught that you get what you deserve and you deserve what you get.

If something good happens, it is God's blessing. If something bad happens, it is God's direct punishment for your evil actions. It serves you right. The way of the righteous shall prosper. The way of the unjust will be hard.

That kind of theology is still around today, from the "prosperity" preachers, who promise that if you live by faith you will get everything you want, to the folks who assume that anyone who is poor, hungry, or homeless is lazy, crazy, or sinful. They assume a direct connection between suffering and sin.

But Jesus gave one unequivocal, stinging response: "No. No, indeed!" At the least this says that life is a complex weaving of cause and effect. Jesus offered no guarantee that comfort comes with goodness, no promise of exceptions for nice people. Suffering is part of the risk of human existence. It can happen to the best of us. There are consequences to our behavior, and we do bring a certain amount of pain on ourselves, but innocent suffering is not the result of the sin of the sufferer. That's why it's innocent: the sufferer didn't necessarily do anything to deserve it. The sufferer just happened to be standing in the way when it came.

"Do you think," Jesus asked, "that these folks were worse sinners than all the rest? That they got what they deserved? No, indeed!" We are all in this life together; it can happen to the best of us.

But someone is saying, "Okay, but what about those difficult words, 'Unless you turn from your sins, you will all die as they did' ?"

Jesus simply described a basic fact of human existence: We are connected with each other. The actions of the many affect the few. The attitudes, values, and assumptions of a society have effects for good or ill. When the result is pain and suffering for innocent people, we'd better be smart enough to turn in a new direction, or sooner or later all of us will suffer under it. That's a general principle.

Here is one example: A pastor was killed by gunfire when he pulled into the wrong driveway while visiting in his parish. Can't you hear Jesus asking, "Do you really think that man was the worst preacher in his town? Do you believe that his death was the result of something he had done? That he somehow deserved to die?" In the light of this text, can't you hear Jesus' resounding, "No! It could happen to any of us."

On the individual level, there was no direct connection between that preacher's death and his goodness. He just happened to be in the wrong place at the wrong time and ended up on the suffering end of another person's hostility. But beneath the event itself is the larger issue of our society's acceptance of violence and guns. We are forced to ask other questions.

What about a society that too quickly resorts to violence to deal with frustration? How many people do you see reach for a gun on prime time television programs? How many people have you watched die on television this week? What about our national attitude toward handguns, our total lack of conscience about weapons, which can only be used to hurt people? What about the efforts of organizations and individuals to block responsible gun control legislation?

To those underlying attitudes, those larger issues that affect every one of us, Jesus would say, "Unless you repent, unless you change your way of thinking and living, unless you turn in a new direction, all of you stand the risk of dying at the hands of violence just as that preacher did."

And what if you are on the receiving end? What if you are the innocent sufferer? The families of the Galileans killed in the

Temple? The spouses of the construction workers killed in Siloam?

The epistle reading is a marvelous commentary on the dialogue in the Gospel. Paul wrote: "If you think you are standing, watch out that you do not fall" (I Cor. 10:12). That is Paul's way of saying, "Don't become presumptuous. The things that happen to others could happen to you." Then he went on to say:

> No testing has overtaken you that is not common to everyone. God is faithful, and he will not let you be tested beyond your strength, but with the testing he will also provide the way out so that you may be able to endure it.

When we are the innocent who suffer, we are not alone. God will give us the strength to remain firm. The God who went to the cross with his innocent Son will go to the cross with us. God will give strength to endure, and so he will provide, if not a way out, at least a way through.

Trevor Beeson stood at the high altar of Westminster Abbey to celebrate the marriage of his daughter, Catherine, to Anthony, aged twenty-three. Nine months later he stood before the same altar for Anthony's funeral, who was killed when his car ran into a wall in East London. Four months later, Trevor returned to the altar beside the coffin of his friend and hero Earl Mountbatten, who died when his fishing boat was blown to pieces by Irish terrorists. Reflecting on the experience, he said he could not blame God for these senseless tragedies. He wrote:

> I should find it impossible to believe in, and worship, a god who arranged for great servants of the community to be blown up on their holidays and who deliberately turned a young man's car into a brick wall. . . . This is not the God of love whose ways are revealed in the Bible and supremely in the life of Jesus Christ.

Beeson found two insights that helped him to cope with his tragedy and to look beyond it: "The first is that, although God is not responsible for causing tragedy, he is not a detached observer of our suffering. On the contrary, he is immersed in it with us, sharing to the full our particular grief and pain. This is the fundamental significance of the cross."

Second, although we naturally ask, "Why did it happen?"

Beeson discovered that the more important question is "What are we going to make of it?"; "Every tragedy contains within it the seeds of resurrection." This is, after all, the whole point of our pilgrimage through Lent, to Good Friday and Easter morning.

Are those who experience innocent suffering worse than anyone else? Of course not. It can happen to any of us.

But is there a connection between innocent suffering and human action? Of course there is, and unless we change our way of living, we may all experience the same suffering.

What does Jesus offer us when we experience this kind of suffering? The power of God to hold us firm, to give us strength, and to see us through.

Suggestions for Worship

Call to Worship (Ps. 103:2, 8, 11):

MINISTER: Bless the LORD, O my soul,

PEOPLE: and do not forget not all his benefits. . . .

MINISTER: The LORD is merciful and gracious,

PEOPLE: slow to anger and abounding in steadfast love. . . .

MINISTER: For as the heavens are high above the earth,

PEOPLE: so great is his steadfast love for those who fear him.

Act of Praise: Psalm 103:1-13.

Suggested Hymns: opening hymn: "I Love Thy Kingdom, Lord"; second hymn: "Precious Name"; closing hymn: "Just as I Am, Without One Plea."

Opening Prayer: O Lord our God, you are the source of all light and truth. You are the source of all patience and encouragement. You are the source of all peace and joy. Through the presence and redeeming power of your Son, our Lord Jesus Christ, forgive our sins, brighten our morning, and strengthen our hearts to praise you now and forevermore. Amen.

Pastoral Prayer: Good Father of us all, your Son has taught us to pray, naming you as our Parent. You have given us all that we have. You are the source of our whole life. Your blessing is our strength. Your appointment gives us work to do and days in which to do it. Your presence is our warmth. Your goodness is our joy. Therefore, give us this gift also: such sure and certain knowledge of your sovereign grace that will cause us to gratefully praise your name, through Jesus Christ our Lord. Amen.

MARCH 29, 1992

□

Fourth Sunday in Lent

Reconciliation and the place of beginning again are the themes of these lessons. How can a rebellious, runaway child come home?

The Sunday Lessons

Joshua 5:9-12: "The manna ceased on the day they ate the produce of the land" (v. 12). At Gilgal, which means "to roll," the reproach of Egypt was "rolled away," and the children of Israel ate the fruit of the promised land.

II Corinthians 5:16-21: "If anyone is in Christ, there is a new creation: everything old has passed away; see, everything has become new" (v. 17). Being reconciled to God, the community of faith is given "ministry of reconciliation." Sins are not counted. Christ has reconciled that account.

Luke 15:1-3, 11-32: The Pharisees criticized Jesus for eating with sinners. Jesus told the story of two sons: the younger, indulgent and prodigal; the older, obedient and self-righteous. The chief actor in the parable is a patient father who waits for a lost son's return and reminds the faithful son that his brother has been found.

Interpretation and Imagination

"Why don't you settle your differences and decide to be friends?" the teacher asked. "I don't ever want to be her friend," sulked one child. The other quickly snapped, "I hate her!"

Reconciliation is easily recommended and often prescribed, but it is seldom truly desired by anyone who feels deeply wronged. Most times, we'd rather blame someone than be reconciled.

A new beginning in a promised land, the new creation in Christ, and the welcome of a waiting father are the themes of these lessons, which reveal a reconciling God.

The words "God was in Christ reconciling . . . and giving to us the ministry of reconciliation," when taken seriously, are some of the hardest words in Scripture. Don't talk of reconciliation if I suffer while another gets special favors in this society. Don't talk of reconciliation when I'm passed over and one less deserving is rewarded. Don't talk of reconciliation when principles central to the integrity of my life and work are crassly challenged by some scoffer. I want thieves and cheaters brought to justice. I want life to be fair. Don't you?

The parable of the prodigal son and the waiting father speaks convincingly of the patience of God. It tells of a forbearing love that goes beyond any sense of rightness. Neither of the sons expected this love. One came with a groveling confession, "I'm unworthy; make me a slave." One complained, "It's not fair." And all the while, a father loved with patient forbearance that sought the well-being of both.

Reconciliation begins with God. It is a manifestation of the patient mercy that is a primary quality of the God revealed by Christ.

THE ELDER BROTHER

Luke 15:1-3, 11-32

A SERMON BY VICTOR SHEPHERD

"You can always tell a person by the company he or she keeps." Can you? Always? "Yes," said the people with shriveled hearts who watched Jesus. "You can *always* tell a person by the company he or she keeps."

Jesus kept company with people whom church folk did not care for, such as lepers. In first-century Palestine, most so-called lepers didn't have leprosy at all—any skin eruption or infection was called leprosy. If you had ringworm, psoriasis, or acne, you were called a leper, and you were an outcast—cast out farther than we can imagine. When we read that Jesus consorted with lepers, we must understand that he befriended those who were most vehemently rejected. Among the rejected were those whose virtue neighbors deemed to have disappeared twenty years ago. Gentiles, whom Jews regarded as spiritually bereft and ethically benighted, were beyond the pale. Jesus welcomed all such people. He dignified them—the poor, the irreligious, those who were viewed as inferior for any reason or who were rejected outright.

Yet, there was one thing Jesus did not do to them. Unlike so many of us, he did not romanticize them.

Many North Americans who are not poor themselves romanticize the poor, especially at Christmastime, when we speak sentimentally of them as the "humble poor." Jesus never romanticized poverty. He knew that poverty is degrading and dehumanizing.

We romanticize sickness. In the twentieth century, Victorian novelists romanticized those who had tuberculosis. Today our society is eager to romanticize those with AIDS. Think of the books that hold up the person with AIDS as an unwitting victim and, therefore, as the new manifestation of courage and fortitude and resilience. Jesus did not romanticize sickness. Jesus looked at sickness as something to be eradicated.

We romanticize criminality. Bonnie and Clyde. Billy the Kid. The "great train robbers." What was great about these criminals? Surely they were as despicable as a person who holds up the corner variety store.

Jesus romanticized nothing—not poverty, not sickness, not criminality, and certainly not sin or sinners. Yet, he always received sinners. He was able to do something that we may find almost impossible: He neither condoned sin nor condemned notorious sinners.

Jesus approached all kinds of people. He pardoned them when their messes were their own faults and when their messes weren't their own faults (the sick, the poor, the outcast), and he gave them hope and freedom from bitterness. They loved him for it. Until he arrived on the scene, the only attention they had ever received was negative, contempt followed by rejection. But now they thought better of themselves because someone had first thought well of them. The transformation in them was nothing less than miraculous. Not only did they now have dignity because they knew someone cherished them, but also, more profoundly, in meeting Jesus they had been set on a joyful, liberated life in God. They rejoiced in it.

But not everyone rejoiced. The superior, disdainful people became uptight when they saw the freedom and high spirits and happiness of Jesus and his friends. They envied what they saw;

they resented seeing in others what they didn't have themselves; and finally they objected that anyone else should have it at all. In no time they were accusing Jesus of befriending the very people whom respectable people knew enough to ignore. The accusation stung. Jesus smarted under it. He responded to the accusation: "You object to what I am doing? You resent my friends? Let me tell you a story." The parable of the two sons is our Lord's defense of himself in the face of accusation. You know the story. We call it the "parable of the prodigal son."

To the prodigal son, home is a drag, dull beyond description. "So give me *now* what will be mine in any case when you die," the younger son says to his father. "I need money for a good time. You might as well give it to me now instead of making me wait until you are dead and gone."

After getting the money, the sons set out for the far country, so far out, compared to home, that his father would have had a coronary had he known what went on there. It is a blast. The son is stoned every night.

His money soon disappears, and he is hungry and getting hungrier every day. He goes to the employment office and is assigned to work for a Gentile. In first-century Palestine there was nothing more humiliating for a Jew than to have to work for a Gentile. Why? There are many reasons, not the least of which was the conviction that Gentiles were ignorant, immoral pagans. When Paul wrote to the church in Ephesus he told of the Gentile world he knew, and he did so in a vocabulary that Jews commonly used of Gentiles in that era:

> They are darkened in their understanding, alienated from the life of God because of their ignorance and hardness of heart. They have lost all sensitivity and have abandoned themselves to licentiousness, greedy to practice every kind of impurity. (Eph. 4:18-19)

There wasn't a Jew who wouldn't have agreed with this description of the Gentile world. How would you feel if you were reduced to penury (itself humiliation enough); had to work for the minimum wage (another humiliation) for an employer whom everyone knew to be godless, insensitive, and vicious; and had to say, "Yes, sir. No, sir. Whatever you say, sir" to that creep every day?

Not only did the young man have to work for a Gentile, but he also had to work with pigs, the symbol of uncleanness for Jews. And not only did he have to work with pigs, but he also became so hungry that even pig food looked good. But the nasty Gentile boss would rather see him starve than let the pigs go hungry!

The fellow knows that things can't be bleaker. He has really messed up. He goes home to throw himself on his father's mercy. He thinks he'll be lucky if his father takes him back as chauffeur or butler. No wonder he is blown away at the reception his father gives him! Not one word is said about the life-style he has wallowed in. He is welcomed without question or qualification. His father cuts short the breast beating and gives him a robe—to the Hebrews a sign of belonging; it is pressed upon the young man that he belongs to the family as son. The father gives him shoes. Slaves went barefoot; only those who enjoyed the privilege of freedom had shoes. And the father gives his son a ring (this was a signet ring, used to make impressions on sealing wax, which gave the son the ability to draw on all his father's resources). And then the party began.

Jesus told this parable to defend himself against the accusation that it was inappropriate for him to welcome so-called inferiors. "Inappropriate?" Jesus gasped, dumbfounded. "What could be *more* appropriate? Look at the transformation my welcome has worked in them! They have come to belong to the family of God. They have been freed from the tyranny of their own sin and from the bitterness of others. They now call upon God, certain that he longs to share his riches with them. Why do you fault me for this?

He was aswered by silence. Dead silence. What could our Lord's opponents say? Nothing! More silence. At last Jesus spoke: "Since you mean-spirited stinkers can't tell me or won't tell me why you fault me, *I* am going to tell *you* why you carp at me and sneer contemptuously at me whenever you see me coming down the road with my ragged rejects."

And so Jesus began the second half of his parable, the story of the elder brother. In a word, the elder brother is the person of any era who hangs around the house of God but has never become part of the family of God. This person works diligently for the church but has never really become acquainted with Jesus Christ. He or she contributes a little money for its upkeep (after all, every village should have a church), but has never discovered what Paul speaks of as "the riches of God's grace" or "the unsearchable riches of Christ" or "the riches of his glory."

The elder brother has confused proximity to the church premises with personal acquaintance with the one whose church it is. You must have noticed how frequently this confusion occurs in the realm of the Spirit compared to how infrequently it occurs elsewhere in life. People who sit in the stands do not think for a minute that sitting there makes them hockey players. Those who read the batting techniques of their favorite slugger do not assume that they are major league hitters. In everyday life we don't confuse observation with participation. The person who regularly confuses observation with participation is hallucinating, and very few people hallucinate.

With respect to knowing, loving, obeying, and following Jesus Christ, however, the situation changes. That's why it is that frequently the person who was baptized at three months and confirmed at fifteen years drifts away but comes back when she or he has children and worries about their fate in our booby-trapped world—and then is gone for good some time after that, telling us that she or he no longer sees any point to religion. I agree with that statement. There is no point to religion! But what about the unsearchable riches of Christ?

From time to time someone who has spent years in a spiritual wasteland comes to self-conscious faith at a public evangelistic meeting or through the ministry of a church that is a little more direct, even bold, than we are about such matters. This person then blurts out that he or she is now possessed of what was missing for all those years when he or she trafficked in the wrappings of religion but never possessed the goods. If we rejoice at this person's spiritual quickening, then we are acquainted with Jesus Christ ourselves. If, on the other hand, we stare at this person uncomprehendingly, then we should ask a question or two of ourselves.

The elder brother rails against his father, "All these years I have slaved for you, and what do I get?" Clearly he thinks that his situation with his father is meant to be that of servant or slave or employee to boss. He expects wages for his work. He wants to be compensated. All the while his father has wanted a son, not an employee; a relationship, not a labor contract. When the elder brother, now embittered, speaks of the younger brother he hisses to his father, "This son of yours," not "my brother." The contempt is undeniable, and his contempt discloses his stony heart.

We must not fool ourselves. "Elder brotherism" is serious business, lethal business, not just for the elder brothers themselves, but also for all those among us who are hesitant about embracing the father because we assume that the father resembles the elder brother. We assume that the brother's character mirrors the character of the father, and we are not about to trust ourselves to a God who appears to be cold and distant.

I regularly correspond with a dear friend in St. John's, Newfoundland. She is a pediatrician by training and a faithful Roman Catholic by persuasion. She has been horrified and saddened because a number of priests have been arrested by the Royal Canadian Mounted Police and charged with molesting boys. Many aspects of this development distress her: that the priests did it at all; that they won't plead guilty when charged but instead perjure themselves only to be convicted anyway; that the boys themselves have likely been damaged irretrievably.

"All these years I have slaved for you and what do I get?" What does the elder bother expect to get? Something? Some *thing*?

In knowing my wife, loving her, trusting her, and being loved by her, I have discovered that the relationship is the reality. There is nothing to be gotten *beyond* the relationship. What could there be beyond a relationship that is so rich as to defy description? If after twenty years of marriage I said to my wife, "I have been your devoted, non-philandering husband for all these years. Now what do I get for it?" she would know immediately that I had missed the reality of the relationship completely.

The younger brother came to know gloriously what it is to be cherished as a son of the father. The elder brother knew only what it is to be a frustrated employee.

There are many varieties of "elder brotherism." We find one variety in the reaction to Jesus' promising the man dying on the cross beside him on Good Friday that he would be in paradise that day with Jesus. "Elder brothers" reply in anger or bewilderment, "But it's not fair! Why should any thug, however repentant, be promised exactly what is promised the saint who has served sacrificially for forty years?" Or they say, "I've lived on the straight and narrow all my life. I had plenty of chances to have my fling, but I kept to the straight and narrow. And what did it get me? My friends are all more prosperous than I."

So very different is the prayer of Ignatius Loyola, founder of the Jesuit order: "Teach us, O Lord, to serve and not to count the cost, to labor and not ask for any reward, save the reward of knowing that we do your will."

The most glorious reward of any profound relationship is simply *the relationship itself*—rendered even more profound. The younger brother came to see this; the elder brother never did. Insisting on a tit-for-tat transaction, he passed up the relationship.

The elder brother never understood grace, which doesn't compromise with sin but invites sinners in the far country to "come to themselves" and come home, where they are no longer slaves or servants but sons and daughters.

Martin Luther understood, as Luther understood so much. His fine hymn is worth hearing in this context:

> 'Tis through thy love alone we gain
> The pardon of our sin;
> The strictest life is but in vain,
> Our works can nothing win;
> Wherefore my hope is in the Lord,
> My works I count but dust,
> I build not there, but on His word
> And in His goodness trust.

Suggestions for Worship

Call to Worship (Ps. 34:1, 3-4):

MINISTER: I will bless the LORD at all times;

PEOPLE: his praise shall continually be in my mouth. . . .

MINISTER: O magnify the LORD with me. . . .

PEOPLE: [He] delivered me from all my fears.

Acts of Praise: Psalm 34:1-8.

Suggested Hymns: opening hymn: "In the Cross of Christ I Glory"; second hymn: "Arise, My Soul, Arise"; closing hymn: "Jesus Is Tenderly Calling."

Opening Prayer: Gracious God, you came to us in the one from Nazareth. You will come in a new manifestation when you conclude human history. You come again and again to us now, as often as the day is new.

Open our ears to hear you.

Open our eyes to see you.

Open our hearts to love you.

Do all of this, we ask, that we might know this day to be the day of your visitation. Amen.

Pastoral Prayer: O saving God, you are indeed the author of the Word of Life. Even as you open our ears to hear it, prepare our hearts to receive it, and fortify our wills to do it. Let that Word fall upon us afresh until our resistance to you crumbles, our frigidity thaws, and we cast ourselves upon you.

Quicken in us a readiness to trust you.

Fashion in us an eagerness to love you.

Foster in us a hunger to know you.

Awaken in us a desire to obey you.

As our Lord has told us of your great generosity, let us take him at his word and believe with renewed confidence that you will give us everything we need at all times and in all circumstances.

We intercede today for those of this congregation who have found the past week tumultuous: those who buried someone dear to them; the people whose illnesses and hospitalizations have left them anxious; the many whose problems cannot be solved and must be endured.

For all these we pray, that in their sadness or fretfulness or somberness they will ever know that you are God, that life is good, that you can be counted on to infuse all of life with your grace and truth. Amen.

April 5, 1992

□

Fifth Sunday in Lent

The victories of yesterday will not win the battles of tomorrow. We press on for the prize of the upward call.

The Sunday Lessons

Isaiah 43:16-21: The song of hope in Isaiah (40–55) refers to the return of the exiles as a second exodus. God's power was previously seen in the crossing of the Red Sea and in the provision of food and water in the desert. Now God's power will be seen in the return of the exiles. "Behold, I will do a new thing" (v. 19 KJV).

Philippians 3:8-14: Some persons in the church at Philippi were confident that they had attained a perfect relationship with God. Paul, who had more reason to be confident than any of them, counted his virtues as nothing. Claiming no perfection, he wrote: "Forgetting what lies behind and straining forward to what lies ahead, I press on toward the goal for the prize of the heavenly call of God in Christ Jesus" (vv. 13-14).

John 12:1-8: Mary of Bethany showed her love for Christ by anointing him with about a pint of costly perfume. She poured it over Jesus' feet and then dried his feet with her hair. Judas complained that the oil could have been sold and the money given to the poor. "Leave her alone," Jesus replied. This anointing was for his burial. The Byzantine tradition, noting that this event precedes the coronation parade of Palm Sunday in John's Gospel, likened it to the anointing of a new king.

Interpretation and Imagination

"Once is enough," he said. The speech described his careful and calculating manner. He'd been there before and assumed he'd seen everything there was to see; that he had heard all there was to hear. However, there was another quality about him that was even more limiting. He resented any extravagance and was so miserly that he wasted nothing. He kept track of everything and kept score of every wrong.

Memory is at times wonderful. It can also become the source of pride, prejudice, and bitterness. Memory at its best gathers confidence, vision, and courage from the events of the past. Throughout Scripture we are encouraged to remember God's mighty acts. But when memory, satisfied with old values and well-worn traditions, never gathers strength for a new dream, it is more hindrance than help.

"Forget the former things; do not dwell on the past," the prophet Isaiah says. Looking forward to a future that belongs to God, he proclaims God's word. "See, I am doing a new thing." Why then, do we think of God's mighty deeds as events of long ago and far away? Is it not that we feel safer that way? The God of yesterday does not cost any of us very much.

There is frightening extravagance in the Gospel lesson. The oil of pure nard that was poured out on Jesus' feet was very costly. It was worth about three hundred denarii. A laborer earned one denarius a day, so it was equal to a working man's salary for a whole year. Yet, the overwhelming extravagance was not the perfume. It was this: the extravagance of Almighty God, who was taking his only Son, heaven's very best, and pouring out his life on a garbage dump outside Jerusalem.

WHAT PRICE GRATITUDE?

John 12:1-8

A SERMON BY VICTOR SHEPHERD

In the early days of my ministry I had supper with a missionary surgeon who was home on furlough. His reputation as a surgeon was matched by his reputation as a gruff, abrasive fellow who was equal parts kindness and sandpaper. We ate together in a steak house. I ordered my steak rare. When it arrived it was so rare it was hemorrhaging. He glanced at it and barked, "Do you want a tourniquet for that thing?"

A few months later I met him again. This time he was speaking to a small group of university students about his work in the Gaza Strip. He was telling us that we North American "fat cats" knew nothing about gratitude. Nothing! On one occasion he had stopped at a peasant hovel to see a woman on whom he had performed surgery. She and her husband were dirt-poor. Their livestock supply consisted of one angora rabbit and two chickens. For income the woman combed the hair out of the rabbit, spun the hair into yarn, and sold it. For food she and her husband ate the eggs from the chickens. The woman insisted that the missionary surgeon stay for lunch. He accepted the invitation and said he would be back for lunch after he had gone down the road to see another postoperative patient. An hour and a half later he was back. He peeked into the cooking pot to see what he was going to eat. He saw one rabbit and two chickens. The woman had given up her entire livestock supply—her income, her food, everything. He concluded his story by reminding us that we knew nothing of gratitude. He wept unashamedly. The incident will stay with me forever.

There is another incident concerning gratitude that will never be forgotten. It's about a woman who poured costly perfume over our Lord as she wiped his feet with her hair. Make no mistake—the perfume was expensive, three hundred denarii, a year's income for a laborer in Palestine. Enough to keep a family alive for the next twelve months.

Why did she do it? We shall come to that. What rejoinder did the deed elicit? With either dismay or disgust—but certainly in vehement disagreement—Judas retorted sharply, "Why isn't something as valuable as this sold for what it's worth and the proceeds given to the poor?" Jesus, as always, did not answer the question he was asked. Instead he rebuked Judas, "Let her alone, let her keep it for the day of my burial. The poor you always have with you, but you do not always have me."

We would misunderstand this Gospel story abysmally if we thought for one minute that Jesus was cavalierly dismissing the poor and their misery as insignificant. We would be people of unspeakably hard hearts ourselves if we were to regard this story as making legitimate the disregard for the poor. Only silly or insensitive people overlook wasted money, which could do ever so much for the wretched of the earth. We must remember that the poor of Jesus' day were not those who had a little less than their neighbors, those whose automobiles were three years old. The poor spoken of in the text were living at the subsistence level.

Judas, the house guest who witnessed the perfume-pouring, made a most telling point. Moreover, he doubtless thought he was merely anticipating what Jesus himself was going to say. After all, our Lord was a faithful son of Israel. And Israel has always had a special concern for the poor, ultimately because God himself continues to have a special concern for the poor and never loses sight of them. The psalmist, in whose poetry Jesus had been steeped since infancy, reminds us that "God does not forget the cry of the afflicted."

If we North Americans think we live under governments that have shown magnanimity toward the poor, then we should listen more closely to the tradition of Israel. The poor in Israel could take grain from the field or grapes from the vine *at any time* if they were without food. (This was not deemed theft on account of the manifest emergency.) When the harvesters went through a field, they had to leave a border of grain intact, which the poor could have. Cut grain that fell out of the harvesters' arms had to be left in the field for the disadvantaged to glean. Every third year 10 percent of the harvest was given to the needy. The poor were allowed to borrow money at no interest. Job said he could not face God if he had withheld from the poor what they needed. Amos said that because of the shabby treatment the poor received God would certainly punish Israel.

The same attitude was found in the early church. James, an apostle, was outraged when the wealthier members of the congregation received preferential treatment. Several months before Jesus permitted Mary to pour a year's income over his feet he had told a rich young man who wanted eternal life to sell what he owned and give the proceeds to the poor. Then it is entirely reasonable that anyone who witnessed the event in the home in Bethany might think he could anticipate the response of Israel's greater son!

When Jesus said, "The poor you have with you always," he did not mean that the poor can be ignored. Still, this misunderstanding has surfaced again and again in the history of the church. "The people lack bread? Then let them eat cake!" said Marie Antoinette contemptuously during the French Revolution. A similar abuse of our Lord's words drove Karl Marx to speak, with more justification than we care to admit, of religion as the drug that tranquilizes the wretched of the earth to the pain of their misery.

The poor matter; in fact, they have a claim on the privileged. To disregard their claim is to violate God. Every Israelite knew this. Jesus knew it, too, and Judas was aware that Jesus knew. Judas's protest is entirely understandable. Then what about Mary? Why did Jesus permit her to do what she did? First, another question: When the missionary surgeon looked into the cooking pot and saw the rabbit and chickens, why didn't he wheel toward the woman and shout, "You fool! How are you going to live now?" But he didn't. And neither did Jesus rebuke Mary for her extravagance.

Mary's act was a spontaneous outpouring not merely of perfume but also of love and gratitude. It was an expression—the most adequate expression she could find—of her devotion to the one who meant so much to her. Does anyone want to suggest that she should have written her Lord a letter, since the postage for a first-class letter costs less than fifty cents? Jesus did not object to her doing what she did once. I have no doubt that had she attempted to do it repeatedly, he would have resisted her gently.

But our Lord knew what now possessed and inflamed Mary's heart. Her brother had been given back to her. Can any price tag be attached to this? The words, "I am the resurrection and the life," now throbbed in her heart in a way she could never have imagined. The one whose words they were, in whom were found the very presence and power of God, had graced her home.

Earlier, when Martha had responded to him sorrowfully yet hopefully, "I know that my brother will rise again in the resurrection at the last day," Jesus had turned last-day hope into present-day fulfillment as Lazarus had come forth. From that moment the sisters and their brother had known that in Jesus of Nazareth the endtime restoration had broken in upon the world. And if it had broken in, they were living in a new reality to which others might yet be inert but that now electrified them.

When the spiritually blind finally see, and see a richness that the most imaginative anticipation can't remotely guess at; when the deaf finally hear so clearly as to discern the redeemer's utterance in the midst of the groans of the anguished and the distractions of the superficial and the blandishments of false prophets; when the newly invigorated can look back on the deadliness of what so many continue to pursue as life-giving—what expression of joy and gratitude can be stipulated as adequate, but not excessive? Then the perfume, however costly, could never be inappropriate!

At the turn of the century a well-known Scottish preacher remarked, "You show me the person who, for the sake of the one she loves, has never purchased a gift she could not afford, and I will show you someone who is not fit for the kingdom of God." At some point we have bought such a gift. Not every week, of course. But one day, as we thought of our dearest, we suspended calculating common sense and icy rationality—and we did it! And did the one to whom our heart had gone out—just because through him or her we had entered that bright new world to which love alone is the key—then remind us of the poor? Anyone who labelled the extravagance "irresponsible" would plainly not know that love is incalculable.

I am always moved as I read the account of our risen Lord's appearance to Peter. Peter insisted that he would never let the Master down, even though others couldn't be counted on. Peter's knees were turned to jelly by a servant girl's recognizing him. And after the rooster had crowed so raucously and persistently, the sound would be the ugliest Peter could imagine. Our risen Lord had one question for Peter: "Do you love me?" The question was repeated, and then repeated once more lest Peter ever be tempted to think that his whole-souled love for his Lord would be insufficient to render him a disciple and might need to be supplemented or shored up. Jesus didn't ask, "Do you think you can prove yourself extraordinarily diligent?" or "Would you like to attempt feats of heroism that might just balance the failures of cowardice?" or "Can you assure me that you will never falter again where you need most to be resolute?" There is one question only to be put to any of us: "Do you love me?"

Then there is one unique expression of gratitude and love for each of us: Mary cannot be faulted.

Yet, she was! Or at least the one upon whom she lavished her attention was faulted—by Judas. The text tells us that Judas was a thief. However, we need not assume that Judas disagreed vehemently with Mary and Jesus inasmuch as he had designs on a large sum of money. After all, when Judas finally betrayed Jesus into the hands of hostile men, the sum of money was scarcely a factor, so slight was it compared to the three hundred denarii. While Judas was indeed light-fingered, his root problem was not that he was prone to shoplifting; his root problem was spiritual obtuseness. He had never discerned that in Jesus of Nazareth the "last days" had drawn nigh, that even now there was a new truth, a new reality, nothing less than a new world, which our Lord's intimates lived for, lived from, and attested to day by day. Judas persisted in living in the age that our Lord's death and resurrection would consign to pass away—the age of calculation, estimation, and manipulation; the age of hatching cagey schemes, co-opting useful people, and arranging workable deals. What preoccupied Judas became apparent at Gethsemane, when Judas assumed he could back Jesus into a corner where Jesus would have to effect what Judas craved to see and what Jesus alone had power to do: rid Palestine of its Roman occupiers.

Mary assumed nothing. For her Jesus was not a useful tool, let alone that tool essential to implementing the fixations born of self-interest. She simply abandoned herself unself-consciously to the very One whom she had seen restore life to her brother, in whom she had found richest friendship for herself, and in whom she had discerned a new age for all who would open their eyes.

"Leave her alone. Let her keep it for the day of my burial," said Jesus. Mary's love, immense as it was, was only the quickened response of a still greater love, for it was on the day of our Lord's burial that love opened its arms wide enough to embrace the entire world.

We still have the poor with us. Our text must never become a pretext for forgetting them, especially since they are so readily forgotten. Cruel dictators—forget them. Dollar-obsessed industrialists—forget them. Ideologically blinded leftists—forget them. Do busy people like us forget them, too? On the contrary, it is as our Lord frees us to lavish upon him all we are and anything we have that our hearts will be knit to his. And just because our hearts are knit to Israel's greater Son we shall resonate with Israel's concern for the poor.

We can do no better than to emulate the woman who poured

herself upon her Master. In doing that she anticipated the death that buried the old age and, therefore, the resurrection that brought forth the new age, whose truth disciples of Jesus hasten to do throughout the world.

Suggestions for Worship

Call to Worship (Ps. 126:4-6):

MINISTER: Restore our fortunes, O LORD, like streams in the desert, the watercourses in the Negeb.

PEOPLE: May those who sow in tears reap with shouts of joy.

MINISTER: Those who go out weeping, bearing only the seed for sowing,

PEOPLE: shall come home with shouts of joy, carrying their sheaves.

Act of Praise: Psalm 126.

Suggested Hymns: opening hymn: "What Wondrous Love Is This"; second hymn: "O Sacred Head, Now Wounded"; closing hymn: "The Lord Our God Alone Is Strong."

Opening Prayer: Eternal God, as we gather before you, subdue the turbulence we have brought with us from the past week; quiet the fears that lap at us even when we are not thinking of them; heal the bruises that appear as we collide with other people.

Speak to us in this hour of worship, for your Word, empowered by your Spirit, will renew us, cheer us, strengthen us, and send us on our way rejoicing. Amen.

Pastoral Prayer: Gracious God, we rejoice today that in your Word preached, your Word made incarnate, and your Word made Holy Scripture, we always encounter the utterance of you, the living God.

Attune us to this Word, we ask. And, like the psalmist of

old, let us hide it in our hearts, for there it will both take root and bear fruit—and ultimately rebound to the praise of your glory.

We praise you for your faithfulness to us in the midst of our betrayals, your goodness to us when we were assaulted by evil, your wisdom for us when we were almost seduced by the less than wise, your patience with us when we were about to give up on ourselves.

Let us find in you all that we need and all that we hope for.

We intercede today for those of our congregation for whom each Sunday's sermon seems to raise more questions than it answers; those whose faith seems to flicker without ever going out, but also without ever flaring up into glorious flame; those whose smiles disguise heavy hearts or numbing discouragement.

For all these people we plead for the touch that is yours alone and for which we look to you now. Amen.

April 12, 1992

□

Palm/Passion Sunday

Jesus, obedient unto death, has been given a name above every name. At his name, every knee should bow. Millions and millions of voices will praise him today. Hosanna, God saves.

The Sunday Lessons

Deuteronomy 32:36-39: This lesson from the song of Moses speaks of God's help for his powerless people. "The Lord will vindicate his people . . . when he sees that their power is gone." He is the only true God. "There is no god beside me; I kill and I make alive; I wound and I heal."

Philippians 2:5-11: Four stanzas make up this early Christian hymn: (1) Christ Jesus did not count equality with God a thing to be grasped; (2) he became obedient unto death; (3) therefore, God bestowed a name above every name; (4) let every tongue confess, "Jesus Christ is Lord."

Luke 22:14–23:56: The Passion narrative is long, and several readers should be used if it is read in entirety. The Last Supper, the prayer, and the betrayal are recorded in 22:1-53. Peter's denial and the trials before the council, before Pilate, and before Herod are recorded in 22:24–23:25. The crucifixion, death, and burial are recorded in 23:26-56. Luke emphasizes the compassion of the dying Christ and speaks not only of suffering but also of saving.

Interpretation and Imagination

Who crucified Christ? The soldiers who drove the nails? The crowds who cried, "Crucify"? Pilate, who allowed it? The Jews who arranged his arrest? No. God did it. The others are only bit players in this mighty drama, which brought in a new age. The sovereignty of God, who says, "I kill, I make alive," is plainly evident.

The crucified one, crowned with thorns, saluted with mockery, and lifted up on a cross, is indeed the messianic king. The final episodes refer to the glorification of God's chosen one and are bound together by prophecies. Judgment is pronounced on the old age (23:26-31). Christ is exalted even as he is crucified (23:32-49).

Ellis writes in *The New Century Commentary:* "It is a story of the eighth day of creation, God's new creation of the messianic age. Thus, on the cross Jesus can say already, 'Today in Paradise.' " The signs that accompany his death point to the end of the old and the beginning of the new. The kingdom is no longer referred to as future.

Piety and devotion are too pale to be appropriate responses to the harsh realities of Christ's death. They easily overlook death-sentence sacrifices, ruthless sin, the passion of God, transcending miracles, and new victory over evil. An individualistic religion of shallow prayers, religious practice, and moral ideas is simply not in touch with God's transcendent activity.

Holy Week is marked by an awesome reality. On the first Good Friday this reality prompted wonder and fear and made people say, "This is the work of God."

YOU CALL THIS SUCCESS?

Luke 19:28-44, 22:14–23:56; Philippians 2:5-11

A SERMON BY JAMES A. HARNISH

Let's talk about men, "real men," and what it takes for them to succeed.

On Ash Wednesday the local newspaper reviewed a book entitled *Ambitious Men: Their Drives, Dreams, and Delusions,* by Srully Blotnick. After studying seven thousand men over a ten-year period, Blotnick concluded that successful American males come in four types: The "Clint Eastwood type" is strong, silent, and direct. He hates phoniness and doesn't care what people think. The "John Davidson type" is articulate, suave, well-mannered, eager to please, and always ready to put people at ease and to court their favor. The "Lee Iacocca type" is the hard-charging, self-made man who wants recognition and draws attention to himself. Finally, the "Saul Bellow type" is the creative loner, the reclusive intellectual.

What, according to Srully Blotnick, is success? "In America, it's fortune, fame, power and prestige. Success is something that can be measured quantitatively through performance and by dollars and cents." Ambition is "the desire for more. More what? you ask. Simple. More of what you already have. More money, more fame, more power, more prestige."

As I read the article, I was impressed by the accuracy of the description and the irony of its appearance on Ash Wednesday, the day of humility and repentance. On this day we remember Jesus' walk on the road to Golgotha. Jesus,

> though he was in the form
> of God,
> did not regard equality with
> God
> as something to be exploited,
> but emptied himself,
> taking the form of a slave . . .
> he humbled himself
> and became obedient to the
> point of death—
> even death on a cross.
> (Phil. 2:6-8)

What would Srully Blotnick do with a man like that? How will ambitious men and women like us respond to a Jesus who turns our ideas of success and failure upside down? While we are so busy clawing our way to the top, what will we do with one who is intentionally making his way down?

Just look at him on Palm Sunday. By Blotnick's standards, Jesus had it made. I tried to imagine how the event might have been reported on the evening news:

> Jesus of Nazareth arrived in Jerusalem today, ushered into the city by cheering crowds who called him King. They waved palm branches, an ancient symbol of Jewish political power. Pious Jews remembered a prophecy that their king would come into Jerusalem on a donkey, which is exactly the way Jesus chose to arrive. Our on-the-scene reporter is being

sent to the scene, where she will interview people in the crowd and, if possible, gain an interview with Jesus himself. In this political season, Jesus is obviously a man to watch; the pollsters predict he is on the way to the top.

That's how it looked as they began the journey down the Mount of Olives and into Jerusalem. No one seemed to notice the tears flowing down Jesus' cheeks. He came closer to the city, and when he saw it, he wept over it, saying, "If you only knew today what is needed for peace! . . . You did not recognize the time when God came to save you!" (Luke 19:42, 44 GNB). Not exactly the Clint Eastwood type, is he?

Listen to him at supper. The conversation turns, as dinner-party conversations so often turn, to matters of success and failure: Who's been promoted? Who is moving up? Who is the greatest? Jesus replied, "The greatest one among you must be like the youngest, and the leader must be like the servant. . . . I am among you as one who serves" (Luke 22:26-27 GNB). He doesn't quite fit the Lee Iacocca model either, does he?

Watch him on trial before Pilate, the Council, and Herod. His responses frustrate his judges, until they say, "We don't need any witnesses! We ourselves have heard what he said!" (Luke 22:71 GNB). Not exactly the people-pleasing John Davidson type, is he?

Follow him through the beating, the mockery, and the naked brutality of the crucifixion, the punishment reserved for disobedient slaves and political revolutionaries. Is it any wonder that the people "went back home, beating their breasts in sorrow" (Luke 23:48 GNB)?

What will we do with a man like that? Where does he fit into our images of success? What would it mean for us to follow this one who, though he was equal to God, emptied himself and was obedient even to death on the cross?

For me, the most disturbing part of the following passage from the Philippian letter is not what it says about Jesus, but what it says about us: "Don't do anything from selfish ambition or from a cheap desire to boast, but be humble toward one another . . . look out for one another's interests, not just for your own. The attitude you should have is the one that Christ Jesus had" (Phil. 2:3-5 GNB).

The Apostle Paul will not allow us to stand off at some safe distance and gaze at an old rugged cross "on a hill far away." It is not enough to honor Jesus; we are called to imitate him. It is not enough to remember the Passion as an event in the past; we are called to live this way in the present. It is not enough to tip our hats to the cross as we pass by; we are called to go to the cross with him, to die to our selfish ambition so that we might be raised to a new life with new desires, new ambitions, new hopes, and a whole new definition of what it means to be a man or a woman in this world. The Gospel calls us to share among ourselves the same mind, the same attitude, and the same spirit that led Jesus to the cross.

What would it be like for us to live that way? Although it would be nice for us to live in the manner of heroic stories of great martyrs and saints, most of us will be called to live this truth in the ordinary, common places of life.

It is not unusual for people to face difficult decisions about career moves. In an upwardly mobile society, it is a constant reality. To climb the corporate ladder usually involves a move to a new job in a new city. But recently several men and women have shared something like this with me: "There was a time when it would have been an easy decision. More power, more money, more prestige—I would have jumped at it. But something is different now. I am asking different questions. What impact will this move have on my family? How will it affect the time I spend with my children or invest in ministry with others? What about friendships? What about my faith? Is there anything in this new position that will contradict my deepest values and highest ideals? How can I find the will of God for my life? What will it mean for me to be obedient to Christ as I face this decision?"

Each person responds in his or her own way, but within each struggle I have sensed the Spirit of one who calls us not to do anything from "selfish ambition or from a cheap desire to boast," but to consider other people's interests as if they were our own. It is the Spirit of one who humbled himself and lived among us as a servant.

It doesn't fit, you know. This model of life that we see in Jesus just doesn't fit with the models of success and ambition that dominate the society in which we live. If it seems as if somebody somewhere has turned the whole thing upside down, as if something about the cross of Christ sounds like a contradiction of everything we have learned about competition and success, as if

Paul is calling us to go in a direction we may not particularly be ready to follow, then perhaps we are beginning to get the point.

Suggestions for Worship

Call to Worship (Ps. 118:24, 26-27):

MINISTER: This is the day that the LORD has made;

PEOPLE: let us rejoice and be glad in it. . . .

MINISTER: Blessed is the one who comes in the name of the LORD.

PEOPLE: The LORD is God, and he has given us light.

MINISTER: Bind the festal procession with branches, up to the horns of the altar.

Act of Praise: Psalm 118:19-29.

Suggested Hymns: opening hymn: "All Glory, Laud, and Honor"; second hymn: "When I Survey the Wondrous Cross"; closing hymn: "Go to Dark Gethsemane."

Opening Prayer: O eternal God, whose love is revealed to us in Jesus, who so freely, so boldly, and so intentionally comes among us, we offer the arrogant realities of our daily lives. May the living Spirit of the living Christ fill our every action, our every thought, and our every motive with a love beyond our own. Deepen our desire to follow our Lord, even though his steps lead to a cross, and that we may also walk with him in the new life of the resurrection. Through Christ our Lord, amen.

Pastoral Prayer: O Lord our God, we acknowledge again our dependency upon you and our deep need for you. Have mercy on us and hear our prayer. Bring us into your holy presence by faith that stirs us to follow and with love that prompts our praise of Christ. We lift our voices in prayer to say, "Blessed is he who comes in the name of the Lord." We open our hearts to cry, "Hosanna, save us now!"

You know who we are, O God, and you know that our faith is both weak and fickle. You know us better than we know ourselves, O Savior, and you know that our love is half-hearted devotion that costs little and risks even less. And you know, O sovereign Grace, those things that belong to a community of faith that is worthy of the name "Christian." It is for these things we pray.

Christ said, "Blessed are the poor in spirit." Grant us a true humility that we may hear.

Christ said, "Blessed are the meek." Quiet us now so that we may receive.

Christ said, "Blessed are those who hunger and thirst for righteousness." Stir within us a deep longing for a right relationship with you, O God, that we will cherish above all things Christ's atonement for sin.

Christ said, "Blessed are the pure in heart." Center our vision now so that we may see your glory.

Christ said, "Blessed are the peacemakers." Open our hearts and our homes, our fortresses and our stubborn ways that all things good and true and blessed may yield the peace of Christ, in whose name we pray. Amen.

April 19, 1992

□

Easter Sunday

The empty tomb made them believe that someone had taken the body away. But there's more. We are not born to die. God has given us new birth into a living hope through the resurrection of Jesus Christ. We have been given an inheritance that can never perish, spoil, or fade.

The Sunday Lessons

Acts 10:34-43: Peter's sermon before Cornelius tells of the life, death, and resurrection of Christ. From Galilee to Jerusalem the disciples had witnessed his life and death, and they ate with him after the resurrection. The risen Christ commanded Peter to preach and testify that he is the one whom God appointed.

I Corinthians 15:19-26: If it is only for this life we have hope, Paul said, we are to be pitied. "But in fact Christ has been raised from the dead" (v. 20). Death came through Adam. Life comes through Christ. He destroys every ruling power, even the last enemy—death.

John 20:1-18 ***or*** **Luke 24:1-12:** Both lessons tell of women who found the stone rolled away and the tomb empty. This news sent Peter and another disciple running to the tomb. The passage from Luke should be read in those churches that have an Easter vigil. John's Gospel should be read on Easter morning. The lesson from John tells of the weeping Mary meeting the risen Christ in the garden. She went and told the disciples, "I've seen the Lord."

Interpretation and Imagination

Scientific proof that is absolutely conclusive is not gentle. It is compelling. It is brutal. One is forced to believe. Signs of wonder and mystery are not so ruthless. To be sure, they claim one's attention, but they only invite belief.

The stone rolled away is such a sign. Mary could have concluded that an angel rolled the stone away, but she did not. Her first assumption was that someone had moved the body.

The empty tomb is such a sign. Peter saw an open grave and used grave clothes, but nothing more. The beloved disciple, John, saw and believed.

We live in the age of science. We like hard evidence. We want the facts, nothing more, just the facts. We're impressed by bone and sinew and flesh, and, like Mary, want to know about the body. When we're confronted with the bodies of our dead, we give first attention to the cause of death and second to preparation for burial.

The question asked on the first Easter, "Why do you look for the living among the dead?" (Luke 24:5) needs to be asked again and again. Easter people, compelled by fact and moved by faith, find joy in the gentle, open, and far-reaching mysteries of life.

A six-year-old child, trying to put together what he saw with what he believed, came to the funeral home to see the body of his grandfather. When the child stood on tiptoe to look into the casket, he blurted out, "He's not here." Then speaking his grandfather's name, the boy said, "Gramp's not here." His grandfather's body was there, and the cosmetic art of the undertaker had made every physical feature lifelike. Death was effectively masked. But the child saw it right. So will all who are blessed with sight that sees beyond the shadows of earth to the light of eternity.

MORE BEYOND

John 20:1-18

A SERMON BY EMERSON S. COLAW

On one occasion I heard a theologian say, in an effort to combat the popular heresy of the "gospel of success," that the story of Jesus was not a success story; it ended on a cross. I affirm his emphasis on the centrality of the cross in Christian theology. But the story of Jesus did not end on a cross. If it had, this congregation would not be gathered in this sanctuary this morning. History has seen thousands of people die for causes in which they believed.

The heroism of those who have given their lives to overthrow oppressive governments is inspiring. Exemplary as this might be, you don't build a religion on it. As Christians, we stand in wonder and awe before the "resurrection drama" and allow it to shape our beliefs. We are people of resurrection victory. The basis for our celebration in worship is the victory of Jesus Christ over the last great enemy, death!

In fact, Easter is more than the story of the resurrection of Jesus. If that were all there were, it would represent an interesting phenomenon but would have little meaning for the human race. The excitement that surrounds this extraordinary event is that it makes a difference for every one of us. It dramatizes for us the fact that we have two worlds where we may find answers to life's questions. Sin and darkness do not have the final word. Easter is the fulfillment of Jesus' promise: "Because I live, you also will live" (John 14:19).

Even though we can never state in precise detail just what happened between sunset and sunrise in the tomb, we can say that Christ's mission was accomplished. The mission of Jesus was to bring life, in all of the full-orbed meaning of that word, to an alienated, suffering human race. The triumph of his resurrection gloriously pierced the darkest corners of our plight with the promise of life renewed, life abundant, and life eternal, which is the victory over every evil, including death.

Death so often seems illogical. The more we love life, the more irrational is death. The really decisive question is whether we are related to something infinite that will make this experience climactic and purposeful. This is why the affirmations about the triumph of Jesus in the resurrection are so reassuring. By rising from the dead he conquered death and meaninglessness.

I read an article by a doctor in which he tried to explain our fears about death. He said there are three fears concerning death: first, fear of pain and of the feeling of anguish that is implicit in dying; second, the sadness of leaving our loved ones and all the things that bind us to the world; third, fear of the unknown.

He then went on to suggest that death is not often accompanied by pain. Furthermore, leaving loved ones and our worldly goods can be less distressing if we also leave goodness and a worthy contribution. But the great fear is that of the unknown. He added this helpful insight: "It might help to dissipate our fear if we remember that, were we endowed with consciousness before birth, we would probably feel the same fear of the unknown when passing from the shadow-world of the womb . . . into the light-world of life, all noise, commotion and cold." What happened when we made that transition? For most of us, arms of welcome and love awaited us. Jesus affirmed that this would be our experience: "I go to prepare a place for you . . . that where I am, there you may be also" (John 14:2-3). Consider the confidence that permeates the following lines from the Apocrypha:

> But the souls of the righteous
> are in the hand of God,
> and no torment will ever touch
> them.
> In the eyes of the foolish they
> seemed to have died;
> and their departure was thought
> to be a disaster,
> and their going from us to be
> their destruction;
> but they are at peace."
> (The Wisd. of Sol. 3:1-3)

The story of the raising of Lazarus (John 11:1-44) exists for the sake of one saying, "I am the resurrection and the life. Those who believe in me, even though they die, will live, and everyone who lives and believes in me will never die" (John 11:25-26).

Taken literally and physically, that saying of Jesus is not true. Every person has or will experience mortality. This compels us to look more closely at the biblical teaching about resurrection. It is not referring to the resuscitation of a corpse. It is the conviction that when we die, we die all over, but that the power of God, manifest in the triumph and resurrection of Jesus, will raise us to eternal life. And the God who gave all forms of life here an appropriate body can obviously be trusted to give an appropriate spiritual body in the next life. How this will be, I do not know. Perhaps someday we shall arrive at the point where the phenomenon of the resurrection is normal. Perhaps we won't. Our failure to do so will not invalidate it. We know that God, who raised up Christ, can swallow our death in an eternal victory. With the apostle we can shout, "Thanks be to God, who gives us the victory through our Lord Jesus Christ" (I Cor. 15:57).

I recognize that not everyone is excited about the idea of "living forever." A man was heard to say, "Heaven is my home, but I'm not homesick." One school teacher, a woman who loved her Lord and her church, was confronting serious surgery. I suppose everyone in that circumstance faces, at least fleetingly, the question: "Suppose I don't wake up?" The thought came to her, and she said, "It is immaterial, for I have long been curious about heaven." But then she added, "Much of what I hear doesn't make it very attractive. Sheep are silly creatures; golden streets would be ostentatious; rivers flowing with milk and honey would attract flies; and it would be dull for a teacher to be in a place where everyone was already perfect. So," she added, "I prayed, 'I'll go, Lord, but I'd rather not tomorrow.'"

But we do not have the option of deciding whether or not we wish to have eternal life. Our Lord said, "Because I live, you too shall live." And in our better moments, when we are facing life's searching questions, we know we do want the gift of everlasting life. I shall suggest two reasons why one life isn't enough.

First, *the justice of God requires it.* Think of all those who are caught short by life, who never have the opportunity to fulfill all their hopes and dreams, to express their potential. There is little to lament when a person dies whose work is accomplished and the long day is done. But it is tragic when death comes so soon that a life has never had time to blossom and to grow. If there is no place where such a life may find its fulfillment, then it does not seem possible to believe in either the love or the justice of God.

Recently I was a guest in a church and met two families who had experienced grief and bereavement. One family's nineteen-year-old son was killed in an automobile accident the previous weekend. He had been a star athlete in high school. More than seven hundred persons attended his funeral service. The other family's daughter, twenty years of age, died on her wedding night. Following the ceremony and the reception, she and her husband drove off for their honeymoon. She was killed in an accident. It seems meaningless for persons so young and so full of personal joy to lose life.

I would be less than honest if I said that the only comfort these families needed was the assurance of Christ's resurrection. In time, that knowledge may become a source of comfort. Yet, if we truly believe we shall see our loved ones after our death, that belief can soften grief.

The justice of God requires that those who have experienced unmerited suffering have some opportunity for things to be set right. The justice of God requires that we have opportunity to fulfill all the ambitions and yearnings God has placed within us. Life eternal is not a compensation for present deficiencies. It is the contagious creative continuation of our new life in Christ. Those who have believed most courageously have labored most valiantly.

We may have everything that we deem important, but we also need heaven. If life is to be full, we must have more than this world can give. Every human being needs God, for only God fills the emptiness in the human heart and plants a melody in the living of every day. Only eternity satisfies the longings, the instincts, the passions of the soul.

Second, *the love of God requires it.* In the Christian conception of God, two attributes exist side by side: God's justice and God's love. Both of them demand another life. God's love affirms our importance, our greatness, and declares that we are precious in God's sight and are not to be lost.

There is reassurance in the phrase "Today thou shalt be with me in paradise." It is personal. Obviously, Jesus believed that when life on earth is finished—be it long or be it short—we are not absorbed back into the storehouse of the universe nor is our identity lost in some all-pervading spirit. You will still be you, and I will still be me. This is the natural and inevitable culmination of the faith that is at the heart of Christianity: the worth of the individual before God. The great news of the gospel is that each person matters to God. As Jesus explained it, "Not a single sparrow falls to the ground without God's knowledge. You are more valuable than sparrows."

Some of us remember a song of yesterday, "I'll be loving you, not for just an hour, not for just a year, but always." There is something so right and sure about that sentiment. John reminds us that God so loved the world that whosoever (that's personal) believes will not perish but have eternal life. Only eternity can satisfy the genuine demands of personal love.

The newspapers once told of a tragic plane wreck. The

passengers knew for several minutes that they were going to crash. One of them used those moments to write a letter to his family and concluded with these words: "The end is near, but I am going to a better place." The letter was found in the wreckage and delivered to his family.

As we face life's ultimate questions, we need the assurance of Easter. Good Friday and Easter go together. Every person has some dark moments, some disappointments, and we need Easter as an assurance of confidence and hope. Every person faces mortality. We need Easter, with its promise of life eternal.

Mary's excitement on that first Easter was the natural amazed incredulity that a person would experience upon discovering that her dear friend was not dead, but alive. But soon Jesus' followers saw the larger truth of his resurrection. It carried a promise for them. "Because I live, you, too, shall live—eternally." And that is the good news of Easter.

Suggestions for Worship

Call to Worship:

MINISTER: Christ is risen!

PEOPLE: He is risen indeed!

MINISTER: The LORD is my strength and my song.

PEOPLE: He has become my salvation.

Act of Praise: Psalm 118:14-24.

Suggested Hymns: opening hymn: "I Know That My Redeemer Lives"; second hymn: "Sing with All the Saints in Glory"; closing hymn: "Christ the Lord Is Risen Today."

Opening Prayer: Almighty God, who through your only Son have overcome death and opened unto us the gate of everlasting life, grant, we beseech, that we who celebrate our Lord's resurrection may also offer the tribute of our praise for the everlasting hopes that rise within our hearts. We also give thanks for the gospel, which has brought life and immortality to life. Receive our thanksgiving, reveal your presence, and send into our hearts the Spirit of the risen Christ. Amen.

Pastoral Prayer: Almighty God, who by the death of your Son Jesus Christ have destroyed death, and who by raising him from the dead have delivered us from the kingdom of darkness into the kingdom of light, we praise you for the hope that because he lives, we shall live also. Inspire us by the example of the cross to serve you with obedience here on earth and at the last to commit ourselves to your eternal mercy and care. Take us through the journey of life as those who can see beyond the journey's end. Give us the faith to surrender our loved ones to your safe keeping, in the blessed assurance that you will raise them to yourself, and in sure and certain hope that they and we together will share the resurrection life of Christ; to Whom with you, O Creator yet personal Friend, and the Holy Spirit be praise and glory, now and evermore. Amen. (Adapted from a prayer by Leonard Griffith).

April 26, 1992

□

Second Sunday of Easter

Sign language has a compelling sign for the name of Christ. The forefinger of the right hand is touched to the left palm; the forefinger of the left hand is touched to the right palm. Nail pierced hands and a touching finger are symbols of a meeting with the risen Christ.

The Sunday Lessons

Acts 5:27-32: The Sanhedrin tried to silence the apostles' teaching, charging that it would "bring this man's blood on us" (v. 28). Peter and others testified to what they had witnessed, saying, "We must obey God rather than any human authority" (v. 29). Crucifixion, resurrection, and exaltation of Christ call for repentance, and they offer forgiveness.

Revelation 1:4-8: John, exiled to Patmos Island by the Emperor Domitian, had a vision. It was introduced by a message to the seven churches of Asia. The greeting from "him who is and who was and who is to come" (v. 4) proclaimed love, freedom from sin, a new kingdom, and his coming so that every eye will see him.

John 20:19-31: This traditional lesson for the Sunday following Easter records an appearance of the risen Christ behind closed doors. His greeting was "Peace." His marks were nail prints and a wounded side. His gift was the Holy Spirit. Thomas, absent when Christ first appeared, would not believe until he could place his finger in the mark of the nails and place his hand in Jesus' side. Eight days later, the risen Christ appeared again, and Thomas believed.

Interpretation and Imagination

A recurring theme that pervades the Acts of the Apostles, the Revelations of John, and the Gospel of John is that the risen Christ is victorious in every circumstance. There are no barriers he cannot bring down, no waters he cannot cross, no valleys too dark for his presence, and no dominion that can thwart his power.

These images suggest a series of sermons for Eastertide that may be called "Meetings with the Risen Christ." The first is "Behind Closed Doors" (John 20:19-31), the second is "Beside a Fire" (John 21:1-19), the third is "In the Valleys" (John 10:22-30), and the fourth is "Through a New Commandment" (John 13:31-35).

Fear had scattered the disciples. They all forsook him and fled. Later, when they gathered again, it was a relatively secret meeting behind closed doors.

The risen Christ meets us in deeply personal ways ("Put your finger here, and your hand here in my side"). The risen Christ is more than personal; yet, not one bit less than personal.

Some things one must do alone. No one else can really see for you. No one can adequately describe for another the feel of a personal touch. No one else can stand in a place of meeting for you. Your believing is like your birth. It's like your death. You have to do it alone. The risen Christ meets us in the solitary places of our own existence.

WHEN DOUBT BECOMES THE FRIEND OF FAITH

John 20:19-31

A SERMON BY EMERSON S. COLAW

"He was crucified, dead and buried" is a phrase in the Apostles' Creed. The enemies of Jesus were exultant; his friends were in despair. The disciples had followed him to Jerusalem even when they knew how dangerous it would be. Now the end had come, unexpectedly, tragically, and apparently irrevocably. The broken body of Jesus had been hurried to a tomb. Exhausted and hopeless, the little remnant of followers had brooded through a long Sabbath. Early the next morning Mary Magdalene, with confidence shattered, went to the tomb to do those last, final things that could be accomplished. She was utterly unprepared for what she encountered.

Mary ran to tell the disciples what she had seen. Most of them dismissed her account as hysterical babblings. But Peter and another disciple believed. They ran to see for themselves.

On the evening of that day the disciples were together in a room with the door shut when suddenly Jesus was in their midst. The scripture says the disciples were glad when they saw the Lord. It seems to me that is one of the world's greatest understatements. I expect they were more than "glad." They must have been beside themselves with excitement, confusion, and joy. But Thomas was not there. When the others shared with him what had happened, he expressed understandable doubt. "Unless I see the mark of the nails in his hands . . . I will not believe" (John 20:25).

Eight days later the disciples were again in the house, and this time Thomas was there. Once more, Jesus came and stood among them. He would not permit Mary to touch him on that first day, but now he invited Thomas to place his hand in Jesus' side. He seemed to be saying, "You want proof? Here it is." Thomas was convinced. He exclaimed: "My Lord and my God."

Our focus in this sermon is on the honest doubt Thomas expressed when he was first told that Jesus had been in the presence of the disciples.

When I was leaving seminary for the pastorate in the late 1940s, Leslie D. Weatherhead was one of the more respected and articulate voices to which preachers listened. In the 1960s he retired and wrote, as his last book, a volume titled *The Christian Agnostic.* I was disappointed in the title. Here was a brilliant thinker who had helped England hold steady during the darkest days of World War II. And now, it seemed to me, he was emphasizing the negative in his valedictory.

But then I read the book. In the preface he stated:

> I am writing for the "Christian agnostic," by which I mean the person who is immensely attracted by Christ and who seeks to show his spirit, to meet the challenges, hardships and sorrows of life in the light of that spirit, but who, though he is sure of many Christian truths, feels that he cannot honestly and conscientiously "sign on the dotted line" that he believes certain theological ideas about which some branches of the church dogmatize; churches from which he feels excluded because he cannot "believe." His intellectual integrity makes him say about many things, "It may be so. I do not know."

Every thoughtful person would admit that there are times when we are baffled by the way some Christian doctrines have been presented. Weatherhead's plea is for modern disciples to start following Jesus of Nazareth and to learn from him, much as his first disciples did. He argues persuasively for acceptance of Jesus Christ as the guide to God and to fullness of life. He pleads that doubters should start here and then let their unfolding experience lead them into wider circles of understanding among the mysteries of our existence. He is confident that a sincere disciple will, in time, develop all the beliefs really needed.

I found myself, when reading the book, protesting many times that Weatherhead was rejecting naive interpretations of church doctrine. Yet, I had to admit that a reverent agnosticism about unessential matters would serve the church well.

The story of Thomas, found in the lesson for this morning, is inserted in the Gospels for an essential reason. It leads to this climactic assertion: "Blessed are those who have not seen and yet have come to believe" (John 20:29). I think it is also there because almost every student of the Christian faith can, at certain times, identify with Thomas.

G. K. Chesterton once remarked that "materialists and madmen never have doubts." An authentic mark of a believer may be the ability to doubt honestly. Real doubt, coming from a reverence for truth, is from God. It does not forbid questions, nor does it answer questions prematurely. Instead, it reaches beyond understanding and asks honest questions. This preparation is essential. If we do not contend seriously with the question we will not understand the richness or the depth of the answer. It is against the horizon of doubt that new understanding bursts forth like the daysprings of a resurrection morning.

The late Carl Michalson once wrote about the *Crisis of Doubt.* He began by saying:

> Conscientious people worry more than needful over their doubts. Often doubt is utterly inoffensive, in some cases it is even indispensable. . . . Doubt either worries weak ideas into exhaustion or exercises them into greater strength. . . . Were it not for doubt's tireless cross-examination, we would find the inertia of our attitudes carrying us

beyond the time of their usefulness. . . . The doubting side of our mind knows we ought not surrender to inadequate ideas and attitudes.

Jesus offered his hands and side for Thomas's inspection. We do not have such objective data available to us.

Once I conducted a preaching mission in a church. The pastor asked whether I would be willing to meet the youth group and answer questions they had prepared for me in their meeting the previous week. When I arrived I was given about thirty-five cards with questions written on them. I was impressed by their quality. It was obvious the group was struggling to understand the faith. One question read: "Can you give proof that Jesus rose from the dead?"

I answered by saying there is no scientific proof to which we can refer. The empty tomb cannot be explained. Many persons become entangled in the thorny, unresolved questions about the nature of the resurrection body and what happened to the physical body. Thoughtful study and discussion are necessary. God does not ask us to believe something that puts in jeopardy our intellectual integrity. We cannot prove the resurrection to those who wish to disbelieve. We must acknowledge a measure of bafflement and lack of understanding.

I said to the young people that while we cannot provide objective evidence that proves the resurrection, we do see everywhere the results that have come from the fact that through the centuries men and women have been convinced that Jesus did, indeed, rise from the dead. We have the testimony of the disciples. When they experienced the risen Christ, doubt turned into conviction. Defeated, discouraged, frightened men became men of courage whose enemies complained that they were upsetting the world. Men who had disgraced themselves in the crisis became the spiritual conquerors of the Roman Empire.

Move into contemporary life. In the name of the risen Lord, churches have been established by the hundreds of thousands all over the world. Hospitals, colleges, and shelters for the homeless have provided ministries in his name. Across the years hundreds of thousands of persons have risked their lives to tell his story in every corner of the earth. The proof is in the conviction that has gripped the minds and spirits of countless millions across the years.

John Wesley once said, "Preach faith until you have it." This is not always sound advice. Within clergy this can produce depression and burnout. In the laity it may lead to alienation from the faith, cynicism, and a feeling of having been betrayed. When doubt is a passion, it cannot be reduced by a simple intellectual act. It must be resolved, as Kierkegaard suggests, by an opposite passion, the passion of faith. Yet, we also remember that a characteristic of the mature mind is that it can act wholeheartedly even without absolute certainty, as one psychologist reminds us. But I like the phrase "Doubt must be resolved by the passion of faith."

Recently I had lunch with a fine couple who are pillars in their church. The husband shared with me his experience of "dying" and then coming back. He described the tunnel, the light, and then seeing his parents, who looked as they did when he was a child, not as they were at the time of their death. Then he described how he awakened and how those who were at his bedside during the time said he was pleading, "Let me stay. Let me stay. I don't want to come back." He could not explain the experience. I do not wish to make more of his experience than I should. Obviously, we are in the presence of a mystery. Perhaps it is a way of confirming our faith.

Raymond Moody, a professor, has talked to over two hundred people who have had this same kind of experience. Elisabeth Kübler-Ross, a psychiatrist who became internationally famous for seminars she gave for dying patients, joined Dr. Moody in his project. In a book on this subject, she says, "Before I started working with dying patients, I did not believe in a life after death. I now believe in a life after death, beyond a shadow of doubt."

One pastor, attending a seminar where Dr. Moody and Dr. Kübler-Ross spoke, had some questions. He wrote:

> At first I felt reassured. It was nice to hear that someone from another discipline had arrived, without benefit of clergy, at a belief in life after death. I was troubled, however, that Kübler-Ross had made not a statement of faith, but what she regarded as a statement of fact, "Beyond a shadow of doubt."
>
> Her certainty might be a welcome boost to the feeble faith of many Christians. For me, her concept of immortality creates serious scientific, theological, and biblical problems. Life after death is, by definition,

beyond the range of scientific research. She confuses believing with knowing.

I believe that Jesus Christ rose from the dead; I don't know that he did. If it were a matter of knowing, then research centers would be more appropriate than worship centers. Our faith is that we will be in God's care. Dr. Kübler-Ross suggests a human-centered immortality fortified by stories of patients who have "died" and reported back and this is not necessarily good religion.

From the beginning, persons have come forth with arguments to prove the existence of God. They talk about the wonders of an orderly universe. But homes have been destroyed, people have been killed, and lives have been disrupted by a sudden, violent display of nature at its ugliest. We can do many things through technology to control nature, but finally nature is capricious, and every year disastrous tornadoes trigger fear and bitterness. Nature's holocausts do not speak of God—in fact, they speak loudly and clearly of ungodliness. There are as many arguments against belief in God from natural evidence as there are for belief in God.

I heard a preacher say that the Jews and many other people of the early world said, "We believe in God, but we don't believe in Christ." But the early Christians said, "We believe in Christ, and because of him we know that there is a God." They reversed it. This same preacher continued: "Because I believe in Christ, I believe in God. As I read philosophy and observe senseless death, suffering, and worldwide trauma, I don't find any good reasons to believe in God except for Christ. If I did not believe in Christ, I could not believe in God." There is a sense in which this pastor is right. The resurrection made belief in God tangible. The early church believed in God because they had seen and touched Christ.

On one occasion I was invited to have dinner with Elie Wiesel and a group of denominational leaders. Elie Wiesel was a survivor of the concentration camps. His parents and sister were murdered at Buchenwald, but he survived and began a career of keeping that memory alive. In fact, he's the one who gave the name *holocaust* to the Jewish experience of suffering in the twentieth century. He is also a writer. If you have read his works, you know that he wrestles with God in search of answers for his questions.

Following dinner, Wiesel gave a speech in a large auditorium to a standing-room-only audience. Questions followed. One person asked why Wiesel and his wife, after years of refusing to have children, finally decided to have a child. His answer, as I remember it, went something like this: He and his wife did not believe the world should be trusted with another Jewish child after what had happened in the Holocaust. But one day, reading the book of Job, he was struck by the fact it said that after all the terrible things that happened to Job and his family, Job still decided to have more children.

Harry Boulware, a United Methodist minister, tells of an interview with Wiesel after it was announced that he had won the Nobel Peace Prize. Wiesel, according to Boulware, had this to say:

> I still do not understand why God allowed the Holocaust to occur. I have not resolved the question. But I have never lost faith in God. . . . Nor can I understand the silence of the eclipse of God in years when we need Him most . . . I would say that sometimes I have been closer to Him for that reason.

Elie Wiesel is a great storyteller in the Hasidic tradition. He tells a story he heard in a concentration camp: Three rabbis put God on trial for being absent from humanity. They find God guilty as charged. When the trial ends, one rabbi looks at his watch and says, "It's time for prayers." The three rabbis who have just condemned God for abandoning them bow their heads and pray.

Let us confess that we live in a world of mystery. What brings faith to some and not to others? Thomas doubted but then believed when he saw the Lord. "Blessed are those," said Jesus, "who believe even though they have not seen." We live in a world where there is little evidence to substantiate our faith. It finally does come down to experience.

As a youngster, I sang the song "He Lives" in the country church my family attended:

> You ask me how I know he lives?
> He lives within my heart.

That is the passion that leads to faith. It is based on personal experience. Doubt turns to faith when Christ becomes a personal experience.

Suggestions for Worship

Call to Worship:

MINISTER: Serve the LORD with fear and rejoice with trembling.

PEOPLE: Blessed are all who take refuge in him.

Act of Praise: Psalm 118:14-24.

Suggested Hymns: opening hymn: "Thine Be the Glory"; second hymn: "Easter People, Raise Your Voices"; closing hymn: "Christ Is Alive."

Opening Prayer: God of grace: in Jesus Christ you have given a new and living hope. We thank you that by dying he has conquered death; and that by rising again he promises eternal life. Help us to know that because he lives, we shall live also; and That neither death, nor life, nor things present, nor things to come, shall be able to separate us from your love; in Jesus Christ our Lord. Amen. (Perry H. Biddle, Jr.)

Pastoral Prayer: Eternal God, thank you for the note of victory that fills our souls today, for the rich heritage of faith that life is ever Lord of death and that love can never lose its own.

We thank you for all things excellent and beautiful that make faith in immortality more sure. For our friends who have loved us, our families that have nourished us, for the heights and depths of the human spirit, full of promise and prophecy, for all victories of right over wrong, and above all for Christ who has brought life and immortality to light, we thank you. Join to our company today those we have loved and who live with you in the house not made with hands.

Replenish with new hope all who are discouraged about the world and who find faith in the ultimate victory of righteousness difficult. So often might triumphs over right, and good is undone by evil. Speak to us and refresh our souls with a new hope. Lift our vision above the immediate and illumine for us that eternal purpose you had in Christ. Say to us this Easter season that no Calvary can finally defeat Christ.

May the living Christ be not only in our creed but also in our experience. Let Christ's victory be a present triumph in our souls. Through faith in him and the reality of his resurrection, enable us to overcome the world through the risen Christ. Amen.

MAY 3, 1992

□

Third Sunday of Easter

The risen Christ met Peter and other disciples on the beach beside a fire.

The Sunday Lessons

Acts 9:1-20: The appearances of the risen Christ were not confined to Jerusalem and Galilee. On the road to Damascus, Christ appeared to Saul of Tarsus and left him blind for three days. Ananias, a disciple, was commanded through a vision to lay hands on Saul, "an instrument whom [Jesus has] chosen" (v. 15). Paul regained his sight, was baptized, and went to the synagogues to proclaim, "He is the Son of God" (v. 20).

Revelation 5:11-14: John tells of his vision at the gates of heaven. He saw the throne and heard the voice of myriads crying, "Worthy is the Lamb that was slaughtered" (v. 12). Every person in heaven and on earth joined in praising the exalted Christ. All creation (the four creatures) said, "Amen."

John 21:1 (or 15)-19: Christ appeared to Simon Peter and other disciples by the Sea of Tiberias. They had fished all night and caught nothing. Following Jesus' instruction, "Cast the net to the right side of the boat" (v. 6), they caught more than they could handle. On shore beside a charcoal fire, they ate bread and fish. Jesus asked Peter, "Do you love me?" He commanded Peter, "Feed my sheep." John recorded this as the third appearance of the risen Christ.

Interpretation and Imagination

No one can live in complete isolation. Sooner or later, like Peter and the disciples, we must leave our hiding places and go out in the world. We have to pay the rent. For Peter it was time to go fishing. The risen Christ meets us, in very public ways in the places where we work and play.

Beside a charcoal fire in the high priest's courtyard (John 18:16 describes Peter as being outside the door), the follower was asked three times if he were a disciple. Each time, Peter answered that he was not and that Christ was a stranger to him. He publicly denied any association with Jesus.

Beside a charcoal fire on the shore of the Sea of Tiberias (note how John employed the Greek name for Lake Galilee), Peter was questioned by the risen Christ. "Simon, son of John," he called him by name and then asked, "Do you love me more than all else?" Now, Peter's answer beside the fire was different. Three times, he declared his love.

Meeting the risen Christ in the public world of commerce and society leaves no room for secret love. The Christ you intend to keep is a Christ you are called to share. Declare your loyalty publicly and feed all his lambs, all his sheep.

WHEN A DRAG FULFILLS A DREAM

John 21:1-19

A SERMON BY RICHARD ANDERSEN

An eleven year-old boy in Blair, Wisconsin, was living out his dream. He had fished every day for more than a year. Sometimes he fished for only fifteen minutes, but other times, mainly in the summer, he fished four to eight hours a day. One day he caught over three hundred fish. When a reporter interviewed him, his answer to nearly every question was, "It's hard to say!" Did he prefer ice fishing in winter or regular pole fishing in summer? "It's a hard to say!" Did he remember how old he was when he first began fishing? "It's hard to say!" When you're living out a dream, it's hard to say what part of the vision is best.

Life can become a drag, a long drawn out dreariness that's filled with dreaded and drab aspects, a nightmare instead of a dream. Jesus would have us see visions and dream dreams, living them out like that young fisherman, however. He would have a drag become a dream realized, a vision actualized.

Are you dragging? Is life weightier now than ever, burdened

with pain and laden with unwanted toil? What are you dragging? Is it something that nurtures hope and sustains joy? Or is it something that is more akin to the ancient mariner's albatross in Coleridge's *The Rime of the Ancient Mariner*—a dead weight tied around your neck? To whom are you dragging it? We never keep our burdens to ourselves. We always lay them on someone else, whether intentionally or not. In this post-Easter episode of Jesus' disciples' lives, some answers are provided that may transform what is ordinarily a drag into a dream.

Are you dragging? Peter was. The disciples had returned to Capernaum, to the Sea of Galilee, but they were as lethargic as they had been in the upper room. Having seen the risen Christ, they should have been ecstatic, but their ecstasy had evidently faded. They were dragging. They didn't know which way to go or what to do. Gloom had engulfed them. Their sorrow over Christ's death clouded their vision of him as the resurrected Lord.

Peter said, "I am going fishing." He was tired of the apathy and the sorrow. He needed a change of pace and claimed it. As one who had fished all of his life, returning to work was not a dreaded task but a continuing dream. He was like the boy in Blair, Wisconsin. It's hard to say when Peter first discovered the value of work therapy, but he remembered, and the rest joined him.

This says something to us about handling our tensions and fears, the burdens of life, our sorrows and disappointments, and all those experiences and escapades that leave us dragging. It's not so much that we should go fishing as it is that we should get back to work, and do so with determination. Peter did not say "I *think maybe* I'll go fishing" or "One day I *hope* to go fishing when I'm over my grief." He said, "I am going fishing." It was a clear, declarative statement.

"We will come with you," said the rest. But they still seemed to be dragging. They toiled all night, but they did not catch a thing, says the Gospel of John. Life can seem so futile at times.

When you're dragging, every effort seems useless, unless God is invited to have a part in it, unless Christ is perceived as giving blessing, and the Holy Spirit is allowed to master the difficulties. A drag, no matter how anguishing, can fulfill a dream.

In *The Old Man and the Sea*, Ernest Hemingway tells what it is like when an old man goes fishing after dragging about, fishless, for a long, long time. He catches the biggest fish he has ever seen, but that, too, produces a battle as whole schools of sharks attack the carcass and rip it apart.

"Half fish," says the old man. "Fish that you were. I am sorry that I went too far out. I ruined us both. But we have killed many sharks, you and I, and ruined many others." He was dragging—from exhaustion, from emotional depletion, from physical weariness, but *something* kept him going. The old man prayed and fought the sharks again and again. There was nothing left of the eighteen-foot fish when he finally reached port, but there was the sense that he had done his best, weary as he was. And he was the marvel of the whole village, for they saw the immense skeleton tied to his little boat.

Peter and the others must have felt like Hemingway's old man. Are you dragging, too? Instead of a nightmare, it can become a dream.

The question no longer is "Are you dragging?" but "*What* are you dragging?"

On the shore, as the sun was beginning to spill over the eastern hills, Jesus was standing, watching his disciples toiling futilely.

"Young men," he called to the tired crew of the boat, "haven't you caught anything?"

"Not a thing," they responded.

"Throw your net out on the right side of the boat and you will catch some," said the Lord. When they did so, their muscles soon ached from the heavy load of fish filling the nets. Their dragging melancholy died. Hope was resurrected. Their dream of a catch became a vision of blessing. Good old Simon Peter was no longer dragging emotionally. Now he was dragging the net ashore full of big fish, 153 of them! The dream was becoming a reality. Hope had not ignored them, nor had victory and joy.

What are you dragging? Is it a catch like that of the fishermen of Galilee? Is it the fulfillment of more than a dream, but the promise of God?

Jesus stands on the shore of our lives to tell us where the harvest is. Are you listening? Are you responding with action? Both factors enabled Peter and his crew to change from those dragging about forlornly to those dragging in a magnificent catch of fish.

In Nikos Kazantzakis' novel *Zorba the Greek*, the aging Zorba tells about seeing a much older man, "an old grandfather of ninety" busily planting an almond tree. Zorba, aghast at this, exclaimed, "What grandad. . . . Planting an almond tree?"

"And he, bent as he was, turned round and said: 'My son, I carry on as if I should never die.' I replied: 'And I carry on as if I was going to die any minute.' " The grandfather was right; Zorba was wrong. The faithful come dragging the harvest, not their bitterness or their laziness. They plant almond trees, not negativism and rancor. They listen for the Lord's instructions, and they follow them. They always look to the future. That's when a drag fulfills a dream.

What about you? What are you dragging? Is it the load of unforgiven wrong, the dismal disappointments of the past, the bitter taste of soured hopes? You've toiled all night. Now, it's time to listen to the man on the shore, to Jesus, who intones, "Throw your net out on the right side."

The right side is the one of trust, of continuing on, of responding to him positively and enjoying the adventure, of getting rid of fruitlessness to become fruitful.

Are you dragging? God-in-Christ has an answer for that. What are you dragging? Is it only disappointment over failure, or elation over blessings? Your outlook can determine how the drag of uncertainty can be fulfilled as a dream. It's a matter that also concerns the one to whom you're dragging your gifts or disappointments. To whom are you taking them?

The disciples pulled the load of fish onboard the boat. Peter, however, dragged his abundant blessings to Jesus immediately when he was invited to do so. The Lord had a fire going and was ready to make breakfast for the disciples. He had bread and fish ready for them. Still he said, "Bring some of the fish you have just caught."

Peter dragged the 153 fish ashore to Jesus. "Come and eat," said Jesus. The disciples knew that man was the Lord. They had seen him in the upper room in Jerusalem and now on the pebble-strewn banks of the Sea of Galilee. But there must have been some hesitation, some momentary reluctance on their part to go to Jesus, for John says that "Jesus came and took the bread and gave it to them and did the same with the fish" (John 21:13).

In the upper room, Jesus took bread and shared it with the Twelve, instituting the Sacrament of the Altar. At Emmaus the two disciples, whose company he sought along the roadway from

Jerusalem that Easter night, recognized him in the breaking of bread. Here once more the disciples saw Jesus fully as their living Lord in the sharing of bread. Jesus is the bread of Life from whom our spiritual and physical nourishment comes.

But he invites us to share the harvest he has given us. We need to listen to Jesus' call to share some of the harvest he provides with him and his Church. A drag remains a drag until we drag it to Jesus, not as ridicule or blasphemy, but as gift and commitment.

Jesus seeks to turn the nets of your dilemmas into harvests of blessings. But it cannot be unless you willingly drag yourself, your time, and your possessions to him—your "fish," in other words—just as Simon Peter dragged the huge haul of fish to the Lord for his use, which he in turn distributed cooked and ready for everyone.

W. Somerset Maugham tells a fascinating story in his novel *The Moon and Sixpence.* It's a story of a stormy artist who abandoned everything to foster his art. Charles Strickland is an unpleasant, unsavory person. Says Maugham, "He was single-hearted in his aim, and to pursue it he was willing to sacrifice not only himself—many can do that—but others. He had a vision." And then the author concludes, "Strickland was an odious man, but I still think he was a great one." His art might be great, but his life is a mess. I can only wonder what it would have been like had he dragged it to Christ instead of down to the depths of deprivation. Jesus welcomes everyone who hauls his or her catch to him, and he blesses it immeasurably.

To whom are you dragging the blessings God imposes? If merely to yourself, no wonder you experience uselessness and depression, but if to God, no wonder you rejoice in the feast he fixes.

A drag can become a dream fulfilled. It depends on who is in charge as well as to whom your harvest is being offered.

Once I was part of a group that went walking early in the morning by the Sea of Galilee before the sun peeked over the eastern slopes and splashed its golden rays across the quiet waters. We witnessed a fisherman examining his nets, which he had placed the evening before. He checked each one. He had caught nothing, so he sped off to deeper water and other nets. We could have called to him from the shore as Jesus did the disciples, he was so close, but unlike Jesus we could not see a school of fish nearby any more than that Israeli fisherman could. It takes more than another dreamer to make dreams come true. It takes one who gives visions and conquers the impossible, to whom death means life and impediments an open door. It takes Jesus.

A few days later, we were at the very spot tradition says Jesus made the breakfast for his weary friends. We ate also. Rather than bread and fish, we shared bread and wine. At an outdoor altar, we heard the Lord call to us and felt his presence. None of us dared ask, "Who are you?" in that experience. We knew it was the Lord. Over and over again, those with me that day have commented about that eucharistic event. Christ was there as fully as when he called to the toiling fisherman that night they labored without a catch. Just as he transformed a "drag," an unpleasant and unproductive time, into the prelude for fulfillment, so also he continues to do for us. Seemingly we could hear him inquire of Peter, "Do you love me more than these others do?" And we could hear Peter's answer, for it was our answer, too, "Yes, Lord, you know that I love you." But Jesus tells us not to content ourselves with the emotion, but to wrap it up in action—taking care of little lambs and fully grown sheep that are beyond our corral, but that are nevertheless his.

What are your dreams? Your visions? Do you seek fulfillment for your labor and joy in your doing? They are yours. Like the boy in Blair, Wisconsin, keep fishing. "It's hard to say" when it will happen, but we know that Jesus is nearby, waiting for our answer when he calls, "Haven't you caught anything?"

Jesus stands on the shore watching all of us as we labor night and day. He is ready to direct us as he did Peter and his crew to the successes that will transform a night wasted into a dawn full of surprises.

Suggestions for Worship

Call to Worship (Ps. 30:4, 5, 11-12):

MINISTER: Sing praises to the LORD, O you his faithful ones, and give thanks to his holy name. . . .

PEOPLE: Weeping may linger for the night, but joy comes with the morning. . . .

MINISTER: [God has] turned my mourning into dancing; [God has] taken off my sackcloth and clothed me with joy,

PEOPLE: so that my soul may praise you and not be silent. O LORD my God, I will give thanks to you forever.

Act of Praise: Psalm 30:4-12.

Suggested Hymns: opening hymn: "All Hail the Power of Jesus' Name"; second hymn: "Jesus, Thine All-Victorious Love"; closing hymn: "I Am Thine, O Lord."

Opening Prayer: Creator-Father, in adoration of your goodness, we gather to pray and to praise you, to hear your word and to find hope for our lives.

In celebration of your love, we recognize the weakness of our love, which has caused us to be unloving toward our neighbor. Inspire us with your forgiveness, so that we may embrace those who offend us as well as be restored to those to whom we have given offense. Make us one as our Lord prayed in the upper room, O Lord.

In the joy your presence gives, renew us to live as your restored believers through Jesus Christ, the resurrected and rescuing One. Amen.

Pastoral Prayer: Let us not sidestep your questions, Lord Jesus, or ignore your signs and wonders or miss the fish or ignore the sheep. Encourage us through the Holy Spirit to be those who love your lambs with the care you instructed us to give. Inspire us by your word to watch over your sheep, nurturing them lovingly—those who live in splendor as well as those who live sparsely and sparingly; those ailing in mind and body as well as those agile and whole; those faithful and generous as well as those faithless and penurious. This day, Lord, show us where the fish and the sheep are so that we may haul in a catch of the former and gladly feed the latter. Help us, Lord, by our actions and expressions to love you as much as did your disciples of the past, and more so, if you will enliven our hearts. To your glory, we pray. Amen.

May 10, 1992

□

Fourth Sunday of Easter

The risen Christ as good shepherd leads his sheep safely through the valleys.

The Sunday Lessons

Acts 13:15-16, 26-33: Preaching in the synagogue at Antioch of Pisidia, Paul told God-fearing Jews, who had received the message of salvation, that an innocent Jesus had been delivered to Pilate to be killed. Though Jesus was laid in the tomb, God raised him up. Paul told of Christ's appearances in Galilee and Jerusalem and declared that what God promised, "he has fulfilled."

Revelation 7:9-17: John's vision describes those who survived the great tribulation (salvation belongs to our God) and came out clothed in white robes. His picture of heaven has images of the throne room of God, the Temple, bread and water in the desert, and a shepherd leading his sheep beside springs of living water. "God will wipe away every tear" (v. 17).

John 10:22-30 The good shepherd image portrays a near presence and care that is inherent in the relationship of the risen Christ with his followers. In this part of the good shepherd discourse, some Jews asked, "If you are the Messiah, tell us plainly" (v. 24). Jesus answered, "My sheep hear my voice. I know them" (v. 27). God's love and power assure eternal life and safe care.

Interpretation and Imagination

The good shepherd texts are traditional lectionary lessons for the fourth Sunday of Eastertide. They remind the church of the caring and personal ways by which the risen Christ relates to our needs. Hunger, lostness, and danger are or will be realities in all of our lives. Christ leads us through the valleys.

This Gospel lesson addresses the issue of uncertainty. Sometimes we're not sure that we know and are known by the one who is from God. We'd like for someone, anyone, and certainly the risen Christ to "tell us plainly." It was winter time when they asked him, at the Feast of Lights, to step out of the shadows and be recognized.

Those who trust enough to follow, those who respond as the shepherd's sheep, know and are known. We are inclined to say, "If I could be sure that he is the one who has it right, I would follow him." The lesson teaches that following comes before one has faith—not after. It is in the following that we are named.

A young mother died, leaving her husband and a six-year-old son. After the funeral, the child was afraid to be in his room alone. He came to sleep in his father's bed, but then feared the dark. "Are you there, Daddy?" he asked. "Yes, I'm here," answered his father. Later, the little boy asked, "But is your face turned toward me?" "Yes, child, my face is turned toward you."

THE THAW OF SPRING IN THE WINTER OF DISBELIEF

John 10:22-30

A SERMON BY RICHARD ANDERSEN

Jerusalem, in the middle of winter, can shiver in the chill of a light snowfall in the morning and then bask in the warm, balmy light of the Middle Eastern sun in the afternoon. Some of these dramatic temperature variations are evident in the visit Jesus made to the Temple for the Festival of the Dedication. They are the temperatures of human temperament, rather than those of the weather—the cool attitudes and cold reserve of disbelieving Jews, rather than the fevered delight and the toasty warmth of ready acceptance that many offered him.

"How can you expect a man who's warm to understand a man who's cold," asks Alexander Solzhenitsyn in *One Day in the Life of Ivan Denisovich*. He suggests that we are to let our work warm us up. "That was your only salvation," he said of that Siberian prison camp where he froze winter after winter. But Jesus has a more effective idea.

We sense the cold wave of faithlessness as well as the bright, beaming burst of warming sunlight shining from Jesus, and in the midst of this hot and cold we find an eager bloom working its way up through the frozen earth of the soul to signal spring's gladly awaited thaw. "No one," says Jesus, "can snatch them away from God's care." He was not speaking of crocuses, but of you and me and all who wish to push their way into the sunlight out of the mud of disbelief.

Many of us, however, have been in the same chill-frosted group as those disbelievers in Jerusalem—doubting Jesus, denying his claims, bickering with his promises, and debating his miracles as if they were attempts at defrauding the public. Many of us have been icebergs of contempt at times. "You," we seem to say to the Lord of life in the amazing winter of our own disbelief, "think you can sell us on the validity of prayer, the purposefulness of faith, the mystery of the cross, the mastery of the grave, and the wonder of grace? Well, we won't have it." Our minds freeze over with the ice of intellectual snobbery; our hearts turn to icicles of spiritual disdain. But in the midst of this sub-zero cold snap, Jesus infuses the warmth of his love, which melts even these frigid chunks. "My sheep hear my voice," he assures us. "I know them, and they follow me. I give them eternal life, and they will never perish" (John 10:27-28). Like a blowtorch, he cuts through the glacier of our disregard, penetrating to the depths of our hearts and minds.

Is your spiritual furnace ignited yet, churning up to a head of steam, ready to spread warmth and light instead of cold drafts and chilly ideas, as will a furnace with an extinguished pilot light and a whirring circulating fan? We all need to experience the thaw of a Jesus-activated spring in the long, drab winter of disbelief, to become crocuses of the crucible of the cross.

There was a time when reference to the relationship between East and West was called the Cold War, a battle that seemed to go on endlessly. That day in the Temple, there was a similar bone-chilling rift between the people and Jesus. "How long are you going to keep us in suspense?" they wanted to know. "Tell us the plain truth: Are you the Messiah?" they insisted. Helmut Thielicke says that "taking God seriously means to take him at his word, giving him the chance to act as he has promised" (*Being a Christian When the Chips Are Down*). But the Temple worshipers that winter's day chose to be like the weather. There was a persistent frost in their attitudes. Disbelief became unbelief.

The cold wave that never warms up, that always is plunged below freezing, that is stuck in double-digit minuses on the spiritual thermometer, becomes arrogantly proud of its icy attitude. No matter what Jesus said to those ice boxes of contempt in the Temple colonnade, they maintained their refrigerated reluctance to believe. Jesus answered them by reminding them that their questions had already been resolved. "But you would not believe me," he said.

Jesus had once acknowledged that "Unless you see signs and wonders you will not believe" (John 4:48). But the bitter coldness of such an attitude is to know the thaw of spring in the winter of disbelief.

The frosty gloom can last only so long before the sun will penetrate the thick gray layers of cloud. It is not only a matter of seeing the sunshine, but also of feeling its warmth. It is not only a matter of hearing the gospel, but also of experiencing its power.

"The works that I do in my Father's name testify to me," explained the Lord (John 10:25). The people's failure to believe was due to their unfortunate ownership, revealed Jesus: "Because you do not belong to my sheep. My sheep hear my voice. I know them, and they follow me" (John 10:26-27).

A young father had made gigantic steps in his career. He had everything—everything but a thriving faith. When his doctor discovered a malignant tumor and the extensive requirements of surgery and treatment were in full play, he heard Jesus' voice and felt the warmth of the sunshine that he had not noticed burning through the ice of what had been. His wife was a Christian, but she did not badger him, nor did his two small boys. They let their love sweep him into the "Sonshine." The voice of the Savior echoed in their everyday language and reverberated against the walls of his conscience like the splash of sunshine reflected in a mirror. He sought baptism and involvement in the church, but he was not razzle-dazzled into the kingdom immediately. It was a thoughtful, deliberate process, steeped in in-depth consideration, because he had heard the Lord calling him like a lost lamb in the wilderness of uncertainty—at first faintly, then booming loudly. The thaw of spring had come in the midst of a winter of unbelief. "No one," said Jesus of his sheep, "will snatch them out of my hand" (John 10:28). And there was the promise of eternal life.

The cold wave of unbelief seems to go on forever until the Son breaks through. It is then that the small bulb planted in the soil of life breaks out of its hibernation to emerge as tiny green leaves poking their way through the snow, even breaking the ice that covers them, to come to bright, full-colored bloom.

This is not what happened in the Temple that day. We know those arctic antagonists were so upset with Jesus that they picked up stones to throw at him. They thought him blasphemous for calling himself God. It was not only the tiny emergence of the leaves, but also the spring flower in full bloom that sprang up from his words: "The Father and I are one" (John 10:30).

Countless others who had lain dormant through their long winter's season of disbelief have come to full flower since that episode in the Temple. They were sheep who heard Christ's voice, bulbs that erupted from their graves of doubt to bloom gorgeously in the thaw of spring, brought on by the warmth of the Son of God. Their names are like the names of some of the most remarkable of a gardener's exotic plants—Alan Paton of South Africa, who as a youth rebelled from Christianity to become an agnostic and then returned to Christ as he heard the Lord summoning him to become one of the forceful opponents of apartheid through his prodigious writings; Raoul Wallenberg, a young Swedish diplomat who heard Christ calling him to rescue the sheep of God's flock being sent to the gas chambers of the Holocaust, managing to rescue over 120,000 Hungarian Jews; and countless others who were dormant "bulbs" that erupted from the soil of their existence at the call of Christ to flower fully.

Every flower needs soil, air, water, light, and a place to grow. Similar basic elements are required to experience the blessing we have to give and experience.

This is the result of the bulb that bursts from its wintry tomb to bud and flower. Not only is it stretching out to meet the joy of the sun-filled sky, but it also has God standing in back of its growth and beauty to ensure its steady strength against the blustering winds. Commitment to Christ is backed up by action and fortified by God's Spirit. It is then that the bulb knows the thaw of spring and triumphs in the winter of disbelief.

The sunshine brought forth those blooms, and that sun continues to shine. Let it work through the ice of intellectual indifference and spiritual apathy to draw you into the flowering of faith. Let your winter of unbelief or disregard become more than it was for those people gathered in Jerusalem during that anniversary commemorating the Temple's dedication. Let it be a spring thaw of joy, one that experiences the blessing and knows that winter's cold cannot destroy it. Listen to Jesus, so that no one may snatch you out of his hand. Listen to him all the way to eternity.

Suggestions for Worship

Call to Worship (Rev. 5:12):

MINISTER: [Sing] with full voice,

PEOPLE: Worthy is the Lamb that was slaughtered

MINISTER: to receive power and wealth and wisdom and might

PEOPLE: and honor and glory and blessing!

Act of Praise: Psalm 23.

Suggested Hymns: opening hymn: "Only Trust Him"; second hymn: "The King of Love My Shepherd Is"; closing hymn: "He Leadeth Me: O Blessed Thought."

Opening Prayer: O Lord Jesus Christ, you are the good shepherd, the one who cares for our souls. Call us to yourself in the sunlight of this morning and lead us in those places where we may gain the life and strength we need. When the shadows close around us, bring us to the safety of your fold. Hear our prayer, O Lord Jesus Christ. Amen.

Pastoral Prayer: O blessed Lord and faithful shepherd, you are the source of all life and love of all succor and safety. Though our devotion is half-hearted and our following is foolish, you do not leave us to ourselves. May your goodness reach beyond anything we deserve and your mercy follow us even when we turn from you.

We pray, O God, that you will be our help and sustaining grace today. You know our needs more than we know them ourselves.

Show yourself to all who are needy. Heal the sick; comfort those who mourn; strengthen those who are facing hard trials; lift up the fallen; reclaim the wanderers; have mercy on those who have sinned. Some of us have grown tired and weak. Raise us up, we pray. Some of us have grown fainthearted and afraid. Give us the faith that will turn back our fears. Some of your children are homeless and hungry and alone. Feed, welcome, and comfort them, and encourage your Church to reach out to the needy in faithful service to you, O Christ.

Let all people know that you alone are God Almighty, Father. Let every creature know that you alone are Savior, O Jesus Christ. And let each one of us know that we are children of your own family and the sheep of your pasture. Through Jesus Christ our Lord, amen.

May 17, 1992

□

Fifth Sunday of Easter

The risen Christ gives a new commandment to those who are left alone.

The Sunday Lessons

Acts 14:8-18: When Paul healed a crippled man at Lystra, the pagan crowds said, "The gods have come down to us in human form!" (v. 11). They named Barnabas "Zeus" and Paul "Hermes," and a priest of Zeus brought sacrifices. The apostles, declaring themselves to be persons of like nature with them urged the people to turn from vain things to a living God and noted that God has never been without witnesses in any nation.

Revelation 21:1-6: John's vision of a new creation—"I saw a new heaven and a new earth" (v. 1)—is the claim of his revelation. The New Jerusalem is a place where God will dwell with people. Tears will be wiped away. Death will be no more. Mourning, crying, and pain will be ended.

John 13:31-35: These words begin Jesus' farewell discourse at the Last Supper. Jesus speaks of the near cross and proclaims that the Father is to be glorified by Jesus' obedience. As he tells his disciples, "Where I am going you cannot follow me now" (v. 36), he gives a new commandment: "Love one another. Just as I have loved you, you also should love one another" (v. 34). Love is the sign by which all may know that one is a disciple of Christ.

Interpretation and Imagination

In a few short hours the disciples would be separated from Jesus Christ. "Where I am going you cannot come," he told them. Thus we are made aware that every human relationship ends, either with one's own death or with the death of those one loves. Final separations are the source of our greatest pain.

The approaching separation was the occasion for Jesus' commandment to "love as I have loved you." He was with his disciples at the Last Supper when, like a father meeting the family for the last time, he spoke tenderly. Then, he gave the new commandment. In the Latin Vulgate, those Greek words are translated "mandatum novum," "New commandment" (Holy Thursday) became the name of the anniversary celebration of the Last Supper (see F. F. Bruce, *The Gospel of John*, p. 294).

Is the commandment to love new? Certainly not. But this kind of love ("as I have loved") had not been known before. Since Christ's resurrection and ascension, it has been the distinctive mark of a true Christian. "By this everyone will know that you are my disciples" (John 13:35).

Tertullian wrote that the early New Testament Christians in the second century were spoken of by the world in these words: "See how they love one another. How ready they are to die for one another."

THE YARDSTICK IN THE KITCHEN

John 13:31-35

A SERMON BY R. CARL FRAZIER, JR.

As I was growing up I always knew where my mother kept the yardstick in her kitchen. It resided between the washing machine and the wall. Often, when she would tell me to bring the yardstick to her, it meant bad news. The rod was not spared at our house if it was necessary—and the rod of choice was the yardstick!

But there were other times when being told to fetch the yardstick was exciting. The yardstick was the instrument of measure to check our growth. We would line up—my brother, sister, and I—along the kitchen wall and be measured. Every inch was, for me, an accomplishment, for my goal in life was to measure up to my father (and maybe even be a little taller). My ambition was to be six feet tall.

But I have discovered a curious thing: Measuring up to my father involves more than just physical height. Measuring up to my dad involves acquiring something of his spirit, of his nature, of his personality. That is something a yardstick cannot measure.

It occurs to me more and more that our relationship with God is similar to that yardstick in the kitchen. We devoutly and hopefully wish to measure up, to love into the image of God into which we are created. So we check our growth against certain standards and values. We embrace the Ten Commandments as a guide for life; we live by the Golden Rule; we seek to discern the secret of the Beatitudes; and we check ourselves to see how we are doing.

Yet, we are faced with a dilemma. Like the yardstick in the kitchen, the very standards that would enable us to grow into God's likeness can be turned against us for chastisement:

Did you lie today? (Yes, white lies count.)
Did you steal today? (Being late for a meeting is robbing someone of his or her time.)
Did you "do unto others as you would have them do unto you" today? (Do you really want someone else talking about you behind your back.)
Are you really "hungering for righteousness"? (Or is that just an act for the church's administrative board?)

In the end, however, we no more participate in the nature of God than when we started. That is, of course, the irony of it: that the standards that we would keep and that judge us do not at last save us or change us. In the end, we still fail to measure up.

So in the lesson from John's Gospel, we find the disciples of Jesus faced with a dilemma: Their common bond, their reason and source for being is leaving them. How can they keep going? What standard will they use to measure their life together? The dilemma is acute and painful, for after life with Christ the old standards simply will not suffice any longer.

In the midst of their dilemma, they discovered that they had been offered something new, something that transcends old standards and values: "I give you a new commandment, that you love one another. Just as I have loved you, you also should love one another" (John 13:34).

It strikes the ear as odd to hear Jesus "command" love. Love, we are taught after all, is not something that can be made to order. It is spontaneous, free, a grace, if you will. Love is found in a glance, a touch, a gesture that comes without request or bidding. Love can no more be commanded than a child can be commanded to hug a stranger. Watch the body language: The child hugs from a distance, pulls away, turns a cheek to the kiss rather than a face, and bolts away at the first opportunity. "You *have* to love each other" makes as much sense as a mother telling two small boys to "kiss and make up."

Yet, there it is, echoing through the air. "I give you a new commandment, that you love one another." Perhaps we do not understand love, so we cannot understand the command. By commanding this, Jesus offers a new standard and guide for life—a new measuring stick. Love is learned in relationship; the relationship in which it is learned is the relationship of the believer to the risen Lord. The command is, after all, to love as Christ loved, and that, for us, is learned behavior, not natural instinct.

I once asked a child of four whose parents wished her to be baptized whether she knew what that meant. "Yes," she answered, "it means I am a follower of Jesus, that he loves me, and that I am supposed to love everybody else." Close enough, I figured, close enough.

To be commanded to love is to allow Jesus to be the measuring stick of our lives, for he is both the source and the standard of the new life the believer receives. Our love for one another is also to be the hallmark of our relationship together here in the church. The church that loves bears the image of Christ and shares the ministry of Christ. The church that loves makes Christian love possible in the world, and, through that church, the world still encounters Jesus. So long as we love as he loved—selflessly, faithfully—we reflect him in ways nothing can measure. And we grow into his image.

As I was growing up, there was a yardstick in my mother's kitchen that we used to mark our growth with and by which I checked my progress toward "being like my father." But then, I realized that measuring up to my dad involved more than just his physical height: It involved acquiring something of his nature, his personality, his spirit. Recently, in the midst of a family discussion about decision-making, my six-year-old looked at me and said, "Daddy, you sound just like Granddaddy." That was something the yardstick could not measure.

We seek to honor our baptism, to live into the image in which we were created. That cannot be entirely measured by laws and standards. It involves grace and love—attributes of the nature, personality, and Spirit of God. Once we claim, then—and only then—can we sing "We are one body in this one Lord."

Suggestions for Worship

Call to Worship (Ps. 145:17-18, 21):

MINISTER: The LORD is just in all his ways, and kind in all his doings.

PEOPLE: The LORD is near to all who call on him, to all who call on him in truth. . . .

MINISTER: My mouth will speak the praise of the LORD,

PEOPLE: and all flesh will bless his holy name forever and ever.

Act of Praise: Psalm 145:13*b*-21.

Suggested Hymns: opening hymn: "For All the Saints"; second hymn: "It Is Well with My Soul"; closing hymn: "Christ for the World We Sing."

Opening Prayer: Holy God, you are near to all who call upon you in truth, and you fulfill the desires of all who fear you. Grant that our hearts may be opened to know that you are near and our lives directed to desire only you. Through Jesus Christ our Lord, amen.

Pastoral Prayer: O God, who is the Alpha and Omega, the source and goal of all life, we give you thanks for the life that we have received from your creative power and the new life we receive from you in Jesus Christ. Come among us again and create us anew that in all things we may seek you and the glory of your holy name.

O God, who wipes away the tear from every eye and who conquers death, we ask your comforting presence in those places of life where grief and pain have their way. Come to the world's places of crying and bring your joy. Come to the world's places of pain and bring your healing. Come to the world's places of death and bring the gift of resurrection.

O God, whose nature and name is love and who has shown us your love in Jesus Christ, we give you thanks that you have given us a share in that love and that you have sought us out for covenant relationship. Grant that your love may grow and be nurtured here and in our lives that we may love one another as Christ loved, and bring that love to bear in our life and witness in the world.

We ask these things in the name and Spirit of Christ our Lord, who lives and reigns with you and the Holy Spirit, one God, now and forever. Amen.

May 24, 1992

□

Sixth Sunday of Easter

Persons risen with Christ have distinguishing characteristics.

The Sunday Lessons

Acts 15:1-2, 22-29: Self-appointed teachers from Jerusalem had come to Antioch and created dissension by insisting that all needed to be circumcised. This prompted the convening of a council at Jerusalem, which decided to choose two men from among them to send to Antioch: Judas and Silas. They were to support the teaching of Paul and Barnabas.

Revelation 21:10, 22-27: John is carried away to a high mountain from which he sees the New Jerusalem. There is no Temple; it was destroyed in A.D. 70. Sun, moon, and stars are not needed. The glory of God is its light, and its lamp is the Lamb. Citizens of the city represent people of all nations. Nothing unclean enters, and no one practices "abomination or falsehood."

John 14:23-29: One of the disciples asked Jesus what he meant when he said, "The world will see me no more, but you will see me." What is the nature of this private revelation? It is not a cataclysmic event. It is not miraculous or ecstatic. Love and obedience are its signs, and peace is its quality.

Interpretation and Imagination

Are there certain standards of conduct that must be followed in the church? Of course! Any religion that has no moral demand, that makes no practical difference in our lives or our communities, is sterile.

Then what are the standards by which members of the Christian community shall be measured? What are our requirements for membership? This question created dissension in the church at

Antioch and prompted the council at Jerusalem. Some believers who belonged to the party of the Pharisees, claimed that circumcision and obedience to the laws of Moses were necessary qualifications for all Christians, both Jew and Gentile.

Following the debate, an agreement was made. It seemed good. "It seemed good to the apostles and elders." "It seemed good to us." "It seemed good to the Holy Spirit and to us." These are the words that introduced the apostles' letter outlining expectations for Christian conduct, which were "no greater burden" than three minimal things: Food sacrificed to idols, meat from strangled animals, and fornication were forbidden.

Two things were apparent in the accord: a quality of graciousness and a sense of reverence before the chief actor in the book of Acts—the Holy Spirit. The revelation of John also refers to the nature of men and women who are risen with Christ. Citizens of the New Jerusalem are moral and clean. Those who see and know the presence of the risen Christ are distinguished by qualities of obedience and love.

AN OLD ROCKER AND A GOOD PROMISE

John 14:23-29

A SERMON BY R. CARL FRAZIER, JR.

In my study at home, there sits an old rocking chair. It's not much of a rocker—when you sit in it you sink almost all the way to the floor, and when you lean back, you don't stop until you are almost prone. It's not much of a rocker, but it is important to me.

That chair was my grandfather's, and while that doesn't mean much to anyone else, it means a great deal to me. I can remember sitting in that chair with Granddaddy and listening to him spin stories. I can remember seeing him come home, late in the day. Exhausted from his work in the fields, he would sit in that chair with his feet up on the ottoman to watch the news. I can remember that the first, and one of the last, cigarettes I ever smoked was in that chair (I was seven and smoked it because I wanted to be just like him, and he, dying from cancer, wanted me to know what it was like). I can remember finding him asleep in that chair when he couldn't get relief from his pain lying down. And I can remember that it was to that chair that I went when we came home from his funeral.

That chair, which even I will admit is not much of a chair, is the only thing I asked of my grandmother when she broke up housekeeping, because that chair reminds me of my grandfather. Even now, when I sit in it, he is in some way present with me. It is a legacy of sorts. It is a gift.

The dying do that, you know. They begin to give gifts to those whom they love. They become concerned with the distribution of what is theirs, and they offer to family and friends concrete and specific reminders of their presence. They offer legacies.

With this understanding, it is not unusual that we find Jesus at a farewell supper with his disciples (who were not fully aware that it was a farewell supper) on the night before his death. At that table, Jesus bequeathed to them his legacy:

> I will not leave you orphaned; I am coming to you. In a little while the world will no longer see me, but you will see me; because I live, you also will live. . . . Peace I leave with you; my peace I give to you. I do not give to you as the world gives. Do not let your hearts be troubled, and do not let them be afraid. (John 14:18-19, 27)

Peace I leave with you. Jesus' last word to the disciples, to the Church, was the promise of peace. The text suggests that peace is the sign and seal of his presence and is his abiding gift. It comes not a moment too soon.

We all search for peace. Perhaps that is what has brought us together. We search for contentment, for something to help us sleep better at night and for something to get us through the day. We seek release from worry and woe. We yearn for something to help us cope with squirming children, an inattentive spouse, soaked fields we cannot plow, the irritating customer, the computer at the phone company that keeps getting the bill wrong—the list goes on. We look for peace as we define it: an absence of conflict; freedom from worry; ease; comfort.

Sometimes, it might seem that we have found it. Some of us find peace in the escapism of television; just turn the thing on and it will entertain you hours on end and ask nothing in return. But when we turn it off, the world is still there, and our problems have gone nowhere. Others of us find our peace in what we own or possess, convinced that if we just had a little more we would have "the good life." Still others of us find peace in controlled substances that give us temporary physical and emotional "highs" but, in the end, leave us low and empty.

Perhaps most seductive of all is the peace that we seek in religion. We come to be told that everything will be all right, that God wants only what "is best for us" and that things will be okay. We come as adherents of the "don't worry, be happy" school of religion.

Some time ago, I received a call that one of my churches had been broken into. Having rushed over to see what was missing, a church member and I went through the building with a police officer and, determining that everything was fine, dismissed the police officer as we began to clean up. When we went outside to leave, I realized that while we were in the building, my car had been broken into and that the robber was still in my car. We called to him, and he stood and pointed a gun at us. I am not at all certain who was more frightened at that point—the robber or us—but I did not care to debate the point. For whatever reason, he chose to turn and run, and we were left to pick up the pieces.

Later, as I shared the story of that event with others, the most common reaction I received was "Somebody was sure watching out for you." More specifically, the reaction sometimes implied, sometimes stated, was that God was watching out for me. At first, that was comforting, but later it made me wonder what that attitude would have said about God if that guy had pulled the trigger.

Peace I leave with you; my peace I give to you. I do not give to you as the world gives. Do not let your hearts be troubled, and do not let them be afraid. (John 14:27)

Jesus' last word to the disciples, to the Church, is the promise of peace. Yet, rather than peace being the sign and seal of his presence, is it not possible that his presence is the sign and seal of his peace? Is it not possible that the peace that Christ offers to his church is something more than the absence of conflict, an end to psychological tension, or a sentimental feeling of well-being? Is it not possible that peace is a gift that relates to our salvation, that peace and faith are somehow inseparable, and that what is promised is not an escape from worry and woe but the power to overcome it?

I am confident that it is. Since the night of the break-in, I have come to realize that the peace that surrounded us even in the midst of knocking knees and thumping hearts would have been just as near had the gun been fired. It would have been so because Christ promised that it would be so.

Our salvation, our peace, is not a shield that protects us. Rather, it is a force that empowers us. Our peace is a confidence that God is God, that God loves the world, that God is for us, and that, in Christ, God has made that love real and visible. Our peace is nothing more or less than the certainty of God's presence in all of life. That is a peace the world cannot give—and that is a peace the Church knows. Those who dare to claim it know the presence of Christ through the Comforter.

It really doesn't look like much of a rocker. And it is not. But for me, it is a legacy—and a presence. In the eyes of the world, it may not look like much of a promise. But for the Church, it is a good promise—and a presence.

Suggestions for Worship

Call to Worship (Ps. 67:1, 5):

MINISTER: May God be gracious to us and bless us

PEOPLE: and make his face to shine upon us. . . .

MINISTER: Let the peoples praise you, O God;

PEOPLE: let all the peoples praise you.

Act of Praise: Psalm 67.

Suggested Hymns: opening hymn: "Immortal, Invisible, God Only Wise"; second hymn: "Savior, More Than Life to Me"; closing hymn "Jesus, the Very Thought of Thee."

Opening Prayer: God of all grace and blessing, grant that your face may shine upon us, that your way may be made known, and your people may praise you. Through Jesus Christ our Lord, amen.

Pastoral Prayer: Gracious God, in creation you caused your light to shine in the midst of chaos and darkness. In Jesus Christ, you gave us the Light of the world, and by your Word you promise that the New Jerusalem will be filled with the light of your glory. Cause your light and glory to shine among us, gathered here out of love for you, that we may carry it into the world and bear its beams to all who dwell in a land of darkness.

Lord Jesus Christ, the Lamb of God that takes away the sins of the world, come swiftly among us with your redeeming power and grant us forgiveness for our sins. Strengthen us, and your whole Church, by faith in you that we may proclaim your love and mercy in all that we say and do.

Holy Spirit, divine Comforter, come to this place and bring your peace. Where there is despair, grant faith. Where there is fear, endow hope. Where there is strife, bring unity. Come, "rule in every heart and ne'er from us depart, Spirit of power."

Gracious God, Father, Son, and Holy Spirit, receive these prayers. Amen.

May 31, 1992

□

Seventh Sunday of Easter

The risen Christ is enthroned with God, yet manifest by the Church. We rejoice in his coming and anticipate his coming again.

The Sunday Lessons

Acts 16:16-34: Paul and Silas, having driven a spirit of divination out of a slave girl, were dragged into the marketplace, tried, beaten, and left chained in a Philippian jail. While they were singing and praying at midnight, an earthquake opened the prison doors and unfastened their chains. The jailer, finding that his prisoners had not escaped, asked, "What must I do to be saved?" He believed and was baptized.

Revelation 22:12-14, 16-17, 20: The book of Revelation ends with a series of sayings—"Behold, I am coming soon . . . I am the beginning and the end"—and exhortations—"Let him who is thirsty come and take the water of life." The lection contains the promise, "I am coming soon," and the prayer, "Amen. Come, Lord Jesus." The passage reads somewhat like an invitation.

John 17:20-26: Jesus' words of farewell to his disciples included this prayer for those who received their word, the Church. He prayed that they might be one, knowing the same unity that exists between the Father and the Son and that they, too, may be one with God.

Interpretation and Imagination

When Dr. Paul Carruth was pastor at Trinity Church in Durham, North Carolina, he would often greet the congregation gathered for worship with the words, "How good it is that you have come." When he spoke this greeting on the Sundays of Holy Communion, the words carried a deeper significance. The Great

Thanksgiving recounted salvation history and reminded us that God had come again and again to save us. But still we prayed, "Come, Lord Jesus!"

The farewell discourse of Christ is obviously an appropriate theme for Ascension Sunday. Lessons that encourage us to believe in salvation, and thus be saved, and that invite us to drink the water of life and, at the same time, pray for Christ's return are also significant for this day. However, they do not lend themselves to a unifying theme.

The passage from Acts provides the question, "What must I do to be saved?" The Gospel of John allows us to hear another person, Jesus Christ, praying for us. At first glance we may not consider unity our greatest need, and it may be scarcely sought. Christ's prayer underscores the value of unity in the Church and the great gift of communion with God.

The "I am coming" and "Amen. Come, Lord Jesus," of Revelation 22 are powerful words of faith. In ordinary ways we rehearse this theme often. We received a phone call from good friends. "We're coming to town next week," they said. "Wonderful! Come by to see use!" we responded. After a delightful visit we said our farewells. "How good it was to have you here," we said. And they responded, "We'll be back." "Yes, come back soon! Don't ever fail to let us know when you are coming this way."

ALL ONE BODY WE?

John 17:20-26

A SERMON BY R. CARL FRAZIER, JR.

Have you ever heard someone pray for you? Have you ever heard someone offer you before God for blessing and grace? If you have, you know that it is an experience that does not leave you unmoved or unchanged. In a parish I once served there was a member of the choir who offered prayer before the service each Sunday and invoked God's blessings on "our shepherd who comes to bring the message." It never failed to move me, to stir me, to lift me.

Have you ever heard someone pray for you? Has a pastor ever

sat by your side, taken your hand, and offered your cares and concerns to God? As a child, did you ever hear a parent pray for you and your growth? If you have, then you know what I mean. If you have not, then I have good news for you.

Jesus prayed for you, for me, and for all who believe in him. Imagine that experience. Imagine the power that this prayer would have to change your life. Imagine that you are in the midst of a gathered community and that you hear Jesus praying for you. And what Jesus prays for you, for me, and for all who believe in him is that we may be one.

At first glance, it seems that the answer to Jesus' prayer still awaits its fulfillment. Look around. One does not have to look far to see a divided Church. In any town, large or small, one can find more denominations and congregations than can be counted on one hand. Denominational differences pull us apart. We argue over modes of baptism, some of us not accepting the baptisms of others as valid. We dispute the means and method of the Lord's Supper. We disagree over structure. We quibble over whether pastors should be called or appointed. And we do it all in the name of Jesus, who prayed that we might be one.

One can even find the church divided within denominations. We are fractured over the interpretation of the Bible, over the ordination of women, over the ordination of gays, and over liberals versus conservatives. And we are fractured in the name of Jesus, who prayed that we might be one.

One can find the church divided within local congregations. A close examination is not necessary to discover the cracks in the façade of unity that we would present outside the church doors. Large or small, disputes arise among us; differences of opinion are commonplace—all in the name of Jesus, who prayed that we might be one.

Perhaps, Jesus is not praying for a unity and oneness as we might seek it. Perhaps the prayer is not for organizational unity or denominational merger. Perhaps the prayer is not that diversity will be stifled and every Christian will look, act, and think exactly alike, as if molded from some blueprint labelled "model Christian." Perhaps the prayer is for something deeper, something far more profound. Perhaps Jesus is praying that those who would follow him would have a unity of heart and purpose. Could it be that John Wesley understood this in his sermon

"Catholic Spirit" when he said, "Though we can't think alike, may we not love alike? May we not be of one heart, though we are not of one opinion?" (Albert C. Outler, ed., *Sermons II 34–70*, vol. 2 of The Works of John Wesley [Nashville: Abingdon Press, 1985], p. 82).

Jesus prays for you, for me, and for all who believe in him that we may be one. Are we one?

Do you believe that Jesus is the Christ, the Son of the living God, the one who bears the divine name? Then give me your hand, for we are one.

Do you believe that love is the hallmark of the relationship between the Father and the Son, the Son and the Church, the Church and the world? Then give me your hand, for we are one.

Do you believe in the faith as we have received it from our mothers and fathers, as we profess it, as we know it—that Jesus suffered and died for our sin, that he was raised for our salvation, and that he, by the power of the Holy Spirit, is with us still? Then give me your hand, for we are one.

Do you seek a way of life in the world that reflects that faith, that offers grace as it has received grace, that is marked by an acceptance of and obedience to the faith? Then give me your hand, for we are one.

Jesus prays for you, for me, and for all who believe in him that we may be one. And that prayer, like most prayers, is answered in ways that we do not expect. We are one where it matters—in our faith. We are one in faith and in belief, and we are united by Jesus' grace. That unity challenges the world, even as Jesus challenged the world. It challenges the world to recognize God in Christ and to recognize Christ in us. It challenges the world to see that the power of love and the power of faith can transcend artificial distinction and difference. It challenges the world to see that unity can exist in diversity. Finally, it challenges the world to believe.

In the spring of 1989, I was privileged to be present at Edenton Street United Methodist Church in Raleigh when the new *United Methodist Hymnal* was consecrated by the Council of Bishops. That night United Methodists gathered from all over the country—white, African-American, Native American, Hispanic—to dedicate a book that celebrates our unity. We sang hymns from the gospel tradition, African-American spirituals, a hymn in Spanish, a hymn in the Greek language, and, of course, we sang

"O For a Thousand Tongues to Sing." We celebrated our unity in that singing, even in our diversity, because we celebrated our faith in one Lord. That was something that the street preachers outside the church on the sidewalk did not understand. That is something that the world cannot understand.

But the Church of Jesus understands, for we are united by his grace and by his prayer. All one body we!

Suggestions for Worship

Call to Worship (Ps. 97:1, 12):

MINISTER: The LORD is king! Let the earth rejoice;

PEOPLE: let the many coastlands be glad! . . .

MINISTER: Rejoice in the LORD, O you righteous,

PEOPLE: and give thanks to his holy name!

Act of Praise: Psalm 97.

Suggested Hymns: opening hymn: "Rejoice Ye Pure in Heart"; second hymn: "In the Garden"; closing hymn: "Nearer, My God, to Thee."

Opening Prayer: Sovereign God, you alone are holy, and your righteousness we have seen. In this hour we bring before you our thanks and praise, rejoicing in our salvation, and seeking your face. Grant that we may know again the goodness of your presence, to the end that you may be glorified in our lives. Through Jesus Christ our Lord, amen.

Pastoral Prayer: Thanks be to you, O God, for the waters of life and for your invitation to come and drink of the streams of grace. Your abundance is the source of our life, and we find in you rest and peace. By your Spirit, refresh us again and remind us of the waters on our brow, which bind us to you in covenant love.

Thanks be to you, O God, for the gift of salvation, which you offer to all who believe in the Lord Jesus Christ. By the power of his resurrection, raise us to new life and grant that we may believe what we have not seen. By that faith, cast out fear and doubt and restore in us zeal and devotion for your kingdom.

Thanks be to you, O God, for the gift of your Church. By its teachings, we have been nurtured in the faith; by its sacraments, strengthened; by its worship, brought to you. Forgive us for those places in our lives that are diversive and fractious. Heal us and make us one—one in faith, one in mission, one in ministry to all the world.

We offer these prayers in the name and spirit of Jesus Christ, your best gift and the Lord of the Church. Amen.

JUNE 7, 1992

□

Pentecost Sunday

Fifty days of Easter have ended. Today we celebrate the birthday of the Church and the coming of the Holy Spirit.

The Sunday Lessons

Acts 2:1-21 *or* Genesis 11:1-9: The disciples had gathered in Jerusalem to celebrate the Jewish feast of Pentecost, fifty days after the Passover. That day the church was born. There was an outpouring of the Spirit of God. It sounded like a rush of wind. Strange speech and understanding left the disciples amazed. Then Peter, taking a text from Joel, preached the first Pentecost sermon: "I will pour out my Spirit . . . [you] shall see visions . . . [and] dream dreams" (Acts 2:17).

Romans 8:14-17 *or* Acts 2:1-21: Paul, discussing life in the spirit, declared that those who are led by the Spirit of God are children of God. Not as slaves, but as sons and daughters, we cry out to God, "Abba! Father!" Bondage and fear are the signs of enslavement. Freedom and the confidence of inheriting belong to those who are God's children.

John 14:8-17, 25-27: Philip asked, "Show us the Father" (v. 8). Jesus answered, "Whoever has seen me has seen the Father" (v. 9). Philip's question is our question, too. We want to know about God, but mostly we want to know God and to be one with the Spirit of God. John's Gospel teaches us that Jesus reveals the Father and that the Holy Spirit, who came upon Jesus at his baptism, will abide with his followers as their counselor. The Spirit "will teach you everything" (v. 26).

Interpretation and Imagination

In 1956 some engineers working with what they called artificial intelligence met to discuss the future of robot technology. They predicted that within a single generation humanity would no longer have to work. Clearly, they were wrong, but their numbers are increasing. *The Wilson Quarterly* (New Year 1986) reports that in 1970 about two hundred robots were operating in factories in the United States. Before long there were more than sixteen thousand. Robots don't tire, take vacation, or require pensions. They function in heat, poisonous fumes, and radioactivity.

Robot monsters and robot guardians have become a major motif in children's television. They fill the toy counters of department stores. Such helpers may impress us as being more real than the Paraclete, the Holy Spirit, who in John's Gospel is offered as a counselor and defender.

Perhaps this contrast can serve to point out a fundamental difference between the age of Pentecost and the age of reason and to reflect our current values. We are ready to be empowered and helped by artificial intelligence (automobiles remind us to close the door, reduce speed, and so on), but we are not sure that God's Spirit is as functional and practical. That's because it can never be captured and contained by the analytical and reductionist methods of a scientific age.

A teacher was heard honoring "truth keepers," but praising "truth seekers." The former adore the facts and the things known. The latter seek and search for truth that is yet unknown.

Again and again, the Gospel of John refers to the disciples' failure to understand. The Holy Spirit will teach you all things. Its presence and power gave birth to the church. On this Day of Pentecost, it still speaks of mysteries just aborning.

PENTECOST

John 14:8-17, 25-27

A SERMON BY MICHAEL T. McEWEN

In the powerful and dramatic words of our Lord found in today's Gospel lesson, we are offered a perspective on what it is to be the people of God through the salvation of Christ and the guidance of the Holy Spirit. If Pentecost is the birth and empowerment of the Church according to the exciting story in the Acts of the Apostles, then we can attend to today's Gospel lesson as our Lord's own explanation of how and why the Holy Spirit would come to make us the Church.

If you will look at several of the various translations of the New Testament that are now available, you will see that many of them have chapter headings and subheadings. These were not in the original texts, of course. They are the translators' attempts to give simple summaries of the content of given sections.

Obviously, there is going to be a limit to the accuracy of these summaries regardless of the editor's skill or insight. Because these headings cannot cover everything, the editors pick out a highlight or main theme. Since different editors may be seeing Scripture in very different lights, a review of headings and subheadings can be quite instructive.

Today's Gospel lesson carries several different headings: "The Promise of the Holy Spirit" (GNB; NCV; NRSV); "Jesus Promises the Spirit" (J. B. Phillips); "The Advocate" (NAB); "Farewell Discourses" (NEB); and "Jesus Promises the Holy Spirit" (NIV), to name just a few.

Reading the lesson through several times keeping a different heading title in mind as a guiding theme provides a means to savor the depth and breadth of its meaning. As I went through this exercise with today's lesson from the Gospel of John, I noticed that the word *believe* seemed to emerge as a foundation stone upon which Christ's message is built.

Believing is what is expected of us *and* what is promised by Christ. In some ways, however, the word *believe* is weak and incomplete.

In John's Gospel, the various forms of the word *believe* appear more often than in the other three Gospels combined. It is a powerful and important word for John. It becomes even more so as it appears in the same teachings as those on the Holy Spirit.

The Greek word for "believe" used in the original versions of the Gospel of John is formed from the root word *pisteuo* (*pis TOY oh*). It does mean "to believe," but it also has other important meanings.

First, believing in Christ means coming to him, realizing that he and no one else is the source of salvation. Believing in this sense is not passive receiving. It is also being pushed, drawn, attracted, and propelled to Christ out of the sheer recognition that he alone is the source of salvation for us.

Second, believing in Christ means receiving him. It means being open so that he can come into our very being. This can be a frightening thought. Do we really want to open ourselves up to the point where the love, compassion, and faith of Jesus will come in? Imagine how your life changes when Christ is inside you. Think about the aspects of your life you might lose if you received Christ. Sure, the gain is great, but the loss may seem so, too. Who will we be if we have Christ in our hearts?

For John, believing meant loving Christ. Loving implies action. In all of John's theology, word and action are inseparable. To love Christ is to do loving things with and for Christ. Here also is a thought that can seem very daunting. We know how seriously Jesus took the commandment to love. If we believe in him, we must love him and love as he does. It does not take much reflection to realize how difficult that is going to be.

In addition to the distinctive uses of the concept of believing that John uses, the word carried additional meanings for him and others of his time, especially Old Testament meanings that were common to the Jewish culture. One of these meanings is to obey. We cannot really believe in Christ if we do not obey him.

Another Old Testament meaning is to trust. If we believe, we will be willing to trust that our Lord will provide; we must have faith in him. A third Old Testament concept is to hope, to have confident belief in God as our Father and Christ as our Savior.

Add up all of the flavors, meanings, and callings that are part of the meaning of *pisteuo* ("to believe"), and the result is very intimidating to consider. How can we possibly believe in the full sense that the term implies? No wonder those around Jesus were always looking for some kind of sign. No wonder Philip asked Jesus in today's lesson, "Lord, show us the Father."

So are we to just quietly withdraw from the scene as many of the fainthearted would-be disciples did? No, and thank God we do not have to, because Christ did as he said, and we have been given the gift of the Holy Spirit.

The coming of the Spirit on the day of Pentecost was a spectacular event, and we do not usually see that when the Spirit comes to us in our daily lives. But Christ is faithful to his promise. We can know that because we can and do believe.

We do not believe perfectly, to be sure. But we and others around us do believe. In our limited, stumbling, and sinful ways, we are still able, through God's grace, to believe. When we allow the Spirit to work in us we come to Christ, we receive him into our hearts, we love as he loves, we obey, we trust, and we have faith. Not always and definitely not perfectly, but we do believe. In those precious moments of prayer, worship, and transcendence, we experience Christ, we feel his forgiveness, and we offer his love to others.

This is the Holy Spirit alive in us. This is Christ's promise fulfilled in our own experience and being. This is the eternal Pentecost. The Church was born on Pentecost as it acknowledged and embraced the Spirit on that great day nearly two thousand years ago. We, the members of the Church, have our Pentecost each time the Spirit works in us, and we find ourselves living out the believing relationship with Christ.

How blessed we are when we compare ourselves to Philip. He had to ask to see the Father. We are the Easter people who have seen and felt the Father, the Son, and the Holy Spirit as we have experienced the resurrection of our Lord.

Dear God, give us more and more the strengthening of your Holy Spirit. Help us to believe. Amen.

Suggestions for Worship

Call to Worship (Rom. 8:14-16):

MINISTER: All who are led by the Spirit of God are children of God.

PEOPLE: For you did not receive a spirit of slavery to fall back into fear,

MINISTER: but you have received a spirit of adoption.

PEOPLE: When we cry, "Abba! Father!"

MINISTER: it is that very Spirit bearing witness with our spirit

PEOPLE: that we are children of God.

Act of Praise: Psalm 104:24-34.

Suggested Hymns: opening hymn: "O Spirit of the Living God"; second hymn: "Holy Spirit, Truth Divine"; closing hymn: "Breathe on Me, Breath of God."

Opening Prayer: Dear Father in heaven, your Holy Spirit is your eternal gift to your children. Yet, we do not always open our hearts to your Spirit. We do not always open ourselves to your healing, loving, and inspiring touch. Breathe into us that same fire of Pentecost that descended on your first disciples. Forgive our sins, and cleanse our hearts that we may spread your love throughout your creation. This we pray through Jesus Christ, who promised and sent your Spirit to be with us. Amen.

Pastoral Prayer: God the Father, God the Son, God the Holy Spirit, stir up the coals that may be smoldering in us. Revive the fire of your Holy Spirit in our hearts. Make us true disciples. Give us the courage and conviction of your apostles. Grant us that same abundant measure of your Spirit that has sustained prophets, martyrs, teachers, and evangelists for all the ages. Bring forth a renewal of the Pentecost spirit in your Church. We ask this in the name of our Lord and Savior and by the grace of your Holy Spirit. Amen.

June 14, 1992

□

First Sunday After Pentecost (Trinity Sunday)

Festival Sundays like Easter and Pentecost recognize a happening in salvation history. Trinity Sunday lifts up a doctrine: God is Father, Son, and Holy Spirit.

The Sunday Lessons

Proverbs 8:22-31: Wisdom, which is sum and substance of God's revelation and action, was before anything else came to be. "The Lord created me at the beginning of his work . . . when he marked out the foundation of the earth, then I was beside him" (vv. 22, 29-30). Wisdom preceded doctrines of incarnate Word and enlightening Spirit.

Romans 5:1-5: "Justified by faith, we have peace with God through our Lord Jesus Christ" (v. 1). The Trinity is apparent in the passage. Christ provides access and gives hope to share the glory of God. God's love is poured into our hearts through the Holy Spirit.

John 16:12-15: The work of the Spirit in relation to truth is the central idea of this text. "When the Spirit of truth comes, he will guide you into all the truth" (v. 13). The Spirit does not teach anything new nor with separate authority. He will "speak whatever he hears. . . . He will glorify me" (vv. 13-14). The doctrine of the Trinity is evident. Truth received from the Father is revealed by the Son and imparted through the Spirit.

Interpretation and Imagination

The Gospel lesson suggests that today's emphasis is on the third person of the Trinity: the Holy Spirit. For some, the doctrine of the Holy Spirit is the most neglected part of trinity teaching. For others, it is emphasized so as to become unitarianism of the third person of the Trinity.

Attention to the context will not allow us to confine our text to the words, "The Spirit . . . will guide you into all the truth," and then claim authority for private opinions and personal beliefs. Neither will the lesson suggest that there is no need for fresh insight and inspiration. The Spirit inspires and enlightens the church again, even as this Gospel lesson is preached and heard today.

How do you know truth? Is it enough to read it or hear it spoken by an authority? Surely not. Is it enough to experience it in natural phenomenon? No. Is truth carefully reasoned and thus known only through rational processes? No again.

To be sure, God is known through Christ. That he is "Father Almighty, Creator of heaven and earth" is known to eyes and announced to ears. Both the truth and mystery of God are perceived through the working of our minds. But there is also intuitive knowing—it is inspiration of the Spirit.

Truth is from God. It's revealed by Christ and made real by the convincing and compelling power of the Spirit.

THE TRINITY

A SERMON BY MICHAEL T. McEWEN

The Trinity, even if it is not a "stumbling block to faith," can certainly be a point of confusion. Clergy and theologians are sometimes tempted to "explain" the Trinity by saying, "It is a mystery. We are not meant to really understand it." That statement is true, as far as it goes, but it is also clearly an attempt to avoid dealing with a complex and difficult issue that happens to be a foundation stone of our Christian faith.

For nearly two thousand years, pastors, teachers, theologians, and laypersons have been offering descriptions and explanations of God and the Trinity. One of the most interesting attempts comes from what may seem an unlikely quarter: the folklore of the American Southwest—"cowboy theology," in other words.

Cowboys, like the rest of us, come in all types. Some are devout believers, some are outright atheists, and many fall somewhere in between. Their comments on religion tend to be like their other observations: succinct and to the point. This includes their thinking on the Trinity, as we shall see.

Thinking about God, the Father and Creator of all, is perhaps the easiest aspect of the Trinity to consider. To discuss the creator or origin of the created world does not seem too abstract. Those who have trouble with this first person of the Trinity are usually not confused in any logical or rational sense, but they may be highly skeptical as far as the existence of God is concerned.

For the skeptic who has doubts about the existence of God the Creator, consider the story of two cowboys who were lounging around their campfire one night. They had finished a hard day on the trail and had just stretched out with their heads on their saddles for a few minutes of stargazing and idle conversation before drifting off to sleep. It was one of those typically clear Southwestern nights when the stars appeared by the thousands, the Milky Way glowed dramatically, and an occasional meteor was seen to streak across the heavens.

Drawn by the incredible beauty above them, the two cowboys began to discuss the nature and origin of it all. The skeptic was entranced by the beauty but stubbornly insisted that it just did not seem necessary to assume that a God was around to create it all. After trying several unsuccessful tacks, his believer friend finally ended the argument with a single observation by saying, "Look, Partner, I don't know of any way I'm going to be able to prove God made all this, but do you really think that what we're seeing up there just happened by accident?"

There is an element of profound faith and of real intellectual rigor in that observation. We must make a decision with respect to the created order. Is it an accident, or is it the deliberate act of a creative and awesome God? Reason, not just skepticism masquerading as rational thought, can lead us to the understanding of and belief in God the Creator.

God the Son is perhaps a bit more difficult to understand. Few people have trouble with the idea of Jesus as a great teacher and prophet, but many balk at calling him the Son of God in the meaning of the term that orthodox Christian theology demands. Why, they ask, would God have to become human and live among us? Why could not God just reveal himself in other ways?

Cowboy theology answers those questions with the story of a young ranch hand who considered himself very much a doubter on the issue of the divinity of Christ. In fact, he never went to worship with his bunkmates, who usually managed to make it into town at least on major holy days.

One Christmas Eve, all the wranglers except this one had gone to church. He did not see much reason to worship at a time when the whole point was acknowledging the incarnation of God in Christ, so he just stayed back at the ranch to enjoy some peace and quiet. As happens sometimes, a really bad blizzard came blowing in from the northwest. Out in the corral by the bunkhouse were some wild young calves that had been brought in from the range just the day before. Being a conscientious stockman, the young cowboy bundled up and went out to the corral to open up the barn so that the calves could get warm and be fed.

Unfortunately, the calves were still so wild that he could not get near enough to them to herd them into the barn, and he couldn't lure them in with hay or feed. After a very frustrating hour of half-freezing without getting a single calf into the warmth and shelter, the cowboy went back into the house, stoked the stove, turned on the radio, and poured a cup of hot coffee.

As he sat there, he said to himself, "I guess they just can't relate to a human being yet. They are just too scared and confused. If I could just have become a calf for a few minutes, I could have been with them and led them into the shelter." Just then over the radio came the familiar tune and words of "Silent Night," and a skeptical young cowboy realized in a moment of crystal clarity why God had to come to us in the form of his Son—so that we could recognize him as one we can trust and follow.

Finally, we have the problem of understanding what is for many people the most difficult aspect of the Trinity: the Holy Spirit. What is this mysterious entity? Why does it have to be God?

A cowboy preacher explained it like this:

> When you get a wild horse off the range you've got a handful of kicking, stomping, biting, resentment, and fury. Contrary to the Hollywood myth, you don't just slap a saddle on him and try to ride him into submission—at least you don't do that unless you are looking for rodeo stock instead of a trusted working horse and partner.
>
> Instead, what you do is begin to communicate with the horse. You talk gently to him, you feed and water him, and when you can, you begin to touch him gently. Your actions become real, tangible proof that you care

and that when you are with him he is in good hands. A bond develops and horse and man begin to become the combined unit that will be able to rope calves, round-up strays, and chase coyotes without conscious thought, one being, horse perfectly conformed to rider's will and acting according to his purpose.

Isn't that what the Holy Spirit does for us? He's the gentling, feeding, reassuring voice, touch, and presence that let's us learn to be the kind of horse God needs us to be, ones that can respond to his direction and do his will. Without that connecting presence, horse never gets to know rider and we never get to know God.

So there we have the cowboy Trinity: God the Father and Creator, which is a lot more likely explanation of creation than to call this universe all an accident; God the Son, who became one of us so that he could lead us to safety as one of us and not by trying to herd us along as a strange and frightening being; and God the Holy Spirit, whose gentle, comforting, and sustaining touch lets us know that he cares and that he is always with us to bring us closer and more perfectly into union with him.

Thank you Father, Son, and Holy Spirit for being known to us as we need to know you and can know you. Amen.

Suggestions for Worship

Call to Worship (Ps. 8:1-2, 9):

MINISTER: O LORD, our Sovereign, how majestic is your name in all the earth!

PEOPLE: You have set your glory above the heavens.

MINISTER: Out of the mouths of babes and infants you have founded a bulwark. . . .

PEOPLE: O LORD, our Sovereign, how majestic is your name in all the earth!

Act of Praise: Psalm 8.

Suggested Hymns: opening hymn: "Holy, Holy, Holy! Lord God Almighty"; second hymn: "Holy God, We Praise Thy Name"; closing hymn: "Love Divine, All Loves Excelling."

Opening Prayer: Almighty God, you have revealed yourself as the blessed and holy Trinity. Help us when our human limits bring us to doubt and confusion about your sacred nature. Help us to know you as you are revealed in Scripture and the breaking of bread so that we may be enlightened in our faith and strengthened to serve you. We pray in your name, Father, Son, and Holy Spirit. Amen.

Pastoral Prayer: Dear Lord, you have made yourself known to us as the Father of us all, as the Savior who lived and died as one of us, and as the Spirit who gives your strength and grace as surely to us as you did to the apostles in ages past. Help us to know and to trust your love for us. Conform us to your perfect will. Help us to praise you forever, Father, Son, and Holy Spirit. Amen.

JUNE 21, 1992

□

Second Sunday After Pentecost

These lessons include some compelling questions. "What are you doing here?" "Who do you say that I am?"

The Sunday Lessons

I Kings 19:9-14: While Elijah was hiding in a mountain cave, the word of the Lord came to him, saying, "What are you doing here?" (v. 9). Convinced that he was the only remaining faithful prophet, Elijah had given up. Then, standing on the mountain as commanded, he witnessed a mighty wind, an earthquake, and a fire, but God was not present in any of them. A still, small voice, like a gentle breeze, caused the prophet to cover his face, knowing that the Lord God passed by.

Galatians 3:23-29: Paul concludes his message of justification by faith. The law, like a "custodian" or "guardian," had been the means of salvation until Christ came. Baptism in Christ sets aside all divisions. "There is no longer Jew or Greek, there is no longer slave or free, there is no longer male and female; for all of you are one in Christ Jesus" (v. 28).

Luke 9:18-24: Peter was the first to declare his faith in Christ. Forbidding them to tell it, Jesus told of his suffering and death and spoke of our taking up the cross daily to follow him.

Interpretation and Imagination

"What are you doing here?" Elijah had to answer for himself, and so do we. "Who do you say that I am?" Peter had to answer for himself, and so do we.

Elijah answered by telling how faithful he had been. Peter answered by declaring his faith. Each of them was confronted by a God who intends that the world be different than it is. Neither of them could stay where they were or remain the same.

Buttrick once quoted Tennyson's words:

Where is one that, born of woman, altogether can escape
From the lower world within him, moods of tiger and of ape?

Then the great preacher gave the answer:

Nobody. There is a mood of tiger in us—a snarling anger. There is a mood of ape—a senseless copying of our neighbors . . . there is a mood of sheep within us—a cowardly scurrying with the mob and a mood of mule—a most stubborn cussedness; a menagerie of moods with days when the whole menagerie is in an uproar.

But, if we wished to be true, we would continue the list still further, and say there is a hero in us, a philosopher, a dreamer and a saint" (Buttrick, *Jesus Came Preaching*, p. 123).

We often declare the need for change in our world and emphasize the social responsibility. Ultimately, such public responsibility becomes private obligation. Give thanks for those mountaintop experiences when the "sound of silence" or the "still, small voice" becomes a compelling call from God to follow on the road of suffering and redemption.

IN SEARCH OF IDENTITY

Luke 9:18-24

A SERMON BY CLAY F. LEE, JR.

A little girl was visiting her grandfather's farm. Her first stop was the barn. As she looked over the livestock, she exclaimed, "Grandpa! What a funny looking cow, where are it's horns?" Her patient grandfather explained, "Well, honey, some cows are born without horns, others shed their horns, and we cut off the horn of some so they will not hurt one another. There are lots of reasons why some cows have horns and others do not, but the reason this particular cow does not have horns is that she isn't a cow. She is a horse!"

Identity is important. A horse does not want to be mistaken for a cow. Jesus was concerned about the same thing. After his disciples had been with him for a period of time, Jesus confronted them with two questions. He wanted to know, "Who do people say that I am?" and "Who do you say that I am?"

Jesus knew who he was. His concern had to do with how others perceived him. The effectiveness of his ministry depended largely on their understanding of who he was. If people thought of Jesus as a recycled Elijah or a clone of John the Baptist, he would not be able to achieve the purpose for which he had been sent into the world. His work would be in vain if people failed to discover his true identity. However, as William Barclay concludes in his study, "If there was any realization, however incomplete, it meant that he [Jesus] had lit such a torch in the hearts of [people] as time would never put out" (*The Gospel of Luke*, rev. ed. [Philadelphia: The Westminster Press, 1975], p. 119).

Jesus did not seem to be upset when his disciples acknowledged the fact that rumors were being circulated about him. He knew how easily crowds jump to conclusions. He understood the human tendency to classify, categorize, and stamp labels on one another. Perhaps this is the reason he often told persons who were the beneficiaries of his divine intervention to say nothing about their experience. What would be the result if the popular notion was that Jesus was only a super magician or a miracle worker?

But this was not the burning concern of Jesus. He portrayed an impatient sense of urgency as he changed the inquiry: "But who do *you* say that I am?" Had he experienced any anxiety in the answers to his first question, now his heart must have leapt with joy as Peter made his confession: "You are the anointed one of God!"

Why would Jesus be so concerned that human beings in that age or any age knew his true identity? He would, of course, know that he had not failed in his God-given mission if people did not know who he was. However, there was an even more significant reason. In discovering the true identity of Jesus, human beings discover their own true identities.

Was this not true of Simon Peter? His story dramatically unfolds in the pages of the Gospels. His confession marks a turning point in his spiritual journey. There would be times when he would waver. He would even deny his Lord, but the more he absorbed of God's anointed One the more resolute he became. He grew into a powerful instrument that God used to bring the church into being. That was also true of the Apostle Paul, whose description of himself was, "For me to live is Christ, to die is gain."

It has never been enough for us to know stories about Jesus. The test of life is not based on the facts about Jesus and his ministry. To each individual Jesus comes asking, "Who do you say that I am?" In knowing Jesus, we are given the opportunity to face the truth about ourselves. In Christ Jesus, one discovers redemption for the sin and failure of one's past life; renewed enthusiasm for that which is true, honorable, just, pure, lovely, and gracious; and an overriding conviction that death is not the final verdict that will be rendered.

Archbishop Janani Luwun knew who he was. Officials of the church rarely take on the leaders of their country, particularly when the leader is the dictator Idi Amin. But Luwun told General Amin repeatedly that his reign of terror was evil in the sight of God, and Luwun paid the penalty for his integrity with his life. Luwun knew that this would happen. According to Michael Green, who tells Luwun's story in his book *The Empty Cross of Jesus,* Luwun quite deliberately chose death rather than his natural desire for safety in order to allow the Lord to rise through his death. That happened very speedily and very wonderfully. The authorities would not release his body for burial, so Luwun's funeral took place around an empty grave on the grounds of the Namirembe Cathedral. Retired Archbishop Erica Sabiti preached to the over twenty thousand people who defied the government's ban in order to be present. His text was appropriate for the occasion, "He is not here: he is risen" (Michael Green, *The Empty Cross of Jesus,* [Inter-Varsity Press, 1984], p. 213)

Philosophers before the time of Jesus taught the concept of self-knowledge. "Know thyself" was the forerunner of Shakespeare's advice during the English Renaissance:

> To thine own self be true,
> And it must follow, as the night the day,
> Thou canst not then be false to any man.
> (*Hamlet,* act 1, scene 3)

However, Christians dare to go a step further. It is both conviction and experience that causes the people of God to affirm that they only know their own true selves as they know Jesus Christ.

Do you know who you are? Psychologist Carl Jung focused on this issue:

Among all my patients in the second half of life—that is to say, over thirty-five—there has not been one whose problem in the last resort was not that of finding a religious outlook on life. It is safe to say that every one of them fell ill because he had lost that which living religions of every age had given their followers. And none of them have been healed who did not regain his religious outlook. (*Modern Man in Search of a Soul* [New York: Harcourt, Brace, 1933]).

What is the essence of Jung's affirmation? He is acknowledging the fact that human life is lost in meaningless meandering until it discovers its reason for being. What the psychologist calls a "religious outlook" Christians believe is the experience of viewing life through the mind and spirit of Jesus Christ.

We use different terms and images, but human beings lose their innocence as they journey through this world. They stand in need of that which will impart stability and hope. The great tragedy as the twentieth century winds down is that we lose our innocence almost before we can get started on the journey. For example, drug abuse is not unique to the modern age. Yet, who dares to suggest that the danger and threat it represents is not greater today than it was even one generation ago? The same thing can be said about sexual irresponsibility. Whatever thread of innocence with which we are endowed as we come into this world is snatched from us almost before we can walk and talk.

What Carl Jung called a "religious outlook," Jesus referred to as "the new birth." Jesus invited those who heard him while he walked on earth to experience "the new birth." He offered them the opportunity to discover who they were by knowing him and the dreams he had for their lives. That is the invitation extended to us. Jesus' question is neither casual nor rhetorical—*Who do you say that I am?*— That question holds the promise of life—life that is both abundant and everlasting.

I once visited with a young woman who demonstrates anew this ageless truth. She was living in a home for young women that was owned and operated by a Methodist church in South America. In many ways Maria is like so many other ambitious, dedicated students. She is studying commercial art. Because of government requirements she will have to teach in public schools after graduation. Her dream is to own a studio of her own and teach privately.

She has not always had such goals. Married before she was twenty years old, she has two sons. Her husband had difficulty finding and keeping jobs and often vented his frustration by beating and abusing his wife. After spending three weeks in a hospital as the result of injuries her husband had inflicted upon her, she decided that to protect herself and her sons she had to divorce her husband. It was during this period that reality began to dawn on her. She had no place to live, no education or skills to get a job.

Through some friends, she was put in touch with the church. Fortunately, the counselors who worked with Maria sensed that hers was a much larger problem than simply needing a place to live and food to eat. She says it took several months, but she began to realize that those people in the church really cared about her. She could not understand why they wanted to help her find herself until she began to remember the stories of Jesus she had learned as a small child. Then it began to make sense. She was being loved and accepted by church people who wanted to reflect their own experience with Jesus. That was a giant step in a journey that is still continuing. She now knows who she is because she knows Jesus.

Identity is important. It is more than simply not wanting to be mistaken for something or someone else. It is the need to know who we are and why life has value and meaning. That need finds its fulfillment in our knowledge and experience of Jesus Christ.

Suggestions for Worship

Call to Worship (Ps. 43:3-5):

MINISTER: Send out your light and your truth;

PEOPLE: let them lead me;

MINISTER: let them bring me to your holy hill

PEOPLE: and to your dwelling. . . .

MINISTER: I will praise you . . . O God . . .

PEOPLE: my help and my God.

Act of Praise: Psalm 43.

Suggested Hymns: opening hymn: "The Church's One Foundation"; second hymn: "God of Love and God of Power"; closing hymn: "Rock of Ages, Cleft for Me."

Opening Prayer: Holy God, stir and strengthen the wills of your faithful people. Bring forth in abundance the fruits of faith and obedience, that we may become more like your Son, our Savior, and that we may receive your gracious blessing. Through Jesus Christ our Lord, amen.

Pastoral Prayer: O Lord our God, you alone can tame and order our rebellious ways and sinful affections. By the power of your Spirit, convict of us of our wrong and convince us of your truth. Help us to love the things that you love and desire that which you promise. Save us from temptations that waste and destroy and bring us through this changing, uncertain world with our hearts truly fixed on the Author and Finisher of faith, Jesus Christ our Lord.

Then name us as your own sons and daughters, children of the household of faith; lambs of your own fold; sinners of your redeeming; servants by your call. Name us with the name that is above every name, that we may share Christ's resurrection and inheritance of eternal life, for it is in his name we pray. Amen.

June 28, 1992

□

Third Sunday After Pentecost

Jesus' steadfast journey toward the cross offered no home on the way, no room for bitterness, and no chance to look back.

The Sunday Lessons

I Kings 19:15-21: Following his vision of God on Mount Horeb, Elijah went to the wilderness of Damascus where he anointed kings and prophets. Seven thousand remained faithful. When Elijah found Elisha and cast his mantle over him, the new prophet at first wanted to escape the call. Then he said, "Let me kiss my father and my mother, and then I will follow you" (v. 20).

Galatians 5:1, 13-25: Freedom is the great benefit of salvation by faith. Freedom is defined not as "an opportunity for self-indulgence" (v. 13) but as love and service to one another.

Luke 9:51-62: Denied hospitality in a Samaritan village, James and John wanted to burn it. Jesus rebuked them. Later, Jesus made plain the fact that he was homeless. Steadfast obedience is the way of discipleship.

Interpretation and Imagination

"Faith journeys" are often discussed in the context of spiritual formation and faith development. Luke, more than any other Gospel, relates the ministry and teachings of Jesus to his journeys—journeys through Galilee and toward Jerusalem. His pilgrimage led to a cross.

The journey to Jerusalem was a significant part of the faith of every faithful Jew. High holy days called them to make the trip often. There were two major routes from Galilee. The longest and most preferred went through Perea. The shorter one went through Samaria. Jews wanted nothing to do with Samaritans, who for the most part would not accommodate travelers who were obviously Jewish pilgrims.

When James and John could not find a place to stay in a Samaritan village, they wanted to destroy it. But the inhospitality of Samaritans was never rebuked by Jesus. Instead, he corrected the sons of Zebedee. His journey toward death never hurt anyone else. He only healed and forgave.

It's hard to join the Christ on his way to the cross. Even if we want to follow and are willing to suffer a little, we would just as soon put it off for a while. Perhaps we can stay back and comfort others who must die. Such a compromising view can't keep up with Jesus.

THE INVITATION HAS NOT CHANGED

Luke 9:51-62

A SERMON BY CLAY F. LEE, JR.

No one has ever accused Jesus of attempting to secure followers under false pretenses. If anything, Jesus was too honest. The requirements he set forth are strict and severe. Today public relations experts would caution against such strategies, particularly if one were making an appeal to the masses. It is doubtful that Jesus would even acknowledge such a word of caution. We do know that his words pierce our comfortable sense of reality: "Let the dead bury their own dead; but as for you, go and proclaim the kingdom of God" (Luke 9:60) and "No one who puts a hand to the plow and looks back is fit for the kingdom of God" (Luke 9:62).

Jesus was not inviting his followers to a picnic. The challenge was to march with him into the very jaws of death. His hands would be pierced, and his disciples should not assume that they would go unscathed. His words were harsh and stinging. The reality of the cross was before him. This was no time to mumble or slur words. No one who looks back is fit for the kingdom of God.

The invitation has not changed. It is the same as the invitation Jesus made to his disciples. It has to do with the task of proclaiming the kingdom. We get at that task by having a single vision, complimented by perseverance, self-denial, and cross bearing. The compassion of Jesus at times causes us to be oblivious to the realism of Jesus. He understood that in a fallen world redemption comes hard. The salvation of a broken planet inhabited by warped people is an uphill climb. Somewhere, sometime, someone must step out from the crowd and thrust himself or herself onto the playing field where the souls of human beings are at stake. Someone must take seriously the claim that loyalty to God is the greatest loyalty.

Fortunately that has happened in dramatic ways throughout history. Many people in today's society are old enough to remember what happened in Germany during the 1930s. Albert Einstein, the world renowned mathematician, reflected on those times when he said:

> When Hitlerism came to Germany I expected the universities to oppose it. Instead they embraced it. I hoped for the press to denounce it, but instead they propagated its teachings. One by one the leaders and institutions which should have opposed the Nazi philosophy bowed meekly to its authority. Only one institution met it with vigorous opposition and that was the Christian Church.

Einstein confessed, "That which I once despised, I now love with a passion I cannot describe."

Contrary to popular opinion, discipleship to Jesus Christ is not a "spectator sport." Discipleship is not being seated in a church, watching the paid professional demonstrate how things are done. Discipleship is bound up in being and doing. We dare not be like the farmer who was asked by a neighbor what crop he intended to plant that year. The farmer replied that he would not plant corn because he understood that the corn borer was a danger. He also was afraid to plant cotton because of the threat of the boll weevil. "Well, what will you plant?" the neighbor persisted. "Nothing," replied the farmer, "I'm going to play it safe."

There is no playing it safe in the kingdom of God. Once our hands are on the plow, we set our eyes on the goal ahead and move in that direction. There is a popular maxim that has relevance: "Nothing risked, nothing gained." That may well be the modern expression of the New Testament affirmation, "You reap whatever you sow" (Gal. 6:7).

My own experience is that people are rarely driven from the church by stern truths and stringent demands. Rather, people become contemptuous and indifferent when the church fails to call for the best that is in them.

In describing the kingdom Jesus used many comparisons. Mark remembered Jesus' saying that it was like a man going on a journey. We are invited to join Jesus on a journey. But Jesus makes it clear that the journey will be demanding. The admonition not to look back means that we must match step for step with Jesus regardless of the danger or difficulty.

After the disastrous charge at Balaklava during the Crimean War, Alfred, Lord Tennyson penned the poem "The Charge of the Light Brigade," which includes these lines:

> Theirs not to make reply,
> Theirs not to reason why,
> Theirs but to do and die:
> Into the valley of Death
>   Rode the six hundred.

Tennyson's poem has often been blasted as nothing more than blind patriotism. However, he enunciates a truth involved in soldiering that is also basic to Christian discipleship: obedience. But it is not blind obedience. It is obedience that is tempered with trust. The old hymn says it best:

> Trust and obey,
> for there's no other way
> to be happy in Jesus,
> but to trust and obey.

There is no compromise in the invitation of Jesus—no postponing, no second thoughts, no looking back. Accepting the invitation to journey with him to the kingdom, we bet our lives that we can trust him. His will is for our good. Obedience may be difficult, but even as he steadfastly set his face toward Jerusalem, trusting God, we can steadfastly obey his will.

Translated into our every day lives, discipleship does not always have the dramatic element. It does, however, involve the element of consistency. One of the most moving testimonies to this spirit was shared by Bishop Kenneth Goodson during the Memorial Service of the Southeastern Jurisdictional Conference of The

United Methodist Church in 1976. Remembering the late Bishop Paul Herrick, Bishop Goodson described the last day of Herrick's earthly life:

> The day before his death he conducted worship services in the United Methodist Building at Dayton, Ohio, in the morning, played a round of golf in the afternoon, had mowed the lawn of a neighbor in the late afternoon, and then after dinner had worshiped at his old church in the annual Thanksgiving service. He retired a bit weary, but jubilant from the rewards of a busy day. When he did not answer the call to come to breakfast his family went to see about him. They discovered that he had gone to have breakfast with the King. Quietly did he live, quietly did he die.

A magnificent vision is shared in the book of Revelation. In what seems to be a part of the great judgment scene, an elder cries out, "Who are these, robed in white, and where have they come from?" (Rev. 7:13). And the answer is

> These are they who have come out of great ordeal; they have washed their robes and made them white in the blood of the Lamb
> For this reason they are before
> the throne of God,
> and worship him day and
> night within his temple.
> (Rev. 7:14-15)

Such is the hope and goal of those who set their hands to the plow and do not look back.

Have you ever wondered what thoughts must have gone through Jesus' mind as he journeyed under the weight of the cross toward Golgotha? I have wondered many times whether Jesus looked back to see if his disciples were walking with him. However, I doubt that he looked back. Such was his trust for those he had invited to journey with him.

The invitation has not changed. The kingdom is still before us. God calls us to be disciples for a new and better world.

I have had the privilege of traveling with a group to work with the Evangelical Methodist Church in Chile. Each day our total group was divided into smaller groups of four to five persons. My small group traveled each day from the city of Concepion to the small seaport town of Penco. Over several days we had some very moving experiences, including a tour of a china factory where workers labored under primitive conditions. There was no ventilation in the building and no safety precautions around the huge furnace that baked the china. The lack of standards and safety for workers would never be tolerated in more progressive nations.

We also visited a community of families living in shacks and lean-tos on the top of a small mountain. They had lived in the forests, but a huge fire had destroyed their homes, forcing them to move. Most of the men had left because they could not find work. Only the women and children were left in the village, trying to eke out a bare existence on a welfare grant of about six dollars a month.

After these experiences, we sat in the church with a number of the local members discussing what we had seen. One of our group posed a question to the members of that church: "Who is Moses? Who is God calling to lead his people to a better and brighter day?" Immediately, a young layman stood and answered, "The Methodist Church in Chile assumed that role a long time ago."

Jesus said, "As for you go, and proclaim the kingdom of God" (Luke 9:60). May we be the faithful disciples who can unite our hearts and voices in response, "We have accepted that invitation and have not looked back."

Suggestions for Worship

Call to Worship (Gal. 5:1, 24):

MINISTER: For freedom Christ has set us free.

PEOPLE: Stand firm, therefore, and do not submit again to a yoke of slavery . . .

MINISTER: those who belong to Christ have crucified the flesh with its passions and desires.

PEOPLE: If we live by the Spirit, let us also be guided by the Spirit.

Act of Praise: Psalm 44:1-8.

Suggested Hymns: opening hymn: "God of Our Fathers"; second hymn: "Onward, Christian Soldiers"; closing hymn: "Beneath the Cross of Jesus."

Opening Prayer: O Lord Jesus Christ, our Savior and Friend, never has it been recorded that anyone who cried to you for help was turned away. Though burdened by our sins, we are inspired by your mercy and are confident in your grace. And so we turn to you for new life. Do not despise our seeking, but mercifully hear our prayers. Amen.

Pastoral Prayer: O holy God, who has enlightened every heart, help us to know our sins and to trust in your mercy. Lead us to right choices. Too often we have chosen what is wrong. Too often we have failed to do good. We have rebelled against your will for us and have disobeyed your laws. We have sinned against you, O merciful God, whom we should love above all.

We seek your help, O God. Help us to a true repentance that will turn us from our sins and will help us to seek just penance and to avoid temptations that led us into failure.

Our Savior Jesus Christ, you are the Friend of sinners. By your teaching and your saving death you have invited us into your kingdom. Make us worthy of your name by your redeeming grace. Then may peace take root in our hearts and bring forth a harvest of love and justice, of purity and truth. Amen.

July 5, 1992

□

Fourth Sunday After Pentecost

The word of God is and shall be the last word in our stories and in history.

The Sunday Lessons

I Kings 21:1-3, 17-21: Naboth had a vineyard that King Ahab wanted. When Naboth refused to sell his inheritance, Queen Jezebel suggested that Naboth be charged with insurrection and killed. Property of an executed criminal would fall to the king. The prophet Elijah found Ahab in the vineyard where he had gone to take possession. Elijah pronounced God's judgment, "You have sold yourself to do what is evil in the sight of the Lord, I will bring disaster on you" (vv. 20-21).

Galatians 6:7-18: Paul's proverbs teach kindness and generosity and warn against self-indulgence. In the concluding verse, Paul challenged the Judaizers, who were proud of the mark of circumcision. He made his boast in the marks of crucifixion.

Luke 10:1-12, 17-20: Hospitality and rejection are themes evident in Christ's commission of the seventy. He sent them out to the villages two by two. Without purse, bag, or sandals, they were to stay in homes that received them. When rejected, the missionaries were not to be vindictive, but rather to make a quick and clean departure. God's judgment would follow.

Interpretation and Imagination

"And that's the rest of the story" are the familiar words of news commentator Paul Harvey. King Ahab and his wicked queen assumed that they had put an end to the contest with the commoner Naboth and that the coveted vineyard was theirs. Then Elijah, "troubler of Israel," appeared. He had the last word. That he was uninvited and unwanted was of little consequence. He was the messenger of God, and God's word would be the last word in the matter. The strongest kingdom in the history of Israel would soon fall.

The villages that rejected the witness of the apostles were not rid of God's truth either; not even when the messengers had shaken the dust from their shoes and left town.

Several issues are evident in the lessons. When another does our sinning for us, are we still responsible? Yes! It was Jezebel's treachery and dirty work, but King Ahab had to pay.

Can one really "possess" the land? It is a fearful thing to assume that we are the owners of this earth or any part of it. We are only stewards. All of it is a gift, and much of it is an inheritance. Naboth's loyalty to his garden and his obvious connection to the land are seen as virtue in the lesson. King Ahab's desire to possess is seen as the beginning of conflict, treachery, and death.

When one says no to the truth of Christ and to the invitation of the gospel, the conversation has not ended. It's still too soon to say, "I am rid of that troubler." The last chapter remains to be written. The rest of the story belongs to the author and finisher of creation and of our faith.

DO YOU HAVE A CONSTITUTION?

Romans 13:1-8

A SERMON BY EUGENE W. BRICE

Do you remember July 4, 1976? It seems but an instant ago for some of us. It was our nation's Bicentennial, and it fell on a Sunday—July 4, 1976. Two hundred years earlier, the Declaration of Independence had been signed, and we were a free nation. Remember the celebrations? The great ships in New York Harbor, the exploding fireworks, the oratory? Our Declaration of Independence was two hundred years old.

Ten years after the signing of the Declaration of Independence, another event happened of equal, or perhaps greater, importance. On September 17, 1786, after years of struggle and debate, the Constitution of the United States was signed and forwarded to the states for ratification. These were two events of monumental significance, but which, in your estimation, was *more* important?

I remember Labor Day Weekend 1948. My own personal Declaration of Independence was issued, if not signed. At age seventeen, after years of devoted service to the king and queen at my house, the yoke of my servitude to them became oppressive, and I declared independence. I was off for college, finding there a freedom that was exhilarating and full. No checking when I came in at night, no reminder of homework, no tips about table manners or dress codes—that first week of complete freedom was a dizzying experience. Then reality set in, and I discovered that I needed to find some sort of discipline, or else I would be returned rather quickly to the dependence of home.

It is thrilling to be independent, to be free, but some sort of order has to be imposed, or that freedom may become destructive anarchy.

So it was with our nation in 1776. Freedom was grand, but it would be lost if some sort of order could not be voluntarily devised and accepted for the nation. So in that critical decade—1776 to 1786—the free and independent nation sought a constitution.

Why did it take so long? Anyone who has sat on a committee trying to decide what color to paint the classroom ought to know. Fierce differences of opinion existed about almost every conceivable issue raised, and negotiations and compromise were necessary at every turn. Those decisions made two hundred years ago have given our nation its cast and character of today.

How should the states be represented in Congress—according to their population or equally? A compromise was reached: The Senate could be apportioned with equal representation, the House according to population.

How should slaves be counted in the population? Illustrating the fact that the decision makers were not perfect, they decided that each slave should be counted as four-fifths of a person. How should taxes be levied? Who should decide on disputes between States? Where did States' rights end and federal authority prevail? How strong should the chief executive be? What roles should the legislative, executive, and judicial branches of government play in the enactment and enforcement of laws?

Again, freedom was heady and exhilarating, but unless the States could accept a Constitution, an order, that voluntarily *limited freedom*, the new nation could not exist. And there were those who fiercely resisted the Constitution and opposed any federal restriction of freedom. Remember Patrick Henry? It was Patrick Henry's fiery words that had led to the Declaration of Independence. Who can ever forget those words spoken in May 1776? "Is life so dear or peace so sweet as to be purchased at the price of chains, of slavery? Forbid it, Almighty God. I know not what course others may take, but as for me, give me liberty or give me death!" Patrick Henry was great at rebellion and revolution, but after the war was over and the United States was struggling for order, or a constitution, Patrick Henry kept right on rebelling. He refused to attend most of the Constitutional Conventions, and when the Virginia legislators considered ratification of the Constitution in 1788, Patrick Henry's fiery oratory rang out against it to the bitter end. He objected, for example, to the way it began—"We the people of the United States"—because the people never got to vote on it, only the state legislatures. So his suggestion was that the Preamble should begin, "We the States. . . ."

Finally, after long and intense struggle in the legislatures of each of the thirteen states, the Constitution was formally ratified in June 1788. What an incredibly creative and significant document the Constitution was and is. For the first time in world history, a harness had been devised to make democracy workable. It was not perfect, of course, but it included devices for careful and ordered change.

No political system, no form of government, can ever substitute for the integrity of its citizens. But the Constitution gave us a way to make democracy stable and workable, and that is what we celebrate and thank God for this week.

Again, it should be stated clearly that freedom is magnificent, but order and discipline have to be imposed or that sparkling freedom turns sour and produces nothing. This principle applies to each of us in our own personal lives. Many a person who has, in a moment of courage, declared independence from some tyranny and gained freedom, has failed to devise a constitution by which to order his or her life—and that freedom has gone bad.

Young single persons experience this struggle more than most others. Once school is over, a good-paying job has been attained, and obligations have been minimized, we experience a period of freedom we haven't known before and probably won't know again. There is no warden closing the gates and ringing the bell. We don't have to keep declaring our independence—it is there, for all to see.

But many find that a glut of freedom doesn't bring the rewards they thought it would, and the order that some impose on themselves, the obligations they freely accept, the chains, if you will, that they wear, seem to bring them more joy than unending, unceasing independence. Only when their declarations of independence give way to some voluntarily accepted constitution, or order, does meaning come.

Often we emphasize our freedom in matters of religion more than our responsibilities and obligations. We declare independence in religion, but we stop short of devising a religious constitution for ourselves, setting forth what we want to be free *for*.

It is easier to devise declarations of independence of religion than it is to devise constitutions. The old evangelical question is "Brother, sister, are you *saved*?" The emphasis is usually on what we are saved *from*—we are saved from guilt, from sin, from death, from eternal damnation. Get saved, and you are free from all these things. But saved for what? At home we sometimes say, "Are we going to save this or that article? Yes? Then put it in the attic if we want to save it." Some would see the church as a sort of religious attic into which saved persons are put—but this is incomplete. Saved for what? What do we intend to *do* with our freedom from guilt, from sin? To be born again means to be born to a life of integrity and responsibility and righteousness, and most persons need some sort of personally ratified constitution to guide them in turning religious freedom into responsible living.

All of us have devised some sort of religious constitution, whether it is written or unwritten, conscious or unconscious.

Does my unwritten religious constitution say anything about how often I worship God?

Does my constitution count people of other races as being four-fifths of a person or as whole people?

Does my constitution ever direct me to the aching needs of hungry and hurting people around the world, or does it prevent me from traveling abroad?

Does my constitution point me in any way to people of this world whose struggle for freedom goes on, or does it focus my gaze on what I've got?

Does my constitution say anything about gossip and slander and fault finding? Does it cover how much of my income I give away? Does it deal with clean language or honesty or decency?

You see why it is that many persons who declare independence in religion *never* create a constitution. No wonder religion, then, is unsatisfying to many persons—they never give it order and structure, and so it can have no strength. In this sense, then, constitutions are more important than declarations of independence, and unless you have one for your life—and until you get one—the freedom you enjoy will be lacking.

John Killinger wrote about a young woman who came to his office with a baby in her arms and a slightly older child pulling at her dress and acting up. She was in a hurry because she was to pick up her third child from preschool. Her hair was uncombed, her dress a bit soiled now by milk and juice and baby food. Finishing the discussion with Dr. Killinger, she readjusted one child on her hip, pacifying the other, and picking up scattered toys from the office floor. Killinger reports her parting words: "Wow! When I think that five years ago I was dying to get married and move out of my parents' house in order to be free, it almost blows my mind!" (John Killinger, *Pulpit Digest* [July 1987]: 299).

And yet, it was in her gladly accepted chains that she found freedom's meaning, fulfillment, and joy.

Back to our nation. The Constitution is in a sense the Dr. Spock for raising justice and freedom. But justice and freedom are messy babies. They spit up on us and cry all night—but they are worth raising.

Thank God, then, for freedom and for those patriots who brought it to us. But thank God even more for our kind of constitution—national or personal—that takes freedom and puts it to work in responsibility.

Suggestions for Worship

Call to Worship (Ps. 5:7-8):

MINISTER: I, through the abundance of your steadfast love, will enter your house,

PEOPLE: I will bow down toward your holy temple in awe of you.

MINISTER: Lead me, O LORD, in your righteousness because of my enemies;

PEOPLE: Make your way straight before me.

Act of Praise: Psalm 5:1-8.

Suggested Hymns: opening hymn: "America"; second hymn: "America the Beautiful"; closing hymn: "Lift High the Cross."

Opening Prayer: O Lord our God, we acknowledge again our constant dependence on you. We praise you for the strength and freedom of our great nation even as we confess our need of you. Therefore, we humbly ask that you will draw near to all who seek you, and that you will seek even those who never acknowledge you. Forgive our sins. Heal our brokenness. Correct our foolishness. Quiet our fears. Restore our confidence. Your love is steadfast, O God, and your power will save us, through Jesus Christ our Lord, to whom be glory forever. Amen.

Pastoral Prayer:
O Holy Christ, purify me.
O saving Christ, forgive me.
O broken body of Christ, heal me.
O crucified Christ, strengthen me.
O risen Christ, from my death call me.
From all evil, protect me and keep me from turning away.
Then I shall know the joy of your salvation. Amen.

July 12, 1992

□

Fifth Sunday After Pentecost

A neighbor is one who, seeking to establish himself or herself, finds a place for others, and who, desiring attainment for himself or herself, helps others to attain, and who, wanting a safer society for his or her own, keeps safe the stranger, the outcast, and the oppressed.

The Sunday Lessons

II Kings 2:1, 6-14: When Elijah was about to be taken to heaven by a whirlwind, he journeyed with Elisha to Gilgal. Elijah parted the Jordan by striking the waters with his mantle. Elisha asked for a parting gift, and Elijah gave his mantle to Elisha. When Elijah was taken away by the chariot of fire, Elisha's ministry began. He took the mantle, struck the water, and the river parted for his return.

Colossians 1:1-14: The Colossians Epistle centers on Christ and the Church. It challenges teachings that threaten the uniqueness and sovereignty of Christ. A prayer of thanksgiving for the young church's faith, love, and hope is followed by petitions that the Colossians may grow in spiritual wisdom and bear fruit in every good work.

Luke 10:25-37: A lawyer asked, "What must I do to inherit eternal life?" (v. 25). Jesus answered with a question, "What is written in the law?" (v. 26). The lawyer, seeking to define the limits of love, asked, "Who is my neighbor?" (v. 29). Jesus answered with the parable of the good Samaritan. The enmity between people like Samaritans and Jews, the failure of religious leaders to practice the law they taught, and the universality of love are evident in the story.

Interpretation and Imagination

"It's your turn to serve," he said. Then, my tennis partner handed me the ball and took his place at the net. He hadn't lost his serve throughout the entire match, but now it was my time to do what I could. That's the way we order most of our games. Your time at bat, your play, your move—that's the way life comes to us.

The great prophet Elijah was gone, and his mantle fell on Elisha's shoulders. The priest, the Levite, and the Samaritan each "came to the place where he was," and it was each one's turn to serve or to pass by.

"I think I'll pass" is part of the way we play our games, too. Often that's the primary way in which we respond to the realities and challenges that confront us. Personally, we choose not to become involved. Politically, we espouse the doctrine of isolationism. Religiously, we warn against excessive meddling in civil affairs.

Being neighbors to everyone is a nice idea, but it is seldom easy. We can always say, "This time I'll pass." Honor belongs to those who don't pass.

CROSSING THE BOUNDARY

II Kings 2:1, 6-14

A SERMON BY LUCY A. ROSE

I want to retell the Old testament story of Elijah and Elisha, found in today's lesson, including verses 2-5. I invite you to let your imagination run free. Try to see the sights, hear the sounds, smell the smells, and feel the emotions that the story conjures up.

The main character is Elijah, a crusty old prophet. He's a loner, a wanderer, and a powerful symbol of God's presence in the land of Israel. The time has come for God to take him up in a whirlwind to heaven. So Elijah and his assistant, Elisha, set out from Gilgal. As they are walking along, Elijah turns to Elisha and says, "Stay here; for the LORD has sent me as far as Bethel." Elisha answers, "As the LORD lives, and as you yourself live, I will not leave you" (II Kings 2:2). So they arrive in Bethel. There a band of about fifty prophets surrounds Elisha. My image is that Elijah is walking ahead of his assistant so that the prophets can approach Elisha by himself. The prophets say to Elisha, "Do you know that today the LORD will take your master away from you?" Elisha answers curtly, "Yes, I know; keep silent" (v. 3). Again Elijah turns to Elisha and says, "Stay here; for the LORD has sent me to Jericho." Elisha answers, "As the LORD lives, and as you yourself live, I will not leave you" (v. 4). So Elisha follows the prophet to Jericho. There another band of about fifty prophets approach Elisha and say to him, "Do you know that today the LORD will take your master away from you?" Elisha answers, "Yes, I know; be silent" (v. 5). A third time Elijah turns to Elisha and says, "Stay here; for the LORD has sent me to the Jordan." A third time Elisha answers, "As the LORD lives, and as you yourself live, I will not leave you" (v. 6).

At this point the story shifts. Up to here the principal focus clearly has been on Elijah and God. The narrator has told us that *God* is about to take Elijah to heaven in a whirlwind. Elijah has told Elisha that *God* has sent him from Gilgal to Bethel to Jericho to the Jordan. The prophets remind Elisha that *God* is about to take his master from him. Do you know the old saying, "Two's a couple; three's a crowd; four on the sidewalk is never allowed"? Well, up to this point, it is as though Elisha has been the unwanted third, a tag-along. But when Elijah leaves Jericho, the biblical language changes.

Now the two go side by side. The picture presents the crusty old prophet and his assistant, trudging toward the Jordan together. Together they stand by the banks of the Jordan. Then Elijah takes his mantle and rolls the mantle up and strikes the Jordan River with it. The water divides in two, half on one side and half on the other side. Then *together* the two men cross over on dry ground. While they are crossing, Elijah turns to his companion and says, "Tell me what I may do for you, before I am taken from you." Elisha answers, "Please let me inherit a double share of your spirit." Elijah responds, "You have asked a hard thing; yet, if you see me as I am being taken from you, it will be granted you; if not, it will not" (vv. 9-10).

On the far side of the Jordan, the two continue to walk along. The biblical wording emphasizes that they were doing very ordinary things, walking along and talking. Suddenly, there appears a fiery chariot drawn by fiery horses. The fiery chariot and its fiery horses separate the two men. Elijah is caught up in a swirling wind, and Elisha does not see him again. Elisha's cry rings out, "Father, my father!" Then Elisha takes Elijah's mantle that has fallen to the ground, he tears his clothes as a sign of deep sorrow, and he returns to the Jordan. Standing on the bank, he rolls up the mantle and, like Elijah, strikes the waters of the river, saying, "Where is the LORD, the God of Elijah?" (v. 14). Once more the waters separate, and Elisha crosses on dry ground.

Elijah became a symbol, like the fiery chariot, of that which crosses from heaven to earth, from beyond to here. Because Elijah did not die, he became a legendary figure who could return to the human realm. Jewish folktales tell of his reappearance to heal the sick and to aid the poor. At a Jewish circumcision the family would set a chair for Elijah beside the godfather. A legend claimed that God had commanded Elijah to be present at every Passover, and one day he would announce the arrival of the Messiah. Even before the end of the Old Testament era, Elijah had become a symbol of the one who would return from heaven to earth. Malachi, the writer of the last book in our Old Testament, claims that Elijah's return will precede the Messiah. So John the Baptist is portrayed in the Gospels as Elijah, preparing the way for Jesus.

Now the first question I want to ask you is this: What are your symbols for that which crosses between there and here? The boundary between heaven and earth, between the sacred and the secular, is an important one for all religions. And for nonreligious people the boundary is uncrossable. For many in our world today, either there is no otherworld or it is unknowable. Nothing crosses the boundary. But for those of us with faith, the boundary is permeable. And my question for you is what, for you, crosses from there to here?

The Christmas carol "It Came upon the Midnight Clear" speaks to those of us who are stooped "beneath life's crushing load," those who find life's way painful and hard. The carol invites us to "rest beside the weary road,/ and hear the angels sing!" The angels' song is another symbol for that which crosses the boundary.

Joan of Arc was the young girl who led the forces of France in military victories over the English. In one version of the legend surrounding her life, the king of France asked her how she heard the voices that advised her about military strategy. Now, the Angelus for the Roman Catholic Church was a prayer time, observed morning, noon, and night. The cathedral bells would ring out across the countryside to signal these times. And the faithful would pause in their work and bow their heads. Joan answered the king, "I hear my voices in the silence after the bells ring out." The king asked, "Why don't I hear them?" Joan replied,

"Maybe you are not listening" (see George Bernard Shaw, *Saint Joan*). Bells brought voices from beyond.

What, for you, symbolizes the presence of the holy in the ordinary?

Let me now shift our focus from the chariot and Elijah to Elisha. In this morning's story, Elisha is somewhat like us. Before meeting Elijah, he was nobody special. He was plowing his father's fields when one day Elijah passed by and threw his mantle across the younger man's shoulders. Elisha left his father's home and followed the prophet.

Apparently, before Elijah's disappearance, Elisha had no experience of the power of God in his own life. Rather, Elijah had been for him the embodiment of the power of God. Therefore, I hear in this morning's story Elisha's fear. The prophets remind him that God will remove his master. And Elisha answers curtly and emphatically, "Yes, I know. Be quiet." Can you hear the fear, edging around the corners of each word? Elijah urges Elisha to stay behind. Elisha responds, "As God lives and as you live, I will not leave you." Can you hear the fear edging around the corners of each word? Then Elijah asks Elisha what he needs to carry on the prophetic work. And Elisha answers, "A double portion of your spirit." I had always heard arrogance in that request; now I hear fear. Elisha feels unprepared. Elijah is his link to divine power, and Elijah is about to be taken away.

After the prophet's disappearance, Elisha returns to the Jordan. He has seen the prophet depart and is thereby guaranteed a double portion of his master's spirit. He stands by the River Jordan. Imitating Elijah, he rolls up the mantle and strikes the water. Listen to his words, "Where is the God of *Elijah*?" Not where is my God. But where is the God of Elijah. Elisha clings to the only symbol of the transcendent he knows, and God rewards his faith through the Holy Spirit.

My second question to you this morning is this, Have you hung on long enough? Have you hung on when all else has disappeared? Perhaps you have identified those experiences of God's presence in your life. Perhaps you have named those symbols of divine mystery in the world. Perhaps you have recognized those places that seem sacred because there you can almost touch the world beyond. Elisha named that symbol in his life as Elijah, and he knew to hold on. When Elijah was present, he clung to him. When Elijah was only a memory, he clung to him.

Sometimes in our fear and our frustration, in our routines and rituals, we let go. God slips away, and the secular world closes in. Sometimes we forget to pray. Sometimes our prayers seem to bounce back to us off the walls. Sometimes the presence of God is only a memory.

So this morning I leave you with two questions. What are your symbols for that which crosses the boundary from heaven to earth? Reclaim them. Name them. Can you cling to them long enough for them to bless you once again with the presence of God? Remember and hold on.

Suggestions for Worship

Call to Worship (Ps. 139:1-2, 4, 6-7, 10):

MINISTER: O LORD, you have searched me and known me. . . .

PEOPLE: You discern my thoughts from far away. . . .

MINISTER: Even before a word is on my tongue, O LORD, you know it completely. . . .

PEOPLE: Such knowledge is too wonderful for me; it is so high that I cannot attain it.

MINISTER: Where can I go from your spirit? Or where can I flee from your presence? . . .

PEOPLE: [Everywhere] your hand shall lead me, and your right hand shall hold me fast.

Act of Praise: Psalm 139:1-12.

Suggested Hymns: opening hymn: "For the Beauty of the Earth"; second hymn: "Leaning on the Everlasting Arms"; closing hymn: "Be Thou My Vision."

Opening Prayer: Almighty God, bless us with a deep sense of your presence with us in this hour. We cannot worship you or sing your praises, we cannot lift our prayers or hear your Word, except by the power of your Spirit. Grant us your Spirit this morning, in our midst as your people and in our hearts and minds. We pray in Jesus' name. Amen.

Pastoral Prayer: God of heaven and earth, of the past and the present and the future, we thank you for Jesus Christ, through whom we know your love for us and all the world. We thank you for Jesus Christ, through whom we know new depths of life here and now and through whom we hope for eternal life.

We thank you for your Holy Spirit, who nurtures and sustains our very being, who reminds us of your presence and love, who inspires us to see in the ordinary occurrences of life glimpses of eternal things.

We pray for those to whom you seem very far away. We pray for those whose faith is faltering, who face life or sickness or death with fear and doubt. Grant them the shelter of your comforting, reassuring Spirit. Grant them courage and renewed faith in Jesus Christ as Savior and Lord.

We pray for our world, in which violence and injustice shatter innocent dreams and distort lives beyond repair. We pray for our world, in which souls die even as bodies live. We pray for our world, in which greed for money and power has hardened human hearts, while the poor die in quiet despair. O God, teach us and your world the way of sacrifice, instead of self-aggrandizement. Teach us and your world the way of community, instead of individual advancement and pleasure. O God, speak loudly and clearly, for our ears have grown deaf. We have tried desperately to shut out the hurting, hungry, war-torn, greedy world.

Forgive our deafness, which refuses to hear and obey your voice. Forgive our blindness, which refuses to see you in the injured neighbor. Forgive our hardness of heart. With fear and trembling we ask for caring hearts and clear eyes and open ears. Give us hope to dream of a different world, in which your will is done. Give us courage to work for your kingdom, which is surely coming because you have promised it. We pray in Jesus' name. Amen.

JULY 19, 1992

□

Sixth Sunday After Pentecost

The need for devotion to something greater than oneself is more profound than the need for companionship or service.

The Sunday Lessons

II Kings 4:8-17: The first of two miracles that Elisha performed for the Shunammite woman who provided him with food and lodging was relief from her barrenness. This wealthy woman, who needed neither provision nor protection, was given the best gift of all: a child. Life—new life—is the gift of God through his prophet.

Colossians 1:21-29: Paul described the church in before-and-after terms. Once you were estranged and hostile. Now, you are reconciled. Boldly, the apostle declared that his ministry was to make the word of God fully known. The mystery, hidden for ages, but now made manifest to the church, is that "Christ in you, the hope of glory" (v. 27).

Luke 10:38-42: The Gospel continues to emphasize the one thing we need: to love God and neighbor. The story of Martha entertaining Jesus in her home focuses on the styles of two sisters—one who was busy serving and one who sat at Jesus' feet, adoring and contemplative (service to neighbor and love for God).

Interpretation and Imagination

Bertrand Russell—ardent pacifist, winner of the Nobel Prize for Literature, brilliant teacher of philosophy and economics, leader in the campaign for nuclear disarmament—was a professed atheist. He once said, "The idea that the world is a unity is rubbish."

The *Wilson Quarterly* (Spring 1986) carried a review of an article written by Robert H. Bell in which he argued that Russell's autobiography, "despite his claim to godlessness, reveals a profoundly spiritual dimension." Bell quoted these words from Russell's diary: "The sea, the stars, the night wind in waste places, mean more to me than even the human beings that I love best. I am conscious that human affection is to me at bottom an attempt to escape the vain search for God."

Sometimes when God is so obviously absent and the needs of neighbors are so obviously present, it seems that Christian faith has only one significant point of contact with reality: love and justice as they relate to the oppressed, the poor, the outcast, and to brothers and sisters in faith. Humanitarian service seems to be the essence of Christian faith.

The context in which Luke placed the story of Martha's busy service and Mary's quiet contemplation (following the parable of the good Samaritan), is a startling challenge to that view. The answer to the question, "What must I do to inherit life?" is "Love God; love your neighbors." Service to neighbor is indeed service to God, but that's only part of our devotion. "Mary has chosen the good portion." A recovery of Sabbath rest and daily meditations will be good for all of us.

A STRANGE AND CURIOUS STORY

II Kings 4:8-17

A SERMON BY LUCY A. ROSE

Biblical texts are like quicksand. If we stand on solid ground and look at the DANGER sign over there, we're probably safe. If we walk closer, holding on to a large tree branch or a strong rope, maybe we'll be able to drag ourselves out again. But if we let go, if we walk forward into the quicksand with nothing to hold on to, we may not get out alive.

Biblical texts are like lassos, and we are like wild ponies. At first we don't realize we're caught. Then there's a steady tug as the text draws us toward the Holy One who holds the other end of the rope. We may resist, kicking wildly, or we may be drawn in docilely. But finally there's an instant of being tamed, if only partially and momentarily, by the Holy One.

I invite you to hear my story of this text's quicksand. I invite you to let the lasso of this story tug on your heart and mind, for it is God who seeks to draw you close.

At first I tried to dismiss this ancient story. Its world is too strange. Elisha is too unreal. He speaks, and miracles happen. God speaks, and a world is created. Elisha speaks, and a baby is created. The passage ends, "The woman conceived and bore a son at that season, in due time, as Elisha had declared to her" (II Kings 4:17). I'm suspicious of modern-day prophets who claim to wield the power of God with a word. Have you heard them? "My prayer, coming over the airwaves into your TV set will grant whatever you ask for. Just put your hand on your television and pray with me." Miracles do sometimes happen. But I'm suspicious of so-called prophets. Elisha doesn't belong in our world.

The passage raises many questions about God. Here's a woman who can't have children. She's overly generous to a man of God. He rewards her with a child. Here's Barbara. She's living as faithful a life as she knows how. Her second pregnancy ends in a miscarriage. No miracle, no child for her. Should she find a prophet to befriend? Here's Maryann. She and her husband are active in their church. They have spent thousands of dollars at fertility clinics. But Maryann can't conceive. No miracle, no child for her. Where's Elisha for her to befriend?

The story is just too strange. How can it speak to us today? I saw it as a sign, but I couldn't make out the letters on the sign. I couldn't read D-A-N-G-E-R. I didn't realize the rope had already caught me.

I left the story alone for a few days, and then, without realizing the danger, I read it again.

This time there was a tug. I felt myself drawn somewhat into this strange world. The woman intrigued me. I had a suspicion that she could teach me something. Listen to this retelling, which focuses on her.

There was once a great woman who lived in the city of Shunem. Probably "great" means "wealthy." If she had no brothers, according to biblical law, she could have inherited her father's estate. But she would have been required to marry someone of her own clan—to keep the property in the family, so to speak. We discover also that she was generous with her wealth.

The story says she saw a wayfarer pass by her house and

constrained him to eat with her and her husband. Probably Elisha was one of many. Whenever she recognized strangers, she honored the ancient law of hospitality and invited them into her home for a meal. Anyone away from home, anyone not among kinsfolk, was unprotected, vulnerable. The law of hospitality was almost universal in the ancient world, though probably few practiced it. To invite the wayfarer in for a meal was to provide temporary protection and sustenance for a potentially dangerous journey. Who was on the road? Merchants, refugees, prophets.

One day this Shunammite woman became convinced that the stranger who continually passed through the town was a man of God. Excited by her discovery, she approached her husband and suggested, "Let's build a little walled room on our roof. And let's put there a bed and a table and a chair and a lamp, so that whenever this prophet passes through our town he may stay with us." She could see the room clearly in her mind, and her vision became a reality. Why did she build the room? Apparently, out of generosity. Did she hope for a reward? Not at all.

One day Elisha turned aside to stay in the roof-room. He rested. Then he said to his servant, "Call the Shunammite woman." Presently she stood before him. He questioned her, "You have cared for us so generously. What shall I do for you?" Did she feel unprotected? Did she need security? Could he speak on her behalf to the king or the general? "No," she answered simply, "I dwell among my own people." She left the prophet's room, but was soon summoned back. She stood in the doorway. The prophet spoke, "By this time next year you will hold a son in your arms." She stammered in disbelief, "No, my lord, do not deceive me." Such a dream was too much for her now. Her husband was old. She had become content with her lot. Oh, she knew the public disgrace of having no children. But she had managed through her generosity to win respect. "I've made my peace with broken dreams." Yet, at that time the following year, she gave birth to a son, just as Elisha had said.

The Shunammite woman has a lot to teach us. We have a lot to learn about being generous. Though hardly wealthy according to a millionaire's standards, we are among the world's rich. The woman's generosity challenges us. Do we share or hoard what money we have? As teachers, do we communicate our insights freely and eagerly? Or are we competitive with colleagues and miserly with students? The Shunammite woman can also teach us about piety. Is our piety linked to reward, either in heaven or here on earth? Do we want others or God to see our good works and grant us success and prestige? And finally, the Shunammite woman can teach us about contentment. She had found her place in the world despite the social stigma of being childless. Sometimes I allow life to turn sour because of uneasy longings in my heart. If only I lived somewhere else. . . . If only I were closer to my best friends. . . . Suppose Elisha were to say to me, "What can I do for you?" Would I be so content that I would have no requests? Does the woman's story have anything to teach us?

The story spoke to me. I recognized places in my life that needed changing. The story made me thoughtful, but it did not transform me. Still, the story drew me into its world, and I was, without being aware of it, in the quicksand, beyond the reach of a rope or a branch. I identified with the woman. I laid my life beside that of the woman. The Holy Spirit had a hold on my imagination.

I then decided to try to identify with Elisha. I would try to play his part. What happened next is hard to describe. It was as though Elisha were a powerful generator and my reaching out imaginatively to touch him released a charge that threw me backwards. The prophet was too "other," too holy, too much like God for me to come close. I had tried to touch the Holy, and I found this Holy One, I found God, inscrutable and powerful. God and the prophet Elisha were both beyond my understanding and my control. God sometimes gives beyond our wildest dreams, giving when we had given up hoping long ago. God sometimes says no to giving us babies or financial security or comfortable life-styles. And I discovered that I am often wrapped up in my personal wishes, stuck on my own dreams, longing for a God who is at my beck and call. My encounter with the Holy has left me with many questions. There are no answers to questions about broken dreams and childlessness and pain and loss.

One last time I looked at the Shunammite woman, and this time I recognized her failing and my failing: She had quit dreaming. She presumably could have asked the prophet for anything—not only for herself but also for her people. She might have asked for abundant harvests for all the people of God, or she might have asked for the Messiah. But she had given up on dreaming. She was content to live among her people. I, too, have been content—not dreaming God's dreams. My encounter with the Holy stirred tentative, timid dreams in my soul. Dare I, dare we, dream of shalom, of wholeness of mind and body and soul? Dare we dream of the end of homelessness and hunger? Dare we dream of a world in which no children are stunted mentally or physically from malnutrition or lack of medicine?

I often hear of God's vision, and I answer, "No, my Lord, don't tempt me with vain hopes." And God says, "The vision is mine. Dream." Dare I, dare we, dream of freedom for all the peoples of the world? Dare we dream of an end to discrimination against blacks and women, an end to homophobia? Dare we dream of a world without crime and child abuse and shattered minds and broken bodies? Dare we dream? Still, my heart begins to cry, "No, my Lord. Do not lie to your people." But I hear a Holy voice, whispering through the pages of the Bible, through the witness of the church down the ages, through the efforts today of countless faithful men and women, "The vision is mine. Dream. Dream. Dream." Through this story of the Shunammite woman and Elisha, God drew me close and spoke a transforming word.

The biblical texts are like quicksand. Stand on the side, or go and take a peek at the sand. But don't go too close.

Biblical texts are like lassoes, God's lassoes. And we are, all our lives, partially wild and partially tamed ponies.

Suggestions for Worship

Call to Worship (Ps. 139:13-14, 16-17):

MINISTER: It was you who formed my inward parts; you knit me together in my mother's womb.

PEOPLE: I praise you, for I am fearfully and wonderfully made. . . .

MINISTER: In your book were written all the days that were formed for me, when none of them as yet existed.

PEOPLE: How weighty to me are your thoughts, O God! How vast is the sum of them!

Act of Praise: Psalm 139:13-18.

Suggested Hymns: opening hymn: "Come, Thou Almighty King"; second hymn: "I Want a Principle Within"; closing hymn: "Happy the Home When God Is There."

Opening Prayer: Creating and saving God, we gather in your presence this morning, knowing that you both comfort us and disturb us. Your ways are not our ways; your dreams are not our dreams. In this hour, draw us close to yourself; touch us and transform us into the image of Jesus Christ, in whose name we pray. Amen.

Pastoral Prayer: Eternal God, sometimes we touch your nearness in this place, in our everyday living, in the secret places of our hearts. Then we recognize your "beyondness," your holiness, your divine love so unlike our own.

You seek to transform us, to sanctify us. And we withdraw into our ordered lives. Forgive us and give us bold faith to lay our lives open to your transforming Spirit.

You call to us repentance and new life. And we withdraw into the safety of our sinful patterns. Forgive us and give us bold faith to confess our failings and misdeeds.

You call us to be instruments of healing in a sin-sick, greed-ridden world. You call us to bring life to the dying, justice to the oppressed, love to hate-filled hearts. And we draw back, afraid of such an adventure into the unknown. Forgive us and give us bold faith to catch a glimpse of your vision for this world and to venture forth in the power of your Spirit.

We pray for those struggling to live with cancer and AIDS and diabetes and other illnesses of body and mind. Comfort and encourage both them and their caregivers. Grant fullness of life even where death threatens. And when death comes, grant safe and fearless passage into your presence.

Hear our prayers, both spoken and unspoken, for the sake of Jesus Christ our Savior. Amen.

JULY 26, 1992

□

Seventh Sunday After Pentecost

"Teach us to pray," the disciples said, and he taught them to believe.

The Sunday Lessons

II Kings 5:1-15*ab*: Naaman, the proud commander of the Syrian army, was a leper. Told about the prophet Elisha, he set out to be healed. The prophet sent a messenger to say, "Go, wash in the Jordan seven times" (v. 10). In anger, Naaman turned away. His servants persuaded him to take the simple step of faith. His confession of faith (v. 15) is the main point.

Colossians 2:6-15: A heresy taught that Christ was just another intermediary through whom humans could communicate with God. Creator and creation were considered separate. Paul contrasted this tradition and its "elemental spirits of the universe" with the sufficiency of Christ. He offered the "fullness of Christ" over against the "empty deceit" of the gnostics.

Luke 11:1-13: When Jesus was praying, his disciples asked, "Lord, teach us to pray." The Lord's Prayer and several teachings regarding prayer followed. The midnight request to borrow three loaves encourages importunity (shameless asking). His instruction is to ask, to seek, and to knock, for the one who asks receives.

Imagination and Interpretation

"It is not what you have that is important. It is what you believe." These words were all that I could see on the page. Reading Margaret Jensen's story about an immigrant Norwegian preacher's wife, *First We Have Coffee,* it seemed that I was reading a part of my story, too.

Life was hard for everyone in the early 1930s. It was especially hard for my parents, Kenneth and Mildred. Our father, "G. K." they called him, had moved us to the cold, barren prairies of northern Montana, where he labored as a missionary preacher. Part of his salary came from the mission board, and the rest came from the offerings of the little struggling church that he pastored. Oatmeal or potatoes were the menu, and patches over patches described our school clothes. But we were rich beyond anything this world can give. We knew, "It is not what you have that is important. It is what you believe."

The power of the story and its compelling message was heard when my preacher father made his last point: "The toughest part was not washing. Not even the leper's healing. It was being willing to be washed."

OUR FOOLISHNESS—GOD'S FOOLISHNESS

II Kings 5:1-19

A SERMON BY LUCY A. ROSE

In one "Peanuts" cartoon, Snoopy is typing on the roof of his doghouse. Charlie Brown comes up and says, "I hear you're writing a book on theology. I hope you have a good title." Snoopy replies very smugly, "I have the perfect title: 'Has It Ever Occurred to You That You Might Be Wrong?' "

The story of Naaman paints with subtle humor the portrait of a man who was wrong again and again. Repeated from generation to generation, this account of an enemy commander surely amused its Hebrew audiences, for Naaman's blunders, though so human, were so foolish.

The real focus of the story is God's relationship to people, specifically to Naaman. Again and again God interfered in Naaman's life through an apparently foolish word. Again and again God rescued him in order to bless him. If we dare to find ourselves in this story, we may confront both our folly and the apparent folly of God's Word.

Naaman was the commander of the Syrian army, a national hero, and one of the king's favorites. Under his leadership the army had been victorious. Yet, for all his public honor, the real hero in Naaman's victory was God. The story is told so that we, the audience, are in on a very sly joke—undercutting Naaman's claim to fame is the activity of God.

Naaman's grandeur is undercut still further. This mighty man of valor (a phrase descriptive of Israel's best warriors from Gideon to David), this brave and strong man, was a leper. He suffered from the disease most feared by people of the ancient world: leprosy. His condition was synonymous with death; the only cure was life itself.

The story begins to move when a captive slave girl from Israel tells Naaman's wife of the healing powers of a prophet in Samaria. The king grants permission for Naaman to make the trip. Being a very worldly king, he makes an understandable, but stupid, mistake. He sends Naaman not to the prophet, but to the king of Israel and commands him to cure Naaman's leprosy. Now the king of Israel quite naturally panics. He cries, "I am not God. I have no powers over life and death. This neighboring king is demanding the impossible. He intends to pick a fight with me." The search for healing for Naaman threatens to precipitate into international disaster.

Here is the folly of seeking the answers to life's misfortunes from the powers of this world, whether political or church powers, without reference to God. Dare we to recognize our foolishness of struggling to be God's people, but constantly lose touch with God and the reality of God's activity and presence in our lives? We trust ourselves and not God, and we wonder at life's confusion.

And here God intervenes. God comes to Naaman through the prophet Elisha. God rescues Naaman from the consequences of human error. Elisha's words to the king are barbed. In effect he says, "Why did you panic? Send the man to me. At least he shall know—even if you have forgotten—that there is a prophet in Israel." Elisha here shifts the thrust of the narrative from the curing of the leprosy to the more important issue of Naaman's knowing that God speaks and acts in human history. The knowledge of God becomes more crucial than the cure.

The next scene opens on Naaman, complete with horses and chariots, no doubt a magnificent sight, standing before Elisha's modest house. Naaman had already envisioned what would happen. He is at center stage, and the prophet comes to stand before him. Gathered around is the audience, the company of his servants. He has imagined it all—that this prophet would call upon his god, waving his hand over the leprosy, magically effecting a cure. Then comes Elisha's disrespectful, almost crude, message: "Go take seven baths in the Jordan River." Naaman's dream had been shattered and his dignity insulted because this command is absurd. If what he needed was a bath, surely the stately rivers of Damascus were far more preferable to the cow-trough of the Jordan. Naaman in a rage turns his back on the prophet's house.

Once again here is the tragedy of a man who dreams himself at the center of his life. When the dream is shaken, he stands helpless, angry, face-to-face with the same problems he had longed to escape. The command of faith humbles. God's word knocks down the pedestal on which humanity seeks to stand. Dare we to face our own folly? Can we acknowledge the dreams that establish us as the hero and God as servant of our needs? Can we admit our anger when God refuses to solve our problems our way? We confront our human folly not only when we ignore God completely, but also when we try to manipulate God according to our own selfish dreams.

Once again God intervenes to rescue through human agents. Naaman's servants, knowing their master will listen to sound advice, come to him and say, "Had the message of the prophet been some great command, you would have done it. So why not such a simple thing as 'Bathe and be clean'?" So Naaman obeys the word of the prophet. The Hebrews must have enjoyed the scene—the noble Syrian dipping himself in the muddy, unmagical waters of the Jordan. But the cure is complete. Naaman's flesh becomes clean, fresh like a young child's. In his gratitude, Naaman returns to Elisha to thank him, to fulfill the prophet's word to the king. He affirms his faith in this God who has cured him. When his gift is refused, he makes two requests in this most ridiculous scene of all. First, Naaman wants two mule-loads of dirt. His reasoning is that, for him, every god is tied to the land, so he thinks he needs to take home a bit of Israel's land to worship Israel's God. It's so understandable, yet so absurd, for Naaman to believe that by taking home dirt, he could more securely worship God in a pagan culture. He does not trust the strength of his new faith or this new God. He seeks a sign, an external token, of God's continuing presence and favor. And he makes a second request:

He begs premature forgiveness for his ritual participation in the pagan worship of the Syrian national god. He wants some authoritative ethical guidance, some approval for his actions.

How human is the tendency to substitute for the open relationship with God some material surety, some code of conduct. A life-style that allows us to live in free response to God as God interacts with us in daily events is too insecure for us. We reject it and cling foolishly to symbols and to definitions of how we and others ought to behave.

The story of Naaman confronts us with our foolishness. We recognize our confusion when we fall from communion with God. We recognize our inclination to manipulate God by our selfish dreams. We recognize our unwillingness to live without worldly supports for our faith.

But we discover in this story also the apparent foolishness of God's word. God says to an unclean man, "Wash and be clean." The divine word sounds no more convincing to us today. We confess our folly. We stand in the need of God's cleansing for our rebellious, destructive behavior. God's word comes to us as this: "In the blood of Jesus Christ you are clean. Repent and believe." How incongruous are these words. We who are not clean are clean. The cleansing power is not in our activity but solely in the activity of God. Only in God are these words effectual—we who are not clean *are* clean.

Just as God says to an insecure man, "Go in peace," so also God says the same to us. We know the temptations of the twentieth century—secular, pagan, hedonistic temptations. We long for guarantees of God's presence and activity, for knowledge of the right way to live. God's Word comes: "Go forth into the conflicts and confusions of your life, secure in your relationship with God, secure in your faith. The security rests not in our faithfulness but solely in the faithfulness of God."

The story of Naaman is the drama of a relationship. Naaman's life, like yours and mine, is a succession of blunders. But God moves persistently from the shadows into the spotlight. God intervenes until the focus of Naaman's life is the relationship of peace with God. In the drama of our relationship with God, our part is not that of the righteous, but of the fool. And God will not let us go. God rescues us again and again from our errors and leaves us with a humanly inconsistent word, "You are made new; go in peace."

Jesus Christ entered the world to rescue sinners. Those who are in him have become new persons altogether. The past is finished and gone; everything has become fresh and new. Go forth into the world in peace.

Suggestions for Worship

Call to Worship:

MINISTER: Let us worship the Lord our God,

PEOPLE: For his glory is great:

MINISTER: Surely God has granted us eternal blessings,

PEOPLE: And made us glad with the joy of his presence.

Act of Praise: Psalm 21:1-7.

Suggested Hymns: opening hymn: "Take Time to Be Holy"; second hymn: "Children of the Heavenly Father"; closing hymn: "Near to the Heart of God."

Opening Prayer: Almighty God you are beyond us in the farthest reaches of the heavens; yet, you are here among us in your Spirit and in your Word. Speak to our hearts in this hour. Calm us; comfort us; challenge us; create us anew as your people. We pray in Jesus' name. Amen.

Pastoral Prayer: Loving God, you are the Creator and Giver of each passing year and each passing day, of sunshine and rain, of workdays and vacation.

Thank you for the variety in your world—for mountains and seacoasts, for pine forests and wheat fields, for cities and countrysides. Forgive us for destroying the beauty of this earth and threatening its very life. Inspire us to care for your gift, the earth. Empower us to change those habits that destroy and pollute.

Thank you for the variety of relationships in this world—for grandparents and grandchildren, for parents and children, for brothers and sisters, for spouses and special friends. Forgive us when we take these relationships for granted, when in selfishness we hurt by withdrawing or lashing out. Guide us to that balance between giving love and accepting love, between serving the needs of others and allowing others to serve our needs.

Hear our prayers for the sick and dying. Be a sure presence in the midst of fear and uncertainty.

Hear our prayers for our president and world leaders. Grant hem wisdom to seek your will. Free them from selfishness and greed for power or wealth. Grant to this world peace with justice.

We make our prayers in Jesus' name. Amen.

August 2, 1992

□

Eighth Sunday After Pentecost

Covetousness and greed lead us to want things we cannot have and to save things that will not last. Bernard of Clairvaux wrote, "Theirs is an endless road who seek for goods before they seek for God."

The Sunday Lesson

II Kings 13:14-20*a*: From his deathbed, Elisha instructed the king to perform two rituals with a bow and arrows. This would determine the number of victories against their enemy—only three. Elisha was furious with the king's poor effort.

Colossians 3:1-11: Aspire to the realm above. Don't let your thoughts dwell on this earthly life. Paul gave a rallying call. Up with your hearts! Covetousness and ruthless greed are to be "put to death" along with all that is of this world.

Luke 12:13-21: A person in the crowd asked Jesus to help him get his share of an inheritance. Rabbis often served as arbitrators in such cases, but Jesus refused to be judge or divider. His warnings against covetousness and greed are supported by the parable of the rich fool.

Interpretation and Imagination

Jesus did not come to reapportion the wealth of the world. His mission was to reconcile and renew. The middle cross on the garbage hill outside Jerusalem was the primary focus of Jesus' ministry. That's where the only One who is truly rich took the place of the poor. The mighty one took the place of the weak. The living one took the place of the dying.

Barth wrote in *Deliverance of the Captives*, "This is reconciliation: his damnation our liberation, his defeat our victory, his mortal pain the beginning of joy, his death the birth of our life." Christ's teaching about the kingdom tells us to cherish reconciliation with God more than any possession and to long for it more than for life itself.

But we don't. Like the rich fool we work for that which perishes and pray for material blessings that will not last. We save things that cannot save us. And all the time we tell ourselves not to trust the treasure of heaven.

Persons who lay up treasures for themselves are in company with those who expect Christianity to redistribute the wealth of the world. The poor are often more covetous than the wealthy and as much in bondage to the tyranny of things as the rich fool.

These lessons gather us all in, the "have nots" who want their share and the "haves" who intend to keep it all. Covetousness and greed can cause us all to neglect the best gift of all.

ABOUT HOLY LIVING: RULE AND RULES IN RUELSVILLE

Colossians 3:1-11

A SERMON BY LARRY E. GRIMES

"Ever see what happens to a wounded chicken, Chipper?" Uncle Lafe asked one sultry summer evening as he sipped his lemonade. "An ugly thing that. Poor creature, already scraped to blood on a barbed wire or some such. Then all the others start pecking at the blood. And pecking and pecking until there's nothing left but scab and scar tissue. Ugly thing to be pecked to death. Mean, cruel, ugly thing."

Of course, I'd seen that ugly sight. You don't get to be thirteen in farm country without seeing nature's worst and best. But it wasn't chickens we'd been talking about that evening. No. We'd been talking about Brother Fitch, the new minister of the Ruelsville Church. Or at least I'd been doing so. The way I'd been talking, I suspect his ears were burning right close to the blistering point.

To say the least, he wasn't on my favorite person list, unless you meant my favorite person to have his car stall on the railroad track with the 3:10 roaring through, or my favorite person to have climb a steel windmill in a zap-crackling thunder storm.

Nor was I alone in my sentiments. Before Brother Fitch's arrival in Ruelsville, we'd had a fine and active youth group in a proud and growing church. Not now. Everything about the church seemed to be dead or dying. Attendance was way down. The youth group had been canceled. A great bitterness oozed out of the controversy in the church into every nook and cranny of our little community.

Controversy is the only name for it, a great controversy. The kind that causes folks to choose sides and come out fighting. This is not to say that the sides weren't already there, because they were.

Now, Brother Fitch had arrived because he'd been asked to come, no saying he wasn't. And he brought real zeal to his work once he arrived. Clearly he was out to save the soul of our town, to save it from itself, to make it a new and better thing. He was a man of principle, a man with a vision. Quickly he let us know from the height and power of his pulpit what it was that Ruelsville should become. Quickly he set in motion plans and programs to achieve this goal.

He liked to say that he preached the gospel of Paul and Silas. "Yes sir," he'd say, "that 'old time religion' is good enough for me."

In Ruelsville he found too much new time religion and too much that just wasn't religion at all. For instance, the youth group was a matter of debates and discussions rather than formal Bible study. And it usually ended with two or three car loads of kids going off to Crawfordsville for ice cream cones, cherry colas, and a few frames at the bowling alley. When he couldn't straighten us or our youth leaders out, he simply canceled the youth program and added a special youth Bible study to the week's round of church events, a study, he announced, that he would in fact lead.

It wasn't just us kids who went a round or two with Brother Fitch. No coward, he even took on the ladies class. The issue was the annual Christmas bazaar. Since he and Jesus, so he said, would have no moneychangers in the temple of God, the bazaar was not to be held.

Well, that did it. Aunt Myrtle, the sweetest soul that ever walked our streets, got her dander up. The bazaar had been her pet project for nearly thirty years. It had been the mainstay of the church's local mission budget, helping family after family through the rough times, and it was often the piggy bank of the church when debts exceeded income at the end of the month. She wasn't going to let it go without a fuss. And a fuss she made by announcing at the board meeting that if it was the money of sinners Brother Fitch wanted to keep out of the church, and if she was chief of sinners for running a bazaar in the basement of the church, then she reckoned the church would be better off if she stopped her giving here and now. There was a round of "here heres" and "me toos" in the wake of her pronouncement. Immediately the budget of the church fell off by nearly half.

You have to know that Aunt Myrtle is Uncle Lafe's wife, but that didn't mean that where one went the other followed. Still Uncle Lafe wasn't what I'd call one of Brother Fitch's folk, though Brother Fitch had some powerful folk in his corner. No, Uncle Lafe was the kind of man who didn't want to be cornered by anyone or be in anyone's corner. So he sat back on the sidelines and watched sadly as the chickens pecked away at one another.

"Scab and scar tissue," he mumbled into his lemonade. "That's what all this church business has come to. Look at Brother Fitch. He's been wounded deeply—the names he's been called. It's cruel and mean. He's a Christian, Chipper. I'll give him that. And I'll call him that. And I'll love him for that.

"Look at Myrtle. Those sad dark eyes. The tired step. The stuffings been taken out of her. Talk about hurt. Her heart's been cut out. She's a Christian, too. No doubt about it.

"And you are, Chipper. And I am. So why all the pecking and picking? Why all the scabs and scars?"

I begin immediately to dissent, to insist that Brother Fitch was no more a Christian than Genghis Khan was. A man who turned the young folk and old folk alike from the church, who stopped its growth, wrecked its budget, killed its morale—how could that man be anything but the devil himself?

But Uncle Lafe wasn't having anymore picking and pecking, not from either side. No, he just leaned back into his porch rocker, sipped his lemonade, and closed his eyes.

"You know, Chipper," he said quietly, his eyes still closed tightly, "sometimes we see most clearly with our eyes closed. Human vision just can't be trusted. No, it can't. That you've got to remember. When you come to think your vision is the true vision, you've just narrowed the world and yourself in a single moment. And that's what's happening here. We've got a conflict of visions, human vision, of what it is to be Christian. Folks are taking their visions to heart and disregarding their blindspots. It's no good us playing at God. Ours is to constantly admit that we see through a glass darkly; ours is to know always that however good our vision may be, God's vision is grander—far grander.

"We have to risk the little kingdoms we build from our visions of the city of God, risk losing them that we might find the God of vision. Ours is to keep dying to the old world and rising to the new. That's what it means to say the kingdom is come and is coming. That's how we learn to love our enemies, to pray for those who persecute us, who make us suffer affliction.

"Small towns are little kingdoms, you know. Little kingdoms with great walls protecting a shared vision of the good and simple life. We don't have many muggings or murders, but we still maim. We maim each other right good because we live inside each other's skin. Our lives get all tangled—family, work, school, play—it all becomes one thing. Then we grow silent with one another, shun one another. Almost like a body shutting one of its systems down. The whole body suffers the loss of a part.

"So you see, there's a lot of rotting and dying going on around here, Chipper. And we need a lot of rising. Nobody's vision of what's good here is good enough. Not Brother Fitch's. Not Myrtle's. Not mine.

"When we catch on to the limits of our vision, we'll begin to see again, if ever so darkly. And then there'll be more praying and less picking. More hands holding hands and less pecking. More breaking bread together, fewer broken hearts. Jesus healed the blind, you know.

"Blessed are those who know they lack vision, for they shall be washed in the light of God's love."

I could tell Uncle Lafe was about to slide into a deep and peaceful sleep there in the quiet land behind his closed eyes.

As he began to snore, I knew human passions would fade. Our feuding visions would give way to human need. God would be present in that need. God always is. And our narrow visions would transcend in that moment. Hands would touch. Scabs and scales would fall away. Wounds would be healed. Kind words would be spoken. We would be bathed in the light and love that is ours in Christ Jesus our Lord.

Now, I wasn't so young or naive as to think this would all happen without painful change in the community. The problems would still have to be solved—at both human and social cost. That was inevitable. Principles might be compromised. One side might just lose outright. But the wise word of God was that this could all be done without costing the kingdom, without losing the love, respect, and dignity that rightfully belong to us all as children of God.

Not, however, without risk—the risk of living the kingdom come; the risk of loving our enemies, breaking bread with all who would eat it, praying for those who persecuted us, speaking always with the tongue of love, reaching out always with hands that would heal.

We must risk the little kingdoms that are our lives—the kingdoms of profession, family, community, and nation—if we are to live even now in the greater kingdom of God that is come and is coming, even here, even now.

Suggestions for Worship

Call to Worship (Ps. 28:7-9):

MINISTER: The LORD is my strength and my shield;

PEOPLE: in him my heart trusts; so I am helped. . . .

MINISTER: The LORD is the strength of his people;

PEOPLE: he is the saving refuge of his anointed.

MINISTER: O save your people, and bless your heritage;

PEOPLE: be their shepherd, and carry them forever.

Act of Praise: Psalm 28.

Suggested Hymns: opening hymn: "Maker, in Whom We Live"; second hymn: "From All That Dwell Below the Skies"; closing hymn: "A Charge to Keep I Have."

Opening Prayer: O Lord, hear us as we confess our sin before you. We are more ready to call upon you to judge our brother and our sister than to bring reconciliation and wholeness to relationships.

We desire more and more possessions with little regard that all things come from you and will in time return to you. Forgive us our selfish and hardhearted ways. Help us to follow more closely the example of our Lord Jesus Christ, for it is through him, who reigns with you and the Holy Spirit, one Lord, that we pray. Amen.

Pastoral Prayer:

Blessed be the LORD,
for he has heard the sound of
my pleadings.
The LORD is my strength and my
shield;
in him my heart trusts;
so I am helped, and my heart
exults,
and with my song I give
thanks to him.
(Ps. 28:6-7)

For generations, O Lord, you have been faithful to your people and have received our prayers. In days of trial and trouble you have been constant and strong. We praise you for your greatness and your desire to come down to be with your people.

In this hour we pray that you would take the hand of the innocent who are encountering those whose ways are cunning and deceitful. Guide the path of those whose pilgrimage in faith leads them into menacing places. Make clear the mind of those who are searching to know you. And carry in your loving arms those who are facing the hour of their death.

O Lord, our Lord, how blessed is your name in all the earth. We praise you and give you thanks that you are our strength and our shield. In all things, keep us faithful to you. In Jesus' name we pray. Amen.

AUGUST 9, 1992

□

Ninth Sunday After Pentecost

When you have things right, you know you're ready.

The Sunday Lessons

Jeremiah 18:1-11: The parable of potter and clay tells of a vessel that was "spoiled." The clay was not discarded, but "reworked." For the prophet it symbolizes the relationship of Yahweh to the house of Israel.

Hebrews 11:1-3, 8-19: Faith is the substance of things hoped for. Substance is the ground beneath you. The faith of Abraham who "set out, not knowing where he was going" (v. 8) secured the promise. Later, he risked that promise when he was ready to offer up his son Isaac.

Luke 12:32-40: Two themes are evident in the passage. The first—"Where your treasure is, there your heart will be also" (v. 34—emphasizes the never-failing treasure of heaven and seeks to quiet anxiety. The second—"You also must be ready" (v. 40)—refers to Christ's coming.

Interpretation and Imagination

"Don't be anxious. You're ready!" I spoke these words to a student pilot about to embark on his first solo cross-country flight. As his instructor, I watched him plan the flight, check the weather, and preflight the airplane. We had already tested his ability to fly, to handle emergencies, and to navigate. From the beginning we had been trying to replace the fear of flying with confidence, and the foolhardy ways of inexperience with a readiness to fly.

Something like that goes on in all of life. "Don't be frantic" is the first teaching of these messages of Christ. The second is "Don't be complacent, lazy, and indifferent. Don't put off doing what needs to be done."

Larsen's commentary on this passage recalls a story about Saint Francis of Assisi. On a day when Saint Francis was hoeing his garden he was asked, "What would you do if you knew you had only one day to live?" "I would keep on hoeing my garden," he replied.

How good it is to have that which is spoiled remade into something beautiful and good. How good it is to have one's house in order, to be ready for the Master's return.

CLAY IN THE POTTER'S HANDS

Jeremiah 18:1-11

A SERMON BY ROBERT E. BERGLAND

When I was young, one of the things I looked forward to with excitement was going to Massachusetts for a month in the summer. My father's brother lived there, but it was my cousins and the old farm that attracted me. The old house and barns had stood for more than a century. The nearby village of Blandford was even older. Everything seemed as if it had been there forever. The farm, the village, and the whole countryside were filled with all the wonder and curiosity of another century. That's where I found the jug.

While rummaging through an old antique store, which was filled with New England relics, my eye caught sight of an old stoneware jug sitting in the midst of a collection of old jugs. It had been turned out by a potter, glazed and fired in his kiln a long time ago. I picked it up and saw the name of the place where it had been made: Bennington, Vermont.

I bought that old jug and gave it to my parents. They still have it—a treasured antique. That old jug reminds me of an old potter and a potter's wheel from another time and place. It came to mind again when I read this text from the Old Testament book of Jeremiah. The prophet liked the potter's house, too.

One October day, I went to a Mountain Crafts Festival. There was a potter who had come from the mountains of North Carolina with his pottery and his wheel. Many people crowded around to see him work his ancient and beautiful craft. At first I was attracted to the finished bowls and vases and jars. They were smooth and without flaw. They were beautifully glazed, hardened by fire, fit for service in the finest of homes.

Next to them were some vases and jars that had just been turned on the wheel. They were not yet hardened by fire or ready for use. Then I watched as the potter reached into his bag of clay, pulled out a lump of clay, sprinkled some water on it, and began to pound the lump of clay on his wheel.

He twisted it, pulled it apart, and pushed it together. He pounded it, rolled it out again, and then, wetting his hands, he started to turn the wheel with his feet. From that round lump of clay, a beautiful vase was shaped beneath this man's gentle and skilled hands.

Watching the potter make the vase and seeing its beauty, I knew that I had to have it. But suddenly, the potter stopped the wheel. The vase sagged a bit, and I watched with surprise as the potter broke out a section of the top and threw it into a pile of discarded clay. The vase was once again a lump of clay. An imperfection had been felt by the sensitive hands of the potter. The flaw would have been disastrous when the vessel was fired in the kiln. The only thing to do was to break it out.

All the clay was not discarded, though. The potter started over again. He kneaded the clay, he twisted it, he pushed it and pulled it, he threw the clay on the wheel, and he began to shape another vase. This time it was perfect—a vase ready to be hardened by fire for service in the master's house.

We have read from Jeremiah today. In this passage we are told that the prophet Jeremiah saw the potter's wheel in a vision of the ways of God. God wanted Israel to be a perfect and obedient people, useful as servants of the Lord. When they proved to be imperfect—marked by selfishness, stubborn pride, and disobedience—they were broken and beaten like a lump of clay on the potter's wheel.

This is what God does with his wayward children. Some of you know about this firsthand. Some of you have seen God shape the lives of others. Let me bear witness to this from my own experience as well.

Growing up the son of a preacher and the grandson of a preacher, I always knew that God was the Creator of all things, the

Sustainer of all things, and ultimately, the Judge of all things. I knew that God's sovereignty was from one end of the universe to the other and that God was certainly sovereign over me as well. But I also thought there might be some chance for me to do what I wanted to do when I wanted to do it. I was stubborn, proud, and rebellious—a wonderful dissenter of the 1960s. I wanted to live my life on my terms, not on God's.

Like a potter at the wheel, the Lord took hold of my life and began to tear away the imperfections in my life. He broke me down, tore me apart, pushed me together, and once again began to shape me into a vessel that could be used—a clay pot that might yet be fit for his service.

Jeremiah's story is my story. And, my bothers and sisters, it is your story, too! You can be sure that if you will trust in God, his love and his truth will work on the imperfections in your life. You will be reshaped into something beautiful and useful for the kingdom.

As a pastor, I hear people share the many sorrows as well as the victories of their lives. Sometimes I hear people ask, "Why?"

"Why am I left with so many broken dreams?"

"Why don't I proposer while all my friends make it big?"

"Why does everything seem to go wrong in my life?"

"Why can't I live out my life in terms that will bring me personal happiness?"

"Why am I so alone?"

Part of the answer to these questions, and to so many other questions, is found at the potter's wheel. If there is a lump in the clay or a spot that is too thin or some inconsistency that will cause the vessel to break or be useless, the potter will not overlook it. The imperfection will be corrected.

There is good news at the potter's wheel, my friends. It is this: The potter does not throw the clay away. The potter discards the imperfect piece, but takes the same clay and reshapes it as though making it anew.

This is like being born again. It is like being made a new creature in Jesus Christ.

There are occasions when I go to my parents' home and pick up that old jug made in Bennington, Vermont, and I think once again about how carefully the potter made it. I think once again about how well it has served and how long it has lasted.

Now I call you to prayer, and I suggest a prayer that I believe fits every one of us. It's for you. It's for me. Pray that each one of us will be open and receptive to the will of God in our lives—to the working of God in our midst. May this be our prayer as we sing the words of our closing hymn:

Have thine own way, Lord!
Have thine own way!
Thou art the potter;
I am the clay.
Mold me and make me after thy will,
While I am waiting, yielded and still.
Amen

Suggestions for Worship

Call to Worship (Heb. 11:1, 3, 8):

MINISTER: Faith is the assurance of things hoped for, the conviction of things not seen. . . .

PEOPLE: By faith we understand that the worlds were prepared by the word of God. . . .

MINISTER: By faith Abraham obeyed when he was called to set out for a place that he was to receive as an inheritance. . . .

PEOPLE: We, too, are looking forward to a city set on a sure foundation, whose maker and builder is God.

Act of Praise: Psalm 14.

Suggested Hymns: opening hymn: "Ye Watchers and Ye Holy Ones"; second hymn: "Trust and Obey"; closing hymn: "Have Thine Own Way, Lord."

Opening Prayer: Almighty God, receive our confession we make now before you. You have taught us to watch and to be ready for the hour of your coming. Still our attention is drawn to those things that will not save us. Still we place our trust in our own power and knowledge to discern the hour of your coming. Forgive us, O Lord, and help us to place our whole trust in you. Keep us ever watchful and prepared for the hour of your coming. Amen.

Pastoral Prayer: Almighty God, we come to you this day, both the very young and the very old. Among us are those whose bodies are strong and vital, and those who know the pain of illness. We come to you this day, those whose lives know victory and those who have seen more defeat than we can bear. We bring with us every hurt, every hope, every joy, every sorrow that life can contain.

Yet, we gather united as your children, who share the common heritage of your steadfast love, passed down to us through the generations of faithful. We give you thanks for the direction their witness shares with us. Help us to be mindful that the burdens we may now be bearing have also been carried by others and that they remained faithful.

We pray that you might give us the strength we need to bear whatever burden we may face; courage to face the uncertainty of the future; confidence to place our trust in your will for our lives.

In Jesus' name we humbly pray. Amen.

August 16, 1992

□

Tenth Sunday After Pentecost

Fire cannot be ignored. It changes things, separating that which endures from that which perishes.

The Sunday Lessons

Jeremiah 20:7-13: Jeremiah declared that the word of the Lord was like a "burning fire shut up in my bones" (v. 9). He had to proclaim God's judgment even though in doing so he would be denounced by his friends. The prophet predicted that his persecutors would stumble and be shamed, but that he would be delivered by the Lord.

Hebrews 12:1-2, 12-17: We are to "lay aside . . . sin that clings so closely, and . . . run with perseverance" (v. 1). Jesus, who endured the cross and despised the shame, is an example. "Pursue . . . the holiness without which no one will see the Lord" (v. 14).

Luke 12:49-56: Fire on the earth is a recurring image in Scripture. It refers to testing and judgment. A critical moment of truth faced Jesus when he proclaimed, "I came to bring fire to the earth. . . . Do you think that I have come to bring peace to the earth? No, I tell you, but rather division!" (vv. 49, 51). John the Baptist had foretold this baptism of fire: "I baptize you with water. . . . He will baptize with the Holy Spirit and fire" (Luke 3:16).

Interpretation and Imagination

The biblical images of human life underscore how temporary and transitory life is: like a flood that rises and recedes; like grass that grows up and withers; like flowers that fade; like sleep that is broken.

The images are compelling. They force themselves upon us by the very reality to which the psalmist refers: "We are consumed" (Ps. 90:7).

Things that are temporary are destroyed by fire. Refiners intend it to be so. They heat their cauldrons until they are white hot and burn away every impurity. Only the pure gold remains.

What endures is hardened by the fire. It is purified by the flame. Luke 12 tells how Christ welcomed such testing. He longed for the time when, by his baptism with fire, the eternal qualities of truth and love would be vindicated. Jeremiah was also willing to be separated from his friends by his commitment.

In our best moments we, too, welcome the tests that divide good and evil. Conflict and loss may result, but so be it. If poison is found in pain capsules, if glass shows up in baby food, we demand immediate change. We don't tolerate filth and contagious diseases that threaten our physical health. The urgency should be even more compelling when people's souls are at stake.

THE TRUE HOWL OF A HUMAN HEART

Jeremiah 20:7-13

A SERMON BY LARRY E. GRIMES

"It was the best of times; it was the worst of times." So Dickens wrote, and so Uncle Lafe recalled of his own life in the late 1930s. He had youth, energy, health, and love. He was also head over heels in debt, having bought a farm in 1931. But even as the depression grew in darkness, Uncle Lafe plodded on. Though he wasn't getting rich, it wouldn't miss the mark to say that in this time of general financial ruin Uncle Lafe was prospering—at a cost. His hours were lonely—4 A.M. to 10:00 P.M. during the busy summer months. He shunned hired help, worked without ceasing, and rode around many a corner on the high curve of his seemingly endless energy. But he did not forget his God. Uncle Lafe was always at church, even on a day the Lord God Almighty seemed to have made for nothing other than putting up hay. And he tithed. Uncle Lafe was never a taker from life, always a giver, a man whose heart rivaled his huge muscles in size and flexibility. Everyone agreed that Uncle Lafe was as fine a young fellow as ever graced God's earth. And I suspect he was, even after it all began to fall apart.

It was in 1938. Uncle Lafe kept everything stretched to the breaking point, from his hard sinewy muscles to his bank account, and he expected others to do likewise. But he did expect them to hold at the breaking point. Not all folks do, and Uncle Lafe learned that the hard way. Because he had managed to prosper a bit he had the capital to extend his energies outside the direct matter of tilling the earth. So over a five-year period he became the largest broker of seed corn and fertilizer in the area. Each year he had a deadbeat or two among his customers, but he sucked up the loss and still made a profit.

In 1939 that was not to be so. Too many farmers had tried for too long to hold out against the failing economy. Too many were up against the wall of debt, and debt refinanced again and again. Then the great drought came. Corn stalks looked like the parched bones of a malnourished people. Ears did not fill on the stalk, and whole fields were nothing more than waste corn for a band of roving pigs. Farmer after farmer folded at mortgage time. Uncle Lafe was no exception. He had borrowed against his plenty to provide the area with seed. They had lost it all, and he lost too. No corn crop, no cash to pay for seed and fertilizer. Left holding the bag, Uncle Lafe made the best deal he could with his creditors. He always told it in a smiling mood, saying he'd been able to keep the house and barn and some acres of hard scrabble grazing land. But the great rich acres of deep black prairie earth were no longer his, nor was he to regain them for years.

All of this was just a beginning. Before that year was over two more disasters were to befall him. First, when the fall rains came they came in torrents, cutting topsoil from the wasted land. Streams became raging rivers. Fields turned into lakes. And Uncle Lafe's son, Stephen, then ten years old, launched himself upon the flood in a raft of his own making. He had hammered it together quickly and set it over old auto inner tubes. Georgie Cole had helped. Then they put out into the great rolling froth, dodging the occasional dead animal and a plethora of tree trunks and limbs. They did fine, or so it seemed, until they rushed toward the first bridge. Caught up in the call of adventure, they forgot that the water was only inches from the floor of the bridge. That had been the end for them. No one saw it happen, but remains of the raft pretty well told the story. Their bodies were found in the flood rubble days after the waters had gone down.

Uncle Lafe's hurt showed, but still he was up at dawn and worked till dusk. His need to do so was larger now. He'd lost most of the fruits of his labor. He'd lost his only child. Still there was food to put on the table and something to pay toward the mortgage. And, great joy and sorrow, Aunt Myrtle was pregnant again—this time it would be with my cousin, Tolliver.

Leaves fell, and the cold rains of November promised an early winter. Uncle Lafe had finished his harvest early, as everyone had, for there was little to glean that year. But there was always something to do. Uncle Lafe was redoing his barn into a dairy barn. He was certain that even with his reduced acreage, careful planning would allow him to make ends meet in the dairy business, though he would be hard strapped in the early years. Among his tasks was one of making the barn loft weathertight for the storage of hay. The barn was ancient, and the roof showed its age. So up he went early each morning, and there he sat until he couldn't see to drive a nail.

On the third day of his undertaking it happened. As I've said, the barn was ancient, and some of the wood was rotten. Uncle Lafe had not, however, expected any of the large timbers to be rotten clear through—but some were. And under the weight of his body and the violent thud of the hammer they gave way, sending Uncle Lafe earthward in a great sprawl. The worst happened, or nearly so: He fell from the apex of the roof down through the open slit in the loft floor where the ladder ascended from the ground floor. The luck that might have landed him on mounds of hay was not there, though a gunny sack of ground corn, rather than the walnut planks of the floor, took his fall. This may have prevented him from splitting his skull open on the floor. But it did not keep him from breaking his back. Of course, he didn't know what damage he'd done in the fall, only that something was terribly wrong and that he lived. He knew no one was at home. Aunt Myrtle had gone to town to see the doctor. So he slowly pulled himself to his feet and began a slow and terrible walk to the house and to phone for help. He had barely completed the phone call and stretched himself full length on the floor before a black wave of emptiness swept over him.

When he awoke he was in plaster from neck to knee. Aunt Myrtle was beside him, weeping tears of joy. The doctors were amazed that he hadn't snapped his spinal cord in the walk from the barn to the house with a broken back. This, at least, he later reflected, God had not allowed.

And so he lay there, immobile, and listened to the doctors describe his new life. Six months in full body cast. No lifting for a year. No bending of the back for a year. How could he farm? How could he keep the farm? How have a child? How could he be himself? The world that had shortly before been yellow in the bright sun of success seemed now to be the red of his own spilled blood. He knew himself now only in weakness and wondered whether he would ever again rise from the bed. Nothing much made him want to do so. He could see no future worth the viewing (only the terror of yet another mouth to feed when he, literally, couldn't even feed his own). He wanted to shut the past from his mind—more hurt was there as he thought of Stephen, of the dark rich earth. The best of life? The worst of life? And all in the course of about six months. A virtual whirlwind of terror had swept him up from the path he would go and dashed him, hope and all, to the ash heap of life.

Uncle Lafe became a study in darkness as he did his time in the big body cast. He said that was when he understood all those Old Testament folks who wanted to curse God and die. And, Uncle Lafe said, he did his best to do both. He didn't eat. He didn't have the will to live. Each day he had at God with tooth and nail. But, as he reflected later, he certainly didn't turn from God or forget God. No sir, God was foremost on his mind—God and all of God's injustice or indifference; God and all of God's cruelty. Uncle Lafe screamed at God. Cursed God. Hated God. And each day he got better. For a while he was convinced that God was sentencing him to live in order to further torment him.

Friends came to visit him, of course. Uncle Lafe was seldom alone, though he said he'd never been lonelier living as he was in a place without light or hope, in a place where he knew the dark truth about life and about God, which no one had ever dared utter to him. There in his wretchedness he listened in anger as friends suggested that he would come, someday, to see that all had been for the best. God works in wondrous ways, they'd say as they left his room, never in their sheltered lives having felt the heavy hand of God upon them. Or the worst among them hinted that God only punished the punishable. The message was clear: Uncle Lafe was a sinner, or God would not have put a hand to him. Some suggested his sin was his pride and his anger before God. Others were quick to assert that his sin was his humanity. Uncle Lafe was not impressed. If these folks were right, then what God did we worship? A God less compassionate than people themselves? A God less just than humankind? He refused to bow before such a God, a God made less than the image of much flawed humanity. So he continued to rage at God, to protest his case, to demand a hearing. Uncle Lafe had learned to pray with a naked soul, and others found it embarrassing to watch—to them it was obscene to hear the true howl of a human heart.

Yet, howl he did. Uncle Lafe's anger with God did not abate until one very unexceptional day a huge smile filled his face. Laughter roared up out of his chest, encased though it was in plaster and tape. He had sat, as he had done so often, for a few moments of quiet silent with Reverend Colfax. That's when Uncle Lafe heard without words the silent voice of God. Before him was the answer to his angry prayers. The answer was a Chinese box of answers, one gently nestled inside the other. Each answer contained within it another answer. All were the answer, and none was the answer. At the end of this regression he heard the troubled laugh of God. But a laugh it was, and not a cynical one—whimsical perhaps, hopeful, more likely—for God had heard Uncle Lafe. Prayer from the naked heart is always heard. God knew the prayer, and God blessed the prayer with holy presence and wrestled with the prayer at the core of being. Then God laughed the laugh of comradery and empathy and hope.

From that time on Uncle Lafe began to reknit his life. He ate again. His bones healed. He walked, then bent his back again carefully and lifted the load of life with caution and zest. A sparkle stayed in his eyes and a smile on his lips. Indeed, folks wondered often at that smile, for it grew largest in moments most ironic. Something he knew about life had lightened his heart and filled him with a spirit of wonder that forever pushed anger and darkness from his heart. Don't get me wrong, Uncle Lafe could get plenty angry and even, sometimes, quite blue. But his anger most red and his funk most blue were somehow only on the surface of his life. His heart remained forever encircled by the laughter of God; his life forever floated on the cusp of a smile.

Suggestions for Worship

Call to Worship (Heb. 12:1):

MINISTER: Therefore, since we are surrounded by so great a cloud of witnesses,

PEOPLE: let us also lay aside every weight

MINISTER: and the sin that clings so closely,

PEOPLE: and let us run with perseverance the race that is set before us.

Act of Praise: Psalm 10:12-18.

Suggested Hymns: opening hymn: "Stand Up, Stand Up for Jesus"; second hymn: "Stand By Me"; closing hymn: "Lead On, O King Eternal."

Opening Prayer: Merciful God,
we confess that we have not loved you with our whole heart.
We have failed to be an obedient church.
We have not done your will,
we have broken your law,
we have rebelled against your love,
we have not loved our neighbors,
and we have not heard the cry of the needy.
Forgive us, we pray.
Free us for joyful obedience,
through Jesus Christ our Lord.
Amen.
(*The United Methodist Hymnal*)

Pastoral Prayer: O God, giver of every good and gracious gift, we come to you with our prayers of thanksgiving this day. We are thankful for the gift of your unfailing grace, which surrounds us so completely. We experience it in the beauty of this season, the smile of a friend, the word of comfort when we are alone, and in the hearing of your Word this day.

There are times when we forget that the gift of your love is freely given for all people. In this world we have been taught that we cannot receive something for nothing. Yet, you gave your Son, Jesus Christ, to die and to be raised up for each of us while we were still lost in sin and separate from you. For this amazing gift of love, we lift our thanks to you.

Among us today are those who have reclaimed the gift of your saving grace. We rejoice with them in their joy and peace. Among us are the weary and the worn who shoulder tasks for your kingdom. It is our prayer that your Holy Spirit would come to them and refresh them as a cool and life-giving stream. Among us are those who have felt the burden of illness and concern for loved ones who are ill. We confess to you that we do not fully understand the gifts of healing and wholeness that you offer, but we simply place our trust in you this day to be to these people a very real presence of wholeness and strength.

In our land and in our world there are those who stand in special need of prayer this day because of famine, flood, and hatred. Help their hunger, their loss, and their pain to become so real to us that we will make it our own and find ways to minister to them. It is in the name of our Savior, Jesus Christ, that we pray. Amen.

August 23, 1992

□

Eleventh Sunday After Pentecost

There are ten thousand ways to be wrong, but only one way to get it right. The door is narrow.

The Sunday Lessons

Jeremiah 28:1-9: These verses contrast the conflicting messages of two prophets. Hananiah promised salvation. Jeremiah foretold judgment and destruction.

Hebrews 12:18-29: The old covenant marked by the fires and tempests of a holy mountain was more forbidding than inviting. Even Moses said, "I tremble with fear" (v. 21). The new covenant, more gracious, rests on the mediation of Jesus. "See that you do not refuse [him]" (v. 25). There was no escape for those who rejected the warnings of earthbound messengers. Much less shall we escape if we reject him who warns from heaven.

Luke 13:22-30: Someone asked, "Will those who are saved be few?" Jesus answered with the teaching of the narrow door. Clear decisions and rigorous discipline are required. The parable of a door closed by the householder and not opened to one's knocking teaches that future opportunities come to an end.

Interpretation and Imagination

Of this you may be certain: Everyone who reads this Gospel lesson or hears it preached wants his or her life to be full, happy, and free. They intend that their endeavors will be rewarded and that their lives will add up to meaning and value. In short they desire good things. None of us wants to be lost or wasted. We want to be saved.

If many desire life and not death, will many be saved, or only a few? Jesus' reply to the question did not answer it. Rather he turned from the question to teach the importance of right decision and clear discipline. The door is narrow.

There are thousands of ways to become lost and thousands of ways to do things wrong. There is one way that leads back to the safety of the sheepfold and one narrow door by which wandering sheep may enter.

In laboratories, scientists try again and again to discover the cause of illness and to find a remedy. Discovery is narrow. Athletes discipline themselves and coaches discipline their teams in an effort to be successful. Discipline is narrow. One cannot be committed to every cause or devoted to every teaching. Devotion is narrow. The choices of activities, friends, and purchases can govern our lives more than our goals, no matter how grand they may be. The teaching asks that we make some right choices today.

GOD'S OPEN-DOOR POLICY

Hebrews 12:18-29

A SERMON BY BERNARD H. LIEVING, JR.

When I saw Private First Class John Smith in the tank maintenance building that cold day in Germany in December, 1971, he said he needed an appointment to talk with me, the unit chaplain. Such requests were not unusual in the United States Army in those days, when drug abuse and racial tensions were at their highest.

John came to see me two days later and explained that while his problem might not seem like much to me it was causing him a great deal of distress. His story was that he had enlisted in the Army to be a tank mechanic, and he prided himself on being a good one. He had been in Germany about two years, serving in that capacity. His trouble started about ten days earlier, when the battalion commander saw some of John's drawings in his barracks room. The commander immediately told him that he was going to make John the unit draftsman. He promised John that the new job would get him out of the cold, drafty maintenance area into warm, comfortable working conditions in which to use his drawing ability on unit projects.

In response to my questioning why this was a problem, John

explained, "Chaplain, I don't want to be a draftsman. I want to be a tank mechanic. That's why I enlisted in the Army. Look, the reason I wanted to talk to you was to ask what you think I should do. I've already talked to my company commander, and he told me I don't have a choice. What do you think I should do?"

Avoiding the trap to give John free and easy advice, I spent another twenty minutes discussing with him his alternatives, which included using the battalion commander's open door policy to talk with him about the situation. I explained to John that all Army commanders must have an open door policy that allows unit members to present concerns or problems of a personal or professional nature that the soldier has been unable to resolve. John decided to make the necessary contacts to see the battalion commander.

About three weeks later John rushed into my office shouting, "Chaplain, it worked! It worked! I am going to be a tank mechanic. The battalion commander said I was needed to do the draftsman stuff and that I had to do it. I went to the brigade commander, and he told me the same thing. I finally asked to see the division commander. It took me a while to see him, but I finally did it. Guess what he said! 'Son, if you want to be a tank mechanic this badly, you need to be a tank mechanic.' Wow! This is great! Thanks, Chaplain."

God also has an open door policy toward his kingdom, the heavenly Jerusalem, the city of the living God where thousands and thousands of angels join in joyful assembly. Both lessons for today are instructive concerning this open door policy.

The Lukan passage picks up Jesus' relentless journey toward the cross as he went on his way through towns and villages, teaching and journeying toward Jerusalem. Someone he met along the way asked one of the questions Jewish scholars had debated for years: "Lord, will only a few be saved?" (Luke 13:23). It was a legitimate question, especially for someone journeying with Jesus and hearing the ever increasing demands of discipleship.

The answer Jesus indirectly gives is that it is God's desire that all his creation, all his children, enter his kingdom. In words we often use in the invitation to the Lord's Table, Jesus declares the universality of the invitation into the kingdom: "People will come from east and west, from north and south, and will eat in the kingdom of God" (Luke 13:29). No one is left out! Even, or more especially, the poor, the crippled, and the blind are invited to the feast in the kingdom, where they will join Abraham, Isaac, Jacob, and all of the prophets at God's table. His kingdom is for the whole human family.

Contrast that openness to the exclusionary policies in private country clubs across America and the machinations of their members to maintain their closed ranks. Marcia Chambers wrote about many, old prestigious clubs that are "seeking new ways to define privacy and shore up their constitutional defenses so that they may remain truly exclusive" (Marcia Chambers, "A Revolution in Private Country Clubs," *Golf Digest* [May 1990]: 122). No nonwhite, non-male, non-American-born need apply. It is not so with God's kingdom—it is for the whole human family.

Hearing Jesus' answer, we would easily tend to develop a false sense of our readiness for kingdom entry. We just show up, and in we go. Not quite! Jesus said there may be some surprises. Elbow rubbing with Jesus will not be sufficient, and casual interest will not be enough to stake your claim to a share of the kingdom. The claim that we ate in his presence and that he "taught in our streets" is not the password. Standing outside and pleading for the Lord to open the gate to us will gain us only the response, "I do not know you; depart from me."

How do we get the Lord to know us? What is the secret? What can we do to gain access to the kingdom? What, then, is the password?

"Strive to enter through the narrow door; for many, I tell you, will try to enter and will not be able" (Luke 13:24). Hear Jesus say, "I am the [door]. Whoever enters by me will be saved" (John 10:9); "I am the way, and the truth, and the life. No one comes to the Father except through me" (John 14:6). There is no secret passage into the kingdom. The way is open to all—through him who stands between sinful persons and loving God and serves as the mediator to bring peace and reconciliation.

Jesus is the one who negotiated a new covenant with God on behalf of God's creation. Previously, one had no more access than the Israelites did at Sinai when God was so unapproachable that no one was allowed near the mountain. If an animal even touched the mountain, it would be put to death. No stronger statement could be given of the inability of the old covenant to provide access to God. Even Moses trembled.

Now, Jesus provides a new covenant, which enables us to be in the very presence of God. He comes between the holy God and our sinful selves and, through his blood shed on the cross, opens a door for us into the presence of the living God in his heavenly city.

The way we get God to know us is through our receiving the gift of his love without imagining that we can somehow measure up to the entrance standards on our own merits. The secret is that the kingdom was founded on grace alone. To gain access we need only trust his promise that the kingdom is ours—and that nothing can take from us the gift he has given. There is no password. Jesus' words pass us in:

> I know who you are. I know where you come from! You have been conceived by the Holy Ghost in holy baptism and are among the firstborn enrolled in heaven. You have believed and come to know that I am the Christ, the Son of the living God. You know that I was put to death in the flesh but made alive in the Spirit, raised again for your justification. Even though you, too, were workers of iniquity, you did not say, 'Be it far from you, O Lord' with Simon, nor with him follow afar, but you followed me on the way to Jerusalem and the cross. I know who you are. You are sprinkled with my blood, the mediating blood of the new covenant. (George W. Hoyer and Wolfgang Roth, *Proclamation 2*, Proclamation: Aids for Interpreting the Lessons of the Church Year, Series C [Philadelphia: Fortress Press, 1974], p. 28)

The day will come when we will know the reality of the heavenly Jerusalem, the city of the living God, when we can say with the thousands and thousands of angels, "It worked! It worked! God made it possible through his Son, Jesus Christ, for me to sit at table with people from the east and west, from north and south, and with Abraham, Isaac, Jacob, and all the prophets." And we will eternally praise God.

Suggestions for Worship

Call to Worship (Ps. 84:1-2):

MINISTER: How lovely is your dwelling place, O LORD of hosts!

PEOPLE: **My soul longs, indeed it faints, for the courts of the LORD;**

MINISTER: my heart and my flesh sing for joy to the living God.

PEOPLE: **Blessed are those who have set their hearts on following you.**

Act of Praise: Psalm 84.

Suggested Hymns: opening hymn: "Stand Up and Bless the Lord"; second hymn: "This Is My Song"; closing hymn: "Make Me a Captive, Lord."

Opening Prayer: We come from all directions and from all circumstances of life to worship you, O God of hosts. We come knowing that even the sparrow finds a home and the swallow a place to nest her young in your house. You have much more here for us because you sent Jesus to give us a covenant of your love. Our hearts sing for joy in your presence. Do not withhold from us any good thing in this hour and in this life until we dwell eternally with you in the heavenly Jerusalem, singing your praises forever. Amen.

Pastoral Prayer: Almighty and everlasting God, we are filled with awe and wonder as we consider your love for us. You made us a little less than yourself and then gave us dominion over the rest of your creation. It is in you that we find strength for life and hope for the future. Through Jesus Christ you assure us of an open door into your eternal city. We praise you that one day in your presence is worth more than a thousand spent elsewhere.

And yet, O Lord, in spite of what we affirm in our praise, we admit that we live as though we don't need your love in our lives. We believe we are self-sufficient, that we can make it on our own. For our failure to acknowledge our need of you and for our taking so lightly the gift of your grace, forgive us, O God.

We thank you that you created all peoples in your image and that you call us all your children. Thank you for the great diversity of cultures and races of this world. We thank you for the firstborn already enrolled in heavenly splendor—our forebears in the faith.

We pray today for this congregation of your people gathered here. Pour out your Holy Spirit on us, that we may follow your Son, Jesus Christ, more closely. Give us wisdom to be the church in this community that reaches out to all people. May the world recognize in us the love you share with us in your Son.

Grant your blessing to all who wear the varied uniforms of the military services of our nation, especially those separated from family and familiar support systems. Give them courage, loyalty, and fidelity to family, home, country, and you.

Hear our prayers for the sick, the grieving, the lonely, and those facing tough decisions, especially those we have named before you and those we now name in our hearts.

We offer our prayers in the name of the One who is the door through which we enter into the city of the living God, even Christ Jesus our Lord. Amen.

AUGUST 30, 1992

□

Twelfth Sunday After Pentecost

If only one can be first, who should it be?

The Sunday Lessons

Ezekiel 18:1-9, 25-29: Judean exiles believed they were cursed by the sins of their fathers. The prophet declared that God deals justly with every individual. Ezekiel set forth a code of conduct for the righteous.

Hebrews 13:1-8: Practical expressions for love are suggested: hospitality to strangers; visiting the ill-treated; and fidelity in marriage.

Luke 14:1, 7-14: At dinner in a Pharisee's house, Jesus spoke of places of honor and an appropriate guest list. To guests he said, "When you are invited . . . go and sit down at the lowest place" (vv. 8, 10). Humility will be honored. Arrogance will lead to humiliation. To the host, he said, "When you give a luncheon or a dinner . . . invite the poor" (vv. 12-13).

Interpretation and Imagination

"We hold these truths to be self-evident that all men are created equal." Thomas Jefferson wrote these familiar words found in the Declaration of Independence and went on to list the inequities that prompted its signers to separate themselves from the king of Great Britain.

Life's inequities have again and again prompted complaints, conflicts, and discontent. Can the counsel of the book of Hebrews be trusted? Is it not a self-evident truth that life's benefits and even life's opportunities are not equally distributed?

The Judean exiles simply accepted their lot as second-rate citizens and slaves, explaining that their fathers' sins had caused it.

Ezekiel did not accept that belief. "God is just," he proclaimed. He assured them that individual responsibility would be rewarded through the even justice of almighty God. We're encouraged to believe that again today. Jesus Christ is always the same; yesterday, today, and forever.

It was once said of the late Charles E. Ashcraft, who for many years was Dean of United Theological Seminary in Dayton, Ohio, "He's always the same." His judgments were marked by the same even qualities that distinguished his teaching, his leadership, and his love for others.

But we prefer privilege to justice even in things as ordinary as a place at the table and names on a guest list. If you want to be first, seek to be first in showing hospitality, obedience, fidelity, and service. Seek to be first in the struggle for equality under the law and first in your confidence in the sovereign grace of God.

KINGDOM ETIQUETTE

Luke 14:1, 7-14

A SERMON BY BERNARD H. LIEVING, JR.

One of the first purchases I made when I came on active duty as an Army Chaplain over twenty-three years ago was *The Officer's Guide*, the "bible" for all Army officers. Its pages contained the authoritative word on all manner of subjects necessary for the acculturation of a new chaplain fresh out of the hills of West Virginia.

My wife and I studied its pages to glean the information necessary for us to make a successful transition into the new world called the Army. We read about the officer image, military courtesy, customs of the service, and the social side of Army life. It tutored us in the right clothes to wear at a variety of functions, the right words to say in a variety of situations, the right size of and wording on our calling cards, and the right order of seating and service at a dinner party. We learned the etiquette, the protocol, the customs, and the taboos. We are probably better persons, having gone through it, although we now laugh at ourselves and the stress we put ourselves under during those first few years, always wondering whether we were correct and proper.

The Gospel reading this morning is a lesson in etiquette, a practical guide on social behavior for dinner guests and hosts. Or is it?

While making his way slowly, but decisively, toward Jerusalem, one sabbath Jesus went to eat at the home of a ruler who was also a Pharisee. Jesus had no more than arrived when he became aware of the furtive glances of the other guests, lawyers and Pharisees. In the social time prior to dinner, the guests crowded closer toward Jesus so they could hear everything he said. Knowing he had a captive audience, and hardly being the model guest, Jesus decided to poke fun at the Pharisees and their religion. "Is it lawful to heal on the sabbath, or not?" he asked them. When they didn't take the bait, Jesus healed one of the guests, a man with such a terrible water retention problem that he could hardly move.

"If one of you has a child or an ox that has fallen into a well, will you not immediately pull it out on a sabbath day?" Jesus asked (Luke 14:5). Again, they didn't say a word. Jesus probably smiled at their discomfort as the hosts called them to dinner.

It is important to interrupt the story here to note that this happened around the setting of a meal. Luke placed great emphasis on the theme of food, upon eating together, throughout his writing. We have greatly devalued the idea of food in our time and have lost much of the meaning of eating together. Not so with Luke and his audience for whom eating together was a religious experience. Luke used food and eating together as the medium for some of his greatest teachings. Responding to the Pharisees' and the scribes' questions about why he ate with sinners, Jesus said, "Those who are well have no need of a physician, but those who are sick" (Luke 5:31). On other times when the scribes and Pharisees murmured against Jesus because he ate with sinners, Jesus told them the parables of the lost ship, the lost coin, and the lost son.

We left Jesus with the Pharisees and lawyers just as they were called to dinner. Jesus the watched became Jesus the watcher, and he saw the mad scramble for the spaces closest to the head table—apparently there were no place cards. Each guest was free to sit wherever he could, based on the level of exertion of elbow and push.

Once the guests were seated and quieted by the serving of the food, Jesus began to speak:

When you are invited by someone to a wedding banquet, do not sit down at the place of honor, in case someone more distinguished than you has been invited by your host; and the host who invited both of you may come and say to you, "Give this person your place," and then in disgrace you would start to take the lowest place. But when you are invited, go and sit down at the lowest place, so that when your host comes, he may say to you, "Friend, move up higher"; then you will be honored in the presence of all who sit at the table with you. (Luke 14:8-10)

If Jesus had stopped there, and if Luke had not told us that Jesus was speaking in a parable, we could believe Jesus was giving good "officer's guide" advice on how to behave as a guest at a wedding feast. But Jesus did not stop there, and Luke did tell us this was a parable. Jesus was not simply discussing etiquette. The table once again became for Luke a place for teaching, a place of revelation about the kingdom. Jesus was talking about kingdom etiquette.

Jesus continued, "For all who exalt themselves will be humbled, and those who humble themselves will be exalted" (Luke 14:11). There it is. Jesus was talking about more than social grace. This parable is about a wedding feast, often Luke's picture of the kingdom. A parable about how the exalted will be humbled and the humble exalted is a glimpse of the heavenly Jerusalem, the city of the living God, where thousands and thousands of angels assemble, and where people come from the east and west and north and south to sit at the table with Abraham and Isaac and Jacob and God's own Son.

What is this attitude toward ourselves to which Jesus calls us? I know what it is not! It is not putting yourself down to the point of worthlessness. It is not an order. It is not a denial of value or ability, a debasing of who God has created us to be.

It is an honest evaluation of ourselves, an acceptance of who we really are. It is recognition of the fact that while God made us just a little lower than the angels—therefore, the highest of his created order—we have no reason to exalt ourselves. We stand before God as sinners, desperately in need of his love and grace, made known to us in Jesus Christ, who humbled himself even to death on the cross, and whom God exalted to the place of honor at his own right hand.

Humility is a quality of life that enables us to know that our real worth cannot be measured by any standard of this world—no promotion, no recognition, no award, no dollar value, no status, no position. Humility is knowing that even while we were yet sinners, God has forgiven us our past, put a robe on our shoulders, a ring on our finger, and sandals on our feet, and has exalted us by inviting us to the wedding feast.

To be humble is to acknowledge our finitude, our inability to save ourselves, our complete dependence on God's grace. Given this meaning, we see these words with a new understanding of how we are able to respond appropriately to the circumstances of life. As human beings we seek to confirm our importance and worth by taking seats in places of honor. Luke tells us that God's love establishes our worth. So when we can say yes to God's love in Jesus Christ, we can say no to the old games of fighting for prestige and security.

What Jesus did on the cross validates our worth. We need only to acknowledge our dependence on God's grace to be exalted, saved, invited to the wedding feast and seated at a place of honor.

Jesus then turned to his dinner host and chided him about his guest list and his motivation for inviting the people seated at the table: "When you give a luncheon or a dinner, do not invite your friends or your brothers or your relatives or rich neighbors, in case they may invite you in return, and you would be repaid. But when you give a banquet, invite the poor, the crippled, the lame, and the blind. And you will be blessed" (Luke 14:12-13).

Jesus' words are more than instructions on social graces. They are guides on kingdom etiquette. Jesus said that members of the kingdom should act toward others as God has acted toward them. God's grace is for all who can give him nothing in return but love. People of the kingdom—that is, those who humble themselves and accept the gift of God's grace—are called to reach out to those whom society considers to be unimportant, the poor, the homeless, the sick—all those who cannot return the favor.

A pastor in Decatur, Georgia, once preached a sermon in which he recalled a layperson's question concerning a position the church had taken on a social issue, in response to what Jesus said in Luke 4:18:

The Spirit of the Lord is upon
me,
because he has anointed me
to bring good news to the
poor.
He has sent me to proclaim
release to the captives
and recovery of sight to the
blind,
to proclaim the year of the
Lord's favor.

The layperson asked, "Why do they pick that one passage of Scripture and make so much of it?" Wilder replied that the church makes so much of it because Jesus made so much of it. Kingdom etiquette calls for us to be concerned about the needs of the poor and the disenfranchised. Christians are called to task wherever people are victimized, whenever individuals are denied their worth and their rights.

Jesus promises that if we live our lives under the banner of lifting up those in need and affirm their eternal worth in the sight of God, we will be blessed. The blessing will not be from other people, but from God. God is ultimately the only One who can bless us, or whose praise matters. And he will bless us as we come to his banquet table—poor, sinful, homeless, deserving of nothing and unable to repay. We will hear God say to us, "Well done . . . enter into the joy of your master" (Matt. 25:21).

When we hear that we can never be the same again. We no longer have to fight to get to the head table because God gives a proper place to all who come in humility. Then we are free to ease the pain, want, and hurt in the world by giving what God has given to us: his love.

Suggestions for Worship

Call to Worship (Ps. 15:1-3):

MINISTER: O LORD, who may abide in your tent?

PEOPLE: Who may dwell on your holy hill?

MINISTER: Those who walk blamelessly, and do what is right,

PEOPLE: and speak the truth from their heart; who do not . . . take up a reproach against their neighbors.

Act of Praise: Psalm 15.

Suggested Hymns: opening hymn: "Marching to Zion"; second hymn: "Break Thou the Bread of Life"; closing hymn: "God Be with You till We Meet Again."

Opening Prayer: O Lord, you call us to walk blamelessly and to do what is right. So much of our lives are spent in blaming others for our shortcomings. You desire us to speak the truth and to treat our friends and neighbors with respect. Our tongues distort the truth, and our actions degrade others. Forgive us, O God. Help us to take responsibility for our actions and give us vision to see the results of our sins. Through Christ Jesus our Lord we pray. Amen.

Pastoral Prayer: O God, you are the same yesterday, today, and forever. Even before the creation of this world, you were God. Far beyond the end of our time here, you will be God, forever and ever. We praise you for being the unshakeable foundation of our often weak, tottering lives. We worship you as Lord and King and offer you all honor and glory.

Most gracious God, who has given us the gifts of your love—the warm sun, the refreshing rain, the hugs of friends, children laughing and playing, a baby's contented sigh, this chance to quiet ourselves before you—accept the praise and thanks of your people.

Holy Lord, you have called us to be your people. We pray for the church in this community. Help us to be doers of your Word and not hearers only. Strengthen us to proclaim your truth and to live your love in our daily walk. We pray for the Church where it struggles for its survival. We do not ask for ease of witness, but for your power to witness boldly and joyfully.

We pray for your people. Dry their tears, heal their hurts, soothe their wounds, give them your peace. Empower those worried with life, afraid of the present and unsure of the future. Make these requests happen through your Holy Spirit and his leading us to care for one another.

Lord God, touch the lives of those who are suffering illness and grief. Minister to those in hospitals and nursing homes through the loving care of the healing team.

We remember the teachers of our children as they plan for and begin a new school year. Grant them patience, wisdom and that special spirit of love that will enable them to inspire and challenge young minds. Give to children a desire for knowledge and a willingness to accept new classmates and affirm old friendships.

Plant the seeds of peace within the hearts of our national leaders and in the leaders of all nations of the world. Nourish faltering leaders who know the good to do, but worry about the consequences. Bless today all your people who suffer the pain of armed conflict. Bring peace to those displaced from their homes and to those who are hungry because of the strivings of people.

Grant us all your peace that we might all be peacemakers—in family, community, and world. Help us in our daily living to find our rightful places of service to you and to our community.

All praise, honor, and glory be to you, loving God, through our risen Lord and Savior we pray. Amen.

September 6, 1992

□

Thirteenth Sunday After Pentecost

The radical demand and high cost of being a watchguard, a fellow soldier, and a disciple are the subjects of these lessons.

The Sunday Lessons

Ezekiel 33:1-11: The word of the Lord came to the prophet, telling him of the responsibilities of a clear warning. If the sentry's trumpet is not sounded, his people will perish. It is God who calls the prophet to be a watchman.

Philemon 1-20: This personal letter from Paul to an affluent Christian asks that he receive Onesimus, a runaway slave, "as a beloved brother." Paul sent the slave back to his master with the message, "If you consider me your partner, welcome him as you would welcome me" (v. 17).

Luke 14:25-33: The cost of being a disciple is no easy bargain. "Whoever comes to me and does not hate father and mother . . . even life itself, cannot be my disciple" (v. 26). Two parables teach the importance of counting the cost.

Interpretation and Imagination

For astronauts, it is not simply a matter of having the "right stuff." Careful preparation, diligent attention to detail, and a willingness to put everything on the line in one great moment of truth are a part of every flight into space. A theological word borrowed from the Christian community is used to describe the time of no return. It is *committed.* When the countdown reaches the final stages, we may hear Houston control saying, "We are committed to flight."

All of today's lessons witness to the cost and the risk of commitment. If a sentry's trumpet sounds an uncertain note, those committed to that sentry's care will perish. If warning or advance knowledge goes unheeded, disaster will follow.

The story of the sinking of the "unsinkable" *Titanic* is legendary. Convinced of the great ocean liner's invulnerability, those in charge provided enough lifeboats for only half the persons onboard. Another ship, the *Californian*, encountered the ice floes, stopped its engines, and broadcast a warning. The *Titanic*, only twenty miles away, sped confidently on. When the lookout on the bridge shouted, "Ice! Dead ahead!" it was too late. But overconfidence still manifests itself. The ship's orchestra continued to play popular tunes. When a command to board the lifeboats was finally given, many passengers refused to believe that the ship was in real danger. The first lifeboats pulled away half empty. More than 1,500 persons perished; only about 700 were saved.

THE COSTS OF LIBERATION

Luke 14:25-28

A SERMON BY WALLACE E. FISHER

Liberation is costly to the liberator; that is obvious. Liberation is also costly to the *liberated*; that is not strikingly obvious. The Gospel lesson for today defines that reality in plain terms. Indeed, it is Jesus himself who spells out the costs of accepting and joining in his liberation work. They are three distinct but integrally related costs, rooted in the nature of biblical faith: (1) self-discipline under the gospel, (2) cross-bearing, (3) obedience to Christ (Luke 14: 26-28). God's promises and his demands are inseparable. Put negatively that means "No Cross, No Crown." How shall we interpret these costs in our time and place?

Jesus calls us to love him more than we love parents, siblings, mate, children, and self. That demand has been misunderstood badly in the course of Christian history. Jesus does not call us to treat others in a cavalier fashion. He calls us to honor these relationships fully, so long as they do not take precedence over the authority of the gospel. Further, Jesus does not call us to flatten our providential gifts as individual selves but to bring our instinctive love of self under an authority above family and self—the gospel of God. He calls us to seek his kingdom above all else. The faith journey inward frees us to make the faith journey outward—service to God and others.

Learning to recognize, appreciate, and use God's providential gifts responsibly, we come slowly but surely to the realization (under the gospel of God) that our most rigorous acts of self-discipline do not alter our deep-seated disposition to be self-serving (see Rom. 7). We discover that acts of the human will do not free us from the demons of pride, envy, greed, anger, lust, sloth, and vain glory. As we learn to discern more clearly God's demands in his law, prophets, and Son, we recognize how desperately we respectable, decent people need a savior to liberate us from sin, the demonic, and death.

As we experience Christ's liberating power in our lives—his power to do for us what we cannot do for ourselves—we discover a deep new desire rising within us—the spirit-prompted desire to have Christ's likeness in us. We discover, too, how gospel faith (Christ in us) produces good works even as a healthy tree produces good fruit. Justification through faith in God's grace and sanctification through his likeness growing in us go hand in hand. So we learn over the years that it is in our recognized and acknowledged weakness that God makes us strong ("My grace is enough"). Acknowledging our need (repentance) and disciplining ourselves under the gospel (faith), we discover that self-discipline is the point at which our journey into biblical faith begins. Sooner or later we learn that we have to work on this discipline until we meet Christ face-to-face in his kingdom.

"Take up your cross." How, we ask ourselves, shall we interpret this cost of discipleship? We need to review the historical evidence in the Gospel accounts for perspective. The cross was not an inevitable event in Jesus' life. It was a voluntary act: "No one takes [my life] from me, but I lay it down of my own accord" (John 10:18). When we ponder the human implications of this reality, we begin to realize that cross bearing is a lifelong series of voluntary decisions made in specific situations to subordinate our wills to God's will. The gospel throws us into a running battle with our human nature and our culture, which prod and encourage us to look out for "number one."

Coming to grips with the New Testament's and church history's concerted witness that taking up Jesus' cross meant imprisonment, exile, and violent death for thousands of his followers during the centuries when Christianity was an outlaw religion, we get a rugged view of cross bearing. Human self-will dies hard; the new self in Christ matures painfully, slowly, unevenly. The good fight of faith is a daily battle. The struggle to become cross bearers brings us into conflict with other selves in and outside our congregations as well as with ourselves and our culture. The biblical narrative and our own modest experiences with cross bearing teach us that these internal and external conflicts recur until we take our last breath on earth. We learn from harsh experience that the moment we relax our focus on Christ for any appreciable period we regress into our old preoccupations with our personal, family, racial, and national interests.

Struggling to understand more fully the historical and existential nature of Jesus' cross, we begin to recognize that Christ himself is demeaned, abused, and crucified anew in every hungering, thirsting, oppressed, exploited, and spiritually empty human being in this world. Realizing that his suffering did not end when he walked from the tomb, we are motivated to open ourselves and our church to all people who are socially, racially, and economically ghettoed in our community; to all people who are spiritually ghettoed in our community's affluent suburbs; and through our intercessory prayers, material gifts, and political decisions to people who are politically and economically ghettoed in other parts of our nation and world. To move from minimal selfhood toward responsible selfhood is to serve Christ above family and self in the world. To bear Christ's cross means to journey outward into the world.

Christian belief can be passive; biblical faith is always active, dynamic. Jesus calls us to follow him. Passive reliance on cheap grace aborts Christ's power to save and to transform us. Repentance and gospel faith go hand-in-hand. Biblical faith is active trust in and obedience to Christ.

Following Christ means precisely that—following. The initiative for Christian witness is Christ himself—his life, teachings, sacrificial death, resurrection, and abiding presence. Those who follow him do not *take* him to non-Christian peoples in other lands or into the public arena. Christians *join* him in all human situations in which people walk in the darkness of spiritual and physical need. The resurrected Christ is present wherever people, rich or poor in material goods, are impoverished in spirit, wherever they mourn, suffer persecution, cry out for deliverance, or are dying. Christ-followers testify to his presence where "cross the crowded ways of life." As obedient Christ-followers, we join him on all the human frontiers of this present life. To follow him is to meet him in biblical preaching, evangelical teaching, the sacraments, Bible study, our closet prayer rooms, and in the world where he, already present, motivates and enables us to share in his ministry. Christ came into the world to save the world. His church is the primary, but not the only, means he uses to save the world; it is, however, the clearest extension of his incarnation into history.

Christ does not trample his followers' freedom or rob them of their individuality. Some Christians, wanting to exalt Christ, adopt a pseudo-humility that obscures God's providential gifts that constitute human individuality. On the other hand, many Christians are disposed to exalt human individuality. Biblical faith teaches us to bring these warped views into a balanced view of reality. All of us need to recall often Paul's description of his personal witness as Christ appealing by him. The authority was God's; the ministry was Paul's. We need to recall often Luther's witness at the Diet of Worms: "My conscience is captive to the Word of God." The authority was God's; the conscience was Luther's.

God offers the treasure of gospel faith to everyone. Those who accept his gift discover slowly, sometimes suddenly, that his Spirit provides a new center, Christ in them, from which each person's individuality is transformed to serve God, others, and self. Christ calls his followers friends. He names them as co-workers with him. He promises that they will be co-heirs in his kingdom yet to come. That is human individuality and human dignity at its highest level!

Following Christ is not validated by calling attention to ourselves, but by pointing gladly to Christ's saving and transforming power in and through us. Following Christ is demonstrated by our disciplined participation in his ministry to the wounded, oppressed, abandoned, and spiritually needy persons in our families, church, community, nation, and world. We journey inward to light the human spirit and to renew it daily. We journey outward to exercise and to mature in the Spirit.

The costs of discipleship are beyond the power of any human being to meet from his or her own resources. The early Christians disciplined themselves under the gospel. They took up their crosses and followed Christ because they relied on God for his providential and redemptive gifts. They "out-loved, out-gave, and out-died" the devotees of the pagan religions in the Roman Empire, not only because they decided in their freedom to bear the costs of discipleship, but also because they decided daily to open themselves to Christ's enabling power to meet those costs.

Getting that reality into our soft heads and hard hearts and acting on it is the essence of Christian discipleship. It all begins when we cry, "Lord, be merciful unto me, a sinner." That opens us to Christ's saving, transforming love.

Suggestions for Worship

Call to Worship (Ps. 94:14-15):

MINISTER: The LORD will not forsake his people;

PEOPLE: he will not abandon his heritage;

MINISTER: for justice will return to the righteous,

PEOPLE: and all the upright in heart will follow it.

Act of Praise: Psalm 94:12-22.

Suggested Hymns: opening hymn: "To God Be the Glory"; second hymn: "Precious Lord, Take My Hand"; closing hymn: "When I Survey the Wondrous Cross."

Opening Prayer: Merciful God, you are attentive to the voice of our pleading. So let us find forgiveness of our sins, comfort in our distress, faith to replace our fear, certainty to quiet our doubts, and courage to carry the cross. Make our faith bold and strong through our Lord Jesus Christ. Amen.

Pastoral Prayer: Lord be merciful to me, a sinner. O broken heart of Christ, broken with love for us, have mercy. O nail-scarred hands of Christ, scarred by the sins of the world, have mercy. O wounded side of Christ, pierced by the evil that seeks to destroy us, have mercy. O crucified and suffering Christ, dying for the sins of the world, have mercy on us. O risen Christ, worthy of all praise, have mercy on us. O reigning Christ, king and center of all things in heaven and on earth, have mercy on us and save us.

And be for us the centering place of wisdom and truth, of hope and joy, of service and repose. You are the delight of all the saints. Have mercy on us. Amen.

September 13, 1992

□

Fourteenth Sunday After Pentecost

There's joy in heaven when the lost are found.

The Sunday Lessons

Hosea 4:1-3; 5:15–6:6: The first part of the lesson refers to a controversy between the Lord God and the people of Israel. Hosea proclaimed that the Lord would forsake Israel until the people repented. God did not want rituals of repentance, but steadfast love and the knowledge of God.

I Timothy 1:12-17: Paul recalled his former conduct and how he had once blasphemed, persecuted, and insulted Jesus. Then he wrote: "But I received mercy . . . the grace of our Lord overflowed for me" (vv. 13-14).

Luke 15:1-10: Pharisees criticized Jesus, saying, "This fellow welcomes sinners and eats with them" (v. 2). This illustrates God's concern for those who cannot find him. Everyone is invited to rejoice.

Interpretation and Imagination

"I will abandon my people until they have suffered enough for their sins and come looking for me" (Hosea 5:15 GNB). This translation seems to be in sharp contrast with parables of a shepherd who goes looking for a lost sheep, and a woman who looks carefully everywhere for a lost coin. *The New Oxford Annotated Bible* makes this comment about Luke 15: "The parable [of the lost sheep] illustrates God's concern for [persons] who lack ability to find him; he seeks them." Which way is it? Does God deliberately forsake his people? Or does God never abandon the lost?

The advocates of tough love suggest that children must

sometimes be abandoned. A teenage addict, who had stolen money and other valuables from her own home, was arrested with a warrant sworn by her mother. "How can you do this to me?" the child cried. The mother knew that her daughter had to turn from the ways that were destroying them all. She hoped that the suffering would cause change.

A lost sheep can almost never find its way home. Surely, a lost coin will never find itself. To be sure, sheep and coins don't repent. A more important message is here. "Christ Jesus came into the world to save sinners." It is not the shepherd that is lost. It is not our responsibility to find him. Prevenient grace means that Christ is looking for us before we realize that we're lost. In spite of our conceit, hardness of heart, foolishness, and falsehood, God does not forget or reject any of us. There's joy in heaven when the lost one is found. Let there be joy in earth as well.

GOD'S SEARCH AND SAVE POLICY

Luke 15:1-10; Hosea 4:1-3, 5:15–6:6

A SERMON BY WALLACE E. FISHER

When Paul declared that God was in Christ reconciling the world to himself, he described luminously the nature and purpose of God's search and save policy toward rebellious human beings. There is nothing like God's policy in human history. Military policy calls us to seek and destroy. Every producer's policy calls us to seek and sell. Our consumer mentality calls us to get all we can. Our undisciplined egos whisper, "Look out for number one." God's policy—search and save—is unique. From the cosmic, earthy stories in Genesis to the sweeping vision of John on Patmos, the message is ever the same: Human beings are lost; God in Christ seeks them, finds them, and gives victory to those who love and serve him. From the time of humanity's first rebellion against its creator, that saving work has been God's primary concern, and it still is. It will continue to be so until he brings in his full kingdom in *his* appointed time.

This search-and-save theme runs through the Old Testament—deliverance from bondage in Egypt, the Jonah story, the psalms, the prophets—but only in the Jesus of history does it come into dazzling focus. He began his earthly ministry with the announcement, "[I] came to seek out and to save the lost" (Luke 19:10). Completing his ministry, he prayed to his Father, "Forgive them; for they do not know what they are doing" (Luke 23:34). Revealing and demonstrating God's search-and-save policy in every act and word, Jesus describes it definitively in the fifteenth chapter of Luke. Four of his best-known parables—the lost sheep, the lost coin, the prodigal son, and the prodigal's ill-tempered older brother—are recorded there. Today's Gospel lesson, incorporating the first two of those parables, points plainly to God's search-and-save policy.

All humans get lost through misusing, abusing, and declining to use their God-given freedom responsibly. None of us behaves at all times like our prevailing social, political, or religious hierarchies think we should. We simply do not fit neatly into others' scheme of things. Consequently, these hierarchies ignore us, criticize us, keep us out of their circles, and occasionally attack us because we behave, believe, and/or think differently from them. The "religious" people of Jesus' day (see Luke 15:1-3) had a "list" of unacceptable people, including tax-collectors, lepers, moral lawbreakers, Samaritans, Romans, Greeks—everyone—who did not honor *their* interpretation of God's law.

Jesus, demonstrating that God loves his whole erring creation, not only shared his message of forgiveness and promise of new life with sinners, but also socialized with them. That was intolerable to the Pharisees. Jesus' criticism of their arrogant disregard for people who were not like them confronts us with the ugly reality that some people are kept out of some churches because of rigid dogmas. Others are kept out of some congregations that deliberately limit and flatten God's inclusive love. Jesus seeks and saves these lost people, if they accept him.

The parable of the lost sheep provides another reason why humans get lost: stupidity and carelessness. Grazing eagerly on God's providential gifts, some of us wander away from the Shepherd and his flock. The lost sheep did not set out to get lost. It simply strayed farther and farther from the flock until, suddenly aware of its terrible aloneness, it bleated pleadingly for the shepherd. How often have you and I gotten lost in just that way? I cannot count the times. I did not expect a particular decision or action to get me lost, but it did. Each of us, suddenly aware that his or her situation is precarious, laments, "I did not intend to get lost."

That is often a true explanation. Our "lostness" began so innocently. Problems with alcohol begin that way. Too often infidelity takes shape that way. Thousands of marriages end, not with harsh accusations and mean acts of retaliation, but with uncomprehending whimpers, "Where and when did our marriage go wrong?" The innate disposition for serving the self without thought of destructive consequences is part of our human baggage. Shakespeare's character, Puck, is right: "What fools these mortals be." Stupidity dogs the learned as well as the unlearned. Jesus searches out the fools (all of us on occasion) and saves us, if we want to be saved.

We also get lost through the wrong teachings and careless deeds of particular persons who are close to us. The lost coin did not lose itself. Its custodian lost it. All of us have a neurosis or two caused in childhood by parents or teachers or peers who deliberately or unwittingly damaged our egos. And millions of young people today are being damaged psychically and physically by individuals they trust.

Jesus searches out these "lost" persons and gives them new life if they *trust* him—and they can. He is trustworthy.

God's love is pluralistic. He loves all his alienated people—whoever they are, wherever they are, in whatever condition of lostness they are. No matter how we get separated from God—lonely because society closes us out; our ill-advised, stupid wanderings in spiritual wastelands; wounded in body and spirit by individuals close to us—he seeks us out.

God's love is person-centered. He calls us by name; he knows each of us better than any one of us knows himself or herself. Jesus called the disciples one by one. He called Zacchaeus from the crowd. He understood and forgave Peter's disposition to crumble under pressure. From the cross he asked John to care for Mary, Jesus' weeping mother. In spite of mounting physical pain and a deepening sense of alienation from his Father, Jesus responded lovingly to the penitent thief dying at his side.

God's love is constant. He seeks all of us until he finds each lost sheep, each lost coin, each isolated, lonely person. Though we make our beds in earthly hells—whether driven there by an uncaring society, drifting there by one careless decision after another, shoved there by our wild and reckless life-styles—God's active love finds us, lifts us into the light, forgives us, and gives us another chance—if we want it enough to repent, to believe, and to go God's way.

God loves us in our lostness. But his love is not a sentimental, ephemeral, surging sea of emotion. His love is structured by his righteousness. We accept God on his terms or go our own way. He does not violate his righteous character or deny his sovereign will. His love is free, but it is not cheap. The Old Testament lesson, taken from Hosea, the prophet of a loving God, reveals his righteousness and sovereign will: "Listen, Israel, to what [God] says: . . . the people do not acknowledge me as God" (Hosea 4:1 GNB); "Perhaps in their suffering they will try to find me" (Hosea 5:15 GNB); "I want your constant love" (Hosea 6:6 GNB). God's love is structured by his righteousness.

God's love is costly to him. That blood-drenched cross on Golgotha is the price he paid to save his lost creation. God's love is also costly for us; we do his will, not ours. How dare we cheapen God's deed by saying airily, as the poet Heine said, "Of course, God will forgive me; that is his business." But we do! How dare we cheapen God's love by separating repentance from gospel faith, justification from sanctification, judgment from grace. But we do! Only those who accept and share God's *whole* counsel (gospel and law, promise and command) are Christ's co-workers. Each person decides for himself or herself whether to pay the high personal cost of accepting God's righteous love.

Another facet of the loving, righteous God is his absolute respect for human freedom. He yearns for our love (see Hosea 6:6); he does not coerce it. He wants sons and daughters who love him freely, gladly, with open hearts, not slaves who are compelled to serve or hirelings who are paid to serve. Real love is always a gift. The other two parables in Luke 15—the prodigal and the prodigal's brother—set this facet of God's person before us plainly. The prodigal son accepted the gift. His angry brother refused his father's entreaties to share in the homecoming.

God loves all people wherever they are, in whatever condition they are in. So we Christ-followers sing with surging gratitude, "There's a wideness in God's mercy" and again, "To those who fall how kind Thou art."

God's pluralistic, person-centered, constant love is structured by his righteous sovereignty; our new life begins when we accept his Son as Savior, Teacher, Friend, Lord. So we sing with solemn humility, "Just as I am, without one plea,/ but that thy blood was shed for me" and again, "In the cross of Christ I glory."

God's love does not crush our freedom to repent and to believe or to go our separate ways. So we Christ followers sing with soaring expectation, "Take my life, and let it be consecrated,/ Lord, to thee" and again, "Jesus, Savior, pilot me over life's tempestuous sea."

Suggestions for Worship

Call to Worship (I Tim. 1:15, 17):

MINISTER: The saying is sure and worthy of full acceptance,

PEOPLE: that Christ Jesus came into the world to save sinners. . . .

MINISTER: To the King of the ages, immortal, invisible, the only God,

PEOPLE: be honor and glory forever and ever. Amen.

Act of Praise: Psalm 77:11-20.

Suggested Hymns: opening hymn: "All Praise to Thee, My God, This Night"; second hymn: "Savior, Like a Shepherd Lead Us"; closing hymn: "Pass Me Not, O Gentle Savior."

Opening Prayer: Gracious heavenly Father, we are here today with needs that cause us to seek you, and you offer yourself always to be found. So let us find you in all the places where you already are—in the fields and hills; in the heavens above and the depths of the earth; in our houses and our temple; on the highways and in offices, classrooms, hospitals, and supermarkets; in the jails, the streets, and the cemeteries. Continue your loving presence with us forever, that the whole world may see your glory. Amen.

Pastoral Prayer: O God, our Father, you keep stars in their courses, rule over the whole universe, and judge the nations. Yet, you number the hairs of our heads. You mark the fall of each sparrow, and you know each of us as though there were only one of us to know. Just now, cross the thresholds of our innermost lives, we pray. You know the anxieties we have. Sickness has found its way into some of our homes. So many of us are poor. Some of us are homeless. Temptations seek to steal our children. We are faced with problems that perplex and tasks beyond our power to do. Our inner lives are full of conflict, and we are tormented by lust and greed, by grief and guilt, by hate and envy. We see within ourselves needs that only your grace can satisfy. We see opportunities that only your power can fulfill. Now for every need send your bountiful supply, through Jesus Christ our Lord. Amen.

September 20, 1992

□

Fifteenth Sunday After Pentecost

The mercy of God leads us to include everyone in our prayers for salvation. It prompts us to prepare for the times when all other securities fail.

The Sunday Lessons

Hosea 11:1-11: Yahweh is like a patient, forgiving father. Israel is like a disobedient child. Israel turns away from God, and bondage becomes her lot. But still the Lord is patient and inclines toward mercy.

I Timothy 2:1-7: God wants all persons to be saved. Christ gave himself as a ransom for all. Paul was appointed to be "a teacher of the Gentiles." The lesson calls us to be universal in our prayers and outreach.

Luke 16:1-13: A dishonest steward is found out. To protect his future, the steward changes records of indebtedness and gains some friends. Jesus commends the steward not because he was dishonest, but because he was prudent and gained security for himself. It is wise to handle the wealth and resources of this life in ways that will help you when mammon fails and you need "eternal habitations."

Interpretation and Imagination

While thumbing through *Compton's Encyclopedia* in search of some trivia, I came across an article on conversation and read again the familiar counsel concerning business contacts: "All you know about conversation will help you when you seek a position or try to make a sale." Then the lesson continued, "Go over the facts. Think about the needs of the person you are to see. Find out about him, so that you may know better how to suit your remarks to him. Whether the interview has been successful or not let the parting be pleasant." It occurred to me that business conversations are significantly more considerate than conversations of children with parents.

Hosea employed the rebellious runaway style of children to express Israel's recalcitrance toward God. And all the time, like a waiting father, God refused to give Israel up. God refuses to give us up, too.

"Do something, say something, give them something, that will make them remember you, even indebted to you," is the counsel provided to salespersons. The unjust steward knew how to cultivate the favor of those who could later help him. His style stands in sharp contrast to our careless neglect of the constant favor of a heavenly parent.

CHRISTIAN WORSHIP

Psalm 145:1-2

A SERMON BY JAMES C. CAMMACK

How many times did you worship last week? Your first reaction might be a mental tabulation of how many times you went to church. "Let's see . . . Sunday morning, Wednesday evening. . . ."

The psalmist broadened our concept of worship when he wrote, "I will extol you, my God. . . . Every day will I bless you" (Ps. 145:1-2). Worship is a continuous process. It is an attitude of the heart that recognizes God in everything we do. It is not limited by place or time. We can and should worship God anywhere and everywhere.

What does it mean to worship? True worship is the human response to the awesome presence of God. We see him in the glory of his natural creation, in the eyes of a child, in the setting sun, or in the the early morning artistry of a new day. But if we recognize God only in the things he has created, we may miss the glory of his living presence. Moses turned aside to examine the miracle of the burning bush, but when he heard the voice of God, he fell down and worshiped Jehovah.

Worship does not come easily to Americans. We have our own secular gods, and we are caught up in the distractions of a multimedia society that distorts the true meaning of worship. Worship is not entertainment. Worship is not a spectator sport. Worship is not an ego trip for a charismatic performer.

Sometimes the most devout Christian may find it difficult to worship—even in church. During the minister's prayer one Sunday, there was a loud whistle from one of the back pews. A little boy's mother was horrified to realize that it was her son who had whistled. She pinched him into silence, and after church asked, "Whatever made you do such a thing?" He answered seriously, "I asked God to teach me to whistle, and he just then did!" While the church may be the ideal place to worship, even there the antics of other worshipers and our own wandering minds distract us from a meaningful confrontation with God.

True Christian worship is a celebration of the good news of God in Christ Jesus. There is one mediator between God and mankind (see I Tim. 2:5). It is a confrontation with the living Savior. Worship is a refining fire that melts the dross of our sinful nature and presents us pure before our heavenly Father. Worship is an experience. It is an encounter with God through the Holy Spirit. It is a costly commitment to Jesus Christ as Lord.

The Christian minister should stand in awe of his or her task as worship leader. No preacher can give at once the impression that he or she is clever and that Jesus Christ is mighty to save. The sanctity of the worship moment is climaxed by the glory of God's revelation of himself. We may enter the sanctuary to praise God, and we may bow down in reverence and humility before him, but we have not truly worshiped if we return to our daily pursuits unchanged in attitude or behavior.

Worship is not limited to one day or to one location. God can perhaps be best worshiped in the church. The psalmist, in a burst of joy, wrote: "I was glad when they said unto me,/ 'Let us go to the house of the LORD!'" (Ps. 122:1). His invitation is to all who will join him: "O come, let us worship and bow down,/ let us kneel before the LORD, our Maker!" (Ps. 95:6). But God can be worshiped anywhere—in the fields, on the freeway, in the office, on a crowded bus, in our homes with our families. Worship happens when every surrounding distraction is erased so that in one glad moment we experience the life-changing presence of God.

Worship should begin at home. American's problem is not

prayer in the schools, but prayer in the home. While the family altar is much more difficult to maintain now than it was in earlier days, that family who do not worship together in the home miss the teachable moment for little children to meet the Lord. Admittedly, most American homes are like a bus station, and finding a quiet moment to worship at the supper table is difficult. One young mother complained, "Getting my kids still at the table is like trying to nail jelly to the floor!" But when a misty-eyed father can say to his pastor, "Billy was saved last night during our family worship," we recognize that the most complicated difficulties of scheduling are infinitely worthwhile.

Worship should be shared with our family of faith. In addition to worshiping at home, every Christian should have a hunger to fellowship with other Christians. The hymns, the prayers, the music, the Scripture—the church house itself—should encourage corporate worship. It was said of Jesus, He went to the synagogue on the sabbath day, as was his custom (Luke 4:16). It was our Lord's habit to worship with other people.

What happens to the family who worships together? Recently someone gave a testimony in church. To the surprise of most of us, this sweet, dedicated Christian overwhelmed us with her honesty. "I was mean," she said. She told of her lack of interest in attending worship with her family, and she shared a secret resentment at having to go to church. "But God intervened in my life, and one night I found myself prostrate on the floor in prayer. Christ came into my life in a new way. Now worship is different. Family is different. Church is different. The world is different. I am different!"

In the same meeting a person rose to say, "Preacher, since we went down the aisle and rededicated our lives to God, my family has prayed together on our knees every night!"

The worship of the living God had brought forth its harvest. It began in the presence of fellow worshipers, but it found its final expression in the personal transformation of their life-styles.

Why is worship so important to us? Worship is important to every Christian because we become like the God we worship. America is literally saturated with modern idolatry. We have fallen down before the gods of secularism, humanism, materialism, and the cultic deity of success. I want men and women everywhere to lift up holy hands in prayer. Don't you?

Isn't it time that Christians in America heard again the psalmist's affirmation of faith: "I will extol you, my God. . . . Every day will I bless you" (Ps. 145:1-2).

Suggestions for Worship

Call to Worship (Ps. 107:1-2, 8):

MINISTER: O give thanks to the LORD, for he is good;

PEOPLE: for his steadfast love endures forever.

MINISTER: Let the redeemed of the LORD say so. . . .

PEOPLE: Let them thank the LORD for his steadfast love.

Act of Praise: Psalm 107:1-9.

Suggested Hymns: opening hymn: "God of Grace and God of Glory"; second hymn: "I Know Whom I Have Believed"; closing hymn: "I Surrender All."

Opening Prayer: Almighty God, you alone are the source of peace and righteousness. Only the warmth of your Spirit can wean us from pride and cause us to pray. Your faithfulness never ends. O Lord, teach us to pray so that we may be helped by your love and guided by your wisdom. Make us one with all your prophets and saints, who have trusted in you and were not ashamed. Amen.

Pastoral Prayer: Almighty Father, enter our hearts, and so fill us with your love that, forsaking all evil desires, we may embrace you, our only good. Show unto us, for your mercies' sake, O Lord our God, what you are unto us. Say unto our souls, I am your salvation. So speak that we may hear. Our hearts are before you; open our ears; let us hasten after your voice, and take hold of you. Hide not your face from us, we beseech you, O Lord. Enlarge the narrowness of our souls, that you may enter in. Repair the ruinous mansions, that you may dwell there. Hear us, O Heavenly Father, for the sake of your only Son, Jesus Christ, our Lord, who lives and reigns with you and the Holy Spirit, now and for ever. Amen. (St. Augustine)

SEPTEMBER 27, 1992

□

Sixteenth Sunday After Pentecost

The reversal of the fortunes of the rich and the poor is a primary theme of these lessons.

The Sunday Lessons

Joel 2:23-30: "Be glad and rejoice," the prophet declares (v. 23). The Lord has given both early and late rains that assure a bountiful harvest. Losses from the years of the swarming locusts will be reversed. Pouring rains will be followed by an outpouring of the Spirit.

I Timothy 6:6-19: Godliness with contentment is the central idea in this passage. We cannot take anything out of the world and should be content with food and clothing. Love of money and the desire to be rich are a snare. The rich of this world are to become rich in good deeds, "thus storing up for themselves the treasure of a good foundation for the future" (v. 19).

Luke 16:19-31: The story of the rich man and the poor beggar, Lazarus, is a portrayal of the reversal of roles. Dives (the name means wealthy) had feasted sumptuously in this world, but in Hades he begged Lazarus to "dip the tip of his finger in water and cool my tongue" (v. 24). Lazarus, whose only relief in this life came from the dogs that licked his sores, finally rested in Abraham's bosom. The great chasm between them could not be crossed.

Interpretation and Imagination

Success stories that tell about someone's move from rags to riches abound. This story is not one of them. The point that Jesus makes with this familiar folktale (found in many cultures and often repeated in rabbinical teaching) is that the rich often fail to use their opportunities. Dives, thought to represent the Sadducees who did not believe in life after death, was intent on using his riches to provide luxury in the here and now. He failed to honor the scriptures that warn that this is not the only life one has to live.

The rich man did not honor justice. He did not expect a time of judgment. Misled by the false creeds of materialism, he was convinced that everything and everyone should serve and comfort him. Even in the midst of torment, his attitude did not change. There, he wanted Lazarus to comfort him; when he failed in that, the rich man wanted Lazarus to serve as his messenger and carry a warning to his brothers. Self-centered arrogance was his style from beginning to end.

Old Scrooge in Dickens's *A Christmas Carol* was frightened by an apparition: the ghost of Christmas past. It caused him to change his attitude toward the poor crippled Tiny Tim. The biblical story does not encourage us to seek or to trust such messages and messengers. If the moral judgments and ethical insights that have been distilled from the long experience of the human race and set down in the teachings of Moses and the prophets are not convincing, no preaching ghost is likely to be either.

HOW TO BECOME AN AUTHENTIC CHRISTIAN STEWARD

I Timothy 6:6-19

A SERMON BY JAMES C. CAMMACK

Have you ever thought of what kind of an epitaph you would want on your tombstone? In a cemetery in Warwickshire, England, there is an epitaph that reads:

> Here lies a miser who lived for himself.
> And cared for nothing but gathering pelf.
> Now, where he is, or how he fares
> Nobody knows . . . and nobody cares!

Christianity is inescapably linked with giving, not with keeping. Not what we have, but how we got it and how we use it are the clues to our understanding of Christian stewardship. Every

Christian who has ever been remembered beyond his or her death has been a person who lived the giving life.

Of course, some of us, with a shrug of the shoulder, don't care to be that kind of Christian, not if it costs us time or involvement—or money.

"Besides," we say, "it isn't natural to want to give away something you have worked hard to earn. Neither is it convenient for me to give up my time and change my schedule to meet someone else's need. The giving life may be for some Christians, but I'm not temperamentally gifted in that direction!"

What if the Apostle Paul had been that kind of Christian? He would never have left Troas to take the gospel to Macedonia. He would never have suffered the hardships and rigors of pouring out his life for Jesus. And the world would have been robbed of his life and testimony. If Paul had been an "apostle of convenience," he could never have shaken the Roman world for Christ or dared to rattle his chains in the governor's court. "Let someone else give his life for the Master!" he could have said.

Or what if God had not been a giving God? The scripture would read differently: "God so loved . . . " that he insisted Jesus stay on in heaven with him, so they could enjoy each other's fellowship. "Let those poor earth creatures grope their own way in the dark," he could have said.

Or the Bible could have read: "The Lord loves a stingy giver." After all, wisdom is first cousin to the prudent, the cautious, the shrewd, the frugal. My hard-earned money wasn't earned to be given away to the shiftless or to the so-called unfortunate, who probably brought poverty on themselves. "The Lord loves a frugal giver!" Let someone else be prodigal with his or her money! I believe God wants us Christians to save our money, not give it away!

Besides, we might argue, it isn't natural to give. When we were children, our parents had to teach us to share, to "give to Billy half of our cookie." Keeping is a natural instinct. Even the animals hoard their food and protect what is theirs.

There is a passage in Scripture that speaks to this attitude of keeping. Paul wrote to the Corinthian Christians: "The one who sows sparingly will also reap sparingly, and the one who sows bountifully will also reap bountifully. Each of you must give as you have made up your mind, not reluctantly or under compulsion, for

God loves a cheerful giver" (II Cor. 9:6-7). God loves the person whose heart is in the gift!

Here is the crux of the matter: Giving is an affair of the heart. If a person's heart is right with God, the person's life will be right. "Those who have been born of God do not sin" (I John 3:9). If a person's heart is right with God, his or her love offerings will be right. God loves a cheerful, willing giver. Moreover, according to Paul, our very giving proves the reality of our faith.

But how do we get our hearts right in the matter of giving? Given that we want to be authentic Christians, how can we become authentic Christian stewards? Let me give you four practical suggestions:

First, acknowledge that *God—not people—is owner of all things.* The cattle are his. The gold is his. "The earth is the LORD's and all that is in it" (Ps. 24:1). Everything is his. We are his!

Now, here is where the problem starts. God created cattle, we reason, so they are his by creation. Gold—well, it was part of the world God made, but it is really only valuable in relation to persons. Some may say, "God may own the earth and the cattle—maybe even the gold—but he doesn't own me." If God created me free to choose my own destiny and determine my own life, then I own me, God doesn't!

Now we reach the second step in how to become an authentic Christian steward: Not only does God own the earth, but he also has the *right to own us.* We are his by creation, and, if we are Christians, we are his by redemption. In Genesis we read that God created us in his own image. That means we are created with a capacity for fellowship with our Creator—a privilege none of the rest of his creation can enjoy. "However," we reason again, "because we are created with the freedom to choose, we can reject God." But the Bible says: "You were bought with a price" (I Cor. 7:23). We are "blood bought." Our redemption cost God the death of his only begotten Son. So if God is to own us as he does the cattle and the gold, we must choose to let him. God does not force his Lordship on us; we can choose to make him Lord—or not. The choice is ours. But the sacrifice was his, and, by Christ's death on the cross, love compels us to surrender.

The fundamental lesson for the Christian steward is to understand that *stewardship is basic to our Christian life and growth.* Sharing is as important as praying. The same Bible that tells us that we ought always to pray also tells us that "just as you did it to one of the least of these who are members of my family, you did it to me" (Matt. 25:40). Giving is as important as going. The same Bible that tells us that by grace we are saved also tells us to make sure that we abound in that grace also. That's the grace of growing in generosity. Growing is as important as going. To live is to give; to withhold is to die. Christian stewardship is much more than giving money. Money alone never made anyone rich. Jesus was more concerned about our need to give than he was with the amount we give. The widow's mite was small in amount, but large in sacrifice. She gave all she had. That's grace giving. When we love God that much, we are willing to give like that. If our heavenly Father owns it all (and he does), as loving children, we gladly offer back to him what he has let us keep for him.

The fourth step in becoming an authentic Christian steward is to let giving become *an act of will.* Knowing about giving is not enough. If we are to receive the blessings of giving, we must first decide that: (1) God owns everything, even us; (2) God's primary concern is not to raise money, but to see us grow as his children; and (3) God does not require us to give. He asks us to give because the spreading of the gospel needs our support, because by giving we grow spiritually, because the love of Christ constrains us to give. We must decide that we will give worthily! That decision is an act of our wills, not of our emotions.

The fact that God has a plan for growing stewards indicates how important he thinks it is for every Christian to become an authentic Christian steward. At first he required that his people give a tithe. Tithing was a discipline for the Israelites. It set a minimum standard for them to follow in bringing an offering as part of their worship. Later, Jesus taught his disciples proportionate, or percentage, giving. We are to give out of love for Christ, as God has prospered us.

So to summarize:

1. God wants all Christians to be authentic Christian stewards—"Trustees" of that which we do not own, but have been entrusted to use.
2. If you have made Christ Lord of your life, you will make him Lord of your possessions as well as your person.
3. Being a good steward is basic to Christian life and growth.

4. We do not become authentic Christian stewards by a process of learning, but by an act of our will. You do not "hope" to become generous; you choose to be!

The challenge of the Lord to each of us, then, is to choose to honor God with our substance, to make him Lord of our family treasury, to begin now, today, to give God gifts that are worthy of his love, and gifts that will grow our souls as they undergird the spreading of his gospel to the ends of the earth. "There is great gain in godliness combined with contentment" (I Tim. 6:6).

Suggestions for Worship:

Call to Worship (I Tim. 6:6-9, paraphrased):

MINISTER: Whoever is wise, let him heed these things,

PEOPLE: And consider the great love of the LORD.

MINISTER: Godliness with contentment is great gain.

PEOPLE: We hope in God, who richly provides all our needs.

Act of Praise: Psalm 107:1, 33-43.

Suggested Hymns: opening hymn: "Holy, Holy, Holy! Lord God Almighty"; second hymn: "Take Our Bread"; closing hymn: "Alas! and Did My Savior Bleed."

Opening Prayer: O God, you have created us in love and saved us in mercy. You have willed that we gather together as a community of faith and as Christ's body, the Church. Now shower us with your blessings, we pray. Make us responsive to the needs of this world and witnesses for Christ in all we say and do. Amen.

Pastoral Prayer: Eternal God, we who live for just a short time turn again toward you. You know how we have sought the fulfillment of our ambitions in the world. Now we bring them to you in this sacred meeting. Let your sanctuary be our courtroom and the eternal hills our jury. Bring all of our ambitions to trial before you, O sovereign Lord. We would see and test them in the light of your countenance.

Let every unworthy and selfish ambition, all covetousness and greed, all pride and false security be arraigned before your righteousness. Let everything within us be tested by the fire of your love and the might and right of your justice. Then, by the cleansing power of your grace, sift and purify every desire, that we may hunger and thirst for you and so be satisfied. Amen.

OCTOBER 4, 1992

□

Seventeenth Sunday After Pentecost

Neither your faith nor your faithful obedience can establish credits for eternity. The creature cannot obligate the creator. The next step is obedience.

The Sunday Lessons

Amos 5:6-7, 10-15: Announcing judgment (vv. 1-3), Amos interrupts his forecast of doom to speak gracious words of hope. The prophet holds out the possibility that God will be gracious to the remnant.

II Timothy 1:1-14: Paul encouraged his younger colleague, Timothy, to "rekindle the gift of God that is within you through the laying on of my hands" (v. 6). Paul said of his own faith, "I know the one in whom I have put my trust, and I am sure that he is able" (v. 12).

Luke 17:5-10: Faith the size of a mustard seed and the parable of the servant who was only dutiful seem unrelated at first glance. The two parables teach that neither faith nor obedience places the Lord God under any obligation. Our relationship to God and our neighbor is seen not as justice (getting what we rightly deserve), but as mercy. The next step is dutiful service.

Interpretation and Imagination

Sunday after Sunday, from Advent to Advent, year after year, and sometimes twice in the same service of worship we pray the prayers of confession. Our need for forgiveness rises not from the wrong we occasionally do, but from the very center of our beings. Our problem, then, in the pilgrimage of faith, is not how to make amends for the wrong we have done, but what to do about our inevitable sin and disobedience.

One of the characters in T. S. Eliot's *The Cocktail Party* says,

"Your business is not to clear your conscience, but to learn how to bear the burdens of your conscience."

Jesus told his disciples, "Occasions for stumbling are bound to come" (Luke 17:1), and he taught them to forgive even one who "sins against you seven times a day" (Luke 17:4). Only faith like that of a mustard seed—blown away, scattered, buried beneath parched ground, and chilled by winter storms—can express the steadfast mercy that prompts new life. Work's righteousness finds no support in these lessons. Jesus calls even a servant who is completely faithful to duty "unworthy."

Roman Catholicism, in its teaching on works of supererogation, suggests that salvation has minimal spiritual and ethical requirements. Good deeds beyond these requirements accumulate merit. In this text no minimum duty exists.

TABLE DUTY

Luke 17:7

A SERMON BY PETER D. WEAVER

(*The first Sunday of October brings the wonderful opportunity to share in World Communion Sunday. The following offering of the Word is set in that context of receiving the Sacrament. Read Luke 17:5-10.*)

What have we done in the world that makes us think we deserve to come to this table? Plenty, or at least so we think.

New ground is being plowed somewhere this week because we have bowed heads in prayers and raised money in offerings to provide farming tools in El Salvador or Zimbabwe. Wide-eyed children will eat, and grandmothers will smile because we've been there, or at least we've helped send some people there, to work. Now we're ready to hear: "Come here at once and take your place at the table" (Luke 17:7). It's World Communion Sunday.

Also, think of all the church meetings we've plowed through! We've changed the contour of some ecclesiastical landscapes in these meetings. That can be tough work, and now we're ready to hear: "Come here at once and take your place at the table."

And then there are the sheep. Like Jesus, we want to reach the lost ones. Wandering alone in the concrete wilderness of some city, a homeless person has been found this weekend and welcomed into the fold of Christian hospitality and shelter. Some great things are happening out in the world in which we have had a part as the servants of God, and now we're ready to hear: "Come here at once and take your place at the table." It's World Communion Sunday.

And when it comes to preparing supper, everyone knows our church is the best. We've raised money for world mission, done the food baskets for the needy, and collected canned goods. Now we've come from the kitchen to the sanctuary, and we're ready to hear: "Come here at once and take your place at the table."

God must be very grateful to those of us who have been working and serving in so many different ways. Now we're ready to hear: "Come here at once and take your place at the table."

But then Jesus stops us short with his troubling question, "Who among you would say to your slave who has just come in from plowing or tending sheep in the field, 'Come here at once and take you place at the table'? . . . Do you thank the slave for doing what was commanded?" (Luke 17:7, 9). Does your boss thank you for doing what is in your job description? When the waiter comes with your food, how many times do you invite him to "come at once" and sit down with you? He has only done his duty.

And what about our duty as God's servants in the world? With all of our plowing, shepherding, and supper preparing, there are still expansive regions of physical and spiritual poverty in our world.

Amos, you were so right. Your words are ancient, but the call is fresh. The poor are still trampled (Amos 5:11). We are still working to "hate evil and love good, and establish justice in the gate" (Amos 5:15). Children beg in Calcutta. Youth sell their bodies on the streets of New York. Mothers and fathers build shanties on the smoking mountains of garbage in Manila. Our work is certainly not complete, nor is our duty done—and we expect to come to the table?

The phone rang, and the pastor, seated in his comfortable office chair, pushed one of the many buttons provided by the latest phone technology. On the line was another pastor who had been working with a neurosurgeon at the university hospital to help Carlos. The doctor had helped Carlos come to a hospital in the United States from Managua, Nicaragua, because Carlos had a very complex brain condition that could not be treated in his home country. Carlos, at thirty-eight and with six children, faced a very uncertain future. Only a few days of tests at the hospital led to the conclusion that surgery would be far too dangerous and that Carlos would have to return to Managua. Because of his condition, he would no longer be able to work. His income had been about $100 a month. Juanita, his eighteen-year-old daughter, was already working during the day and trying to complete high school at night in order to help support the family. Carlos, who attended a small evangelical church near his home, was sure that "Jehovah would provide." Would it be possible, the pastor on the phone asked, for several churches to receive a special offering in order to send Carlos home with the equivalent of six-months' salary, $600?

On Sunday morning, just before the offering, the pastor told the congregation about Carlos and asked for their help. "Put an additional offering, if you can, in a pew envelope to help us raise six-months' salary, $600, for Carlos and his family." Some thought that maybe $200 would be contributed on such short notice, but when the offering was counted, over $600, more than enough, had been given. Wouldn't Carlos and God be grateful! Carlos was, but I'm not so sure about God.

Wasn't that congregation only doing what God would expect of any of us? Its duty? And even at that, when we consider that the average income in that congregation was many times that of Carlos's and that the congregation members drove to church in at least a million dollars worth of automobiles and were dressed in thousands of dollars worth of fine clothes and had combined bank accounts worth hundreds of thousands of dollars, what is so great about $600? Might it be more appropriate to confess: "We are unworthy servants; we have only done what was our duty"? We do not receive an invitation to come at once to the table because of the work we have done in this world.

So how is it that we dare come to this table if trying to follow God's commands and to do our duty are not the key?

The invitation to come to this table arises out of what precedes our work in the Christian life: faith. As surely as the mustard seed precedes the productive plant, so faith comes before our commitment to productive duty. While our works will never be perfect enough or large enough to guarantee us a place at this table, even the smallest seed of faith in the grace and love of Christ is enough to uproot us from our sin and unworthiness and plant us in the "wideness in God's mercy, like the wideness of the sea." By faith we are swept up in that grace and love and carried to this table. Christ calls us to "come at once" to the table, not because we have plowed or shared food or given $600 or done our duty, but because he loves us just as we are, with our tiny faith and unworthy works. Come!

In his poem "The Death of the Hired Man," Robert Frost introduces us to Silas, who plows and digs in the fields for Warren. When old and weary, Silas shows up at the house, and Warren is reluctant to welcome him in. After all "off he goes always when I need him most." Warren, concerned with commands and duties done, is not interested in having Silas at his table. But Warren's wife, Mary, invites the hired man in and gives him tea and a place for dying, because he has had faith in them and has come "home," "something you somehow haven't to deserve."

This table is not a deserved reward for duties done. Indeed, we confess that, like Silas, what help we are in God's work, "there's no depending on." But it is by faith in Christ that we come back home to this table. And Christ welcomes us because this is "something you somehow haven't to deserve."

So what have we been doing out in the world that makes us think we deserve to come to this table? Nothing.

Nevertheless, come at once to the table. In the words of a traditional Communion invitation, "Draw near with faith, and take this Holy Sacrament to your comfort" (A Service of Word and Table IV, *The United Methodist Hymnal*).

Suggestions for Worship:

Call to Worship:

MINISTER: We will sing of your love and justice, O God.

PEOPLE: To you, O LORD, we will sing praise.

MINISTER: Count us among the faithful in the land,

PEOPLE: For we would silence the clamor of wickedness among us.

Act of Praise: Psalm 101.

Suggested Hymns: opening hymn: "When We All Get to Heaven"; second hymn: "Dear Lord and Father of Mankind"; closing hymn: "Grace Greater than Our Sin."

Opening Prayer: Almighty God, you have called us to faith and have surrounded us with a great cloud of witnesses. You have encouraged us by the good examples of your saints. You have provided the way through the life and death of your only Son, our Savior. Through his broken body and shed blood you have gathered us at table. Grant to us, we pray, the saving mercies of Christ, that we may at last inherit your eternal joy through Jesus Christ our Lord. Amen.

Pastoral Prayer: O God of bread and wine and tables everywhere, draw us together around your table today. Grant us the vision to see at this table our neighbors around the corner and around the world. Open our ears that we may hear in new accents the varieties of language, words and images used to express your love for all of us. Quicken our taste that in the texture of bread and the flow of wine we may sense your goodness through the common things of life. Liberate our tongues that we may sing your praises, speak your truth and give voice to your good news in ways that will nourish our world. Prepare our hands to receive this sacrament and then to reach out in sacramental love to our world.

As the gracious Host who calls the world to your banquet, give us open, welcoming spirits in order to embrace those who are lonely or doubting or different. May we be sensitive to the needs of those who cannot be, or choose not to be, at your table this day. We lift them now in prayer. (*silence*).

With sisters and brothers gathered about this table from Brazil and Britain, China and Chad, Italy and Iceland, the United States and the Soviet Union, we offer our prayer in the name of Christ, who is the bread that satisfies us and the vine that links us. Amen.

OCTOBER 11, 1992

□

Eighteenth Sunday After Pentecost

Those who know that they have no right to expect anything are the ones most grateful for life and blessings.

The Sunday Lessons

Micah 1:2; 2:1-10: The Lord will be both judge and witness against Samaria and Jerusalem. The people's evil, oppressive ways, described by Micah, will lead to ruin.

II Timothy 2:8-15: Paul, wearing prison chains, wrote, "But the word of God is not chained" (v. 9). Exhorting Timothy to faithfulness, the Apostle recalled an early Christian hymn (vv. 11-13) that one can trust. "If we are faithless, he remains faithful" (v. 13).

Luke 17:11-19: Jesus healed ten lepers. One gave thanks, and he was a Samaritan. The outsider among the outcasts was the only one who returned to express gratitude.

Interpretation and Imagination

Two virtues are essential for the person who wants healing and wholeness. The first is humility, a willingness to be changed. The second is faith, confidence that one need not stay the way he or she is. Commenting on this lesson, Bishop William R. Cannon wrote, "Gratitude is akin to humility and faith. It, too, is a necessary virtue."

In Russian Orthodoxy, a common religious practice is going on a pilgrimage. Seeking a deeper life with God, pilgrims leave home and family and reduce their daily needs to those that may be met through incidental jobs or acts of kindness toward others. An anonymous man wrote of his wandering and self-emptying journey. He always sought the lowest place, following the example of Christ. His writings, *The Way of a Pilgrim*, have become a spiritual classic.

In one home where this Pilgrim was a guest, he read to his hosts from Peter of Damascus.

The Apostle says, "Pray without ceasing." That is, he teaches men to have the remembrance of God in all times and places and circumstances. If you are making something, you must call to mind the Creator of all things; if you see the light, remember the Giver of it . . . If you put on your clothes, recall whose gift they are and thank Him who provides for your life. In short let every action be a cause of your remembering and praising God, and Lo! you will be praying without ceasing and therein your soul will always rejoice (*The Way of the Pilgrim*, p. 86).

STONE WALLS DO NOT A PRISON MAKE

II Timothy 2:8-15

A SERMON BY PETER D. WEAVER

"I am exposed to hardship, even to the point of being fettered like a criminal; but the word of God is not shut fettered." (II Tim. 2:9 REB)

Have you ever been in prison? The iron doors slam behind you with convincing authority, sending a shudder through your soul. Foul smells and ugly sounds assault your senses. The food is terrible, the company worse. And these are only the reactions of a prison visitor, who knows he or she will soon leave.

The faces in prison are fascinating. Some are hard and expressionless; others smile and seem at peace. These are faces not unlike our own faces. Although very few of us, if any, have been incarcerated behind prison walls, most of us know what it is to feel imprisoned. The chains that bind us are not generally iron links, but rather links of despair and fear and prejudice that confine us and keep us from growing freely into the persons God would have us to be.

We may feel imprisoned by guilt. Things we have done, said, or been stack up like heavy boulders to create the imprisoning walls of guilt. We have not been found guilty by any court other than our own heart and conscience. We know that we have been faithless. While we may "plead the Fifth" when we get to church, the ironclad moralizing we often indulge in creates the bars that cage us even more firmly in our guilt. We are imprisoned.

Sometimes we are imprisoned in fear about the future. What will I do with my life? What happens after retirement or graduation or when the children leave home? What kind of future does this deteriorating relationship have? We may feel unable to break out into the new future God is opening. We may be utterly afraid to leave the security of the present, even though it may be extremely confining. We are in our own prison.

Paul was apparently in prison among the sounds and smells and slamming doors as he wrote the second letter to Timothy. There was nothing pleasant about it. "I am exposed to hardship," Paul wrote, "even to the point of being fettered like a criminal." Yet, see his face behind those bars. Sense the assurance, confidence, and liberation of spirit: "The word of God is not fettered!" Even in that first-century prison, Paul had an extraordinary sense of freedom.

The irony, of course, is that Paul the prisoner was probably the freest person there as he preached and lived the unfettered word of God. On the other hand, so many of us who are outwardly free live imprisoned in our fear and guilt.

Richard Lovelace, a seventeenth-century English poet and a deeply dedicated follower of Christ, was locked in the Gatehouse Prison at Westminster because of his religious beliefs. At the age of twenty-four, he wrote the poem "To Althea, from Prison." You may remember his well-known lines:

> Stone walls do not a prison make,
> Nor iron bars a cage;
> Minds innocent and quiet take
> That for an hermitage;
> If I have freedom in my love
> And in my soul am free,
> Angels alone, that soar above,
> Enjoy such liberty.

Freedom is finally a matter of the soul, not of the body. Whether it was Paul in chains writing to Timothy, or Lovelace writing to Althea from prison, or Bonhoeffer writing from a concentration camp, or Martin Luther King, Jr., writing a "Letter from Birmingham Jail," the word of God made them free.

How do we experience this freeing of our imprisoned spirits? In

II Timothy 2:8-15, Paul suggests two edges to the key to our freedom: remembering and trusting.

"Remember the theme of my gospel: Jesus Christ, risen from the dead" (II Tim. 2:8 REB). This edge of the key faces the past. There is powerful liberation from the boundaries of present circumstances through remembering. The prisoner of war survives the cruelty of his or her captors by remembering home. The hostage maintains freedom of spirit by remembering passages of Scripture.

"Remembrance is a form of meeting," wrote Kahlil Gibran. As Christians, we remember Sunday after Sunday, day after day, that Christ is risen, and we meet him again in resurrection. Christ died and arose to set us free from our guilt. Stones begin to roll away, and iron bars swing open, the dawning of liberated life awaits us. Remember Jesus Christ!

In the Gospel lesson from Luke, there was one who remembered Jesus—and this remembrance produced a time of meeting again. Already released from the chain of leprosy, which was sometimes associated with the guilt of sin in that day, the leper received Jesus' invitation to freedom: "Stand up and go on your way" (Luke 17:19 REB).

Down in the "pit" of a century-old urban county jail the prisoners were crowded onto the wooden benches for worship. At the end of the service the preacher asked if anyone had a testimony to share. Near the back a young man, who some might ostracize as a twentieth-century leper, moved down to the front. In the midst of the foul smells and ugly sounds and slamming cell doors, he faced and retraced his past of crimes and guilt. Then he spoke of Jesus. Remembering Christ's love and forgiveness and renewal, he said, "I want to tell you I'm free today!" "Amen." "Amen." "Amen," echoed around the pit. Quietly, almost imperceptibly, he began to sing:

> Why should I feel discouraged,
> Why should the shadows come,
> Why should my heart be lonely
> And long for Heav'n and home,
> When Jesus is my portion?
> My constant Friend is He:
> His eye is on the sparrow,

And I know He watches me. . . .
I sing because I'm happy,
I sing because I'm free,
For His eye is on the sparrow,
And I know He watches me.

He remembered his mother singing it, and in doing so he remembered Jesus. In that moment of feeling imprisoned in guilt he met again the One who sets us free to sing! When we are imprisoned in our guilt, we need to remember and meet Christ again.

Trust is the other edge of the key. Trust faces the future and promises liberation from our fear of what is yet to come.

Here is a saying you may trust:
If we died with him, we shall live
with him;
if we endure, we shall reign with him."
(II Tim. 2:11-12 REB)

What of the future? You can trust it; we shall live; we shall reign. What a release for the future comes with the ability to trust.

A parent playfully lifts his or her child high into the air, and the child giggles with delight, unafraid of what the next moment will bring, for the child trusts the parent. An infirm adult rests back into the pillow of the nursing home bed, trusting God to see her or him through. A middle-aged executive decides to enter seminary and pursue ordained ministry because she or he trusts God's call. And there is freedom and adventure in trusting God, who goes with us beyond the stone walls that would otherwise limit us and the future.

Christopher Columbus faced the future trusting. When we remember that Columbus came into a world totally unknown to him and his European kin, we marvel at his daring, which opened a dramatic new future for the world. George Santayana mused poetically in "O World, Thou Choosest Not":

Columbus found a world, and had no chart,
Save one that faith deciphered in the skies;
To trust the soul's invincible surmise
Was all his science and his only art.

The faith and trust that freely propelled his journey beyond the confines of Europe and the past was rooted in Christ. He trusted in the destiny of his name, Christ-bearer. Thus, remembering Christ and trusting in him, Columbus did not fear the future. His uniqueness was not in the belief that land could be reached by sailing west, for Aristotle had suggested that nearly three centuries before Christ. Columbus, however, trusted these beliefs enough to want to test them out. Even in the face of repeated disappointments, he was not imprisoned by the past, but free to risk the future.

His trust in God helped Columbus, like Paul, to endure it all (see II Tim. 2:10). Through the harrowing journey and his sailors' lack of faith, which resulted finally in mutiny, Columbus's liberated spirit continued to trust and to endure. Two days following the attempted mutiny, the sailors spotted land. It was a new world and a new future.

By 1500 Columbus's fortunes had changed, and he was imprisoned and sent back to Spain in chains. In spite of leg irons and neglect, his trust in God kept him freely open to the future, even at the end. "'Lord, into thy hands I commend my spirit,' were the words of Columbus," wrote the noted historian George Bancroft, "as on Ascension Day, 1506, he breathed his last. His great discovery was the triumph of free mind" (*History of the United States*).

What imprisons you and limits your freedom to be the person God wants you to be? Stone walls do not a prison make! Guilt and fear of the future are among the more devastating chains that bind us. But we, like Paul, are people of God's Word, which can never be fettered. Remember Jesus Christ. Trust.

Suggestions for Worship

Call to Worship (Ps. 27:2-3):

MINISTER: Prove, O LORD, and try me;

PEOPLE: test my heart and mind.

MINISTER: For your steadfast love is before my eyes,

PEOPLE: and I walk in faithfulness to you.

Act of Praise: Psalm 26.

Suggested Hymns: opening hymn: "Sing Praise to God Who Reigns Above"; second hymn: "Leave It There"; closing hymn: "And Are We Yet Alive."

Opening Prayer: O God of all the adventures of life, as we enter into this worship, liberate us from all that binds us so that we may journey with you into new worlds of the spirit. Open us now as our worship opens. Place in our hands the key that will set us free. Amen.

Pastoral Prayer: God of all time and space, who brought creation out of chaos and has filled darkness with light, we celebrate your presence in this time and place. Out of the sometimes chaotic pieces of our existence, we pray that you will shape new creations of purpose and commitment in our living. Where darkness threatens to overwhelm us, grant us your light for our way.

We thank you, God, that you are not aloof and removed from the circumstances of our lives. You feel our pain with us. You know the decisions we face. You see our brokenness and hear the cries of all your children. May we dare to walk as closely with you as you do with us. Abide in our homes, arrive at our work place, accompany our travels, be present in this church, that all we say and do and are may reflect your will and love.

Even as we are more and more aware of your presence here and now, we pray that our sisters and brothers in all places may experience your love, which is always available and unlimited. May we be as generous in the expressions of love with one another as you have been with us. We pray in the name of Jesus, in whose light and love we flourish. Amen.

October 18, 1992

□

Nineteenth Sunday After Pentecost

Sometimes it seems that God neither hears nor acts. Stubborn, persistent faith is a Christian virtue.

The Sunday Lessons

Habakkuk 1:1-3; 2:1-4: This passage is a dialogue between the prophet and God. Habakkuk asked, "How long shall I cry for help, and you will not listen?" (1:2). The Lord answered, "If it seems to tarry, wait for it; . . . the righteous live by their faith" (2:3-4).

II Timothy 3:14–4:5: Paul encouraged Timothy to be faithful to Scripture. All too soon, people wanting to hear what they like to hear will find teachers that satisfy their "itching ears." The Apostle urged Timothy to "always be sober, endure suffering . . . carry out your ministry fully" (4:5).

Luke 18:1-8: The parable of the unjust judge and the persistent widow teaches disciples to "always pray and not lose heart." The question behind the story is whether God hears and acts. Is God faithful and responsive? Yes! God is faithful. When Jesus returns, will he find faith on earth?

Interpretation and Imagination

A woman whose prayers were unanswered and whose cries for help seemed unheard grew discouraged. "If God doesn't hear, and God doesn't act, what's the purpose of faith?" she asked. Then she began to question her image of God. "Is God all powerful? Does God love us? If he is love, he must not have power. If he has power, he must not have love," she reasoned. A god of love and power would surely respond.

Jesus faced persons who had grown weary in praying and who

wondered whether God was indeed faithful to his people. He did not discuss the ways of God, nor did he rebuke the questions. Instead he spoke of the ways of men and women—the ways of prayer. He likened God to an unjust judge who was unconcerned about being either fair or dependable. Yet, the poor widow was vindicated.

The parable's central message is simply this: Never give up; continue in prayer. Be persistent in matters of faith. It is often said that God knows what we need before we ask and that he is more willing to give than we are to receive. The implication is "Don't beg!"

In this parable, Jesus teaches that we are to persist in prayer. If we are aware of our need and are serious about God's ability to help, our constant prayers will demonstrate it.

PREVAILING PRAYER REWARD?

Luke 18:7

A SERMON BY MILFORD OXENDINE, JR.

And will not God grant justice to his chosen ones who cry to him day and night? Will he delay long in helping them? (Luke 18:7)

The lectionary readings for today and next Sunday share two parables on prayer. Luke 18:1-8 is the parable about the widow who is persistent as she prevails constantly upon the unrighteous judge, who finally yields to her request. Luke 18:9-14 informs us about the sinful pride of prayer—I should say the proper attitude versus the improper attitude of prayer. Thus the emphasis today and next Sunday is on prayer.

To set the theme for today's sermon, let me share with you the following story.

Jules Verne, the pioneer of science fiction, completed his first novel when he was twenty-five. He offered the manuscript to fourteen publishers, all of whom rejected it. Finally, the fifteenth, a publisher named Hetzel, took the manuscript in order to read it. Ten days later Hetzel not only agreed to publish the novel but offered Verne a contract for twenty years for a book each year. The ability to prevail is one of the astonishing resources of life. (See

Glendon E. Harris, "Prevailing Wins," *Pulpit Resource* 2, 4 [1983]: 11.)

In the parable reading today, one finds a widow constantly wearing out her welcome as she tries to overcome the justice of an unjust judge. Notice through her constant and prevailing approach how the window receives what she needed and deserved.

Luke 18:1-8 is closely related to the parable of the friend at midnight (Luke 11:5-13). Both teach the necessity of being patient and persistent, and of preserving prayer. An argument is founded on the complete and infinite contrast between God and persons. Also, there is evidence that God yields to a Christian's argument and persuasion. Further, there is the same influence that God never fails us as friends quite often do. Both parables state that God will avenge the wrongs of the unjust. But as the just await deliverance and the unjust get weary, prevailing prayer will be the just's refuge and resource for patience. Remember, God will answer those prayers offered in accordance with his own will.

In his book *The Gospel of Luke,* William Barclay states these facts about the judge: He was not a Jewish judge; instead, the judge was a paid magistrate who had been appointed by Herod or by the Roman government. His character was that of a bad, notorious beast. He was a godless man who cared only for himself. Also, he was shamelessly corrupt. Herbert Lockyer, in his *All the Parables of the Bible*, agrees with Barclay's characterization of the judge, stating that he was callous and dead to pity. He was hardhearted, a man of no principle. He would even accept a bribe.

On the other hand, the widow was poor and defenseless. She had no influence and money to bribe the unjust judge, which he would have gladly accepted, so she was helpless. She had been wronged, and she was an object of pity. The scripture does not tell us whether she had committed a crime or what was the reason for her urgency in constantly coming to plead her case to the judge. Therefore, we can only say that she needed simple justice in the matter of her adversary. It appeared that her case would never be settled. So the only thing she could do was to exhaust or to weary the judge. The words *exhaust* and *weary* connote physical, bodily damage; therefore, the judge, after the widow's persistent bothering of him, feared that she would give him "a pair of black eyes" if he didn't do something soon (Lockyer, *All the Parables of the Bible* [Grand Rapids: Zondervan, 1963], p. 300). So the judge, after coming to see himself as Christ saw him, vindicates the widow. Thus her persistence won the day; her persistence prevailed. In the end, she received from the reluctant judge the justice she sought and demanded.

The message Jesus was attempting to relay in the parable is quite simple. He was saying, "If, in the end, an unjust and rapacious judge can be wearied into giving a widow woman justice, how much more will God, who is a loving Father, give his children what they need?" (Barclay, *The Gospel of Luke* [Philadelphia: The Westminster Press, 1975], p. 222).

Yes, it is true. However, it is no reason why we should expect to receive whatever we pray for. A parent may have to deny the request of a child because the parent has a strong feeling that what the child has asked for will hurt the child much more than it will help. God is like that, too. As humans we do not know what may happen to us in the next minute, let alone the next hour, week, month, or year. Only God sees time whole. Thus only God has the insight to determine what is good for us in the long run. This is the reason why Jesus reminds us that we should never get discouraged by praying. We should never grow weary or exhausted in praying.

The twentieth century has provided us many studies in human tenacity. Wilbur Wright prevailed over air when he finally flew in a plane at Kitty Hawk, North Carolina, on December 17, 1903; Sir Francis Chichester prevailed over the sea when he alone sailed the sailboat "Gypsy Moth" around the world; Admiral Richard E. Byrd prevailed over frozen nature when he spent a long, lonely winter at Antarctica; and Edmund Hillary prevailed over the highest point on earth when he climbed Mt. Everest.

We cheer and applaud these triumphs, but we also should give the same due to the spiritual conquerors of history: Abraham, who prevailed in a foreign land; David, who prevailed against Goliath; Paul, who prevailed over the forces that arrayed themselves against his monumental work of establishing the church; Augustine, who prevailed over the sensuous nature of his own body; Martin Luther, who prevailed against the evils that had infested the church; and the minorities around the world who are gradually prevailing against the injustice thrown against them.

Today we still fight to prevail against such bedevilments as nuclear destruction and other hazards and fears that call up the human spirit to entrench, defend, and ultimately overcome.

The widow did not prevail because of her elaborate or eloquent plea. She used only five words: "Vindicate me against my adversary." Her cry for help was short and straight to the point. At no time was the subject of her widowhood, family, or divine judgment against an unjust judge mentioned. All she wanted was one important thing—justice for her adversary. And this she received.

Does God answer unwearied or prevailing prayers? Yes, he does. God has assured you and me that he hears and answers prayer. Therefore, this should convince and entice us to continue asking; to have confidence that if we ask, believing, we will receive. Remember that Scripture declares: "Ask, and it will be given you; search, and you will find; knock, and the door will be opened for you" (Luke 11:9). There lies the secret of a reward: One must prevail.

Suggestions for Worship

Call to Worship (Ps. 119:142-44):

MINISTER: Your righteousness is an everlasting righteousness,

PEOPLE: and your law is the truth.

MINISTER: Trouble and anguish have come upon me,

PEOPLE: but your commandments are my delight.

MINISTER: Your decrees are righteous forever;

PEOPLE: give me understanding that I may live.

Act of Praise: Psalm 119:137-44.

Suggested Hymns: opening hymn: "Come, Thou Fount of Every Blessing"; second hymn: "My Hope Is Built"; closing hymn: "Near to the Heart of God."

Opening Prayer: Lord, we come to you with a sense of continual personal need. Sometimes there is an unfailing desire in our hearts to receive what you see that we need. Often we have an unshaken faith that you have what we need in your promises. We still understand that though you withhold for a while, you love to be asked and asked again. Grant us a firm belief that if we ask believing, we shall receive. Amen.

Pastoral Prayer: Almighty God, you spoke through your Son, Jesus Christ, the words "people ought always to pray." Just as the widow cried day and night to the unjust judge, may we who labor under injustice and oppression offer our prayers to you. If a mere selfish feeling prevailed with the bad judge, we are made certain that you will give good gifts to those who ask. If the importunity and perseverance of the widow at last prevailed, how much more will these virtues prevail with you? If we are on the right terms with you, then we know you will avenge and answer us. We expect better treatment from you, a God of love, than that from a heartless judge. As we ask, we believe you will act. When you withhold the help for which we plead, continue to send your wisdom and love as we wait with patient hearts. Our solemn charge, in spite of avowed opposition and trails, is to keep the faith. Amen.

October 25, 1992

□

Twentieth Sunday After Pentecost

To be so self-satisfied before God that one seeks no blessing and asks for no mercy is to stand before God unwilling to ask and unable to receive.

The Sunday Lessons

Zephaniah 3:1-9: Jerusalem would not accept correction. The officials, judges, prophets, and priests were all corrupt. The prophet declared that judgment and reform would follow.

II Timothy 4:6-8, 16-18: Contemplating his death, the Apostle Paul declared boldly, "I have fought the good fight. . . . I have kept the faith" (v. 7). Though he was deserted by all his friends, imprisoned and expecting to die, Paul's message was one of hope and confidence.

Luke 18:9-14: The parable of the Pharisee and the publican contrasts a "righteous" man (one who obeys Jewish laws and ritual observance) with a "sinful" man. The tax collector left the Temple justified, accepted by God. Self-righteous satisfaction and pride are condemned.

Interpretation and Imagination

Pride is the first of the seven deadly sins. One falls into pride when one lacks trust in God and his mercy and becomes arrogant, hypocritical, and self-centered.

Reinhold Niebuhr, who has been referred to as the twentieth-century theologian of sin, summed up humanity's basic sin—our unwillingness to acknowledge our creatureliness, our self-elevation—in one word, *pride.*

Neibuhr described four types of pride:

1. The pride of power wants power to gain security for self or to maintain a power position considered to be secure.
2. Intellectual pride rises from human knowledge that pretends to be ultimate knowledge. It presumes to be final truth.
3. Moral pride claims that its standards for virtue test and measure all righteousness. Niebuhr observed that most evil is done by "good" people who do not know that they are not good.
4. Spiritual pride is self-glorification. It claims that "self's righteousness" conforms to God's righteousness.

A woman, faithful in the attendance of worship, complained about the ways in which hymns are rituals ask us "to mourn our sins," "acknowledge and bewail our wickedness," and suggest "weeping, grieving, confessing." When she said that she didn't feel that way at all about her sins, her pastor replied, "I have to admit that you seem to be bearing up under this burden with considerable cheerfulness."

THE PRAYER GOD DELIGHTS TO HEAR

Luke 18:13*c*, 14*b*

A SERMON BY MILFORD OXENDINE, JR.

God, be merciful to me, a sinner . . . for all who exalt themselves will be humbled, but all who humble themselves will be exalted." (Luke 18:13*c*, 14*b*).

We are so glad that God, our Father, is a prayer hearing and answering God. By this, we do not mean that God grants every prayer or request that is sent to him. When people pray to God in sincerity, God answers when he is ready—yes, no, not now, wait, or even silence. There is one prayer, however, that God always answers with a resounding yes. It is the prayer offered in humility out of a deep sense of need: "God be merciful to me a sinner." He will never fail to hear and grant that prayer, because our Lord has said: "Anyone who comes to me I will never drive away" (John 6:37*b*). Mercy is what we all need—no, what we must have, or else we will never make it.

In the background of our text, our Lord Jesus Christ painted a word picture of a Pharisee in deep contrast to a publican at prayer. One had an arrogant, "holier than thou" air about him: "Lord, look how good I am." Of sins to confess and spiritual needs, he apparently had more. The Pharisees are still with us today, wanting to boast to us of their supposed goodness, wanting to be seen and heard by others. The Pharisee avoided evil behavior, not extorting, dealing unjustly, or "committing adultery." Oh, he was so much better than the publican. The Pharisee fasted, and he tithed. Yet, he was the type of person that no one could get along with. He took note of other persons' sins, but never considered his own. He was too good to associate with other people. He must have forgotten that there is Adam in all of us—that we are all sinners.

A part of the order of worship in many churches is the call to confession, a short period in which worshipers confess their sins to God. One prayer of general confession has the words of truth that pluck at my heart strings with a strong ring of authenticity:

> Almighty and most merciful God,
> we have erred and strayed from thy ways like lost sheep.
> We have followed too much
> the devices and desires of our own hearts.
> We have offended against thy holy laws.
> We have left undone
> those things which we ought to have done,
> and we have done
> those things which we ought not to have done.
> But thou, O Lord, have mercy upon us.
> Spare thou those, O God, who confess their faults.
> Restore thou those who are penitent,
> according to thy promises declared in Christ Jesus our Lord.
> And grant, O most merciful God, for his sake,
> that we may hereafter live a godly, righteous, and sober life;
> to the glory of thy holy name. Amen.
> (*The United Methodist Hymnal*)

If we are at all honest with ourselves and with God, do not we need to pray this prayer daily in sincerity to God?

In Romans 7, we find Paul's great prayer of confession. How can we read it and fail to see a picture of ourselves? Paul says: "I do not understand what I do; for I don't do what I would like to do, but instead I do what I hate" (7:15 GNB). In verse 21, he says: "I find then a law, that, when I would do good, evil is present with me" (KJV). Then in verses 23-24 we read: "But I see in my members another law at war with the law of my mind, making me captive to the law of sin that dwells in members. Wretched man that I am! Who will rescue me from this body of death?"

Both Paul and the publican had something in common. They offered the prayer God likes to hear—"God be merciful to me a sinner." They, too, realized they were sinners.

To drive this thought further, a sincere prayer must come from the heart as we *exalt*, *abase*, and *humble* ourselves. We are, at best, mere sinners saved by the forgiving grace of God, which is always available, but must be continuously claimed and received. God's Word makes it ever so plain in John 1:12: "To all who received him . . . he gave *power* to become children of God" (italics added). Are we ever without need of this power?

Now, what is sin? What does it mean to be a sinner? It means simply that we fail *to do* and *to be* all that God wants us to do and to be. In the light of this great truth, are we not all sinners? Who among us is all that he or she ought to be or what God wants him or her to be? Who does all that God wants us to do? Listen again to Paul: "The saying is sure and worthy of full acceptance, that Christ Jesus came into the world to save sinners—of whom I am the foremost" (I Tim. 1:15). Why must we be reminded that we are sinners? We must be sincere. We must be realistic and honest, or else what hope is there? How can we be forgiven unless we acknowledge, confess, and repent? There is no other way.

The Pharisee failed at this point. Like too many today, he felt that he was okay; he had no spiritual needs! The Pharisee worshiped himself; self had first place in his life. Too often we think money, position, possessions, reputation, and popularity are what is important. Hence, we fail to be our best selves. We lose our way, and that is what sin is all about. We need to offer our prayers of confession. Despite our utter sinfulness, we know that God loves us, and whenever we pray in confession and repentance, God forgives and receives us.

What the Pharisee needed to hear was this: "So if you think you are standing, watch out that you do not fall" (I Cor. 10:12). Listen to Psalm 138:6:

> For though the LORD is high, he
> regards the lowly;
> but the haughty he perceives
> from far away.

We get a picture of the two men praying in Jesus' parable, one ever so lowly—feeling too lowly and sinful to draw near, too humble and contrite to lift his head toward heaven. He beats his breast and prays what he needs to pray and what God wants to hear and never fails to answer. The publican is a merciful person, but not so the Pharisee.

Being a Christian isn't claiming that one's life is dramatically different from the lives of others. The Christian has the same struggles, problems, headaches, heartaches, tensions, and temptations as others. Being a Christian is resting our very lives and our needs upon the mercy and grace of God and leaving them there. It is believing that God in his mercy and love will accept us as we are.

So, then, we are ever in the process of becoming what God wants us to become. John wrote the glorious good news of the gospel, which is revealed to the publican and to those of like mind, but never to the Pharisee and his counterparts: "Beloved, we are God's children now; what we will be has not yet been revealed. What we do is this: when he is revealed, we will be like him, for we will see him as he is" (I John 3:2).

Serious goodness and true worship must always begin, not with the Pharisee's boast, "Lord, I thank you that I am not as other people," but rather with the publican's prayer—"God, be merciful to me a sinner." Notice that one humbled himself and he was exalted. The other exalted himself, and he was humbled. So shall it ever be!

Suggestions for Worship

Call to Worship (Ps. 3:4-5, 8):

MINISTER: I cry aloud to the LORD,

PEOPLE: and he answers me from his holy hill.

MINISTER: I lie down and sleep; I wake again,

PEOPLE: for the LORD sustains me. . . .

MINISTER: Deliverance belongs to the LORD;

PEOPLE: may your blessing be on your people!

Act of Praise: Psalm 3.

Suggested Hymns: opening hymn: "A Mighty Fortress Is Our God"; second hymn: "I Stand Amazed in the Presence"; closing hymn: "Amazing Grace."

Opening Prayer: O Lord, our God, forgive us, for we have a Pharisee's attitude. We have failed to understand that our religion may be our ruin. The very strictness of life has resulted in perdition, as we have prided ourselves on our religiosity and morality, blinding us to the fact that we are sinners as we stand or bow before the throne of a holy God. Forgive us. Remind us that there is absolutely nothing in ourselves to glory about. Let us pursue and accept divine righteousness by and through faith, through Jesus Christ we plead. Amen.

Pastoral Prayer: O God, let us hear your words of wisdom once more: "Every one that exalteth himself shall be abased; and he that humbleth himself shall be exalted." We, too, ask for the praise of humility. As Jesus placed much emphasis on this virtue and demanded it of his followers, allow us to do the same. Grant us the wisdom to understand that without humility we are counterfeit or below the standard Jesus set for us. Speak and remind us of the virtue "He that humbleth himself shall be exalted." We know that you abominate haughtiness while you ask for humility and reward it with exaltation. Allow us, through your wisdom, to learn that the only way up is down. Amen.

NOVEMBER 1, 1992

□

Twenty-first Sunday After Pentecost (All Saints)

The epistle speaks of retribution—affliction for those who afflict you. The Gospel lesson speaks of restitution—repayment fourfold.

The Sunday Lessons

Haggai 2:1-9: The prophet's message refers to the Temple, still in ruins, (520 B.C.) even though exiles began to return to Jerusalem in 536. Reminding his hearers of God's promises, he proclaimed a further promise of God: "The latter splendor of this house shall be greater than the former" (v. 9).

II Thessalonians 1:5-12: The Thessalonian church was born and grew in the midst of persecution. Paul wrote, "It is indeed just of God to repay with affliction those who afflict you" (v. 6).

Luke 19:1-10: Tax collectors were considered to be traitors. The crowd questioned Jesus' association with Zacchaeus. A changed man, Zacchaeus promised to give to the poor and to repay those he had defrauded.

Interpretation and Imagination

Retribution and punishment are the controlling principles of our courts. We sentence persons to pay fines, to serve jail sentences, or to be put to death. Restitution is sometimes ordered, but seldom possible. A convicted felon, converted in prison, spoke of paying his debt to society. Yet, he could not restore to his victim what he had taken.

When Kenneth Hucks was sentenced to life in prison for slaying a jeweler during a robbery, he said to the jeweler's widow: "I have compassion and remorse for the tragedy of your losing a loved one. If it wasn't for Jesus Christ, I wouldn't have been able to sit here without crying. If it wasn't for his grace and love, I wouldn't feel free."

Nothing can make this man innocent. We cannot make anyone innocent. We may be forgiven, but we are still sinners saved by grace. We know that the grace of Christ, who pardons our sin, is a free gift. If we take it, he will claim all we have and all we are. The late Carlisle Marney taught us that we are called to be responsibly guilty.

For Zacchaeus, conversion meant restoring fourfold. Though not a convicted criminal, he wanted to restore with interest all he had taken through fraud. Such desire certifies his conversion. He was a changed man.

UP A TREE

Luke 19:1-10

A SERMON BY ROBERT L. BALDRIDGE

You've all heard the delightful children's song about a wee little man named Zacchaeus, which retells our Gospel lesson. It happened in Jericho, the "city of palms." This rich oasis, surrounded by desert wasteland, was once a gift from Mark Antony to Cleopatra. Because it had a warmer climate than Jerusalem, King Herod made Jericho the site of his winter capital. After Herod's death, his son Archelaus chose it for the location of a magnificent palace. It was *the* stopping place on the caravan route from the north to the east. It was a noisy, busy, frantic place, filled with travelers and soldiers.

Jericho was the home of Zacchaeus, whose name meant "the pure one" or "the righteous one." But because of his profession, the name didn't fit. Zacchaeus was a tax collector; therefore, he was number one on the Jericho hate list. Robbers, murderers, and tax collectors all were lumped together on the list of those banned from the synagogue. We can understand that. Just how many tax collectors do you know who have fan clubs? Zacchaeus worked as a collaborator for Rome as well. As they felt about all tax collectors, the people believed that he "skimmed off" something for himself every time he made a collection. They were probably right. Zacchaeus was not just a tax collector, but he was a "chief" tax collector. He was rich. The economic strength of Jericho made him wealthy. But money wasn't everything. In his case, it didn't buy happiness.

Zacchaeus must have known how people felt about him. It probably hurt when they called him thief and traitor. He saw the way they acted when he came down the street or entered the room. Their hate was so intense that he had to watch out whenever he left his home or office. Crowds meant added danger. He was nervous. He had to have eyes in the back of his head.

The day that Jesus came to town, there was a huge crowd. Luke says that since Zacchaeus was short and couldn't see over the heads of people, he climbed up into the branches of a sycamore tree. Was he curious? Did he have some longings that he hoped Jesus could fulfill? Did he wonder, "Can Jesus really do the things that I've heard he's done? Can he really open unseeing eyes and make the lame walk? Is he really as good a preacher as they say? Can he really give the gift of new life?" Could there have been some other reasons why Zacchaeus was up a tree, other than the fact that he was short? Remember that the citizens of Jericho hated him. They didn't want to be around him, and he probably didn't want to be around them. He probably hated himself.

Have you ever been "up a tree"? Has there ever been a time when you didn't know which way to turn? Has there ever been a time when you felt abandoned, even by your family and friends? Has there ever been a time when you were positive that nobody loved you? Has there ever been a time when you felt that nobody understood? Has there ever been a time when you felt like a total failure? Has there ever been a time when you felt that you were totally inadequate and couldn't cope with all of the pressure? If you can answer yes to any of these questions, then you know what it's like to be "up a tree."

A story has been told about a little town in the state of Maine that went by the name of Flagstaff. (See Robert E. Luccock, ed., *Halford Luccock Treasury* [Nashville: Abingdon Press, 1963].) Some months before the town was flooded by the large lake created by the new dam, the townspeople stopped making improvements and repairs to their homes. Why paint the house if the area would be covered over by water in six months? Why paint a fence? Why straighten a sagging shutter? Why pick up any litter? Why cut the grass? Why do anything when the whole town would soon be wiped out? Conditions quickly went downhill. One person commented, "Where there is no faith in the future, there is no power in the present." The people of Flagstaff had no faith in the future. For them there was no future, and because there wasn't, there was no power in the present. "Where there is no vision, the people perish" is the way Proverbs puts the same truth (29:18 KJV). Zacchaeus was "up a tree" in this way as well. Because he lacked faith in the future, he was powerless in the present. Whenever we lose our faith in the future, we are "up a tree."

All around us are people who are "up a tree." Everywhere we turn there are people who are powerless in the present because they have no faith in the future. So many people feel excluded. We could easily make a long list of factors that turn us into tree climbers: the loss of a loved one; the breakup of a special relationship; the loss of a beloved community or a home due to a job change; the loss of the family farm, business, or home; racism; sexism; ageism; illness; unemployment; underemployment; addiction; a handicapping condition; physical, emotional, or sexual abuse; and on and on. There are many, many people "up a tree" today.

Zacchaeus wanted to see "who" Jesus was. When Jesus came along, he looked up, and in the branches of a tree he saw a thief and a traitor. But he also say a son of Abraham, a brother to those who hated him so. Jesus could see a little child in the midst of a mob of people. How could he miss seeing a grown man sitting up in the branches of a sycamore tree? Jesus called, "Come down. Zacchaeus, come down from your isolation! Come down from your agony! Come down from your wasted life! Come down, I want to go home with you!"

How did Zacchaeus respond? He climbed down out of the tree. When Jesus invited himself to Zacchaeus' house, the tax collector hadn't counted on such a thing taking place. Look at all of the "righteous" people in town that day. "Who was he, whose name meant 'righteous,' to have Jesus as a house guest?" But we read that Zacchaeus "hurried down and was happy to welcome [Jesus]" (Luke 19:6). That's when the people said, "He has gone to be the guest of one who is a sinner" (Luke 19:7). This wasn't the first time Jesus had done such a thing. It was rumored that he actually ate with sinners and tax collectors (Luke 15:2). We know what they said: "Birds of a feather flock together" and "People are known by the company they keep." Such prejudicial murmurings are still uttered today. Slander can ruin almost anybody, but somehow Jesus rose above it.

Zacchaeus came down from the tree, took Jesus home with him, and then confessed his sin. He told it all; he didn't hold anything back. He offered to make restitution to those who had been overcharged. There probably wasn't enough evidence to convict him of stealing, but still Zacchaeus promised to return what wasn't his own. According to the law, only when robbery was a deliberate and violent act would fourfold restitution be required. The law (see Exod. 22:1) said that a person convicted of stealing a sheep must return "four sheep for the one sheep." So Zacchaeus decided to return fourfold what he had taken from people. Jesus didn't tell Zacchaeus to make any such restitution; it was his own idea. Zacchaeus also said that he would give half of his wealth to the poor. The law said nothing about giving anything to the poor. Zacchaeus was going the second mile, and Jesus told him that he and his house had found salvation that very day. What a glorious ending to such a delightful story!

Jesus has given us an example. He was a friend to the isolated and outcast, the dregs of society, people like Zacchaeus, people who are "up a tree." We, who have been called to follow Jesus, are to go and do likewise, because so many people today are shunned and turned into outcasts because of their race, sex, creed, color, national origin, economic condition, wealth, health, or age.

Did you notice that after Zacchaeus confessed his wrong, he made a generous response? Conversion results in acts of uncommon generosity. Genuine repentance bears fruit. God's grace always calls forth our very best gifts. Think about those who have responded in a generous way to their release from being "up a tree." It might be that you count yourself as being among them.

On the day that Jesus came to town, Zacchaeus, a little man, became a giant. He was big enough to confess his sin. He was big enough to make restitution for his wrong. He was big enough to become generous with his wealth. Salvation is wholeness. It's a right relationship with God, others, and self. The message of Zacchaeus to us is that new life is possible, here and now! His story needs to be heard by all those who lack motivation and by all those who have no direction, no radiance, no hope, no faith in either themselves or the future. The story of Zacchaeus is *our* story; it is the story of every Christian. Zacchaeus had wealth, but still went lacking. But when he came down out of the tree he found everything he needed. And so it is for us today.

Hurry and come down; for I must stay at your house today. What will be your generous response when our Lord invites you to "come down"?

Suggestions for Worship

Call to Worship (Hag. 2:6-7):

MINISTER: Thus says the LORD of hosts: Once again, in a little while, I will shake the heavens and the earth and the sea and the dry land;

PEOPLE: and I will shake all the nations,

MINISTER: sot that the treasure of all nations shall come,

PEOPLE: and I will fill this house with splendor, says the LORD of hosts.

Act of Praise: Psalm 65:1-8.

Suggested Hymns: opening hymn: "Heralds of Christ"; second hymn: "Hymn of Promise"; closing hymn: "There's a Wideness in God's Mercy."

Opening Prayer: O God, forgive our unwillingness to believe that we are called to repentance, faith, obedience, and a life of holiness. Forgive us for ignoring, turning aside, and excusing ourselves because we are "only human." Help us this day to faithfully hear and obey your call upon our lives. Through Jesus Christ our Lord, amen.

Pastoral Prayer: God of all creation, you have planted a great longing within us, and that longing has brought us to this time and place of worship. We dare to believe that we have been created in your image. At the same time, we believe that we have marred that image. We come, confessing our many faults and failures. You have given us so many good gifts, but we have refused to acknowledge most of them. We confess with sorrow that we have refused to share our bounty with those who are in need. We have received a vision of what life might be, but we have let the dream fade and die. We have turned aside from the straight and narrow way, which leads to life, and instead have chosen the path of least resistance.

We have been surrounded by friends and loved ones who have made great sacrifices for us, but we, in turn, have failed to show them our gratitude. We have let watchful eyes lose their sparkle and waiting hearts lose their hope because we did not care enough. With humility we confess our selfishness, our indifference, and our lack of love. Our secret sins are made known in these moments of quiet. God of love, accept our penitence. Pardon our wrongness. Deliver us from our sins, that we might be set free from the past to find newness of life.

We long to be set free from the grave of yesterday. We long for a broader vision. We long for a new spirit of adventure. We long to blaze new trails and welcome new friendships and respond to new opportunities for service. We want to reach forward to the things that lie ahead of us. We know that today can be a day of new beginnings for us, and for this we are truly thankful.

Your sheep are scattered on many hillsides. We pray for your children, our sisters and brothers, who are anxious, lonely, troubled, hungry, sick, and suffering because of physical, mental, and spiritual pain. We pray that all might know that beneath the cares of life are the everlasting arms, lifting, giving constant support and courage.

From the ending of each old chapter of life's story to the beginning of each new chapter, help us all to trust in your goodness. This we ask in the spirit of the one who came to set us free, Jesus Christ our Lord. Amen.

NOVEMBER 8, 1992

□

Twenty-second Sunday After Pentecost

"Inanimate things may have a Creator, but only the living can have a God." (G. B. Caird, commenting on Luke 20:38)

The Sunday Lessons

Zechariah 7:1-10: The Temple was destroyed in 587 B.C. For seventy years the faithful had observed a ritual of mourning and fasting. Now, worshipers were rebuilding the Temple. Should the fast continue? The prophet moved from interest in piety to social concern. God requires justice and kindness.

II Thessalonians 2:13–3:5: Writing to a church he honored, the Apostle urged them to "stand firm," to "hold to the traditions," and to become established "in every good work and word."

Luke 20:27-38: An old Levite law provided that a brother marry his brother's sonless widow to provide an heir (Deut. 25:5-6). To discredit belief in life after death, the Sadducees offered a riddle concerning a woman who married seven brothers, but bore no children. Jesus declared, "He is God not of the dead, but of the living" (v. 38).

Interpretation and Imagination

Heaven, although a spiritual kingdom, is often described in earthly terms that suggest gratification of our senses and release from bodily pain. We thus reduce the realm of God to human categories.

Religious traditions, begun as reverence for God, become more important than the Creator. Vital faith, like real hope and love, depends on a true I-Thou relationship with the God of the living.

When Emil Brunner gave the Earl Lectures at Pacific School of Religion in 1955, he related faith, hope, and love to the three dimensions of time—past, present, future. Faith has to do with the ground on which we stand. Hope is the reaching out to what will be. Love is being there now and acting it out. Brunner warned against atheism and secularism, which find little of God in the past and none in the future.

Brunner spoke of humankind's error in assuming that moral progress in civilization resulted from something inherent in human nature, "not realizing this progress was due to the Christian religion." He proposed an honorary Th.D. for Adolf Hitler.

I would not object to giving the doctor of theology degree posthumously to Adolf Hitler, because he has done more than anybody else to awaken Europe to the consciousness of its Christian heritage by creating a world without Christianity. Let me take this opportunity to say to the American people that if we continue on the road of secularism, which means atheism, as we have during the past fifty years, we will surely end with totalitarianism. This is proved by history; it can be proved by philosophy. (See Brunner, *Faith, Hope, and Love*, pg. 42.)

TRADITION

Luke 20:27-38

A SERMON BY ROBERT L. BALDRIDGE

Tevye, the main character in the musical *Fiddler on the Roof*, said that everyone in his little Jewish village of Anatevka was like a "fiddler on the roof, trying to scratch out a simple tune without falling and breaking his neck." He said, "Maybe you ask how we keep our balance. I can tell you in one word, 'tradition.'" According to Tevye, his people have traditions for everything—what to eat, how to sleep, how to work, and how to dress, including the wearing of prayer shawls. He said, "You may ask, 'How did this tradition get started?' I'll tell you, I don't know. But it's a tradition! Because of our tradition, everyone knows who he is and what God expects him to do."

The word *tradition*, which comes from the Latin *tradito*, meaning "handing over," is defined as "the transmission of knowledge, opinions, doctrines, customs, and practices from generation to generation, originally by word of mouth and by example." We've all inherited traditions from our ancestors, which will be passed on to future generations. Traditions are important.

We're looking forward to Thanksgiving and Christmas, seasons laden with all kinds of special traditions—visit to the relatives; a turkey dinner with all the trimmings; the use of a creche; a specific time and way to decorate the tree; the sending of cards; the way we exchange gifts. A church might also have traditions, such as Christmas Eve candlelight communion service or a Christmas pageant. We love and honor such traditions.

But anything can be carried to extremes, and the extreme of honoring traditions is known as traditionalism: "A system of faith founded on tradition; adherence to tradition; especially, undue reverence for tradition in religious matters." Sometimes we do what we do without knowing why we do it. Tevye said, "Maybe you may ask how this tradition got started? I'll tell you. I don't know. But it's a tradition."

The new husband watched in disbelief as his bride took her first baked ham out of the oven. Both ends were missing! He asked, "Dear, why did you cut the ends off of the ham?" She said, "I don't know. My mother always does it." It wasn't very long before the couple visited the wife's parents. He asked her mother, "Why do you cut the ends off of a ham when you bake it?" She said, "I don't know. My mother always does it." The first time the newlyweds visited the wife's grandparents, the husband asked the grandmother, "Why do you always cut the ends off of a ham when you bake it?" She said, "I don't know. I guess it's because my mother always did it. But I think it was because she had a very small oven and most hams wouldn't fit." Now *that's* traditionalism—doing whatever we do without knowing why we do it, but continuing to do it anyway.

Jesus had a lot of trouble with people who were bound to tradition. He had cleansed the Temple of the moneychangers and now was locked in a series of controversies with the Jewish leaders. Two questions had already been asked. The first had to do with the source of his authority. The second had to do with paying tribute to Caesar. Then a third question was asked, having to do with the resurrection of the dead.

The Sadducees were of the priestly class. Many were aristocratic and wealthy. They were the "old believers," who clung to ancient religious tradition. They said that there was no resurrection because it is not taught in the Scriptures, which to them was only the first five books of the Old Testament: Genesis, Exodus, Numbers, Leviticus, and Deuteronomy. What wasn't found in them wasn't authoritative. The Pharisees, on the other hand, believed that there was an oral as well as a written tradition about resurrection from Moses. The Pharisees said that those who denied the resurrection had no share in the world that was to come. In this, they were just as inflexible as the Sadducees. The resurrection was often a subject of heated debate between the two parties (see Acts 23:6-10), and in our Gospel lesson we find the Sadducees playing a game with Jesus.

The third question they asked Jesus was about a woman who married seven brothers, who each died, leaving her to marry the next brother in turn until all seven had died. The question was, "Whose wife will she be in the resurrection?" The Sadducees based their question on Deuteronomy 25:5-10, which describes the levirate law of marriage and defines the duty of a man toward his deceased brother. It was important that the deceased man have a son to succeed him. But if the resurrected life is only an extension of this life, it would make for some heavenly domestic problems. Imagine the deceased wife finding seven former husbands waiting for her at the pearly gates! It was an absurd question. The Sadducees knew the answer before they asked the question, but they were so bound to their tradition that Jesus couldn't change them. But he tried.

Jesus explained that conditions in the next life can't be compared with life here and now. He told them that they really didn't know the Scripture, which, when studied, reveal a divine power that is far greater than our deepest longing. The resurrection is God's gift to us. The resurrected life isn't a poor reflection of this present life. God isn't the God of the dead, but the God of the living. Marriage is appropriate in this life because that's the way the human race is continued. But there will be no need for such an institution in the resurrection. The Sadducees carried tradition too far!

Traditionalism is wrong, but isn't tradition important? It

certainly is! The Apostle Paul said: "Stand firm and hold fast to the traditions that you were taught by us, either by word of mouth or by our letter" (II Thess. 2:15). By traditions Paul meant the whole body of teaching, practical and doctrinal, that he shared either by word of mouth or by letter. There are Christian traditions that we need to know, and that have their origin in the life, teachings, death, and resurrection of Jesus Christ. Since the time of the apostles, these Christian traditions have been transmitted through preaching and teaching. Where the reception is only outward or formal, these Christian traditions become lifeless, even meaningless. Christian traditions are to be received in such a way that the receiver participates in the power of the original event. In the case of our Gospel lesson, the original event was the resurrection of our Lord and Savior, Jesus Christ. Tradition must leave room for revelation, for the Spirit blows where it wills. That was the problem in Jesus' day. There was no room for revelation.

A well-known theologian has said that "any church that is alive lives on the edge of heresy," meaning that its members won't refuse new ideas or new programs or new structures or new opportunities for ministry simply because there are those who say, "We've never done it that way before." Those have been called "the seven last words of the church." The church is to be an agent of change. Its purpose is to change the world and to change people in the world, not to keep everything the way it was. We believe in the salvation of the world, not the salvation of the church. The church is to be God's tool in bringing about change. It is to be used up for the sake of the world. It isn't to be a storehouse of resistance to change. The life or death of any church depends on the response of its members whenever the battle cry of traditionalism is raised: "We've never done it that way before."

Let's not confine Jesus to our sentimental memories of childhood. Let's not lock him up in memories of the church as it used to be, where we sang the same old songs and prayed the same old prayers and used the same old words and phrases. Things will never be like that again. The world is constantly changing, and Christ can't be entombed in the past. He's alive, and his Spirit is at work in our world.

It is for us to acknowledge God's ownership of all things. It is for us to seek God in the events of every day, for there we are tried and tested. The cry of traditionalism, "We've never done it that way before," could be the last words of the church. Our response could mark a point in time when God blesses us with renewal. Remember that Tevye said: "Because of our tradition we know who we are and what God expects us to do."

Suggestions for Worship

Call to Worship (Zech. 7:9-10):

MINISTER:	Thus says the LORD of hosts: Render true judgments,
PEOPLE:	**show kindness and mercy to one another;**
MINISTER:	do not oppress the widow, the orphan, the alien, or the poor;
PEOPLE:	**and do not devise evil in your hearts against one another.**

Act of Praise: Psalm 9:11-20.

Suggested Hymns: opening hymn: "We Gather Together"; second hymn: "Leaning on the Everlasting Arms"; closing hymn: "There Is a Balm in Gilead."

Opening Prayer: Gracious God, we come to you as those who long to walk along your pathways of grace and love. But many times we get discouraged. We are afraid of difficult experiences. We despair at the challenges that come to us. The roads often become steep and rocky, and we become weary. We let a feeling of hopelessness get the best of us. O God, care for us on our journey. Help us to know that your love is always with us, sustaining us and surrounding us with care. O God, today take our road-weary lives and transform us into your new people. In the name of Jesus Christ our Savior, amen.

Pastoral Prayer: God of love, today we know that prayers for ourselves are not enough. Today we would remember the lonely of the world. We see lonely people every day. We know something of what they feel, but we confess that we are often insensitive and uncaring. We see others trying to cover up their loneliness, but we go on our merry way, indifferent to the need that is all around us. O God, open us up to a new ministry of caring to the millions of people close at hand and around the world who are lonely.

Today we would remember the world's sick. When we are in good health, we forget what it's like to suffer. When we go to school or to work or about our daily routine each day, we forget what it's like to be confined at home or in the hospital or in a nursing home. When we sit down to eat an abundant meal, we forget all about those who are unable to eat because of illness. O God, forgive us and open us up to a new ministry to the world's sick and to those who are shut-in.

Today we would remember the world's sorrowing masses. Death might seem far removed from us, but death is a destroyer for so many. Many seek to be free and are willing to protest and to suffer for that freedom. We would remember those who sorrow because of accidents or natural disasters. Many are unable to cope with life. O God, open us up to a new ministry to those close at hand and around the world who suffer and sorrow today.

Once Jesus prayed for his followers that they might be one. Our prayer is that today we might be one people and so show your redemptive love through all we do and say. In the name of Jesus Christ our Lord, amen.

NOVEMBER 15, 1992

□

Twenty-third Sunday After Pentecost

A great day is coming; a great and terrible day. For some it will bring vindication and joy, for others destruction and distress.

The Sunday Lessons

Malachi 4:1-6: Some persons had argued that the wicked not only prospered, but also escaped judgment. Malachi proclaimed the coming day of the Lord, when evildoers would be burned.

II Thessalonians 3:6-13: Expecting the Lord to come soon, some Thessalonians had stopped working. Paul's response is harsh: "Keep away from believers who are living in idleness" (v. 6).

Luke 21:5-19: Jesus joined his prediction of the Temple's destruction with a description of the coming of the Son of Man. For some persons this day will be one of vengeance. For the faithful, it will be a day of redemption.

Interpretation and Imagination

"The time has come," the nurse says as she takes an expectant mother to the delivery room. "The time has come," the conservationist says as he sets free an eagle, recovered from a wound. "The time has come," a soldier says as he kisses his wife good-bye and boards the airplane.

The words are repeated and should convince us that all finite things have an end time. Yet, we only half believe that *the time will come* and that we shall meet the great and terrible day of the Lord.

Our belief concerning the day of the Lord is shaped by our views of history, which are many. Some believe that we are only marking time, waiting for an imminent cosmic happening. Others believe that history repeats itself in never ending circles. Still others believe that history has no rhyme or reason.

The gospel teaches that God has been and is at work in history and that all time shall end at his feet. We are taught that he used Christ as an instrument in a recorded time and place to begin a new age. We are taught that all who honor their baptism are also called to be instruments in a mission still not finished. As Christians we are players in a story still being written. We live in a time to bear testimony.

Therefore, let us not preach that the end has come or even that it is at hand. Rather let us say, "The days will come when nothing we have built, intending it to last forever, will remain." God's truth abides still.

THE TIME HAS COME

Luke 21:5-19

A SERMON BY ROBERT E. BERGLAND

During the late 1960s, the folk group Peter, Paul, and Mary had a hit song called "Leaving on a Jet Plane." If you were alive during that period of upheaval and uncertainty, you probably remember this song. It was a popular song on military bases. Why, we may ask?

One verse of the song goes like this: "Now the time has come to leave you . . . close your eyes, I'll be on my way."

Many soldiers heard these words and found them to be a description of the time when they would board a plane to be carried to war. For some it meant a final farewell, for others the beginning of something that would change their lives forever. The time had come to leave.

We have all heard the words "The time has come" before in our lives. In the labor and delivery rooms of our hospitals the words get action. They carry with them relief and expectancy: "The time has come for the baby to be born." Things will never be the same from this moment on in the life of this family, for a child will be born.

The conservationists often remind us that "the time has come" for us to begin to clean up our environment or lose it forever. Or "the time has come" for the eagle to be set free. It has recovered from its wound.

In the Intensive Care Units of hospitals the words "the time has come" are spoken heavily. It means that only the life support systems sustain life. There is no hope for recovery, and final farewells are at hand. The time has come to surrender to the finality of death.

The time has come. The words remind us that everything finite has an end time. Created things don't last forever. Even the mountains will change.

Why, then, do we only half believe the words of Jesus, who says, "The time will come when you shall all meet the great and terrible day of the Lord"? Beliefs concerning the day of the Lord are shaped by our views of history, which are many.

Some believe that we are only marking time, waiting for an imminent cosmic happening. For many, this kind of marking time is based on various interpretations of the book of Revelation.

Throughout the twenty centuries of the Christian faith, people have been looking for signs, trying to make interpretations of Jesus' coming, even marking on the calendar a specific day and time for the end to come. History has shown that they have miscalculated; they have marked the end too soon.

In our nuclear age, people fear a terrible time of nuclear war or nuclear accident. Our world could end with a cosmic catastrophe. Some say we are only "marking time" until this will happen.

Another belief held by many is that history simply repeats itself. Therefore, we are caught up in a kind of never ending circle. How often have you heard someone say, "Those who forget the past are doomed to repeat it"? It is a belief that time is only cyclical. We are born, we live, we age, and we die. What goes around comes around.

Still others believe that history has no rhyme or reason. We are merely cast into the chaos of life and have to make the best of what we have. Things merely happen, and there is no purpose in any of it. However, the gospel teaches that God has been at work in history, is at work in history, and that all time shall end at his feet.

In our text today, Jesus and his disciples are visiting the Temple, which was being rebuilt by Herod the Great. Construction had begun forty years earlier, but was not yet completed. This beautiful Temple was the center of the Jewish nation and at the heart of its faith and identity. The immense wealth that was put into its construction made it, in its own right, one of the wonders of the world. Some of the huge blocks of marble measured 67 1/2 feet in length, 7 1/2 feet in height, and 9 feet in width.

The eastern front and part of the side walls were covered with gold plate, flashing in the sun, and the rest was covered with gleaming white marble, which, from a distance, made it appear to be a mountain of snow.

It was marvelous. The disciples, caught up in the beauty of the Temple, were speaking of its beauty and magnificence. They must have thought, "This is none other than the house of God, and this is the gate of heaven."

But what was said in innocence prompted a response from Jesus that was more than they expected. What they saw was not what Jesus saw. Beneath all that seemed to be established for the ages was the ever-present reality of change and decay. "As for these things that you see, the days will come when not one stone will be left upon another; all will be thrown down" (Luke 21:6). Jesus was predicting the fall of the Temple, a fall that would occur in A.D. 70. It was shocking, for the fall of the Temple meant to the Jews the collapse of their whole world.

Imagine that someone told you today that not one stone of the Capitol Building or the White House would remain upon another. It would mean the weakening of our great nation. It would bring radical change to life as we know it now.

Your immediate response would be much like that of the disciples. "When will this be?" and "How will we know what will be the sign when this is about to take place?"

Jesus responded to their questions with five predictions: "Nation will rise against nation, and kingdom against kingdom; there will be great earthquakes, and in various places famines and plagues; and there will be dreadful portents and great signs from heaven" (Luke 21:10-11).

Much of this can now be related to events associated with the fall of Jerusalem. After Roman Emperor Nero's death in A.D. 69, one year before the fall of the Temple, four of his captains battled among themselves for the right to rule over the empire. There were wars, and kingdoms did rise up against one another. Also the volcano Vesuvius erupted in A.D. 73, bringing great destruction and death. All through the land there were places where people suffered from famine and pestilence. Believers saw great signs of terror as early Christian martyrs were being killed and tortured.

Some scholars believe that Luke added these verses in order to show that the predictions were being fulfilled. Since he wrote his Gospel around A.D. 80, he would have known about these events. But we should not try to rationalize or ignore these predictions to gain comfort. They are still true today. They signal the reality that change and decay are all around us.

In the eighteenth century, Jonathan Edwards preached his famous sermon "Sinners in the Hands of an Angry God." As people listened to his description of people being held over the fires of Hell like vermin in the hands of an angry God, they were moved to fear. Many were convinced that eternal death was imminent. The time for them to change was now; the day of judgment was made immediate.

My sisters and brothers, the time has come for us to realize that nothing we have built (hoping it would last forever) will remain—not our monuments, our churches, our corporate structures, our cities, our wealth, or our nation. Like the Temple of Jerusalem, these will not last forever.

But this is a message of hope for Christians. It says that in spite of all the endings that will occur, in spite of the fact that you may be "delivered up by family and friends," in spite of the fact that you may even lose your life, by your endurance, your faith in Christ, you will gain your lives.

In his letter to the Romans, Paul wrote these words of encouragement:

> Through [Jesus] we have obtained access to this grace in which we stand; and we boast in our hope of sharing the glory of God. And not only that, but we also boast in our sufferings, knowing that suffering produces endurance, and endurance produces character, and character produces hope, and hope does not disappoint us, because God's love has been poured into our hearts through the Holy Spirit. (Rom. 5:2-5)

The mission of Christ's Church is not yet finished. The time has come for us to once more find courage, strength, and hope that God's truth still abides in a world filled with evils, uncertainties, and terrors.

In chapter 21 of his Gospel, Luke recognizes troubled times, but trusts in the sovereign grace of God to keep all who trust and believe in him.

We can be sure that the temples will come down, that earthquakes will split this world. Above all, be sure of this: The day will come when Christ will return in triumphant victory to receive his people to himself.

Hear the words of Jesus again, "By your endurance you will gain your souls" (Luke 21:19). Amen.

Suggestions for Worship

Call to Worship (Mal. 4:2, 6):

MINISTER: For you who revere my name

PEOPLE: the sun of righteousness shall rise, with healing in its wings.

MINISTER: You shall go out leaping like calves from the stall. . . .

PEOPLE: He will turn the hearts of parents to their children

MINISTER: and the hearts of children to their parents.

Act of Praise: Psalm 82.

Suggested Hymns: opening hymn: "Great Is Thy Faithfulness"; second hymn: "America the Beautiful"; closing hymn: "Now Thank We All Our God."

Opening Prayer:
Eternal Beauty, shine brightly in the midst of chaos.
Eternal Truth, judge rightly in the midst of confusion.
Eternal Goodness, deliver us from evil.
Eternal Power, rule and reign throughout the whole world.
Eternal Mercy, grant us your peace, through Jesus Christ our Lord. Amen.

Pastoral Prayer: Almighty God, all time is your time. Our lives stand in the appointment of your will. Our harvests are dependent on your faithful providence. The order of our days is only certain because you remain steadfast. O great God of seedtime and harvest, of creation and of destiny, in the morning you send us forth, and in the evening you are our sustenance and hope. We acknowledge you as Lord of our lives today.

Your mighty hand, O God, remains majestic in power. In the greatness of your might you have thrown down all those who have opposed you. Your burning judgment will consume every evil thing like stubble. There is no god like you, majestic in holiness, awesome in glory, working wonders. And your unfailing love continues to lead the people you have redeemed. It is your love that has called them to this sanctuary. Now pour out upon us the converting grace and purifying power of your holy spirit. Raise us up today to be numbered among the faithful, a devout and obedient people among the nations. Bless your church today and make it grow into the stature and fullness of our Lord Jesus Christ, who died and rose again and reigns forever at your right hand. Amen.

NOVEMBER 22, 1992

□

Last Sunday After Pentecost (Christ the King)

It is unusual when two kingdoms willingly seek the rule of one king, even if that king is David. Christ the king unites all things, whether on earth or in heaven.

The Sunday Lessons

II Samuel 5:1-5: For seven years David ruled over the southern kingdom of Judah. Then representatives from the tribes of the northern kingdom asked him to be their king, too. David reigned as king of Israel and Judah for thirty-three years.

Colossians 1:11-20: God, having delivered us from the dominion of darkness, has transferred us to the kingdom of his Son. An ancient hymn praises the sovereignty of Christ the King.

John 12:9-19: Some wanted Jesus to be king. Others wanted him dead. After Jesus raised Lazarus, many Jews believed in Jesus; however, the priests plotted his death. The disciples did not understand Jesus' real authority until he had been glorified.

Interpretation and Imagination

Two kingdoms are evident in the Old and New Testament lessons. David brought Judah and Israel together beneath a single sovereignty. The epistle speaks of the reconciliation of heaven and earth beneath the rule of a cosmic Christ. The Gospel lesson contrasts the clamor of a crowd for a king and the plots against him.

We fail to recognize the total rule of Christ the King when we assume that two realms (heaven and earth) and two kingdoms (the cause of Christ and our cause) exist. Barth makes this point in his discussion of the Lord's Prayer. The first three petitions refer to God: his name, his kingdom, and his will. The last three refer to our need for daily bread, forgiveness, and deliverance. If both parts were not joined in the prayer "there would be, on the one hand, an ecclesiastical, theological, metaphysical sphere, and, on the other hand, a sphere concerned with money, sex, business, and social relationships. There would thus be two compartments" (Karl Barth, *Prayer*, p. 41).

Barth went on to say, "Often ministers imagine that there are the two (compartments): . . . God's cause and ours. However, they are linked together; we pray for the two as a whole. Such is the case because it is Jesus Christ who invites us to pray with him, because in him these two causes are one."

CHRIST THE KING

John 12:9-19

A SERMON BY ROBERT E. BERGLAND

Today is not only the Sunday before Thanksgiving, but it is also the last Sunday of the Christian year. Today we celebrate with Christians around the world the festival of Christ the King. It is a high holy day in the Christian church, but one that is often neglected. It's a humble kind of festival, compared with Thanksgiving or Christmas. But we have a humble king.

Isn't it strange to read a lesson from John that portrays our king as one who rides in his coronation parade on a borrowed donkey? Surely, a great king would command a more stately presence.

The prophet Jeremiah promised that a righteous branch would shoot forth from the tree of David, the greatest king of Israel. David was not born a prince, but he became king! As a lowly shepherd boy, he fought and killed the Philistine giant Goliath. As a singer of songs he consoled King Saul. Then at age thirty he became king of two kingdoms, all of Israel, and ruled with power and might. But David was gone. Now the prophet promised a new king to come from David's line. The children of Israel had a reason to hope.

But Jesus, riding into Jerusalem on a borrowed donkey, wasn't what they had in mind.

Yet, Jesus wanted to be king. Although he was a servant, he was a man who wanted to be king. Sometimes we fail to see this. We know that David wanted to be king. He fought for it, schemed for it, and finally celebrated his sovereignty. But Jesus also wanted to be king. That is the reason he went to Jerusalem; that was not by chance. Long before Jesus came into the holy city on a donkey, the Scripture tells, "he set his face to go to Jerusalem" (Luke 9:51). When Jesus first came to the royal city, he wept over it, saying, "If you, even you, had only recognized on this day the things that make for peace! But not they are hidden from your eyes" (Luke 19:42). Jesus wanted to be king. The kingdom he offered, however, was altogether different. David was a king who conquered and ruled with a mighty army and his strong sword. Jesus came to be a king with humility and suffering, bringing peace and love.

Let's change the time frame of our thoughts now. Most of us have come here today, wanting to be more than we are. We have come here with dreams of greatness. We, perhaps, don't talk of it much, but we'd all like to be a bit more grand and wonderful. Sometimes dreams come true. We hope that will be true today.

Occasionally, a commoner marries a member of the royalty and becomes royal. Occasionally, a poor farm hand, through hard work and honesty, becomes the president of the United States. But this is the exception, not the norm.

Each of us to some degree is an achiever. We dream dreams, make big plans, hold ideas about a great future; but then something strange happens. Just when we encounter the challenge of grandeur, just when we begin to shape our dream, we confront discouragement.

You have seen it happen. Perhaps you've experienced it yourself. It's like this: A person begins to boldly follow a dream. He keeps it alive for years. Then, just when he comes to the moment of decision, instead of acting with determination and boldness, he backs away. Worried that it won't work, he gives up. Again and again we try to buy victory with compromise and certainty with doubt.

This is not limited to the lives of individual men and women in secular society. It is also the way the church often responds in terms of leadership and mission. Rather than acting like people for whom the victory is already won through Christ, we act as though we are a defeated army. We hang our heads and say our "if onlys" and act like losers. We are timid when given opportunities to witness to the might and right of Jesus' kingdom. We are afraid to become wholly identified as God's people. We do not demonstrate the confidence that rightly belongs to a people who belong to a great king.

Stanley Hauerwas and William Willimon, in their book *Resident Aliens: Life in the Christian Colony*, contend that life in the Christian colony "does not mean that we settle in, make our claim, stake out our turf, and put up fences." We are not called to act in a defensive and isolated manner, seeming "to imply that we are satisfied with our little corner of the world." In this way we are defensive in our proclamation.

John Wesley, the founder of Methodism, did not take a defensive position. He boldly declared, "The world is my parish."

Hauerwas and Willimon contend that "life in the colony exists and will continue to exist as we take an offensive posture in spreading the Good News." When God broke into human history in the person of Jesus Christ, when God became Emmanuel, God with us, it was, and continues to be a message to the world that, "God refuses to stay in his place!"

My sisters and brothers, if there is one thing we need to hear today, on this last Sunday of Pentecost, it is the fact that Jesus Christ was not born a loser! He was not born to be defeated! He was born the first of all creation. In Christ all things were created, in heaven and on earth, visible and invisible, whether thrones or dominions or principalities or authorities—all things were created through him and for him. Jesus Christ is the head of the body and of the church; he is the Alpha and the Omega, the beginning and the end.

Jesus was not, is not, and will never be a loser. He is not defeated. It is true that he died on a cross, but that was because he would be king. It is true that Jesus suffered and was humiliated, but he suffered and was rejected because that was his mission.

Jesus did not set out to become king in a safe, easy, and comfortable way. He was in conflict throughout his ministry, and the truth, forgiveness, and love of God that he shared with all of creation was scorned. Now on this day that we call the Festival of Christ the King we celebrate this pilgrimage. Our king comes to us on a borrowed donkey, lowly, but not a loser.

Christ is not king in a limited way. May we never be found to be limiting the vision he had for his church. May we never lose sight of what we are called and empowered to be as citizens of his kingdom—that is, reaching out to those who are searching for truth, preaching the good news to those who are sorrowing, ministering to the sick, bringing back to the fold those who have wandered away, making a place for those who have no place to be, and offering salvation freely to all who so desperately turn to so many things that cannot save. We offer Jesus Christ to the world.

It is our eternal loss when we fail to see the grandeur and creative possibilities in Christ's vision of unity for the church. Our lives are made sparse when we become consumed by trivial things and personal ambitions so that we no longer rejoice in the universal nature of the church. It's an inclusive kingdom, united as one body through sovereign grace. And when we, as the church, ravage our unity and tear at one another with partisanship, special interests, and mistrust, we have earned the fear and discontent of rebels in the kingdom.

Remember today what the vision is, what the mission is. Do not lose sight of the glory Christ has revealed to us and will yet reveal to us. Do not lose faith!

We have considered the church. Now come further to consider the place of each member of the church, each citizen of Christ's kingdom. We are amazing creatures. It is amazing what things these bundles of flesh and bone that we call bodies can do. We can build towering structures with the strength and ability we have. We can discern the smallest parts of atoms and understand with some degree of certainty their purpose and function in creation. We can encompass a vast range of emotions from love to hate, from joy to sadness. We are amazing creatures.

But beyond any of this, we know that God is with us. God is just as near to other things in creation, but they do not know it. We know it, and it is a part of the wonder of our being. We are made in the image of God and are called to be like him, to be imitators of Christ.

Jesus Christ wants each of us, his subjects, to be like him. We have a magnificent king, and he deserves magnificent subjects. Being magnificent doesn't display itself through bemoaning all kinds of troubles in our hearts or by seeing ourselves as not worth very much or having any real influence in the world. We are called to wonderful joy. Just as Jesus came to dead Lazarus and called him forth to live again, so also Christ calls each of us. We are called forth to come out of our tombs vital and free.

Jesus Christ is a courageous king, and he deserves courageous subjects. We are to be courageous no matter what the odds against us are, for we are already victors through our endurance and our sharing in the victory Christ won over sin and death.

Jesus Christ is a rich and generous king and he deserves rich and generous subjects. We must be people who will share what we have and who will be extravagant with our possessions, no matter how large or small. We must be wealthy in our style because of our assurance of the unending resources of Christ the king.

Jesus Christ is a beautiful and gentle king, and he deserves beautiful and gentle people. We should walk with grace every day, speak gently, stop to help others, and go lightly through life as though it were a magic kingdom, full of amazement and splendor.

And Jesus Christ deserves subjects who will be holy as he is holy. Being holy does not mean being haughty or making yourself appear to be better than others. Holiness is a life-style of acknowledgment and reverence. Christ the King is crowned; he's alive in our hills and valleys, our homes and hearts. We worship him, adore him, and praise his holy name. Holiness is the constant awareness that we are in the presence of Christ, surrounded by the love of God.

We are called to be more than we are because Jesus Christ is King. Thanks be to God. Amen.

Suggestions for Worship

Call to Worship (Ps. 95:1-3):

MINISTER: O come, let us sing to the LORD;

PEOPLE: let us make a joyful noise to the rock of our salvation!

MINISTER: Let us come into his presence with thanksgiving. . . .

PEOPLE: For the LORD is a great God, and a great King above all gods.

Act of Praise: Psalm 95.

Suggested Hymns: opening hymn: "Crown Him with Many Crowns"; second hymn: "The Battle Hymn of the Republic"; closing hymn: "The Head That Once Was Crowned."

Opening Prayer: Almighty God, in your mercy hear the confessions of your people. We confess our quickness to proclaim you King and Lord when we are caught up in the enthusiasm of the crowd. When the emotion fades and the reality of discipleship confronts us we are more reluctant with our confession and praise. Our lives are not lived as faithful disciples should live. Forgive us, O God, and guide us to be the people you intended us to be. In Christ's name we pray. Amen.

Pastoral Prayer: In the stillness of this moment, O God, we knit our hearts to you. Take away all the things that lay claim to our thoughts and emotions in this moment, and help us to know your nearness.

We give you our thanks for the blessings of your creation; its wonder and beauty are beyond our imagination. From the rising of the sun to its setting in the evening we look out and are reminded that you are God of all things. As we gaze upon the wonders of the heavens at night we are humbled, for we look upon the courts of your kingdom. O God, you are truly a wondrous God of the universe.

Yet, you also reign over our individual and personal lives. We give you thanks for the blessings of health, both of body and of mind, that you give to us. We thank you for those moments of insight and contemplation that make us aware of how near you are to us. We thank you for our homes that shelter us, our families that love us, and our friends that surround us.

Help us to be compassionate and concerned about the men and women who do not know you or the wonder of your kingdom. Help people to know the peace of your presence and to feel your touch, which makes even the heaviest burden light—those who look upon each new day as a new burden that they must carry alone and upon each night with terror; those who know only the pained existence of sickness and uncertainty; those who, because of their own doing or because of the actions of others, do not have homes to shelter them or the love of family and friends. O God, use us in ways that will minister to these people so that we might be one in your name.

Keep watch over us, that we may be loving and bold witnesses for your kingdom, O God. In all things keep us faithful. It is in the spirit and name of Jesus Christ that we pray. Amen.

November 29, 1992

□

First Sunday in Advent

Morbidity encourages no one to watch for the end. Expectation and longing belong to those who are ready.

The Sunday Lessons

Isaiah 2:1-5: The prophet Isaiah proclaimed the Lord's reign. He prophesied that the mountain of the Lord (where the Temple stood) would become the highest mountain. The Lord will establish justice among nations. Peace will prevail.

Romans 13:11-14: Paul's moral exhortations begin in chapter 12. Because of God's grace, Paul appeals for obedience. He urges Christians to "cast off the works of darkness" and to "put on the armor of light."

Matthew 24:36-44: The coming of the Son of Man will be at a day and hour that no one knows. In Noah's time, ordinary routines of eating, drinking, marrying, and giving in marriage were interrupted when the floods came. The lesson teaches, "Therefore, you also must be ready, for the Son of Man is coming at an unexpected hour" (v. 44).

Interpretation and Imagination

When met with disaster, defeat, or destruction we usually expect to recover. The human spirit has a resiliency that prompts us to replant, rebuild, or regroup. Jerusalem was indeed destroyed, and the land made desolate. But today Israel is reclaiming barren land.

When disaster comes, we expect to be surprised. Floods and earthquakes come unexpectedly. So life goes on, and for most persons every day is an ordinary day. We're not making any special preparations. We will be surprised, but deep in our hearts we believe we can reclaim the land, reestablish the foundations, and rebuild our cities.

That view was present in the teachings of the prophets who predicted the destruction of Jerusalem. They expected some would be taken, but some would be left as a remnant people.

However, another view predicts a cataclysmic event that will be the end of time. The destruction and changes of that day will be irrevocable. It is the final consummation of history (like the possibility of nuclear destruction) to which civilization as a whole is totally indifferent. As in the days of Noah, a blind tranquility rests over the populace as we go about our ordinary occupations.

The imminent threat is one for which we prepare. Fire trucks and rescue vehicles are always ready. Security systems on our borders and in our homes are watching. The ultimate threat, the final interruption still claims little attention. Those who belong to the kingdom trust a God who in the beginning authored time and watched over the first day. They long for the day when eternity will touch the temporal. They watch for the day of the Son of Man.

WALK IN LOVE

Isaiah 2:1-5; Matthew 24:36-44; Romans 13:11-14

A SERMON BY LOUISE STOWE JOHNS

The three-year old yells "mine" as she pulls the toy from her playmate's hands. The playmate grabs the toy back. Then, with great speed, the little girl hits her playmate over the head with a wooden block. He screams, and that brings the girl's mother promptly into the room. Assessing the scene quickly, she sees the boy crying and her daughter looking victorious. The mother pulls her child up to her feet and spanks her sharply, while saying, "I've *told* you not to hit!" Two crying children and one angry mother make a sad spectacle.

There is no clear connection between a high ranking officer reprimanding two soldiers and a parent scolding two children trying to exercise their territorial rights. But it's not too farfetched to see a relationship. The mother's message was not as mixed as it appears: the small girl understands somewhere within herself that big people may do what they wish and that ultimately the big person wins. International relations begin in the living room, the kitchen, the backyard, the school, and the streets of our communities. In the global arena, it's no longer the big person who wins; now the basic principle is that the big country wins.

Imagine with me a dissimilar scene in which representatives gather together from all nations. They greet one another warmly, without hostility or suspicion, and take their places in the large circle. They have gathered for a celebration and a service of praise. The unity they have attained has come through their worship of one God, and that unity has brought them through their passionate and arduous negotiations.

A signal from a delegate hushes the intensity of conversations. The ambassadors of peace stand and read in unison:

> We . . . reject war as an instrument of national foreign policy and insist that the first moral duty of all nations is to resolve by peaceful means every dispute that arises between or among them; that human values must outweigh military claims as governments determine their priorities; that the militarization of society must be challenged and stopped; that the manufacture, sale, and deployment of armaments must be reduced and controlled; and that the production, possession, or use of nuclear weapons be condemned. . . .
>
> We believe in the present and final triumph of God's Word in human affairs, and gladly accept our commission to manifest the life of the gospel in the world. Amen. (*The Book of Discipline of The United Methodist Church* [Nashville: The United Methodist Publishing House, 1988] pars. 75, 76.)

A voice sings out: "Goin't' lay down my sword and shield," and the assembly responds with enthusiasm, "Down by the riverside." Each phrase is more fervent until they sing:

> Goin't' lay down my sword and shield,
> Down by the riverside . . .
> Goin't' study war no more.

As the next verse is sung, "Gonna shake hands around the world," it is an unaffected and loving passing of the peace. The women and men are moving about, greeting, smiling, laughing, and singing,

Gonna walk with the Prince of Peace,
Down by the riverside . . .
Goin't' lay down my sword and shield . . .
Goin't' study war no more,
Ain't goin't' study war no more . . .
Ain't goin't' study war no more.

First one diplomat and then the others affirm the source of their solidarity. It is not cultural. It is not racial. It is not linguistic. And it is not nationalistic. What rivets these delegates together is their firm conviction that there is one Judge of the universe, one Creator, one author of peace: God.

Truly what I have described and have called us to imagine is a picture of shalom, which seems as far from our grasp as it did to Isaiah in the seventh and eighth centuries B.C.E. How likely is it that a people would give up their weapons of sword and spear for the instruments of a peaceful, agrarian state, with its plowshares and pruning hooks? How likely is it that nations that have the balance of power will disarm and plant crops to feed the world and build decent housing to provide security and comfort? Without walking in the way of God, the probability is nonexistent.

The prophet Isaiah declared the invitation

"Let us go up the hill of the
 LORD,
 to the Temple of Israel's God.
He will teach us what he wants
 us to do;
 we will walk in the paths he
 has chosen.
For the LORD's teaching comes from Jerusalem;
 from Zion he speaks to his
 people."
He will settle disputes among
 great nations.
They will hammer their swords
 into plows
 and their spears into pruning
 knives.

Nations will never again go to
war,
never prepare for battle
again
Now, descendants of Jacob, let us walk in the light which the Lord gives us! (Isa. 2:3-5 GNB)

Staying allegiant to the God of Abraham and Sarah was far from automatic for the people who were to become the great nation of Israel. Long before Isaiah spoke, the Israelites had trudged through the wilderness, wandering for years. At the edge of the Jordan, Moses reminded the people: "From the day you left the land of Egypt until you arrived in this place, you have been rebellious toward the Lord." (Deut. 9:7*b* NAB).

When they came to the Promised Land, their conviction was that God was the author and finisher of war. The Israelites fought battles that they considered holy, and slowly they claimed the countryside and city states. But as they conquered, ultimately they were conquered: first the northern kingdom, then the southern. Their running after other gods and goddesses had not lessened as they grew into a definable nation. The prophet Isaiah said, "No more!"

Isaiah spoke of two weapons that were known well by the people of his time. The sword and the spear were designed to slash, stab, thrust, and kill; they were not weapons of self-defense. If your blade from your plow is taken to make a sword, your plow becomes useless. Or if the cutting edge of your pruning hook is mounted on a wooden shaft, the vines will grow wild. Micah portrays what happens when one is at peace:

> One nation shall not raise the sword
> against another,
> nor shall they train for war again.
> Every man shall sit under his own vine
> or under his own fig tree,
> undisturbed. . . .
> But we will walk in the name of the
> Lord,
> our God, forever and ever.
> (Micah 4:3-4, 5 NAB)

Are we willing to turn our nuclear arsenal into instruments for healing? Can we transform the keenest military strategists into strategists for a just society? The rejoinder is yes, *if* we are "taught the ways of God" and "walk in God's paths" (Isa. 2:3). The familiarity of the word *walk* should not suggest glossing over its intent.

The writers of Scripture tell us many times that we should walk in God's statutes, in God's law. The verb *walk* can connote "behave," "live," or "follow." Walking is not an indifferent, unspecified action. It is action that embodies the life that God desires for us. There is a steadiness, an everyday quality to walking.

The drums of war and the bugle call stir the blood. Isn't peace forgotten? The former is more appealing if one delights in maiming, death, and destruction. Pacifism, the effort to have peace as an alternative to war, has something in common with passivism—although they do not have the same meaning. The root of *passivism* is the same as that of *passion,* which means to endure or to suffer. In the process of the extremely exacting discipline of pacifism, we may suffer. Our walk may lead us into a lion's den, but if that walk is by God's Spirit, by faith, as children of the light, and *in love,* the way we walk is precisely the place where God led us to be.

Some say that Isaiah's prophecy is not possible or even expected until God's physical reign with us. I wonder how much more blood will stain our earth before the ground cries out enough? How many more "holy" battles will rage before our hands are no longer holy?

We have given birth to too many babies to let them die. We have yearned in vain for the sight of our loved ones. We have been robbed of your best friends. To all we must say: "Rise up! Let us walk in light, and in love. Let us live in accordance with God's truth and walk in God's path. Rise up and call others to the holy mountain of Isaiah's beautiful revelation of shalom.

Suggestions for Worship

Call to Worship (Rom. 13:11-14, paraphrased):

MINISTER: The hour has come for you to wake up from your slumber.

PEOPLE: Because our salvation is nearer now than when we first believed.

MINISTER: The night is nearly over;

PEOPLE: The day is almost here.

Act of Praise: Psalm 122.

Suggested Hymns: opening hymn: "Let All Mortal Flesh Keep Silence"; second hymn: "Come, Thou Long-Expected Jesus"; closing hymn: "Lift Up Your Heads, Ye Mighty Gates."

Opening Prayer: Dear God, we need to be honest with ourselves; yet, that can cause discomfort when we take a close and candid look at ourselves. It is only in knowing your mercy that we have the courage to pray. Being aware that you call us to introspection and our communal responsibility, we pray together now.

We confess that as we begin Advent we are less concerned about our spiritual shape than about our preparations, which often become frantic. We recognize that we are more excited about our round of parties, presents, and all we will consume than about attending to our inner hunger. We even confess that there are days when we wish Christmas would go away!

We admit, as we anticipate the coming of the Prince of Peace, that it is easier to blame the world for military build-up and war than to concede that we ignore the build-up of anger within our own homes.

We acknowledge that, rather than seeking peace by walking in your way, we are wayward, straying from your course, or running toward other paths.

May our confession not be a ritualistic response or thoughtless repetition, but a freeing of our souls from slavery to unresolved guilt and an opportunity for self-awareness. May this awareness not be a source of despair, but a spring of hope.

In that hope of renewal and forgiveness we pray. Amen.

Pastoral Prayer: O God, we thank you for the lives of your faithful servants who waited for the advent of your Son. We thank you that their witness speaks to us today. We give you thanks that we do not have to wait as did Abraham and Sarah, and Ruth and Boaz. We do not have to rely on the prophecy as did Isaiah. Their prophecy is the source of our memory.

While we wait in expectation, knowing the outcome and the miracle, our excitement should not be diminished. Although it's with sadness that we admit, even with that knowledge, we often act as if there has been no revelation.

So we come before you, asking that as a woman carries and nourishes within her a new life, may we allow to flourish within us a yearning for peace, which we will nourish, birth, and nurture. As a woman prepares for the contractions of childbirth, may we not shrink from discord, which is inevitable in our passage toward peace. Help us not to be afraid to attempt impossibilities of humanity because we have lost sight of what is possible with you.

May we teach our young the courage of pacifism, so that from our homes and our streets we may shape a world of respect and mutuality—free of learning war.

In the name of those who have waited, that we might know this day, we pray. Amen.

DECEMBER 6, 1992

□

Second Sunday in Advent

A new shoot rose from the stump of Jesse. God's Spirit would bring a new day.

The Sunday Lessons

Isaiah 11:1-10: This familiar messianic prophecy lists the gifts of the Spirit: the spirit of wisdom and understanding, of counsel and might, of knowledge and fear of the Lord. Justice and peace are the themes of the passage. A new Messiah from the stump of Jesse will "decide with equity for the meek of the earth" (v. 4). Wolf and lamb will dwell together. "They will not hurt or destroy on all my holy mountain" (v. 9).

Romans 15:4-13: The truthfulness of God's promises to the patriarchs was evidenced by Christ's coming as a Jew. The salvation he has brought is for both Jew and Gentile. All peoples shall praise him. "In him the Gentiles shall hope" (v. 12). Both the strong and the weak, the faithful and the half-faithful, share this hope and with one voice glorify God.

Matthew 3:1-12: Each of the Gospel writers records the preaching and baptism of John in relationship to the beginning ministry of Christ. Matthew notes the correlation of the work of John to the work of Christ. John promised; Christ fulfilled. John spoke of a coming judgment; in Christ truth itself has come among us. John called for preparation through repentance; Christ teaches repentance as a way of life. John baptized with water; Christ baptizes with the Holy Spirit and with fire.

Interpretation and Imagination

The text speaks of two kinds of baptism: John's baptism with water and Christ's baptism with the Holy Spirit and fire. If you were to ask contemporary Christians to describe two kinds of baptism, how do you think they would respond? Most persons would speak of sprinkling and immersion; infant baptism vs. believer's baptism. Moreover, in my city, so greatly influenced by Baptist preaching, I sense an underlying conviction that believer's baptism (immersion) is thought to be more compelling, its requirements more rigorous.

There are three familiar modes of Christian baptism, and each employs a powerful symbol. Being immersed suggests that one is buried with Christ and raised to new life in him. Pouring symbolizes an outpouring of God's Spirit. Sprinkling symbolizes an anointing akin to the first-century ceremonies of welcome, whereby a stranger or a newcomer was given a place in the household. The baptisms are the same; only the symbols differ. But the baptism of John was significantly different from the baptism of fire and Spirit.

There was a time when the only word from God was the word delivered through a prophet, a voice crying in the wilderness; when the only revealed truth was a message about truth; when the only baptism was a baptism provided by an agent. Then came the day when God himself came among his people. His word became the incarnate Word. His truth was evident as lived out Truth. His baptism was not symbolic, but the thing itself: fire that destroys the temporary and refines the eternal, the Holy Spirit, and the very presence of the Lord God.

PEACEABLE KINGDOM

Psalm 72:1-8; Isaiah 11:1-10; Matthew 3:1-12; Romans 15:4-13

A SERMON BY LOUISE STOWE JOHNS

Admiral Sir William Penn conquered Jamaica; his son, another William Penn, chose an alternative form of conquering. The son's fame and influence have far exceeded the father's. On land granted to his father as payment of debt by the king of England, the young Penn established Philadelphia and the colony of Pennsylvania. He must have been a disappointment to his father. Raised an Anglican, he became a pacifist Quaker and was expelled from Christ Church College, Oxford, for his nonconformist views.

But that did not stop him from rebelling against the world of his upbringing. After his conversion to the Society of Friends, he was imprisoned at the age of twenty-five for publishing a work on Quaker beliefs.

When Penn came to the colonies, he didn't take by force from the Native Americans the land by the Delaware River. Rather, he stayed faithful to the Quakers' opposition to war by negotiating a peaceful and amicable settlement with the Native Americans who lived on the land. Some of the colonists had viewed the Native Americans as a natural enemy, but Penn's vision of a society of peace overcame that perception and created a harmonious order. Unfortunately, that order was broken years later by others who lived by self-interest.

In Isaiah 11, natural enemies are described in an unnatural, but remarkable, way:

> Then the wolf shall be a guest of
> the lamb,
> and the leopard shall lie down with
> the kid;
> The calf and the young lion shall
> browse together,
> with a little child to guide them.
> (Isa. 11:6 NAB)

About one hundred years after the establishment of Pennsylvania, a child born in Pennsylvania became an admirer of William Penn. Edward Hicks, a sign painter, Quaker preacher, and artist brought together Isaiah's discernment of accord in the kingdom with Penn's peaceful treaty with the Native Americans. Hicks admired Penn because he dealt fairly with Native Americans and because, through his leadership, the Colony was given an unheard of religious and civil liberty.

Because of his fascination with Penn's treaty and Isaiah's prophecy, Hicks produced an estimated one hundred oil paintings of *The Peaceable Kingdom.* In the foreground of one version, painted sometime in the 1830s, is the cast of characters from Isaiah: the wolf, the lamb, the leopard, the kid, the calf, the lion, the fatling, the cow, the bear, the cub, the nursing child, whose hand is over the snake's nest, the older child with her hand over the snake's den, and the child leading the lion.* Many of Hicks's renderings of *The Peaceable Kingdom* are full of animals, tightly packed, but each has its own place as it stares out at the viewer, challenging human beings to the same kind of harmony and tranquility the animals share.

In the background of one of Edward Hicks's paintings, Hicks included what he perhaps considered to be a realization of Isaiah's words: William Penn and the Native Americans are shown by the Delaware River, amicably negotiating a treaty to transfer land from the Native Americans to the new colonists. Hicks depicted a small group of Native Americans and Englishmen—no preference shown for either culture as they are approximately equal in number and in space occupied on the canvas.

In a sermon he preached in 1837, Hicks described his assessment of human nature by employing Isaiah's description of a peaceable kingdom in comparing predatory and domesticated animals. Hicks believed that all people are born with a "savage disposition," like the leopard, the bear, the wolf, or the lion. If undisciplined, self-destruction is inevitable. Hicks told the people that salvation depends on a willingness to allow the divine will to reign over self will. The resulting rebirth turns a person into a creature of gentleness, like a cow, a lamb, or a kid. Hicks's explanation of self-denial was a statement of the goal of the Society of Friends. Isaiah's portrait of the ideal community challenges the reader to deny selfish inclinations, which cause disunity.

The book of Isaiah is held in very high esteem by both Jews and Christians. It is not because it presents a lovely picture of the world during the times in which it was written. It is because it calls us all to holiness and to a return to the intention of God's creation. The passage for today describes a restoration, a regaining of paradise in which the world is a totally new creation living in equanimity.

There is no doubt that the scene described by Isaiah is most amazing: the carnivorous, stalking, dangerous wolf, leopard, lion, and bear all have turned aside from their ways and are living

---

*Because the painting *The Peaceable Kingdom* may not be familiar to all persons and because seeing it would greatly enrich the hearing of the Scripture, show a slide or poster of the painting as you preach. You may obtain a slide or poster from one of these sources: (1) To order a slide of the 1826 version, call Rosenthal Art Slides of Chicago, 312-324-3367 (order number PMA-107); (2) To order a poster of this slide, call the Philadelphia Museum of Art, 215-787-5452.

serenely alongside animals that were used for sacrifice in the Bible: the lamb, the kid, the cow, and the calf. There is a new mandate: The calf will no longer be food for the lion, but the lion will eat straw just as the calf does. The lamb will no longer be prey for the wolf, nor will the leopard hunt the kid.

How is all of this possible? It is possible today because of God's intervention in history, God's sending of Jesus as the greatest exemplar of peace we have ever had. And God also has sent people like William Penn, whose lives have been holy, peaceful, and peace aspiring.

There is a dream, an uncommon vision, that tells us that we can have a world of peace. Advent, these four weeks before the Christmas season, is not a time of false hope, some impractical dream that looks good in a painting, but has no reality. Edward Hicks's painting of *The Peaceable Kingdom* reminds us that the belief of one person can make a difference, and that, in the realm of God, it is fitting.

Up to this point we have heard a narrative about animals that are natural enemies, existing side by side. We have been reminded of Penn's treaty with the Native Americans, which respected their claim to the land. But other than noting Penn's Quaker convictions, we have not yet identified the illuminating source for such peculiar behavior. The passage from Isaiah tells us that the animals

> . . . will not hurt or destroy
> on all my holy mountain;
> for the earth will be full of the
> *knowledge* of the LORD
> as the waters cover the sea.
> (Isa. 11:9, italics added)

There is the key! To know the Lord means there is a deep comprehension of a right relationship with God, which makes it possible for us to identify with God. Knowledge is not a simple musing over some supreme being that is far above us. When we are full of the knowledge of God we recognize and are submissive to our Creator, whose actions within our world are carefully designed. (See E. C. Blackman, "Know, Knowledge," *A Theological Word Book of the Bible*, Alan Richardson, ed. [New York: Macmillan, 1950], p. 121.)

In the Matthew 3 passage for today, John the Baptist minces no words with the Pharisees and Sadducees, who probably came out more for the show by the Jordan than to get baptized. He called them poisonous snakes and told them that if they had any interest in avoiding the winnowing fire, they had best show the fruits of their repentance. He told them that no secondhand faith from Abraham (from ancestral fathers and mothers) would suffice.

The knowledge of the Lord that our parents may have had cannot be passed on to us, because knowledge involves being Christlike, and that means being obedient. The person who lives near you, attends church, or teaches your Sunday school class cannot give you his or her knowledge. The church staff, your spouse, your parents, and your friends may all live with a knowledge of God, but it is up to you to seek the Lord for yourself. That is the only way to have paradise restored.

From a human standpoint, Isaiah is too optimistic. From a divine aspect, God requires us to be like Isaiah, to give up our enemies, to live in accord with them, to return to the pure and uncorrupted state of our birth, to live in peace.

That strange-acting man, John the Baptist, cried out, "Turn around! Time is short, because the one who comes after me, is cleaning house. Refuse will be burned" (see Matt. 3:1-12). Paul's voice was gentler, urging hospitality, harmony, rejoicing, and hope (see Rom. 15:4-13). The eyes of the blameless lamb beside the reformed wolf inspect and question us from the canvas of Edward Hicks's painting and from the poetry of Isaiah.

Do we venture to hope that during this Advent season the earth will be full of a knowledge of God, so that there will be no destruction or hurt in all of God's holy and glorious dwelling? We dare not.

Suggestions for Worship

Call to Worship (Rom. 15):

MINISTER: Everything that was written in the past was written to teach us,

PEOPLE: that through endurance and the encouragement of the Scriptures, we might have hope.

MINISTER: May the God of hope fill you with all joy and peace as you trust in him,

PEOPLE: So that you may overflow with hope by the power of the Holy Spirit.

Act of Praise: Psalm 72:1-8.

Suggested Hymns: opening hymn: "O Come, O Come, Emmanuel"; second hymn: "Hail to the Lord's Anointed"; closing hymn: "Joy to the World."

Opening Prayer: God of history, we gather this Sunday in continued anticipation of celebrating that moment when you split history through a mother's pain, a husband's obedience, and a baby's first cry.

Prepare our hearts to welcome you into our lives as you welcome us with your mercy. Teach us how to live faithfully as you are ever faithful to us. Amen.

Pastoral Prayer: We give you thanks, God, for the stirrings in our world that have liberated minds and lives. We praise you as the author of earthly governments of peace. Although we may perceive of ourselves as being incapable of affecting countries and cultures far from our own, we lift our voices in petition for the continued breaking out of peace. As regimes become less restrictive and fledgling democracies grow stronger, endow the people with patience and courage, with wisdom and vision. May we not as a nation be absorbed in an act out of self-interest, but devote ourselves to empowering their independence.

We pray for those within our community and church family whose homes are filled with dissension, discord, and even violence. We beseech you to provide physical and psychological safety for family members who feel trapped. We pray for your healing of those who perpetrate that violence. Create in us a willingness to extend ourselves with equal compassion and energy to the offender and those offended.

May our eyes not look aside. May our resolution not wane. May we seek your discernment and mercy in being representatives of your restorative love.

In the name of the innocent babe of Bethlehem we pray. Amen.

DECEMBER 13, 1992

□

Third Sunday in Advent

Who is Jesus? Is he the one God sent, or shall we look for someone else?

The Sunday Lessons

Isaiah 35:1-10: A thousand miles of desert faced the exiles on their return to Zion. Isaiah promised joy: "The desert shall rejoice and blossom" (v. 1). Lebanon, Carmel, and Sharon, places of beauty and flourishing fields, would all turn to see the glory of the Lord when "the burning sand became a pool" (v. 7). Those with weak hands and feeble knees (the exhausted former slaves) were told, "[God] will come and save you" (v. 4).

James 5:7-10: Throughout his letter, James encouraged believers to act out the word of God. He concluded with this counsel: "Be patient. Strengthen your hearts, for the coming of the Lord is near" (v. 8). Some examples of persons who have this kind of hope are farmers waiting for the fruits of harvest, suffering prophets, and the steadfast Job.

Matthew 11:2-11: John the Baptist, hearing about the deeds of Christ, sent a message from his prison cell, asking "Are you the one who is to come?" (v. 3). Jesus responded with evidence that the blind, the lame, the outcast, the deaf, and the poor now had reason to rejoice. John the Baptist is likened to Elijah, who was expected to return to announce the coming of the kingdom of God. Neither a reed rattling in the wind nor a courtier from the palace had prompted the crowds to seek John. He was God's messenger, one who came to speak God's word.

Interpretation and Imagination

The phenomenon of the desert mirage is legend. Thirsty, dehydrated, dying travelers longing for water suddenly see an oasis—pools of cool water and inviting, shady trees amid burning sands. Encouraged by the vision, they hurry on, filled with expectation, but they discover that their salvation was only an illusion, a mirage.

When John the Baptist began to preach throughout the Jordan Valley, people were looking for a Messiah. John's appearance, his manner, and his message of repentance reminded the people of the prophets of old, and they went out to see this messenger from God. The evangelist Luke wrote that "the people were filled with expectation, and all [were] questioning in their hearts concerning John, whether he might be the Messiah" (Luke 3:15; also see John 1:19-20). John denied that claim concerning himself. But the longing seemed contagious. From prison, he sent a delegation to Christ to ask him, "Are you the one?"

One way to learn about the identity and mission of a person is to ask someone about that person. "Who is he?" "What's she trying to do?" A better way to find out about a person is to go directly to that person and ask, "Who are you?"

Late one Saturday night, I went into the sanctuary to pray. It was mid-December, and the church was arrayed with the colors and symbols of the Advent season. Signs of the expectation of Christmas visits, gatherings, and gifts were everywhere. I wondered and then prayed, asking, "Are you the one?" The words of an Advent hymn came as an answer to my prayers:

> Lo, how a Rose e'er blooming
> from tender stem hath sprung! . . .
> To show God's love aright,
> she bore to us a Savior,
> when halfspent was the night.

FEAR NOT! HE COMES TO SAVE

Isaiah 35:4

A SERMON BY PHILLIP LEACH

> Say to those who are of a fearful
> heart,
> "Be strong, do not fear!

He will come and save you."
Here is your God. . . .
He will come and save you."
(Isa. 35:4)

Jesus comes to save us from fear. He comes to free us, whose hearts are frightened, from our fears.

Fear is one of the most controlling emotions of modern life. Most of us don't like to think of ourselves as fearful people. We prefer to think of ourselves as strong and independent; as though we have the world by the tail, as if we can take on any comer. And yet, that's simply not true. We all fear.

One of the premier spiritual writers of our day, Henri Nouwen, a Dutch priest, wrote an intriguing book in which he says that "fear is the single most important and tragic emotion in our lives." I think he's right.

Usually we make the mistake of assuming that fear is something "out there." "I'm afraid of somebody over there." "I'm afraid of something out yonder." "*What if* this happens?" "*What if* that takes place?" We play that ridiculous "what if?" game all the time because we are so controlled by our fears.

When I read in one of Henri J. M. Nouwen's books the statement that "*fear* is the single emotion that controls us most often," I immediately recognized myself, and many of you as well.

I could name a thousand fears that you and I have. But I'm not going to do that today. Rather, I want us to focus on one fear that so often controls our lives as Christians, and especially those who are in the Roman Catholic Church: *We are afraid to go to confession.* I really do believe that most of us are terrified at the prospect of celebrating the sacrament of reconciliation. We may have "nicer" and "easier" words to describe it, but the bottom line is that we're afraid to go to confession.

We read articles in magazines and newspapers about the decline in the frequency of confession among Roman Catholics. The professionals are asking why we do not go to confession as frequently as we used to, and they come up with all sorts of "reasons"—some psychological, some sociological, some theological. I'm sure that many of those reasons may be valid, but at the base, stripped of all the fancy language and theories, I'm convinced that we don't go to confession because we're afraid.

I thought about that when I read today's first reading from Isaiah. Remember those marvelous words from the prophet? Listen again when he says:

> Say to those who are of a fearful
> heart,
> "Be strong, do not fear!
> Here is your God. . . .
> He will come and save you."

I read those words and thought, "Ah ha! Isaiah is speaking to me. He's speaking to all of us." We're afraid of the One who comes to save us. Why else would the archangel Gabriel tell Mary not to fear? For what other reason would the heavenly host give the shepherds, watching over their sheep, that same message? He comes to *save* us in word and sacrament, and yet we are afraid. Even in this sacrament, through which we receive the tenderness of God's reconciling love, we are filled with fear.

We claim to be especially afraid now that the church asks us to celebrate the sacrament of penance "face-to-face." It was a little easier, maybe, when we could hide behind a screen; that wall protected our anonymity. The priest didn't know us or *our* sins. But in honesty, that nostalgia is just an excuse. We were afraid back then, and we're afraid now. I don't care how many years we have lived; we remain frightened little children. We're afraid that the priest or minister will look at us and say, "You did *what*?" We're afraid because none of us wants to admit our sins to God, to ourselves, or to the minister of the church.

An experience from my life helps to illustrate this point. Years ago, when I was thinking about becoming a Roman Catholic, the priest overseeing my instruction told me how wonderful the sacrament of reconciliation was. Theoretically, I agreed. When I actually decided to become a Roman Catholic, he said, "Of course, Phillip, before you are received into the Church, you need to go to confession." I said, "Yes, of course!" But to myself I thought, "Not in a million years will I admit all that stuff to a priest!"

Although I had countless perfect opportunities to make my first confession, I found an equal infinity of reasons that kept me from doing it. I had so much work to do, so many books to read, so much shopping to get done, so many friends to see, so much relaxation to catch up on—all perfectly good *excuses.* I simply couldn't face the prospect of sitting down, across from a priest—another human being—and admitting all the many ways I desperately needed God's forgiveness and salvation.

My priest friend never mentioned it again—until the very night that I was to be received into the church. At supper, surrounded by priests and other friends, he asked me, "Did you make your confession while you were on retreat in Washington?"

"Uh, no," I stammered.

"That doesn't matter," said he. "All that counts is that it be done."

Caught! I had been found out! What was I to do? I decided in that moment on the radical course of telling him the truth. He responded with absolute calm, "I'll hear your confession right after dinner." My stomach was in a knot; my palms were so sweaty that I couldn't hold the fork; my head was swirling.

After dinner, my friend and I went into a private room, away from all the other persons, for my first confession. He put his head in his hands and said, "Go ahead."

"Bless me, Father, for I have sinned. This is my first confession. I've lied. I've been uncharitable, and—uh—for all the other sins of my past life that I can't remember right now, I am truly sorry." He gave me my penance and absolution.

When I left that room, I felt stupid because I hadn't told the truth. Well, to be sure, I *had* lied. I *had* been uncharitable. But there were so many other things that I wanted and needed to tell him and, mainly, to tell God. I so wanted to hear the words of the prophet: "Here is your God. . . . He will come and save you."

I had been denying myself the uniquely wonderful opportunity of hearing those consoling words of salvation, and I was ashamed of myself. Fortunately, though, God did not allow my sinful stupidity to ruin that evening. The memory of being received into the Roman Catholic Church is a glorious one for me, and for that I am deeply grateful to God.

My need to go to confession, to hear those words of comfort, did not go away. Still I found so many excuses not to go. My fear of telling the truth about myself continued to control me. I found excuse after excuse, until a little more than a year later. My mother's doctors had found a cancer in her; they said she wouldn't live out the year. I knew I wanted to approach God to beg him to be merciful and gracious to my dear mother. But I also knew that the sin on my heart prevented me from approaching him in freedom. Finally, I had the compelling reason I *needed* to let God save me from my fear. A priest, who is also my friend, had heard that first *real* confession. Oh, to be sure, I had received the grace of the sacrament before. But, I knew, in those previous times, my fears had controlled the half-truths and evasions that had passed for a genuine, complete confession from my needy heart.

We sat in beanbag chairs that day, looking at each other. I told him *everything*—all those things that had been locked away inside of me for my whole life, all those things that I had never wanted to admit to myself, much less to any other living person. Then it was over.

My priest friend said, quite simply, "God loves you very much, Phillip." No recriminations, no lectures, no outraged judgments. He just said to one whose heart was frightened: "Be strong, do not fear! Here is your God. . . . He will come and save you."

I had been set free from all those fears and anxieties that had controlled me. "Do not fear! Here is your God. . . . He will come and save you." That is the message of all of the sacraments; it is particularly the message of the sacrament of penance.

Celebrating this sacrament is the best way I can think of to prepare for Christmas. When we celebrate the sacrament of reconciliation during the Advent and Christmas seasons, we live the words of the prophet Isaiah:

> Be strong, do not fear!
> Here is your God. . . .
> He will come and save you.

As we come to the altar today to receive the body and blood of Jesus, who was born of Mary to save us, who comes to free us from all of our fears, we must beg him to give us the courage to celebrate the sacrament of reconciliation.

Suggestions for Worship

Call to Worship (Ps. 146:5-6):

MINISTER: Happy are those whose help is the God of Jacob,

PEOPLE: whose hope is in the Lord their God,

MINISTER: who made heaven and earth, the sea, and all that is in them;

PEOPLE: who keeps faith forever.

Act of Praise: Psalm 146:5-10.

Suggested Hymns: opening hymn: "Angels from the Realms of Glory"; second hymn: "Lo, How a Rose E're Blooming"; closing hymn: "There's a Song in the Air."

Opening Prayer: Eternal God, you sent your only Son, Jesus Christ, to be our Savior. Through him, we have come to know the joy of salvation. You have promised to be with us, and we have experienced the strength of your presence through the Holy Spirit. You have taught us through Christ that you will come again, and we have been made confident. Hear us, Lord God, as we confess our need for you and our unworthiness of you. Then graciously prepare our lives, within and without, to receive the blessings of the Savior's birth. Amen.

Pastoral Prayer: Almighty God, Father of us all and Father of our Lord and Savior, Jesus Christ, you are the source of everything. You support everything. You shelter everything. You welcome everything. You endure everything. You reveal truth, and you remind us of what is truly sacred. You point us to the highest and the best, and you send us back to the ordinary ways of our life. You bring together shepherds and angels, the holy mother and a manger, stardust and stable straw. You bring together the eternal and the here and now.

On this winter day, when we will have seen the sun setting early, and in all our daily rounds, when we have been too much impressed by the sun's setting, we want to behold a new day. Let us see a new light shining—the light of Christ and his holiness. Let us experience a new age dawning, an age of freedom and justice. Let us rejoice in a new government of all people, a government of peace and love.

On this Sunday in Advent, let us wait with patience and hope for the light and life of Jesus Christ. Our guilt needs his forgiveness; our weakness needs his strength; our poverty needs his blessing; our loneliness needs his nearness; our sickness needs his healing; our hostilities need his peace; our death needs his newness of life. We have watched the sun setting for too long, and we have lamented the dark for too long. Come, Light of the world, and fill us with your light. Amen.

DECEMBER 20, 1992

□

Fourth Sunday in Advent

Mother and child are a picture of peace. The holy infant is our source of hope. The child shall be called "Emmanuel" (God with us).

The Sunday Lessons

Isaiah 7:10-16: This well-known prophecy, a "young woman [virgin] is with child and shall bear a son" (v. 14), is quoted by Matthew as part of today's Gospel lesson. Ahaz, a weak king, asked for no signs from God. The prophet, in promising a successor from the Davidic line, proclaimed that the Lord would give a sign: A maiden would bear a child called Immanuel ("God is with us").

Romans 1:1-7: Paul's salutation to the Romans introduces his main theme: The sovereign grace of God saves all who have faith. Christ came into the world as a descendant of David. His resurrection from the dead marked him as the Son of God. His gift to the whole world is proclaimed in Paul's greeting: "Grace to you and peace" (v. 7).

Matthew 1:18-25: The message of this passage is spoken often as a part of the Apostles' Creed: "I believe in Jesus Christ his only Son our Lord: who was conceived by the Holy Spirit, born of the Virgin Mary." He was named Jesus (Savior) because "he will save his people." Matthew presents Jesus as the fulfillment of Isaiah's prophecy. A betrothed virgin who willingly lay with a man other than her future husband was to be stoned to death. Joseph intended only to divorce Mary quietly. When it was revealed that the Holy Spirit was the agent of her conception, Joseph took her into his home.

Interpretation and Imagination

My father's discipline was more severe than my mother's scolding, and his judgments were more feared. As children, we often heard words like "When your father gets home, you must tell him what you've done." Sometimes he returned as a benefactor, "When your father gets home, he will help you."

Israel expected the coming of the Messiah to be a time of saving and blessing. Isaiah warned that Immanuel, God with us, would mean the very presence of a righteous judge. It would be a time when Israel and all nations would be faced with settling accounts with God.

When Matthew bore witness to the life and ministry of Christ, he recalled Isaiah's name for the Messiah, "Immanuel." We may be sure that he knew Isaiah's warning concerning judgment, but he also told of another name, "Savior."

It was only through great faith and insight that the Gospel writer could speak of Immanuel. That he dared to call him "Savior" is extraordinary. Jerusalem had been destroyed and its people defeated. The Temple lay in ruins; soldiers were in charge. Long years had passed since Jesus had been condemned by Jewish leaders and crucified by Roman authorities.

Yet, with a boldness that befits Advent, Matthew proclaimed:

> "Look, the virgin shall conceive
> and bear a son,
> and they shall name him
> Emmanuel."
> (Matt. 1:23)

He spoke it to link Isaiah's prophecy to the Spirit's witness concerning the Christ. "She will bear a son, and you are to name him Jesus" (Matt. 1:21). "God with us" meant, and still means, he is with his people and not against them. He has come to save.

Many have debated the correct translation of the passages from Isaiah and Matthew. Should we read "virgin" or "young woman"? Matthew told of a supernatural birth, but some say that Isaiah spoke of a natural birth. Our central concern should be for the life and witness of the child when he became a man. The compelling message is that in him "God is with us."

DECEMBER 20

HOW FAR IS IT FROM NAZARETH TO BETHLEHEM?

Matthew 1:18-25

A SERMON BY JUDITH CRAIG

How far is it from Nazareth to Bethlehem? When I was a child participating in the yearly Christmas pageant, it was about as far as from one side of the church gymnasium stage to the other. It was a journey of imagination for me and my friends, lived out in our minds in simple trust of the bare-bones story told to us by those dependable adults who were our Sunday school teachers. Only from the perspective of adulthood, now equipped with life experience of my own "journey," did the distance from Nazareth to Bethlehem begin to take shape in my mind. The distance is not measured only in miles or kilometers from this adult perspective. Now I have come to know that the distance of journey is more than physical; it is emotional, ideological, experiential.

Modern scholarship teaches us that the birth narratives were the last part of the Gospel records committed to writing. They are an addendum of sorts, written decades after the fact, the late memories of aging eyewitnesses. We have pieces of story, created out of memory preserved by word of mouth, penned long after the event. Time and experience of those who remember colors what they tell overlaid with their own faith understanding. The birth narratives are as much confessions of faith as they are historical accounts, as interested in the "who" and "why" of the birth as the "where" and "how."

But in the midst of their mystery and wonder, in the fabric of their revelation of gracious divine participation in human events, they tell us something else of great significance: Jesus was born humanly, just as you and I were born. Jesus was born of a human mother in that natural process of life regeneration set in place with the foundation of creation. To be sure, God was involved in a unique and wondrous way, noted by signs and portents mysterious. It was a human birth, yes! But it was much, much more.

Yet, in all that mystery there were human beings, persons whose responses, actions, and reactions are keys to truth and mirrors of faithfulness into which I can gaze for instruction concerning my own experience with life. Many of the events include journeys—from the Far East to a manger side, from a field to a place of birth, from a hometown to a census city. Some of the journeys are physical and some are internal—journeys of wonder, confusion, and trust. We are people who journey—physically from one place to another, mentally from one idea to another, emotionally from one reality to another. In the journeys of the Christmas narratives, I find guidance for my own pilgrimages—through Advent expectation to Christmas surprise, through ordinary days to extraordinary revelations, through plans thought to point in one direction to results facing another.

That link of human identity between the characters of the Christmas narratives and my own character becomes a point of renewal and encouragement for me as I make the journey of faith each year toward the celebration of Christmas. One of those journeys is especially helpful to me: the journey of Joseph from Nazareth to Bethlehem.

How far is it from Nazareth to Bethlehem? Actually it is about ninety miles—a long way for foot travel, with a donkey to carry a woman nearing the time of delivery. But it was even further than it sounds from those caught up in a drama beyond their comprehension. Long before they "hit the road" their journey had begun. There was mystery and discovery from the moment Mary announced her pregnancy, through all the decisions to be made, the actual trip, and through the marvel of the birth with its strange spectators.

The journey is part of the story because of Joseph. You know Joseph—the bit part in the Christmas pageant—the one who stands silently behind the manger in the tableau. We know so very little about Joseph. A descendant of David, he must have been a carpenter, since Jesus is referred to as the carpenter's son. Joseph is a shadowy background person. How many times do we read his name? In Matthew, twice: when he is told to take Mary to be his wife and when he is told to flee to Egypt. When the wise men arrive, he is not mentioned. In Luke he is named as the one to whom Mary is betrothed, his ancestry the reason they have to go to Bethlehem. When the shepherds arrive, he is included in the list of those they found. He is alluded to by the use of plural pronouns in the presentation of the child at the Temple and the visit to the Temple when Jesus was twelve. That's all there is to the identity of Joseph in the Gospel accounts.

Who was this mysterious, underdeveloped character? What was he really like? What have you thought about Joseph? Jesus used the imagery of father in a way that makes me think Joseph was a positive model. What words would you use to describe Joseph? We read that he was just and kind. Matthew reports that when he discovered he had been shamed during the period of betrothal, he decided to correct the wrong quietly, bringing no more public shame and stir than necessary.

Think about that a while. Joseph's dreams were dashed. His honor was smudged. He was embarrassed and wronged according to the law. Yet, he decided to react quietly without further embarrassment to Mary and others involved.

From that I deduce that he was a man of restraint and dignity born of compassion. I also deduce a man of such sensitivity as to have been devastated by the discovery of Mary's pregnancy. What pain and anguish did he feel until he was led to understand? What terrible moments of heartbreak and anger were his companions?

How would you describe Joseph? I would say he was strong, for he must have been able to withstand considerable ridicule, criticism, and questioning. He must have been scorned and taunted. He took to himself one who was thought to have shamed him, or whom he had shamed. I also think Joseph was compassionate, caring for Mary, protecting her from what must have been cruel tongue wagging in Nazareth. The laughter there must have been as pointed as the stillness in Bethlehem was comforting.

Above all else, I believe Joseph was open to great possibilities and leadings of the Spirit of God. He trusted visions and insights, responding to the activity of God in mind and heart. He was not one to brand strange insights and experiences as indigestion or bad dreams. He was one to whom God could relate because he was open to being so engaged.

To accept what he was told meant going through the days of anguish and misunderstanding without question. It meant throwing aside his life for the life of one who was destined to be something he couldn't imagine. It meant setting aside his own desires and rights to claim his wife as his own, living with her in celibacy until the birth. It meant accepting, caring for, providing for, and loving a child whose origins he was not sure he understood.

Ah, Joseph. What a journey from Nazareth to Bethlehem, from first knowledge to fullness of time. From the moment Joseph knew of Mary's pregnancy, he was on a journey, a question of how and why and when and who. It was perilous traveling between trust and doubt, threading his way around pits of anger and frustration, fighting disappointment and skirting broken dreams.

I came across some lines that reflect much of my wondering about whether God really planned all those strange occurrences around the birth, or whether God set up the broad scheme and then helped the main players work out the details of the emerging situation—the way I believe God operates in our lives every day.

Maybe God planned it that way all the time.
  A worried almost-mother in birth pangs,
  A frantic almost-father, out of breath,
  Running the rounds of jampacked inns and
  Finally settling, just in time,
  For soft hay and ground-cover blankets.
Maybe God worked it all out in advance.
  Only shepherds to hear and visit,
  Only some wise men, outside the family
  To worship this child, and by their coming
  Stir some others, a few perhaps,
  To notice and wonder—a while.
But maybe God was acting on the spot.
  Out-caring the busy and the blind,
  Out-loving the selfish and heedless.
  The complacent establishment was defeated.
  In this makeshift delivery room
  By the ultimate extemporizer.

Yes, I think there was much room in that whole event for human adaptability under the extemporizing guidance of God. I believe that is the nature of life: an overall plan with lots of room for unique development, life by life, situation by situation. God extemporizes with me all the time, and with you, too! I see God doing the same with Joseph and am reminded of how it is so.

Joseph's character allowed God to do that. He trusted God to be able to extemporize, to join a faithful person in making the best of whatever circumstances emerged. Joseph remained steadfast when it appeared everything was coming loose. Just then Joseph listened, trusted, and obeyed.

Nothing happened the way Joseph planned it. Not the wedding, not the public celebration and approval. Not the bearing of children with the help of a midwife in the secure shelter of a home he had provided. Instead there was shame and scorn. There was an uncomfortable journey to a place with no room. And there was the birth with no one in attendance but himself and some strangers he would never see again. It just wasn't the way he had planned it at all. All his dreams faded away, but there emerged what, with God's involvement, was more wondrous than he had ever imagined.

Somehow I think Joseph never really knew despair in the working out of those circumstances. I think he knew heartache and disappointment. I think he knew fear and confusion. But no despair, for he knew God, and God was partner in the working out of new events amid the shards of old plans.

That's why I think Joseph is an important part of the Christmas cast for us to study. His experience with things going awry, turning out so differently from the expected, is so like our life experiences. We think things will go this way, and they fly off that way. We think it will work according to this plan, and the product ends up matching blueprints we never saw before. We start our journeys in Nazareths and find ourselves in Bethlehems—extemporizing. The difference between hope and despair is whether we recognize God as our companion extemporizer.

I do not believe that God creates trouble or disappointment for us. I do believe that God stands ready to extemporize with us in the face of all our altered expectations.

Whatever else we can say about Joseph, he was a man of unwavering confidence that God would work with him to provide. Hence Joseph was always listening for the next set of instructions, and he was able to be led to resources appropriate for every circumstance. His strength, compassion, and courage all flowed from his constant faith in God's accompaniment.

In this Advent-Christmas season—as we wonder at Mary's quiet calm, as we admire the tenacity of the wise men in their trek, as we share the excitement of the shepherds—let us also look to the quiet figure of Joseph. Let us draw from him a lesson of unwavering trust that will enable us to take the disappointments, the surprise circumstances, the changed plans, and the devastating realities of life and trust God to extemporize with us a victory in the face of every apparent defeat.

It was a long, long way from Joseph's first awareness of Mary's being with child in Nazareth to the moment of exhilaration and wonder of birth in Bethlehem. We all know Nazareth from time to time—hearing news we don't want to face, accepting realities we want to deny, altering plans frustrated by circumstances beyond our control. In the face of such discoveries, we have the option of learning to walk with Joseph toward Bethlehem, there to find God in the midst of altered circumstances, bringing new possibilities for the likes of you and me.

Joseph may stand quietly in the Christmas pageant, having few lines to say and a lot of standing to do. But in Joseph's character resides the model of faithful confidence that even the most surprising and distressing journey-twists are not outside the companionship of the extemporizing God of Bethlehem and your town and my town. Thanks be to that God!

Suggestions for Worship

Call to Worship ("Come, Thou Long-Expected Jesus"):

MINISTER: Come, thou long-expected Jesus,

PEOPLE: Born to set thy people free;

MINISTER: From our fears and sins release us,

PEOPLE: Let us find our rest in thee.

Act of Praise: Psalm 24.

Suggested Hymns: opening hymn: "O Come All Ye Faithful"; second hymn: "What Child Is This"; closing hymn: "Hark! the Herald Angels Sing."

Opening Prayer: O Lord our God, you show your mighty power through your abundant mercy. You show your righteousness through steadfast love. You show your love for us through the gift of your only Son. Grant unto us, we pray, such a longing for your grace that we will seek you early and follow your commandments in faithful obedience. Through the grace of Christ our Lord, let us become partakers of your heavenly gifts, for it is in his name we pray. Amen.

Pastoral Prayer: Our hearts are strangely warmed, O God, by all the sights and sounds of Christmas. The familiar carols and the sacred lessons remind us of that holy night when the One who made everything that is was born of a woman and cradled in a manger, was safeguarded by a poor father and sheltered in a stable.

We kneel before this Christmas mystery, O God, and give thanks to you for every reminder of your mercy. Your saving love has been manifest among us. Now by the prompting of your Spirit, grant to each one of us this gift within—love that is pure, love that is blameless, love that is real, love that never fails.

We rejoice today in the peace and joy of Christmas. Forbid that they should find room in our hearts only for a brief time. Rather cause the spirit of Christmas to stay with us in all the ordinary places of our lives—in our poverty, our brokenness, our human frailty, and our responsibilities.

May all we do and say in the Christmas season bring honor to your name. Forbid that any of our festivities dishonor the Child we adore and bring sadness to countermand his cheer. May the goodwill and lovingkindness that have so markedly changed our homes and neighborhoods these days also change us, that the birth of Christ becomes nothing less than new birth for all who bear his name.

In the name of Christ, who came to save his people from their sin, we pray. Amen.

DECEMBER 27, 1992

□

First Sunday After Christmas

The joy and wonder of the Christmas birth are soon challenged in the flight to Egypt and the obscurity of Nazareth. God's saving acts in history seem to move in slow and uncertain ways toward fulfillment.

The Sunday Lessons

Isaiah 63:7-9: Isaiah's psalm of lament begins by recounting God's saving acts. His great goodness and steadfast love are seen first in the call of his people Israel: "Surely they are my people" (v. 8). He became their Savior, suffering their affliction, lifting them up, and carrying them "all the days of old" (v. 9).

Hebrews 2:10-18: The book of Hebrews was written for persons about to give up their Christian faith and return to Jewish faith. It compares the two, showing the superiority of the work of Christ. Though superior to angels, Christ embraced human suffering and was "not ashamed to call them brothers and sisters" (v. 11). His concern was for humankind, not for heavenly beings, and he was made like them in every respect.

Matthew 2:13-15, 19-23: Joseph was warned in a dream that Herod intended to kill the holy infant. Joseph took the child and his mother and fled into Egypt. When Herod died, another dream told Joseph to bring Jesus back to Israel. He went to Nazareth in Galilee rather than to Bethlehem in Judea because Herod's son ruled Judea. Prophecies were fulfilled.

Interpretation and Imagination

In his great sermon "Christmas Day," Phillips Brooks asked his hearers to identify with one of the three groups recorded as being present at the birth of Christ. The first group were those nearest to

Christ, his parents and especially his mother. "Mary taught us of the dignifying of humanity through the Incarnation," Brooks said.

The second group were that company of wise men from the East, often referred to as the three kings. "They teach us of the true place of humanity in obedient subjectship to the Incarnate."

The third group were the shepherds who heard the angels' song and went to Bethlehem to "see this strange thing." They remind us of those who are "hungry, needy, empty, wanting a Savior . . . and found Him (Christ) all they wanted."

There are other players in the Christmas drama whose responses to this time-shattering event are more negative than positive, more evil than good. Herod heads the list of these. His desire to kill the child, followed by his edict that all boy babies be destroyed, stands in stark contrast with the blessed story of angels and wise men, mother and child, shepherds and stable stock. The record of this weak king who thought he was strong, this short-sighted king who thought he had a plan, this man of history who is remembered so badly, reminds us today that the light shines in the midst of darkness. So soon the Savior became a refugee child in Egypt.

The tragic and comfortable silence of humanism, which expects no appearing of the Son of God and seeks no Savior, is equally damning and is more effective in doing away with the child.

THE HIGH PRIEST WHO IS THE SACRIFICE

Hebrews 2:10-18

A SERMON BY JAMES R. McCORMICK

At Christmas God gives us the gift of his Son, the Messiah, the Promised One. The story of the baby Jesus in the manger never fails to excite our imagination and elicit our approval. Who among us does not love that beautiful tale? But the full value of God's gift is not seen at the manger in Bethlehem. For that we must journey to Gethsemane, to Calvary, and to a garden of resurrection.

The persons in ancient times who awaited the coming of a Messiah would have been quite comfortable with the Christmas stories of angelic choirs, guiding stars, and astrologers traveling long distances to bow down before him. Such accounts are quite consistent with their understanding of the Messiah who was to come. But, as it turned out, Jesus became a quite different kind of Messiah, and it may well be that this is why they turned against him and finally insisted on his death.

As the Gospel story unfolds, we see Jesus accepting the identity of Messiah, but breaking free from the narrow confines of popular expectations. More and more, Jesus talked of the necessity of his suffering and death. Of course, a great many people had difficulty with that. That was no way for a Messiah to act. A Messiah was supposed to be powerful, and he was supposed to win!

Even the disciples had not grasped the full meaning of his being the Messiah. Jesus had tried again and again to tell them of his coming rejection and death, but they refused to hear. Such things do not happen to messiahs. Messiahs are not put to death; they put their enemies to death!

But the writer of the book of Hebrews went so far as to declare that it is precisely his suffering that "perfects" Jesus for his task of redemption. In the Greek, the word translated "perfect" is *teleios*, meaning "perfect" in the sense of being complete, being perfectly adequate for an intended purpose. The writer insisted that Jesus' suffering and death, instead of hindering his mission, was essential to it. Jesus' humanity was not a weakness exploited by the ancient enemies of sin and death. Rather, it was the means by which God, once and for all, decisively defeated those enemies. It was all a part of God's grand design for the salvation of the world!

One of the earliest debates in the history of the Church was the debate about Jesus' nature. There were those who said that Jesus was not really a human being. He was God, dressed in human flesh, just pretending to be human. But the early Church saw the danger in that and declared it to be heresy. God was uniquely present in Jesus, that's true, but whatever else he was, Jesus was fully human. They were sure about that. He received no exemptions, no special privileges. He experienced life in every way exactly as we experience it. The only difference was that he was perfectly obedient and without sin. He became hungry and sleepy and tired. He experienced pain and disappointment and sorrow and, yes, even death. Jesus really died, and his death was necessary to accomplish God's purpose.

Here we see something new in the history of religion. In Judaism and in other religions there had been talk of powerful gods, holy gods, righteous gods, even loving gods. But here, for the first time, we are introduced to a vulnerable God, a God who suffers, a God who dies. Most of the people could not understand it or accept it. It was scandalous!

But we Christians don't apologize for that. We glory in it! The writer of Hebrews even says that it is indispensable! Just think about it: a God who so loves his people, a God who so identifies with his people that he takes upon himself our human flesh and enters into our kind of life in this world. Jesus was one of us, experiencing life exactly as we experience it.

That means that Jesus knows and understands. "Because he himself was tested by what he suffered, he is able to help those who are being tested" (Heb. 2:18) So, however difficult life has been for us, it was difficult for him, too. However painful life has been for us, it was painful for him, too. He understands. I can get close to someone like that. I can feel the loving warmth of someone who cares enough to share my kind of life.

Perhaps that is at least part of the truth the Scripture is getting at. We may admire and respect someone who is remote, above it all, powerful, competent, and self-sufficient. But we cannot get close to someone like that. If redemption is what I think it is; if redemption is taking those who have been separated from God through their sin and bringing them back into a loving, trusting relationship with him, then I can understand God's vulnerability being indispensable to that. I think it is a law of life; we deeply touch one another not at the places of our strength, but at the places of our weakness. Something happens to us when we become vulnerable and touch one another in our weakness.

Perhaps that is the experience in which Christmas meets Good Friday. An all-powerful, creator God seems so remote, so unreachable, so threatening. But a baby—who is afraid of a baby? We can all feel close to a baby. A God who cares enough about us to become vulnerable and to enter into our humanity, who shares our struggles, our pain, and finally, our death—we can feel ourselves being drawn to a God like that, can't we?

Jesus saw so clearly that his Messiahship required suffering and death. Jesus had to suffer and to die to let loose in the world the greatest saving power there is: the power of suffering love! The writer of Hebrews refers to Jesus as "a merciful and faithful high priest," making "atonement for the sins of the people" (Heb. 2:17). What a compelling image!

In ancient Judaism, in accordance with the provisions of the old covenant, the high priest would make a sacrifice for his sins and for the sins of the people, and he would enter the "Holy of Holies" to intercede with God on their behalf. The high priest was chosen from among the people to go before God to make a sacrifice on their behalf. The animal to be sacrificed was to be as nearly perfect as possible, without spot or blemish. You don't offer shoddy gifts to God! The sacrifice was to effect atonement, *at one ment*, reconciling God with the people of God. But that sacrifice was always less than perfect, so it had to be made again and again.

Jesus is the faithful high priest of the new covenant. He, too, comes from the people. He is "one of us," but instead of offering a sacrifice for us, he *is* the sacrifice for us. Under the old covenant, the high priest offered a sacrifice to God. Under the new covenant, God offers the sacrifice, and God *is* the sacrifice! Since Christ is sinless, the sacrifice he offers is sufficient for all time, never needing to be made again. Instead of entering the "Holy of Holies to intercede for us, our high priest has gone on to heaven, to sit in glory at the right hand of God, to intercede for us there. The writer of Hebrews pleads with wavering first-century Christians to remain faithful, arguing the superiority of Christ as our high priest. But the essential point is that our high priest loves us enough to identify with us, to share our vulnerable humanity with us, and to suffer with us and for us! That kind of high priest deserves our loyalty and is worthy of our trust!

I am convinced that you and I have been made in such a way that we cannot be brought back into relationship with God by argument or by punishment or by coercion. We can only be reconciled to God by the power of a forgiving Father's love. Nothing needs to be done to make God more accepting, more willing to forgive us and to claim us as his children. But something does need to be done to soften our hard hearts and to bring us back to the Father. More than anything else, the thing that cuts through all our defensive armor plates, the thing that seeks us out in all of our favorite hiding places and gets to us in our depths is God's suffering love, seen supremely at the cross.

Do you understand, then, why Jesus' suffering "perfected" him for the task of redemption? Nothing else could reach us. Nothing else could save us.

I experienced the redemptive power of it early in my life. As a child, there were times when I misbehaved. My parents believed in punishment, and I have vivid memories of times when they meted it out. I hopped from one foot to the other, crying out, "I won't do it again. I won't do it again." I am sure that physical punishment did not leave any permanent scars, either physical or emotional, and there may have been some behavior modification as a result. But those experiences did not change me deep inside. I'm sure of that. Punishment, threats, and coercion do not have the power to effect that kind of change. There were other times, however, when my misbehavior was handled differently, usually by my mother. She would call me in, sit me down, and simply talk with me. She told me of her dreams for my life, of how disappointed she was in my behavior. Sometimes she would begin to cry. That got to me, down deep, because I knew that my mother was suffering because of her love for me. That got through to me in a way that all the punishment in the world could not. That shaped my life in a profoundly redemptive way, and I am a different person today because of the suffering love of my mother!

God reaches out to us like that. God approaches us not with the arm twisting of divine imperialism, but with the persuasive power of suffering love. There is no doubt about it: It is the most redemptive power in all the world!

Once we experience it, and once we respond to it in faith, it saves us. And that is the gospel!

Suggestions for Worship

Call to Worship (Luke 2:10-11, 14):

MINISTER: I am bringing you good news of great joy

PEOPLE: for all the people:

MINISTER: to you is born this day in the city of David a Savior,

PEOPLE: who is the Messiah, the Lord. . .

MINISTER: Glory to God in the highest.

PEOPLE: and on earth peace among those whom he favors!

Act of Praise: Psalm 111.

Suggested Hymns: opening hymn: "Good Christian Friends, Rejoice"; second hymn: "Jesus Loves Me"; closing hymn: "The First One Ever."

Opening Prayer: Loving God, there is something deep within us—a yearning, a restlessness, a homesickness—that speaks to us of God. We sense that we are not complete and life is not whole until we are yours. So meet us now in this experience of worship. Claim us again as your children. Make us open to the word you want to say and receptive to the experience you want to give us. Nourish us now with your grace. Inspire us to become more faithful disciples of Christ and more loving servants of human need. In the Master's name we pray, amen.

Pastoral Prayer: Loving God, we are grateful for the many good experiences of Christmas. For the time we are privileged to spend with family and friends, for the joy of giving and receiving gifts of love, for times of inspiration and closeness with you, we give you our thanks. Especially we are grateful for your gift to us at Christmas: the gift of your Son and our Lord, Jesus Christ.

We are grateful that we are coming to one in prayer who is never too busy for us, but is always ready to listen, always willing to love us and forgive us, always able to give us what we need. We do not deserve such gracious care, but we need it, and we are grateful for it. And, when we are at our best, we sense that our best hope in life is in reaching into your storehouse of love and allowing you to give us the gifts you want to give.

Father, we are grateful for the way your love has already blessed our lives. You have called us into being and have given us a good world in which to live. You have touched us by the caring concern of families, teachers, and friends. You have ministered to us through your Church. You have guided us when we were confused, forgiven us when we were failing, comforted us when we were hurting, come to us when we were alone, strengthened us when we were faltering, and again and again loved us into new life. We know, when we are thinking clearly, that all we are and all we ever hope to be, we owe to you and to the generosity of your great love.

Help us now to share that love with others. Help us to know that love spoils and loses its power when we try to hoard it selfishly. Give us the Spirit of our Lord. Give us a love big enough to love, and thus help to bring new life to this hurting world.

Use this service now to do something good for us and to prepare us for service in your world. We pray in the name of Christ, who loved the world so much that he gave his life for it. Amen.

Section II:

□

SERMON RESOURCES

LESSON GUIDE:
BASED ON *THE NEW COMMON LECTIONARY*

Sunday	Sunday	Gospel Lesson	Gospel Theme	First Lesson	O.T. Theme	Second Lesson	Epistle Theme	Psalm
1/5/92	2nd After Christmas	John 1:1-18	Word became flesh	Jer. 31:7-14	Return of exiles	Eph. 1:3-6, 15-18	Predestined to be children	147:12-20
1/12/92	Epiphany 1	Luke 3:15-17, 21-22	Baptism of Jesus.	Isa. 61:1-4	Good news to the poor	Acts 8:14-17	Sorcerer wants power	29
1/19/92	Epiphany 2	John 2:1-11	Water changed to wine	Isa. 62:1-5	No longer called deserted	I Cor. 12:1-11	Spiritual gifts.	36:5-10
1/26/92	Epiphany 3	Luke 4:14-21	Jesus reads in the synagogue	Neh. 8:1-4*a*, 5-6, 8-10	Ezra reads the law	I Cor. 12:12-30	One body, many parts	19:7-14
2/2/92	Epiphany 4	Luke 4:21-30	Rejected at Nazareth	Jeremiah 1:4-10	Call of Jeremiah	I Cor. 13:1-13	Love—best way of all	71:1-6
2/9/92	Epiphany 5	Luke 5:1-11	Disciples called	Isaiah 6:1-8 (or 13)	Isaiah's call	I Cor. 15:1-11	Resurrection of Christ	138
2/16/92	Epiphany 6	Luke 6:17-26	Sermon on the plain	Jer. 17:5-10	One who trusts	I Cor. 15:12-20	If Christ not raised	1
2/23/92	Epiphany 7	Luke 6:27-38	Love for enemies	Gen. 45:3-11, 15	Joseph makes himself known	I Cor. 15:35-38, 42-50	The resurrected body	37:1-11
3/1/92	Last of Epiphany (Transfiguration)	Luke 9:28-36	Transfiguration	Exod. 34:29-35	Moses returns from mountain	II Cor. 3:12–4:2	Where there is freedom	99
3/8/92	Lent 1	Luke 4:1-13	Temptation of Jesus	Deut. 26:1-11	Firstfruits and tithes	Rom. 10:8*b*-13	Confess and believe	91:9-16
3/15/92	Lent 2	Luke 13:31-35	Sorrow over Jerusalem	Gen. 15:1-12, 17-18	Covenant with Abram	Phil. 3:17–4:1	Stomach their god	127

Sunday	Sunday	Gospel Lesson	Gospel Theme	First Lesson	O.T. Theme	Second Lesson	Epistle Theme	Psalm
3/22/92	Lent 3	Luke 13:1-9	Parable of the unfruitful tree	Exod. 3:1-15	Before the burning bush	I Cor. 10:1-13	Warnings from Israel's history	103:1-13
3/29/92	Lent 4	Luke 15:1-3, 11-32	Prodigal son	Josh. 5:9-12	Reproach rolled away	II Cor. 5:16-21	Message of reconciliation	34:1-8
4/5/92	Lent 5	John 12:1-8	Anointed at Bethany	Isa. 43:16-21	Doing a new thing	Phil. 3:8-14	On toward the goal	126
4/12/92	Lent 6 Palm Sunday	Luke 22:14–23:56 *or* Luke 23:1-49	Triumphal entry	Isa. 50:4-9*a*	His back to the smiters	Phil. 2:5-11	Obedient to death	31:9-16
4/19/92	Easter Sunday	John 20:1-18 *or* Luke 24:1-12	The empty tomb	Isa. 65:17-25 *or* Acts 10:34-43	A new faith; God raised him up	I Cor. 15:19-26 *or* Acts 10:34-43	Resurrection of the dead	118:14-24
4/26/92	Easter 2	John 20:19-31	Doubting Thomas	Acts 5:27-32	Obey God rather than people	Rev. 1:4-8	Who is, to come	2
5/3/92	Easter 3	John 21:1(or 15)-19	"Peter, Do you love me?"	Acts 9:1-20	Saul's conversion	Rev. 5:11-14	Worthy is the lamb	30:4-12
5/10/92	Easter 4	John 10:22-30	My sheep follow	Acts 13:15-16, 26-33	Paul preaches resurrection	Rev. 7:9-17	Multitude in white robes	23
5/17/92	Easter 5	John 13:31-35	A new commandment	Acts 14:8-18	We are not gods	Rev. 21:1-6	A new heaven and earth	145:13*b*-21
5/24/92	Easter 6	John 14:23-29	One who loves obeys	Acts 15:1-2, 22-29	Letter to gentile believers	Rev. 21:10, 22-27	No night there	67
5/31/92	Easter 7	John 17:20-26	That they may be one	Acts 16:16-34	Paul and Silas in prison	Rev. 22:12-14, 16-17, 20	Coming soon	97
6/7/92	Pentecost	John 14:8-17, 25-27	The Spirit of truth	Gen. 11:1-9 *or* Acts 2:1-21	Tower of Babel; Day of Pentecost	Rom. 8:14-17	We are God's children	104:24-34
6/14/92	Trinity Sunday	John 16:12-15	Guide into all truth	Prov. 8:22-31	Wisdom's place in creation	Rom. 5:1-5	Justified by faith	8
6/21/92	2nd After Pentecost	Luke 9:18-24	"Who do you say I am?"	I Kings 19:9-14	Elijah on the mountain	Gal. 3:23-29	The law and the promise	43

Sunday	Sunday	Gospel Lesson	Gospel Theme	First Lesson	O.T. Theme	Second Lesson	Epistle Theme	Psalm
6/28/92	3rd After Pentecost	Luke 9:51-62	Dead bury the dead	I Kings 19:15-21	Call of Elisha	Gal. 5:1, 13-25	Life by the Spirit	44:1-8
7/5/92	4th After Pentecost	Luke 10:1-12, 17-20	Sending out seventy-two	I Kings 21:1-3, 17-21	Naboth's vineyard	Gal. 6:7-18	One reaps what one sows	5:1-8
7/12/92	5th After Pentecost	Luke 10:25-37	The good Samaritan	II Kings 2:1, 6-14	Elijah taken up	Col. 1:1-14	Hope stored up for you	139:1-12
7/19/92	6th After Pentecost	Luke 10:38-42	Mary and Martha	II Kings 4:8-17	The Shunammite's son raised	Col. 1:21-29	Mystery of the ages revealed	139:13-18
7/26/92	7th After Pentecost	Luke 11:1-13	Jesus teaches prayer	II Kings 5:1-15*ab*	Naaman healed of leprosy	Col. 2:6-15	Endurance and patience	21:1-7
8/2/92	8th After Pentecost	Luke 12:13-21	The rich fool	II Kings 13:14-20*a*	Elisha's final challenge	Col. 3:1-11	On things above	28
8/9/92	9th After Pentecost	Luke 12:32-40	Watchfulness	Jer. 18:1-11	At the potter's house	Heb. 11:1-3, 8-19	By faith	14
8/16/92	10th After Pentecost	Luke 12:49-56	Not peace, but division	Jer. 20:7-13	Jeremiah's complaint	Heb. 12:1-2, 12-17	God disciplines his children	10:12-18
8/23/92	11th After Pentecost	Luke 13:22-30	Mustard seed, yeast, narrow door	Jer. 28:1-9	False prophet prophesies peace	Heb. 12:18-29	Kingdom that cannot be shaken	84
8/30/92	12th After Pentecost	Luke 14:1, 7-14	At the banquet	Ezek. 18:1-9, 25-29	Soul who sins will die	Heb. 13:1-8	Let love continue	15
9/6/92	13th After Pentecost	Luke 14:25-33	First count the cost	Ezek. 33:1-11	Ezekiel, a watchman	Philemon 1-20	Plea for a runaway slave	94:12-22
9/13/92	14th After Pentecost	Luke 15:1-10	Lost sheep and coin	Hos. 4:1-3, 5:15–6:6	Charge against Israel	I Tim. 1:12-17	God's grace	77:11-20
9/20/92	15th After Pentecost	Luke 16:1-13	The shrewd steward	Hos. 11:1-11	God's love for Israel	I Tim. 2:1-7	Instructions on worship	107:1-9
9/27/92	16th After Pentecost	Luke 16:19-31	Rich man and Lazarus	Joel 2:23-30	Rend your heart	I Tim. 6:6-19	Money is the root of evil	107:1, 33-43

Sunday	Sunday	Gospel Lesson	Gospel Theme	First Lesson	O.T. Theme	Second Lesson	Epistle Theme	Psalm
10/4/92	17th After Pentecost	Luke 17:5-10	Faith and duty	Amos 5:6-7, 10-15	Seek good and not evil	II Tim. 1:1-14	Encouragement to be faithful	101
10/11/92	18th After Pentecost	Luke 17:11-19	Ten lepers healed	Micah 1:2; 2:1-10	Planning iniquity	II Tim. 2:8-15	A worker approved by God	26
10/18/92	19th After Pentecost	Luke 18:1-8	The persistent widow	Hab. 1:1-3; 2:1-4	Habakkuk's complaint	II Tim. 3:14–4:5	In season and out of season	119:137-144
10/25/92	20th After Pentecost	Luke 18:9-14	Pharisee and tax collector	Zeph. 3:1-9	The future of Jerusalem	II Tim. 4:6-8, 16-18	Finished the course	3
11/1/92	21st After Pentecost	Luke 19:1-10	"Zacchaeus, come down!"	Hagg. 2:1-9	Glory of the new house	II Thess. 1:5-12	Thanksgiving for their faith	65:1-8
11/8/92	22nd After Pentecost	Luke 20:27-38	Whose wife in the hereafter?	Zech. 7:1-10	Justice and mercy; not fasting	II Thess. 2:13–3:5	Encouragement and hope	9:11-20
11/15/92	23rd After Pentecost	Luke 21:5-19	Signs of the end	Mal. 4:1-6	The Day of the Lord	II Thess. 3:6-13	Warning against idleness	82
11/22/92	Christ the King	John 12:9-19	Entering Jerusalem	II Sam. 5:1-5	David becomes king	Col. 1:11-20	Supremacy of Christ	95
11/29/92	Advent 1	Matt. 24:36-44	Suddenly, like a thief	Isa. 2:1-5	Future reign of God	Rom. 13:11-14	How critical the moment	122
12/6/92	Advent 2	Matt. 3:1-12	John the Baptist	Isa. 11:1-10	New king and kingdom	Rom. 15:4-13	God of hope	72:1-8
12/13/92	Advent 3	Matt. 11:2-11	Should we expect another?	Isa. 35:1-10	Flowers in the wastelands	James 5:7-10	Patience and prayer	146:5-10
12/20/92	Advent 4	Matt. 1:18-25	Angel appeared to Joseph	Isa. 7:10-16	Virgin's son called Immanuel	Rom. 1:1-7	Descendant of David	24
12/24/92	Christmas Eve	Luke 2:1-20	Born in Bethlehem	Isa. 9:2-7	To us a child is born	Titus 2:11-14	Glorious appearing of Savior	96
12/27/92	1st After Christmas	Matt. 2:13-15, 19-23	Flight into Egypt	Isa. 63:7-9	Became their Savior	Heb. 2:10-18	Shared their humanity	111

A SCHEDULE OF HYMNS

Sunday	Opening Hymn	Second Hymn	Closing Hymn	Sunday
1/5/92	Go, Tell It On The Mountain	We Three Kings	Who Is He In Yonder Stall	2nd After Christmas
1/12/92	Jesus! the Name High over All	Majestic Sweetness Sits Enthroned	We've a Story to Tell to the Nations	Epiphany 1
1/19/92	See the Morning Sun Ascending	I Love to Tell the Story	Spirit of Faith, Come Down	Epiphany 2
1/26/92	When Morning Gilds the Skies	Standing on the Promises	O Zion, Haste	Epiphany 3
2/2/92	O For a Thousand Tongues to Sing	Sweet Hour of Prayer	Take My Life, and Let It Be	Epiphany 4
2/9/92	Jesus Calls Us	Lord, I Want to Be a Christian	Take Up Thy Cross	Epiphany 5
2/16/92	My Faith Looks Up to Thee	Blessed Assurance	O Come and Dwell in Me	Epiphany 6
2/23/92	Christ for the World We Sing	In Christ There Is No East or West	Where Charity and Love Prevail	Epiphany 7
3/1/92	Christ, Whose Glory Fills the Skies	Ask Ye What Great Thing I Know	Jesus Shall Reign	Last of Epiphany
3/8/92	Guide Me, O Thou Great Jehovah	I Am Thine, O Lord	By Thy Birth and By Thy Tears	Lent 1
3/15/92	Come, Christians, Join to Sing	All the Way My Savior Leads Me	Only Trust Him	Lent 2

Sunday	Opening Hymn	Second Hymn	Closing Hymn	Sunday
3/22/92	I Love Thy Kingdom, Lord	Precious Name	Just as I Am, Without One Plea	Lent 3
3/29/92	In the Cross of Christ I Glory	Arise, My Soul, Arise	Jesus Is Tenderly Calling	Lent 4
4/5/92	What Wondrous Love Is This	O Sacred Head, Now Wounded	The Lord Our God Alone Is Strong	Lent 5
4/12/92	All Glory, Laud, and Honor	When I Survey the Wondrous Cross	Go to Dark Gethsemane	Lent 6 Passion/Palm Sunday
4/19/92	I Know That My Redeemer Lives	Sing with All the Saints in Glory	Christ the Lord Is Risen Today	Easter Sunday
4/26/92	Thine Be the Glory	Easter People, Raise Your Voices	Christ Is Alive	Easter 2
5/3/92	All Hail the Power of Jesus' Name	Jesus, Thine All-Victorious Love	I Am Thine, O Lord	Easter 3
5/10/92	Only Trust Him	The King of Love My Shepherd Is	He Leadeth Me: O Blessed Thought	Easter 4
5/17/92	For All the Saints	It Is Well with My Soul	Christ for the World We Sing	Easter 5
5/24/92	Immortal, Invisible, God Only Wise	Savior, More Than Life to Me	Jesus, the Very Thought of Thee	Easter 6
5/31/92	Rejoice Ye Pure in Heart	In the Garden	Nearer, My God, to Thee	Easter 7
6/7/92	O Spirit of the Living God	Holy Spirit, Truth Divine	Breathe on Me, Breath of God	Pentecost

Sunday	Opening Hymn	Second Hymn	Closing Hymn	Sunday
6/14/92	Holy, Holy, Holy! Lord God Almighty	Holy God, We Praise Thy Name	Love Divine, All Loves Excelling	Trinity Sunday
6/21/92	The Church's One Foundation	God of Love and God of Power	Rock of Ages, Cleft for Me	2nd After Pentecost
6/28/92	God of Our Fathers	Onward, Christian Soldiers	Beneath the Cross of Jesus	3rd After Pentecost
7/5/92	America	America the Beautiful	Lift High the Cross	4th After Pentecost
7/12/92	For the Beauty of the Earth	Leaning on the Everlasting Arms	Be Thou My Vision	5th After Pentecost
7/19/92	Come, Thou Almighty King	I Want a Principle Within	Happy the Home When God Is There	6th After Pentecost
7/26/92	Take Time to Be Holy	Children of the Heavenly Father	Near to the Heart of God	7th After Pentecost
8/2/92	Maker, in Whom We Live	From All That Dwell Below the Skies	A Charge to Keep I Have	8th After Pentecost
8/9/92	Ye Watchers and Ye Holy Ones	Trust and Obey	Have Thine Own Way, Lord	9th After Pentecost
8/16/92	Stand Up, Stand Up for Jesus	Stand By Me	Lead On, O King Eternal	10th After Pentecost
8/23/92	Stand Up and Bless the Lord	This Is My Song	Make Me a Captive, Lord	11th After Pentecost
8/30/92	Marching to Zion	Break Thou the Bread of Life	God Be with You till We Meet Again	12th After Pentecost

Sunday	Opening Hymn	Second Hymn	Closing Hymn	Sunday
9/6/92	To God Be the Glory	Precious Lord, Take My Hand	Jesus Keep Me Near the Cross	13th After Pentecost
9/13/92	All Praise to Thee, My God, This Night	Savior, Like a Shepherd Lead Us	Pass Me Not, O Gentle Savior	14th After Pentecost
9/20/92	God of Grace and God of Glory	I Know Whom I Have Believed	I Surrender All	15th After Pentecost
9/27/92	Holy, Holy, Holy! Lord God Almighty	Take Our Bread	Alas! and Did My Savior Bleed	16th After Pentecost
10/4/92	When We All Get to Heaven	Dear Lord and Father of Mankind	Grace Greater than Our Sin	17th After Pentecost
10/11/92	Sing Praise to God Who Reigns Above	Leave It There	And Are We Yet Alive	18th After Pentecost
10/18/92	Come, Thou Fount of Every Blessing	My Hope Is Built	Near to the Heart of God	19th After Pentecost
10/25/92	A Mighty Fortress Is Our God	I Stand Amazed in the Presence	Amazing Grace	20th After Pentecost
11/1/92	Heralds of Christ	Hymn of Promise	There's a Wideness in God's Mercy	21st After Pentecost
11/8/92	We Gather Together	Leaning on the Everlasting Arms	There Is a Balm in Gilead	22nd After Pentecost
11/15/92	Great Is Thy Faithfulness	America the Beautiful	Now Thank We All Our God	23rd After Pentecost

Sunday	Opening Hymn	Second Hymn	Closing Hymn	Sunday
11/22/92	Crown Him with Many Crowns	The Battle Hymn of the Republic	The Head That Once Was Crowned	Christ the King
11/29/92	Let All Mortal Flesh Keep Silence	Come, Thou Long-Expected Jesus	Lift Up your Heads, Ye Mighty Gates	Advent 1
12/6/92	O Come, O Come, Emmanuel	Hail to the Lord's Anointed	Joy to the World	Advent 2
12/13/92	Angels from the Realms of Glory	Lo, How a Rose E're Blooming	There's a Song in the Air	Advent 3
12/20/92	O Come All Ye Faithful	What Child Is This	Hark! the Herald Angels Sing	Advent 4
12/27/92	Good Christian Friends, Rejoice	Jesus Loves Me	The First One Ever	1st After Christmas

INVITATIONS TO CHRISTIAN DISCIPLESHIP

□

Response to the Word

(*Responses may include one or more of the following acts: invitation to Christian discipleship, followed by a hymn of invitation or response; baptism; confirmation; reaffirmation of faith; or other reception of members.*)

While reflecting on his preaching in Ireland, John Wesley wrote in his journal, "Many have been deeply convinced, many converted to God, and some perfected in love" (*Journal,* May 13, 1789). This kind of response to the preaching of the Word is still evident in the Church. From the ancient rites of penance and reconciliation to the altar calls of revivals and the invitation to discipleship of Sunday morning worship, the Church has moved through varieties of ways that invite hearers to signify their response. Many preachers are like the good Reverend Shelton of whom Wesley wrote: "That able and laborious divine, not having clear views of the method of a sinner's justification, few, if any, received the forgiveness of sins" (*The Works of John Wesley,* vol. 18, Journals and Diaries, p. 75)

We do not imply that forgiveness depends on a method, nor would we suggest that one can settle all of the religious issues at an altar of prayer following an invitation; yet, we value opportunities in worship that provide ways for hearers to respond when the Word of God is preached and heard. The following prefaces will help ministers to lead into an invitation to Christian discipleship or a call to prayer.

1. "These days of lent have been times of spiritual discipline and prayer. We have met today so that we might turn our lives to the way of the gospel."

2. "Every time the Lord's Prayer is prayed, the Christian asks

for forgiveness and prays for deliverance from evil, and so we pray again."

3. "Many of our hymns praise God for grace that is greater than our sins. The words of this hymn of invitation open wide the doors of the church."

4. "There are moments in every Christian's life that are special. They are sacramental times of safety and harmony and hope; times when we turn from everything that steals, kills, and destroys to the good Shepherd who gives abundant life. I invite you to claim this sacred moment as your own."

5. "Repentance and reconciliation are constant and lifelong. We cannot settle our conflicts with sin once for all time. Every day there is some failure or need made known by the spotlight of God's righteousness. Every day there is something in our lives that needs the grace of Christ. God's grace is new every morning, and I invite you to claim it in a new way today."

6. "There are many ways to symbolize a covenant. Sometimes we sign our names or join hands or kneel in prayer or give and receive rings. Today there are some here who want to seal their covenant with a simple act of devotion."

7. "We are so many, and all of us are so different, that I don't know how to instruct your prayers. But I know how to invite them. The altar is a good praying place. Christ have mercy on us."

8. "The church is quiet now as we bow in prayer. We seek God's pardon; we confess our regret and sadness; and we pray that Christ's love and mercy will be known."

9. "Sin that is personal is not private. Our sins have hurt and wronged others. But now let those who want to regain peace with God and restore friendship with every neighbor use this time of prayer for reconciliation. Come alone or

come with another, but come now that the grace of Christ may mend the brokenness of our relationships and restore us to wholeness and peace."

10. "We have heard the good news: God is love, and in him there is no anger or hostility toward any one of us. The Father's love invites us all, but love can be complete only when it is received and returned. You've said it before. Will you say it again? 'Lord Jesus, I love you.' "

11. "Let us bring our gifts, our commitments, and ourselves to the altar. Let us give thanks to the Lord, for he is good."

12. "As a tangible sign of your need, an outward sign of your desire to be identified, and to evidence your intention to unite with the church, I invite you to come and. . . ."

13. "Let us respond to the gospel with an examination of conscience. Jesus Christ said, 'When you stand praying, forgive, if you have ought against any.' Jesus said, 'Judge not.' Jesus said, 'Love your enemies.' Jesus said, 'Do unto others as you would have them do unto you.' Jesus said, 'Enter in at the strait gate.' "

14. "I have been your preacher; now let me be your priest. I invite your prayers of repentance so that I may proclaim for everyone who has faith, 'In the name of Jesus Christ, you are forgiven.' "

15. "May the Holy Spirit, who is our friend and counselor, help us to know our sins and to trust Christ's mercy."

16. "May Christ the Savior, who is the friend of every sinner, be your friend just now. He frees from sin, forgives our iniquity, heals our brokenness, and speaks peace to our souls. May Christ's peace take root in your heart and grow into a harvest of love, goodness, and truth."

17. "There are some things that cannot be settled at an altar of

prayer or in any act of penance. The prophet Isaiah said, 'This is the fasting that I desire. Set free the oppressed. Share your bread with the hungry. Shelter the homeless. Clothe the naked and never turn your back on your own."

18. "Let the power of Christ's cross be among us today. Let our obedience be like his. Let us love as he loved and serve as he served. Let each of us bear a cross, and bear it in the power of the cross of Christ."

Offertory Scripture

□

Deuteronomy 28:12: The Lord will open for you his rich storehouse, the heavens, to give the rain of your land in its season and to bless all your undertakings. You will lend to many nations, but you will not borrow.

I Samuel 2:8: He raises up the poor from the dust; he lifts the needy from the ash heap, to make them sit with princes and inherit a seat of honor. For the pillars of the earth are the Lord's, and on them he has set the world.

I Chronicles 29:12: Riches and honor come from you, you rule over all. In your hand are power and might; and it is in your hand to make great and to give strength to all.

Proverbs 3:9: Honor the Lord with your substance, and with the first fruits of all your produce.

Proverbs 22:4: The reward for humility and fear of the Lord is riches and honor and life.

Malachi 3:10: Bring the full tithe into the storehouse, so that there may be food in my house, and thus put me to the test, says the Lord of hosts; see if I will not open the windows of heaven for you and pour down for you an overflowing blessing.

Matthew 6:2-3: So whenever you give alms, do not sound a trumpet before you, as the hypocrites do in the synagogues and in the streets, so that they may be praised by others. Truly I tell you, they have received their reward. But when you give alms, do not let your left hand know what your right hand is doing.

Matthew 25:37, 40: Then the righteous will answer him, "Lord, when was it that we saw you hungry and gave you food, or thirsty and gave you something to drink? . . . 'Just as you did it to one of the least of these who are members of my family, you did it to me.'"

Mark 10:45: For the Son of Man came not to be served but to serve, and to give his life a ransom for many.

Mark 12:17: Jesus said to them, "Give to emperor the things that are the emperor's, and to God the things that are God's."

Luke 6:38: Give, and it will be given to you. A good measure, pressed down, shaken together, running over, will be put into your lap; for the measure you give will be the measure you get back.

Luke 12:33: Sell your possessions, and give alms. Make purses for yourselves that do not wear out, an unfailing treasure in heaven, where no thief comes near and no moth destroys.

John 6:27: Do not work for the food that perishes, but for the food that endures for eternal life, which the Son of Man will give you.

John 13:34: I give you a new commandment, that you love one another. Just as I have loved you, you also should love one another.

Acts 17:25: Nor is God served by human hands, as though he needed anything, since he himself gives to all mortals life and breath and all things.

Acts 20:35: In all this I have given you an example that by such work we must support the weak, remembering the words of the Lord Jesus, for he himself said: "It is more blessed to give than to receive."

Romans 8:32: He who did not withhold his own Son, but gave him up for all of us, will he not with him also give us everything else?

Romans 11:35: Who has given a gift to God, to receive a gift in return?

I Corinthians 4:2: It is required of stewards that they be found trustworthy.

II Corinthians 8:7: Now as you excel in everything—in faith, in speech, in knowledge, in utmost earnestness, and in our love for you—so we want you to excel also in this generous undertaking.

II Corinthians 9:7: Each man of you must give as you have made up your mind, not reluctantly or under compulsion, for God loves a cheerful giver.

Galatians 6:9: Let us not grow weary in doing what is right, for we will reap at harvest-time, if we do not give up.

Revelation 4:11: You are worthy, our Lord and God, to receive glory and honor and power, for you created all things, and by your will they existed and were created.

Subjects and Texts for Funerals

□

Take Your Inheritance

Then the king will say to those at his right hand, "Come, you that are blessed by my Father, inherit the kingdom prepared for you from the foundation of the world." (Matt. 25:34)

God So Loved

For God so loved the world that he gave his only Son, so that everyone who believes in him may not perish but may have eternal life. (John 3:16)

That I Shall Lose None

And this is the will of him who sent me, that I should lose nothing of all that he has given me, but raise it up at the last day. (John 6:39)

The Ultimate Will of God

This is indeed the will of my Father, that all who see the Son and believe in him may have eternal life; and I will raise them up on the last day. (John 6:40)

Bread of Always

I am the living bread that came down from heaven. Whoever eats of this bread will live forever; and the bread that I will give for the life of the world is my flesh. (John 6:51)

Christ—The Resurrection and the Life

Jesus said to her, "I am the resurrection and the life. Those who believe in me, even though they die, will live, and everyone who lives and believes in me will never die. Do you believe this?" (John 11:25-26)

Something You Can Trust

The saying is sure: If we have died with him, we will also live with him; if we endure, we will also reign with him; if we deny him, he will also deny us. (II Tim. 2:11-12)

They Rest from Their Labor

And I heard a voice from heaven saying, "Write this: Blessed are the dead who from now on die in the Lord." "Yes," says the Spirit, "they will rest from their labors, for their deeds follow them." (Rev. 14:13)

Where to Find Help

I lift up my eyes to the hills—
from where will my help
come?
My help comes from the LORD,
who made heaven and earth. (Ps. 121:1-2)

Better Than Life

Because your steadfast love is
better than life,
my lips will praise you.
So I will bless you as long as I
live;
I will lift up my hands and call
on your name. (Ps. 63:3-4)

Waiting

I wait for the LORD, my soul
waits,
and in his word I hope. (Ps. 130:5)

Dying Alone, but Never Alone

We do not live to ourselves, and we do not die to ourselves. If we live, we live to the Lord; so then, whether we live or whether we die, we are the Lord's. For to this end Christ died and lived again, so that he might be Lord of both the dead and the living. (Rom. 14:7-9)

Not Yet Known

Beloved, we are God's children now; what we will be has not yet been revealed. What we do know is this: when he is revealed, we will be like him, for we will see him as he is. (I John 3:2)

Brought Home with Him

For since we believe that Jesus died and rose again, even so, through Jesus, God will bring with him those who have died. (I Thess. 4:14)

The Shroud Destroyed

On this mountain the LORD of
hosts will make for all
peoples
a feast of rich food, a feast of
well-aged wines,
of rich food filled with
marrow, of well-aged wines
strained clear.
And he will destroy on this
mountain
the shroud that is cast over all
peoples,
the sheet that is spread over
all nations;
he will swallow up death
forever.
Then the Lord GOD will wipe
away the tears from all
faces,

and the disgrace of his people
he will take away from all
the earth,
for the LORD has spoken.
It will be said on that day,
Lo, this is our God; we have
waited for him, so that he
might save us.
This is the LORD for whom we
have waited;
let us be glad and rejoice in
his salvation. (Isa. 25:6-9)

And in the End

I know that my Redeemer
lives,
and that at the last he will
stand upon the earth. (Job 19:25)

Clothed with Immortality

For this perishable body must put on imperishability, and this mortal body must put on immortality. When this perishable body puts on imperishability, and this mortal body puts on immortality, then the saying that is written will be fulfilled:

"Death has been swallowed up
in victory."
"Where, O death, is your
victory?
Where, O death, is your
sting?"

The sting of death is sin, and the power of sin is the law. But thanks be to God, who gives us the victory through our Lord Jesus Christ. (I Cor. 15:53-57)

A Funeral Sermon

□

KNOWING THE WAY

John 14:1-7

A SERMON BY JOHN B. PETERS

There is a quality about "doubting Thomas" that we admire. He was willing to risk putting into words what many of us would only dare to ponder. Thomas asked the question, while all the other disciples acted as if they knew the answer. They probably had their doubts, too, but Thomas had the courage to express his reservations and uncertainty, while the others simply pretended to understand Jesus, whom they had so often misunderstood.

When Jesus said, "You know the way to the place where I am going," Thomas stopped him: "Lord, we do not know where you are going." Jesus answered by offering a great statement concerning his identity: "I am the way, and the truth, and the life. No one comes to the Father except through me" (John 14:4-6).

What do we know of *the way*? If you have ever had the experience of being lost and have asked directions, only to be given landmarks you couldn't locate and street names that seemed not to exist, you recognized that simply being told to travel in a particular direction would not suffice. To be told to go north, south, east, or west was not enough.

Lord, how can we know the way? Jesus didn't tell Thomas to go to Jerusalem or to Bethlehem or to Jericho, and you'll know the way. He wasn't talking about a particular direction in which to travel. *The way* is not simply a road or a town. It is not a geographical point.

Neither is *the way* simply a style of life. All of us appreciate a life well-lived, one that people point to and say, "Now that's how one ought to behave." To be wholesome, respectable, admired by the community, and law abiding are all characteristics we may admire. They may make us good citizens of the community. But they may have absolutely nothing to do with *the way* of which Jesus was speaking.

You see, *the way* is nothing less than the person of Jesus Christ. To know *the way* is to know the Master. It is to see that the truth about God is revealed in Christ. Jesus is the way to God. He alone can lead people into the presence of God.

We can live our lives ever so well when we know the way we are going. ______ lived such a life. She/He knew the way because she/he knew the Lord all her/his life. Jesus' way was her/his way; her/his reason for being. He/She passed on to his/her family the principles of a faith so deeply ingrained in him/her throughout life; learned from parents as a child; complimented by an adoring spouse; reiterated in his/her experience as a Christian.

When our passion is for *the way,* Christ's way, surely our passion will it lead us to eternal life. ______, through faith and commitment, has known a quality of eternal life in this life. Can there be any doubt that ______ knows it now in the kingdom of God?

Today, let us not weep too long for ______. God has called home one of his truly faithful; one who has lived all of her/his life ready to go wherever God would call. ______ was well prepared, whether God would have her/him live in this life or the next life. ______ is one who has known *the way* because she/he has known the Master. May we, too, seek to live our own lives so as to give evidence that we have learned the answer to Thomas's question, "Lord, how can we know the way?" When Christ's way becomes our way, then we'll know *the way.*

From Text to Sermon

□

Eight Steps

JOHN K. BERGLAND

A young rabbi once asked an older rabbi, "How can I preach the Torah?" After a long silence, the old rabbi replied, "Turn yourself into a giant ear."

If you intend to be a faithful biblical preacher, your first task is to listen to the text. That means you should never assume that you know more about life than the text does. You don't have better questions. You don't have better answers to life's problems than the Scripture has. There is great wisdom and power in biblical literature. The preacher's first task then, is to hear what the Scripture says.

Where should you begin? Should you let the text rest where it is and bring the hearer to it? Should you let the hearers rest where they are and bring the text to them? Schleiermacher's image, and preaching textbooks agree, is that there are two choices: one may begin in a contemporary life situation (hearers) or one may begin with a historical situation (text).

Lectionary preaching, which is based on assigned Sunday lessons, begins with the text. You will maintain the tension between the historical and the contemporary, but the starting place is in the text. You need not look for a text; the text has already found the hearer. The next step is to move from the text to the sermon.

There are many ways to hear and study a text. There are many questions you can ask, many themes for which you may listen. The following guideline is one more "hearing aid" for those who want to prepare to preach the Sunday lesson.

1. *The text.* Read the text from at least three good translations. Note the variations and then note significant agreements.

2. *The context.* Study the context of the passage. Note what precedes and follows it. Note similar passages and sources

throughout the scripture. Is there any significance in the context of this passage? Why has the author placed it where it is?

3. *Key words.* Consult Bible dictionaries, word-study books, commentaries, and concordances to probe the meaning of key words. Clarify important concepts within the passage.

4. *Presuppositions.* What assumptions does the author make about God and about his hearers? Try to understand his worldview, his cosmic view, and his prejudices.

5. *Purpose.* State the purpose of the passage in its canonical shape. If the text or parts of the text are found in another context, determine the purpose of the passage there also.

6. *Situation.* Describe as vividly and concretely as you can the life situation of the author and the people for whom he wrote. Try to live into the writer's situation, his conflicts, his faith, his needs, and the issues that confronted his hearers.

7. *Main idea.* Identify the central concept of the passage. State the main thought as clearly and concisely as possible. Reword the message of the author in contemporary terms. This may lead you to the controlling theme of the sermon.

8. *Present situation.* Seek to bring the message to bear upon your own life and the lives of persons you know in the present. This process uses both interpretation and imagination and is a time of meditation. Ask yourself questions such as these:

Where is the real life issue that is found in the text evident today?
In what ways does my situation resemble or differ from that of the writer?
Am I included in the judgment and/or correction of this lesson?
What claims does this message place upon my life?
What grounds does this text give for thanking and praising God? (Luther used this test.)
What are the evidences of God's grace?
What does the text encourage me and others I know to expect from God?
What kind of God does this text assume there is?
What am I encouraged to expect of God?
What does this passage say to me now?

Eugene Carson Blake wrote:

> The beginning of a sermon with me is that moment when a spark is struck by the steel of the Word in the Bible on the flint of some human need. The spark is an idea, a fresh insight, a heightened emotional and intellectual response to a passage of scripture; or the flash of the Gospel's answer to some troubling human problem. Some begin with the Word. But it is no sermon unless flint strikes steel. (Donald Macleod, *Here Is My Method,* Revell 1952, page 25)

Sermon Contributors

□

The Rev. Dr. Richard Andersen
Sr. Minister St. Timothy's Lutheran Church
5100 Camden Dr.
San Jose, CA 95124

The Rev. Robert L. Baldridge
Rockingham District Supt. UMC
P.O. Box 1588
Laurinburg, NC 28352

The Rev. Dr. Ralph K. Bates
Sr. Minister First United Methodist Church
518 North 19th Street
Birmingham, AL 35203

The Rev. Robert E. Bergland
Senior Minister Grace UMC
800 Smith St.
Clinton, NC 28328

The Rev. Dr. John K. Bergland
Sr. Minister Haymount UMC (Editor)
1700 Fort Bragg Road
Fayetteville, NC 28303

The Rev. Dr. Eugene W. Brice
Sr. Minister Country Club Christian Church
6101 Ward Parkway
Kansas City, MO 64113

The Rev. Dr. James C. Cammack
Pastor Emeritus Snyder Baptist Church
2805 Millbrook Rd.
Fayetteville, NC 28303

Bishop Emerson S. Colaw
Homiletics Prof. United Theological Seminary
1810 Harvard Blvd.
Dayton, OH 45406

Bishop Judith Craig
Michigan Area Bishop United Methodist Church
21700 NW Highway Suite 1200
Southfield, MG 48075

The Rev. Dr. Wallace E. Fisher
Pastor Emeritus Holy Trinity Lutheran
85 Briarwood Circle
Pinehurst, NC 28374

The Rev. R. Carl Frazier, Jr.
Pastor St. Francis UMC Cary
2971 Kildaire Farm
Cary, NC 27511

The Rev. Dr. Larry E. Grimes
English Prof. Bethany College
P.O. Box C
Bethany, WV 26032

The Rev. James A. Harnish
Pastor St. Luke's UMC
4851 S. Apopka-Vineland Rd.
Orlando, FL 32819

The Reverend Louise Stowe Johns
Prison Chaplain Tutwiler Prison
4037 Strathmore Dr.
Montgomery, AL 36116

The Rev. Phillip Leach
116 Oak Street
Hope Mills, NC 28348

Bishop Clay F. Lee, Jr.
Bishop Holston Area UMC
P.O. Box 51787
Knoxville, TN 37950-1787

Colonel Bernard H. Lieving, Jr.
Main Post Chaplain Ft Bragg, NC
Office of the Chaplain
Fort Bragg, NC 28307-5000

The Rev. Dr. James R. McCormick
Senior Minister Parkway Heights UMC
2420 Hardy Street
Hattiesburg, MS 39401

The Rev. Michael T. McEwen
Rector Emmanuel Episcopal Church
1819 North Pennsylvania
Shawnee, OK 74801

Chaplain Milford Oxendine, Jr., LCDR, CHC, USN
Native American Chaplain US Navy
178 Rockey Court
San Clemente, CA 92672

The Rev. John B. Peters
Braddock St. United Methodist Church
115 Wolfe Street
Winchester, VA 22601

The Rev. Dr. Reginald W. Ponder
SEJ Ad Council Ex. Sec. United Methodist Church
Box 67
Lake Junaluska, NC 28745

The Rev. Dr. William K. Quick
Senior Minister Metropolitan UMC
8000 Woodward Ave.
Detroit, MG 48202

The Rev. Dr. Lucy A. Rose
Homiletics Prof. Columbia Theo. Sem.
PO Box 520
Decatur, GA 30031

The Rev. Dr. Victor Shepherd
Sr. Minister Streetsville United Church of Canada
274 Queens St. South
Streetsville, Ontario
CD L5M 1L8
CANADA

The Rev. Paul T. Stallsworth
Assoc. Dir. Rel. and Society Institute
338 E. 19th St A
New York, NY 10003

The Rev. Dr. Thomas H. Troeger
Homiletics Prof. Colgate Rochester
1100 South Goodman
Rochester, NY 14620

The Rev. Dr. Peter D. Weaver
Sr. Minister First UMC Pittsburgh
Center and South Aiken Avenues
Pittsburgh, PA 15232

Section III:

□

INDEXES

Scripture Index

□

OLD TESTAMENT

Luke, *continued*

John

General Index

□